Leonard Miracle
WITH MAURICE H. DECKER

Book of Camping

OUTDOOR LIFE · HARPER & ROW
NEW YORK

Contents

PART 3 · In the Woods

Introduction

CAMPING OPENS AND CLEANSES MAN'S SENSES, just as a warm bath opens and cleanses his pores.

Campers see more clearly in the woods beyond the cities and suburbs. Ears dulled by the endless clatter of machines pick up subtle and soothing sounds. The sense of smell, jaded by exhaust fumes, is awakened by the tingling odors of lakes and forests and meadows. The skin gains a sharp awareness of warm sun, cold water, the soft pressure of wind.

There is something basic about the acuteness of these senses. It has to do with being fully aware and alive.

Outdoor camps are thinking places, too, but most men who try to explain their devotion to camping speak in terms of senses. The sound of horse bells, say.

If you are lucky, you will hear those horse bells at night as you sit by a fire in the fringe of pines at the edge of a high mountain meadow. You will be peacefully tired from the trip up a mountain trail with pack and saddle horses. Your tent will be up behind your fire. And the warm light of the fire will spread through the open front of the white tent and dance on the sleeping bags unrolled and ready inside.

You have finished a banquet of trout from the clear mountain stream in the meadow. The dishes are done, the last cup of bucket-brewed coffee poured. You have matches aplenty, but you light your pipe or cigarette with a twig held in the fire.

Then you sit on a saddle blanket in the circle of warmth that holds back the chill of the high-country air. Bustle and laughter have subsided now. The loud tales have been told. It is quiet now, except for the soft purring of wind through the pines. A pocket of pitch in a pine firelog sputters and flares. There is the steady tinkle of creek water spilling over rounded rocks. The moon lights a great granite peak high above camp.

This is the time when you listen to horse bells. They are strapped to the necks of the natural leaders among the little herd of pack and saddle animals grazing in the moonlight on the meadow. The front feet of the horses are hobbled to keep them from straying too far in this fenceless wilderness, and the jingle of the bells will guide you to the herd if it is hidden in heavy timber when you ride out on your camp-hitched roundup horse next morning.

Now, in that hour before bedtime, the bells tell you that your trail-hungry horses are feeding quietly. The grass is good here and cool water just a step away. The white mare is full and resting already, her bell sounding only when she shifts her weight to favor one aging leg or another. The bell on the bay rattles softly as he raises his head from grazing, chimes louder as he walks, then rattles as he massages a bridle-sore ear against a willow clump.

Your eyes are on the fire, but your ears will tell you all is well with the horses, and the soothing pulse of the bells will make gruff men smile as they sleep.

There are other sounds and senses that move other campers.

Ben Lily, "last of the mountain men," was a hiker who roamed the far places of the Southwest with most of what he owned on his back. Lily remembered the feel of his feet settling firm and sure on the ground as he picked a path to a new camp in some roadless range. He walked "like a b'ar," planting his feet with measured steps that explored the texture of the earth.

Car campers know how headlights sweep curving woods' roads in the hour before daylight. There is a campsite ahead by a lake where the fishing is best at dawn, and your car's yellow lights are whisking away the darkness to hurry you there.

How many slumbering senses are awakened by wild geese passing overhead through wind and rain and clouds?

Those are a few of the thousands of things campers go afield to find. Some want their wilderness wild. Others are equally happy at the lake near home. City dwellers will always treasure camp life for its quiet places, for sight of uncluttered skylines, for the change to air that is conditioned by sun and rain and filtered through trees. All well-managed camps are health resorts. They treat the whole person, body and soul.

All campers, however they travel, wherever they go, need a basic store of equipment and knowledge. This book is designed to serve as an encyclopedia of camping lore. It will tell the beginner where to start, remind the expert of the knot, recipe, or formula that has slipped his mind. Carry it with you when you go.

Preparation and Equipment

PART I

Preparation and Equipment

1 · Planning the Camping Trip

WHEN YOU BEGIN TO THINK ABOUT TAKING A TRIP into the outdoors it pays, as in all other activities of life, to plan ahead as far as possible. What you actually do, when the first pangs of restlessness occur, is get out your bank book and count the money in it. If it was an African safari you had in mind, chances are the trip is off. But there may be more than enough to rent a canoe for a two-week wilderness fishing venture or one of many similar outdoor trips.

Keeping the financial considerations in mind, there are two essential steps in the sound planning of a trip. The first is to decide where you want to go and what you want to do. The second is to find out all you can about what your trip will involve—equipment, traveling, reservations, local regulations and conditions.

These are things you need to know *before* you hop the train for the North Woods or bundle your family into the car at dawn and set out for a campground. For the man who plans ahead will not drive his family the five hundred miles to that campground only to find it has been closed to campers since his visit two years ago.

And he won't make the long trip to a wilderness lake only to find that the dock operator from whom he expected to rent a canoe was burned out and left the country last spring. It is a good bet the man who does get caught in this situation will try to salvage his trip by spending money. Perhaps the lumberman down-river will rent out his personal canoe—at his own price.

One determined deer hunter from a big eastern city took a train to a town in the Maine woods on the spur of the moment. Finding it impossible to make last-minute connections with a hunting camp, he hired a taxicab to drive him fifteen miles to the hunting area next morning and instructed the driver to come back for him that evening. This hunter wasn't a rich man—just a stubborn citizen who had not learned the economy of scouting ahead with a letter or a telephone call.

Planning ahead need not be complicated. A simple letter or telephone call made in advance of your trip will save you more money than all the skimping and bargaining you may do over grub, clothing, and equipment. Call the friend who made a similar trip. If you lack a friend who can tell you about an area strange to you, there are many other quick and easy sources of advance information. Many major newspapers have outdoor experts in their sports departments who will furnish a wealth of free information to anyone who picks up the phone and calls them. Or try your local game warden. Finally, in many areas a local telephone call will put you in touch with an office of the U.S. Forest Service.

If time is short, a few dollars' worth of long-distance calls can work wonders. Say you live in Kansas City and want to take a pack trip with horses into the Wyoming Rockies. Pick up your phone and ask your local operator to connect you with the operator in Cody, Wyoming. Ask the girl in Cody to connect you with a local pack-trip outfitter. Two minutes later that outfitter or his helper will ask in a western drawl if he can help you. He can.

Small-town telephone operators will know the ropes in such matters. So will the village chamber of commerce or the postmaster, if you are asking by mail. He will usually forward a letter addressed to him to a local guide or outfitter.

Or you can write to the editorial departments of the several outstanding national outdoor magazines, whose staff members can give you expert advice on camp-trip planning. The advertising pages in the backs of these magazines are filled with information about camping services and equipment. These advertisers are interested primarily in selling tents or outfitting hunters after big game, but many of them will pass out free information to outdoorsmen who are potential customers for their products or services.

STATE CONSERVATION DEPARTMENTS

A letter to either the conservation department or the fish and game department of any state will yield all necessary information about camping in state forests or parks as well as about licenses or permits for hunting and fishing. They will know about specific regulations governing the cutting of trees or building campfires during dry seasons. These state offices are in the capital cities of each state. They will get any letter addressed to them with the correct city and state.

If you are planning a Montana trip, for example, your letter of inquiry would be addressed: Montana Fish and Game Department, Helena, Montana. Some states use the title "Conservation Department." A letter addressed either way will get to the proper offices, and routine information furnished by the state conservation or fish and game departments is free.

TRAIL CLUBS

Two of the major mountain chains in the United States—the Pacific Crest chain and the Appalachian system—have a vast number of hiking trails. It is possible to hike for 2,050 miles on the Appalachian Trail, a marked path which runs from Mount Katahdin in Maine to Mount Oglethorpe in Georgia. The trail snakes through New England's Green Mountains, the White Mountains, the Berkshires, down through the Catskills, the Allegheny, the Blue Ridge, and the Great Smoky ranges. There are established campgrounds and shelters along part of the route, real wilderness areas in some stretches.

A pamphlet titled "Suggestions for Appalachian Trail Users" is published by the Appalachian Trail Conference, 1916 Sunderland Place, N.W., Washington 6, D.C. The club charges 35¢ for this booklet to meet the expense of getting it out. The booklet is a fact-packed bargain for anyone planning to camp along the Appalachian Trail.

In the far West, campers can follow the Pacific Crest Trailway from Canada to Mexico. It runs through the Cascade Range, the Sierra Nevadas, and the Sierra Madres—offering 2,156 miles of outdoor adventure. Those are high, wild ranges.

Anyone planning an outing along this western trail would be off to a good start by writing for the advice of the Sierra Club, 1050 Mills Tower, San Francisco 4, California.

GOVERNMENT INFORMATION OFFICES

For information about camping in national parks (Yellowstone, for instance), write the National Park Service, Department of the Interior, Washington, D.C.

Campers heading for any one of the country's many national forests can get advance information by writing the U.S. Forest Service, Department of Agriculture, Washington, D.C. Ranger stations located within those forests will furnish the same information, along with specific information about particular areas. Visit or call the local ranger station on your way into the national forest if you have specific questions about such things as fire rules and trail conditions. A friendly ranger or his assistant will go so far as to tell you what dry fly will take the trout in a certain lake.

New and popular camping areas have sprung up all over the country at large lakes formed behind dams built by the Corps of Engineers of the U.S. Army. Most of these lakes offer good boating, fishing, and swimming, and many of them have provisions for tent camping. For specific information about any of these government-managed projects, write the Corps of Engineers of the U.S. Army in the particular state or district.

Trips to Canada, Mexico, or remote foreign countries can also be smoothly planned by mail. Get in touch with one of the travel bureaus found in all major cities. The offices of airlines flying to foreign countries supply the same kind of information. Most countries with a lot of outdoor resources have professional guides and outfitters, who advertise in the sporting magazines and supply information about their services to large outdoor equipment stores.

WHERE TO GET MAPS

The cheapest guide service available to campers heading for unfamiliar territory is provided by a pair of good maps. One map should show the whole state or region. The highway maps that oil companies offer free at their service stations will serve that purpose. The second map should show the details of the comparatively small region where you will camp. The best detail maps are those available for less than a dollar each from the U.S. Geological Survey, Washington, D.C. They show every minor creek, peak, and trapper's cabin in an area. Seldom does an outdoorsman have a chance to buy so much reliable information so cheaply.

The U.S. Forest Service maps of specific parts of the national forests are equally good sources of precise information about trails, roads, ridges, rivers, altitudes, and so forth.

Detailed maps of the seacoasts of the United States can be obtained from the U.S. Coast and Geodetic Survey, Department of Commerce, Washington, D.C., while maps of navigable rivers are available from the Corps of Engineers, U.S. Army—both for a nominal fee.

Canadian maps can be had from Map Distribution Office, Department of Mines and Technical Surveys, Ottawa, Ontario, Canada. Those are complete and precise. General maps of Canada are available through the Government Travel Bureau in Ottawa.

For maps of Mexico, write Dirección de Geografía y Meteorología, Tacusaya, D.F., Mexico.

Perhaps the best maps of other foreign countries are those published by the National Geographic Society, 16th and M Streets N.W., Washington 6, D.C.

If your camping plan involves a long auto trip—a jaunt from the East to West coast, say—it is a good idea to get a marked road map from an automobile club or from one of the major oil companies. The American Automobile Association (check your telephone book for its local address) specializes in such services. Most of the major oil companies will chart your auto trip in the same way as a public service.

For a list of state offices that furnish free advice on camps and camping, see the appendix at the back of the book.

2 - Tents

THE WANDERER ACQUIRES A PLACE OF HIS OWN when he stops and builds a fire. When his tent is up, he has a home.

For all its light, fragile appearance, a well-pitched tent is a stable and protective structure. Many of the world's nomadic tribes have found no housing more suitable than their tents in two thousand years of tribal housekeeping. These tent homes withstand Sahara sand storms and brave the blizzards of Mongolian heights. Large families live their lives in them.

The modern camper's first concern in choosing a tent should be its suitability *for his specific needs*. The teepee used by the Plains Indians, for example, was an ideal shelter for their purposes. But it required twelve or more straight poles 10 to 14 feet long to support it.

Plains Indians hitched their teepee poles to horses and pack dogs to sled their gear from camp to camp. Transporting such a load of long and awkward poles would be ridiculously impractical, however, for today's auto camper or hiker. It is equally impractical to obtain that many long, slender poles at a campsite. Most established campgrounds have strict rules against cutting green trees. Many wilderness areas have no saplings long and straight enough for good teepee poles. Few white men will ever again live the kind of nomadic wilderness life for which the Indian teepee was the perfect shelter.

What the camper wants is enough tent to provide adequate shelter without needless bulk, weight, and trouble. Some summer hikers can get by with a nylon shelter half which will fold to fit in a jacket pocket. The auto camper with a large family may be happiest in a fabric home with porches, patios, and bedrooms. These are available, too. (See Chapter 14 for specific information on tents for auto campers.)

WALL TENTS

The wall tent is the modern substitute for the Indian's teepee. It is fairly spacious, has ample head

The wall tent is a rugged, roomy shelter for semipermanent camping. This one is pitched with factory-made poles and pegs. *Courtesy of Fulton Cotton Mills.*

room, and will accommodate a wood-burning stove. Properly pitched, a wall tent will shed torrents of rain and stand warm and sturdy through blizzard or gale. It is the work-horse tent of the U.S. Forest Service. The Army has relied on wall tents for more than a century. Many of the Indians who still roam the Canadian Rockies hunting and trapping have switched from tee-pees to wall tents.

A large wall tent with a board floor and a stove can be made as satisfactory a wilderness home as a cabin. The boom towns of Gold Rush days had streets lined with board-floored wall tents, some in the same location for several years. With the end flaps closed, the simplest tin-box stove will keep a wall tent with a 10-by-14-foot floor area as warm as a furnace room in temperatures well below zero.

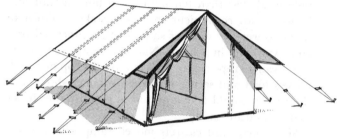

A canvas tarp, or fly, across the roof of a wall tent provides insulation for hot-weather camping and extra protection against rain.

A tarp also provides shade and shelter at the front of the tent. Here, a window of airy mosquito netting has been stretched across the back.
Courtesy of Eureka Tent Co.

With the end flaps tied up to let the breeze pass through, a wall tent is a cool summer shelter. In particularly hot climates, a large tarp can be stretched over the roof of the wall tent to form an air space of 4 to 6 inches between tent and tarp. This is a fine combination for camping in an area where both rain and heat are severe. A lot of cooling air will circulate through the large panels of insect netting used to cover the ends of a wall tent pitched where mosquitoes or other insects are a summer nuisance.

The camper who uses a long rope in place of a ridge pole needs less than ten minutes to hoist a wall tent between two convenient trees and stake it down in shape to weather summer showers. One practiced trail crew working in Challis National Forest in Idaho could yank a rope-ridged wall tent off the top of a pack horse's load and secure it against summer showers in the time it would take a person to get into the slicker tied behind his saddle.

Since these trail clearers moved camp often, it was important for them to have a wall tent rigged to set up or come down in a hurry. If a heavy storm with high winds set in with the promise of lasting for some time, they would bolster their tent by putting up shear poles at the tent ends and lashing the tent ridge to a sturdy ridge pole. If the rain was gentle and short, they saved the time and trouble of cutting a full set of stakes and poles.

A wall tent *can* be a light and easily handled outdoor shelter, but it is mainly a tent for groups of three or four persons who need and can easily carry a heavy-duty outfit. A wall tent is ideal for big-game hunters packing into the Rockies in late fall. They can heat it with a sheet-metal stove small enough to go on a pack horse. Campers who drive to established campsites and

The two-room cottage tent provides adequate space for families or groups camping for lengthy periods. *Courtesy of Morsan Tents, Inc.*

pitch their tents beside their cars will like the roomy wall tent, and they can easily carry precut or factory-jointed poles to support the shelter.

Sizes of Wall Tents

Wall tents are ordinarily available in sizes from 6½ by 6½ to 16 by 20 feet. Larger ones can be made to order or bought from Army surplus stores. Some of the latter are as large as 16 by 50 feet.

Side wall heights run from 2 feet in the small models, made of light fabrics for hikers or canoe campers, up to 4 feet for the cabin-sized models. Three-foot walls are standard with many makers of wall tents.

Wall tent heights at the center or ridge peak are generally standardized between 7 an 7½ feet. Adults need that much standing room, so be sure to check that dimension on any tent you plan to buy. Some of the cheaper tents with standard floor space are made with lower roofs. This robs the buyer of head room and gives him a flatter tent roof which is not as efficient at shedding rain or snow.

Except for outdoorsmen traveling light and far, a wall tent with a 7-by-9-foot floor space is the smallest comfortable size for two men and their gear. It will house two beds and a small stove in cold weather, with a little room left over for duffel. Three fall hunters and a stove need a wall tent with at least a 9-by-12-foot floor space. With larger parties, it is far easier and more pleasant for all hands to have two or more average-size tents than one circus-size canvas shelter. Privacy is also valuable in the wilderness, and the party with several tents can use certain tents for specific purposes—one for cooking, another for sleeping, a third to store equipment.

Pitching a Wall Tent

The best way to pitch wall tents in the back-country camp where they are at their best is the seven-pole rig.

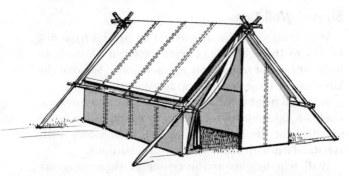

Pitched with a seven-pole rig, a wall tent will withstand rough weather. Shear poles do away with obstructing center poles.

This means that two shear poles are lashed in an inverted V shape at each end of the tent to support a ridge pole. The shears at either end of the tent are connected by a pair of poles running along the eaves of the tent. Guy ropes are tied to the eave poles. This seven-pole rig is stanch in strong winds, and it is simple

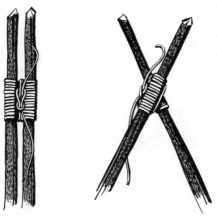

Lash shear poles for the seven-pole rig side-by-side, finishing off with a square knot. Scissor action of spreading the poles tightens the rope and secures the lash.

to adjust the tightness of the tent fabric when it shrinks in rain or loosens in fair weather. The best wall tents have outside tapes for using a rough or crooked sapling as an outside ridge pole.

Most top-grade wall tents have a sod cloth, which is a right-angle extension of the fabric at the lower edge of the walls. It lies flat on the ground inside the tent as a barrier against drafts and bugs. Poles, stones, or extra equipment will hold it down in wind. Campers in cold climates sometimes order extra-wide sod cloths which can be run out on the ground outside the tent and weighted down with blocks of snow. This eliminates the need for a dozen or more side wall stakes a good-sized wall tent ordinarily requires in stormy weather. Long poles stapled or tied to tapes at the bottom of the side walls will also save cutting and driving a great quantity of stakes. This is a particularly useful dodge for any tent pitched on rocky or

A wall tent can be pitched quickly and securely between two trees using a rope as a ridge pole. After running the rope under the ridge of the tent, secure an end to one tree. Throw the other end over a branch of the other tree and hoist the tent, leaving some slack in the ridge, and tie it temporarily. Erect the eave poles the height of the eaves about 2 feet outside the tent area.

Peg down the four corners. Then pull the ridge rope taut and tie it securely around the tree. Tie guy ropes to the eave poles (see guy-line hitch, p. 17), and finish pegging down the sides.

Tie guy ropes to the eave poles with the guy-line hitch. Ropes may be adjusted by sliding the lower knot up or down. The hitch can also be used when tying guy ropes to tent pegs.

frozen ground. Wall tents pitched on sand—by surf fishermen, for example—can be anchored by tying the guy ropes to bundles of brush buried in the loose soil.

The many stakes and poles needed for the wall tent limit its usefulness for many roadside campers. There are tents of other models that can be set up more quickly and easily, and they are sturdy enough for casual camps in mild weather.

UMBRELLA TENTS

Known also as the "auto" or "marquee" tent, the umbrella model is tops for the motorist who carries his own shelter when he tours the country. No other design serves so well for roadside camping as this straight-sided, pyramid-roofed job.

The umbrella tent is roomy with a head room that lets you walk erect to sides or corners and dress or perform other chores without stooping. And yet with the single exception of its door awning, this tent has no large flat surfaces to catch snow or hold water. Ventilation is ample: a large door and a window in one or more sides prevent the structure from becoming stuffy on even very warm nights. Occupants are well

The umbrella tent, ideal for auto campers, has plenty of head room. Screen door and sewn-in floor ward off insects and snakes. This one is pitched with an inside center pole. *Courtesy of Fulton Cotton Mills.*

protected by storm shutters; tight mesh screens exclude flying insects, and the sewed-in waterproof floor turns away drafts, surface moisture, and crawling pests. A doorsill strip from 4 to 6 inches high discourages small animals and snakes from entering. All of these protective features are especially prized by women and girls. It is no surprise then that the umbrella tent is one of the two most popular and best-selling models currently made.

Properly staked and guyed, the umbrella tent can resist high winds, and its peaked roof easily sheds torrents of rain. When the door shelter is propped horizontally, it provides a sheltered area where campers can work, cook, and eat. Umbrella tents are erected and dismantled quickly, and one man can do the job easily. Even the larger sizes can be made ready for occupancy in as little as four or five minutes—a definite advantage when a storm is imminent.

Sizes and Weights

Only one feature keeps this tent from enjoying wider acceptance for other camping—its weight. Umbrella tents weigh from 30 to 65 pounds, depending upon

Supported by an aluminum framework, this type of umbrella tent allows added room by the omission of the center pole. *Courtesy of Eureka Tent Co.*

the size and the type of pole support. That is no handicap when duffel is moved by car, but it is quite out of the question when campers travel afoot or by canoe. (NOTE. Umbrella tents are lighter today than in the past since some makers use aluminum, instead of steel, supports and thinner, lighter cloth.)

The extra weight of an umbrella tent, compared to that of other designs, is due mostly to the special poles and corner braces that keep the walls and top taut. These must be factory-made and fitted; you cannot cut them in the woods as you can poles for a wall or wedge type of shelter. Two kinds of bracing are usually available: one has a center pole; the other is a so-called "poleless" design which actually has four poles or trusses which fit into the corners and leave the center of the tent clear.

Your choice of pole design depends on how much room you really need and how much money you wish to spend. Poleless tents cost more and are heavier but may provide more inside room. However, in many cases a center pole or support is no real handicap since beds can be set on either side of it and it can be used as a clothes tree or rack or to support a curtain when

Pitching Umbrella Tent with Corner Pole Assembly

First, lay tent out on ground and peg down the four corners. Extend one of the corner poles and mount the arm assembly on top of it. Using it temporarily as a center pole, raise the tent on it, and set arms into the corners.

Place the three corner poles in position. The center pole becomes the fourth corner pole when it is detached from the arm assembly. The ends of the arms lock into the tops of the poles.

Pull the sleeve of the arm assembly into locking position, thereby spreading the arms and making the roof taut. Tent is now fully erected.

privacy inside the tent is desired.

Umbrella tents are made in sizes to accommodate two to six people. For a couple, shelters measuring 7 by 8 or 8 by 8 feet are usually large enough. Four campers find a 9½-by-9½ or 10-by-10-foot model about right, and these larger shelters will house five if some of the occupants are children. No inflexible rule need be followed; only be sure that the floor area will accommodate the number of beds needed. A pencil sketch drawn to scale of both tent floor and beds will help you determine this. It is not necessary to allow much room for storage in an umbrella tent used for auto touring. During the day you gain working room by stacking one bed on top of another, and at night the daytime gear can be put in the auto.

Pitching

When you buy an umbrella tent, note how walls and roof are folded over the floor to make a neat compact package and how the floor is rolled on the outside for protection. Use this same arrangement when you take your tent down and break camp. To erect an umbrella tent, stretch the floor out tight and square and stake its four corners. Get inside and raise the top with whatever pole system you are using. Then drive in the bottom stakes that go between the corners, secure the rear guys, and put up the front awning. Do not pull the awning ropes too tight. If you do, the strain gradually draws the tent forward, warps it out of shape, and may cause leaking. Large umbrella tents should have two rear guy ropes attached to upper corners to counteract this strain.

Pick level ground for the tent site—ground that is free of stones, roots, or any sharp objects that might damage the floor. Do not force any pole in place. If a pole seems too long, this means the ground there is higher than it is at other spots. The remedy is to turn back the floor and scoop away a little dirt from the place where the pole stands. Add some soil there if the pole seems short and fails to stretch wrinkles from the tent sides and roof.

It is wise at night to lower the front end of the door awning, so that it cannot fill with rain, putting extra strain on the tent. It is possible, too, to hit your head against such a pocket and get an unexpected shower. Carry two sets of umbrella tent stakes, one 6 inches long for hard ground, the other 10 or 12 inches for wet or sandy soil.

When you strike an umbrella tent, use a small hand broom to brush dirt from the underside of the floor as it is folded. The floor is usually sufficient protection for a tent in transit; if, however, your model is made of one of the special light fabrics, you should keep it in a tent bag. The unbagged, folded tent can be tied at each end with ropes or web straps for easy packing and handling.

WEDGE TENTS

Wedge tents, so named because of their shape when erected, are simple structures with three great virtues: low cost, ease of erection, and weatherproof design. Because of its low cost, the wedge model known as the "pup tent" is commonly the tent owned or used by boys on their first outdoor trips. The simplicity and soundness of the design caused the Army to use the pup tent as a standard two-man bivouac shelter in many of its infantry operations.

There are at least half a dozen wedge-type tents with as many different names: the pup tent, "A" tent, Hudson Bay tent, snow tent, and so forth. They have ap-

A wedge tent pitched with an outside ridge pole suspended by a rope between two trees is a sturdy, rain-shedding shelter.

proximately the same faults and virtues. They are generally light and easy to carry, and simple to erect. Wedge tents are superb shedders of rain and snow. They are easily screened against insects, which is of vital importance to campers in regions infested with mosquitoes. It takes a gale wind to bowl over a well-pitched wedge tent. The weaknesses of these tents are lack of head room and the heating problem in cold weather. A campfire in front of a wedge tent will send

The light, inexpensive mountain tent with a netting door and sewn-in floor is a favorite of many hikers. Courtesy of Morsan Tents, Inc.

some heat into the open front, but there are other fabric shelters that reflect campfire heat much more efficiently. It is possible to heat a large wedge tent with a wood-burning stove, but a wall tent handles such a stove better. A small, tight wedge tent can be warmed with a gas stove or even a lantern, but the camper using such a small heater in a very tight tent must be careful to let in a fair amount of fresh air to avoid asphyxiation. A wedge or any other snug tent will become clammy with body vapor from the campers inside if it is sealed too tight and made of fabric woven or waterproofed so that air cannot pass through it.

PYRAMID TENTS

Tents of this shape are best of all for shedding rain or snow. When solidly staked at the base and supported by a rigid center pole or an outside tripod of poles, a pyramid tent is supremely stable in windstorms.

Pyramid tents are easy to pitch and light and compact to carry. Simplicity and rugged durability make them a present-day favorite with such professional campers as western sheepherders and prospectors; in fact, one well-known type of pyramid tent, much used by roving mineral hunters past and present, is known as the "miner's tent."

One of the smaller pyramid tents, with a floor area measuring 7 by 7 feet, is a sound and durable sleeping and shelter tent for campers traveling light in remote country. It is not a good campfire or wood-stove tent, however.

All pyramid tents are poor campfire tents, and the small ones won't handle a wood stove. They are rather cramped and stuffy freezing-weather shelters when heated with a small gas, oil, or alcohol stove. The large

A pyramid tent can be pitched without a center pole by suspending it from a tripod of saplings (left) or a convenient tree branch (right).

pyramid tents that can be heated efficiently in winter weather lose the virtues of light weight and easy pitching.

BAKER TENT

This shelter is basically a wall tent with one wall raised to form a front awning. It is roomy, like the wall tent, and the open front makes it a very good campfire tent. With a campfire in front of it, a baker tent is a snug shelter in temperatures well below freezing. Rocks or green logs stacked behind the fire will reflect heat into all but the farther corners of this open-fronted tent.

Hunters camping in high country in late fall can

weather most any storm with a baker—as long as they keep their fire going but under control. To cope with flying sparks, the baker should be treated with one of the waterproofing solutions containing fire-resistant chemicals. Too much fire or an awning pitched too low can cause trouble in any event.

The baker tent is airy in summer and, with a reflecting fire going in front, is warm in chilly weather. *Courtesy of Fulton Cotton Mills.*

The relatively flat roof of the baker requires tight-woven fabric or a good waterproofing job with chemicals if it is to shed heavy rain without leaking. And the baker tent is more vulnerable to strong winds than pyramid, wall, and wedge tents. For that reason a baker tent chosen for rough going and stormy weather should be made of top-quality fabric and sturdily reinforced at seams and corners. Face it away from prevailing winds. Anchor it with long stakes when a storm is expected, because a strong wind sailing into the open front of a lightly pitched baker can fly it high as a kite—or split it open, if ropes pull tight against weak fabric or seams.

A good size for a baker tent is 6 by 8 feet; this will sleep two persons comfortably or shelter three who are good friends. A tent maker will turn out a larger baker-style tent on request. The snug utility of the tent starts to suffer, however, when its size is increased. Do not count on a campfire to warm the interior of a baker larger than 8 by 10 feet.

The open baker tent is a poor choice for camping where mosquitoes, no-see-ums, or other biting flies are plentiful. A screen of netting or cheesecloth can be fitted to cover the wide front opening, but individual bed nets will be more convenient for most baker-tent campers. They can rely on the smoke of the fire and the fine modern insect repellents to keep the bugs at bay until bedtime.

Despite its weaknesses, the baker is a long-established tent pattern which a host of aged-in-the-woods campers will defend with wild emotion. Much of their fondness for the tent is based on memories of basking with old friends by its warming campfire. And they know how the baker, unlike closed sleeping tents, gives the feeling of being constantly outdoors.

You can see the stars from a bed in a baker tent. Or watch the rain fall. Or hear the coyotes howl.

FORESTER TENT

This small tent may be best of all for go-light campers who want a small shelter that can be warmed by an open fire. The roof angles of the neat little forester are superbly planned to reflect heat into the interior.

The forester is quickly and solidly pitched on a tripod of poles as shown in the illustration. It will stand a lot of wind and shed buckets of water. The weight of a standard-sized forester tent made of Egyptian cotton or light duck is not enough to hamper a small Boy Scout on a good trail.

Warren H. Miller, a dedicated outdoorsman who designed the forester tent in the early nineteen-hundreds, has said that a pack of hounds paid his invention its most profound compliment. In a cold-weather hunting camp where two other open tents were facing the same campfire as Miller's was, the shivering hounds invariably sneaked into Miller's tent to sleep for the night. He was no special friend. The dogs were simply choosing the warmest of the three tents.

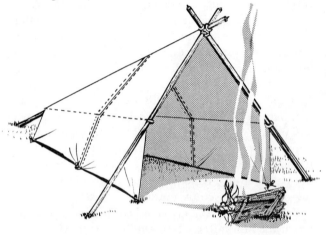

The light, sturdy forester tent pitched on a pole tripod absorbs a lot of warmth from a reflecting campfire.

The conventional forester is a small tent—about 8 feet deep and 6 feet wide at the front. The inside space is triangular, narrowing to a point at the rear. This allows reasonable sleeping space for two campers, possibly for a third small one in an emergency. The rig is at its best as a one-man tent, which allows room for groceries and gear that should be sheltered.

Separate bed nets are the best insect protection in a forester tent in bug season.

EXPLORER TENT

This type of tent, as its name suggests, is for out-doorsmen traveling light in far places. It is especially suitable as a sleeping tent for one or two persons in areas plagued by mosquitoes, for the explorer tent, with sewed-in floor and a netted front door the size and shape of a large porthole, is about as bugproof as any tent you can buy. For that reason the explorer has for years been the favorite tent of surveyors and other working campers in the mosquito-clouded northlands of Canada and Alaska.

Mosquitoes can be as think as fog in the lowlands of those regions in summer, so that a tent like this is nearly a life and death matter. The camper rids his clothes of insects by standing in the campfire smoke for a few minutes before bedtime. Then he crawls through the sleeve of close netting fitted to the porthole door of the explorer. Tying the netting sleeve shut behind him, the mosquito-wise woodsman checks the tent's interior with candle or flashlight to be sure there are no infiltrators, for two mosquitoes buzzing your face, then hiding in a dark tent, can spoil half a night's sleep.

Once the camper is in and the mosquitoes are out, however, the well-made explorer tent is a priceless refuge. The steep-walled design sheds rain efficiently. It also stands stanch in wind. An explorer with a 7-by-

The explorer tent with its netted door or porthole is a good choice for mosquito country. *Courtesy of Laacke's, Milwaukee.*

7-foot floor space will weigh only 10 or 12 pounds if made of some tough, light-fabric like Egyptian cotton or the similar high-grade cotton fabric called balloon silk. It packs into a small bundle which will almost fit into a roomy coat pocket.

Explorer-style tents made of nylon or Dacron are more durable and lighter than those made of cotton. Because they form compact sleeping shelters requiring few poles and stakes, these featherweight tents have been widely used with good results for overnight camps in the Arctic. The tightly woven synthetic fabrics are poor "breathers," but an open porthole will give the sleeping camper enough air in extremely cold weather.

TARP AND LEAN-TO SHELTERS

A great many summer campers who use tents would be just as secure and less burdened with simple canvas tarps or shelter halves. These are just square or roughly square sheets of fabric with hemmed edges and loops or eyelets for supporting ropes.

These can be the cheapest, lightest and simplest of all shelters. Yet they can be pitched in half a dozen different ways to provide adequate shelter for campers in warm and moderate weather. Summer campers in arid southwestern states, for example, have every reason to expect a week or more without a drop of rain to dampen unsheltered beds and equipment. For them, an 8-by-10-foot fly of waterproof fabric or tough plastic is a sound, almost overcautious provision. Though a bit of pessimism is safer in this matter, rain is rare all along the great chain of Rocky Mountains from July into September. In fact, the tentless gambler has a good chance for a dry weekend anywhere in the country from July to September. But the odds are equally good that when rain comes, it will be a cloudburst.

A canvas tarp is a suitable shelter for hikers in dry country. It can be pitched in a variety of ways.

That is when the tarp or shelter half becomes a priceless possession. Drape it over a pole to form a simple pup tent. Angle it higher to form a baker type of shelter roof with a front awning. Raise it as a flat roof if it is of sturdy material and completely waterproof. Heavy canvas tarps properly waterproofed will hold pools of water without leaking a drop when pitched to form roughly flat roofs over camp gear. Most untreated woven fabrics will leak at once and badly if pitched flat, and they will often leak when raised at a forty-five-degree angle if you rub against them from below. The touch of a finger to the under surface of untreated cotton fabrics will often start a spot leak.

The light, thin plastic sheeting now available everywhere has several virtues for shelter-half use. It weighs next to nothing, is completely waterproof, and is so inexpensive that a ripped sheet is a trifling loss. Disadvantages: it wilts or burns near fire, deteriorates in strong sunlight, and is easy to puncture or tear. Do not seal yourself in a tightly closed plastic shelter. It is so airtight that you will be drenched with vapor from your own body.

SPECIAL LIGHT HIKER TENTS

In addition to the tarp and lean-to shelters just described, outfitters supply special small tents which appeal strongly to hikers and other campers desiring a light pack load plus good protection from weather and insects. The most popular of these special designs is the cruiser, actually a small edition of the explorer tent. The ground size of the cruiser is 5 by 7 feet which is ample room to accommodate two single air mattress beds. The waterproof sewed-in floor excludes surface

Hikers camping at high elevations favor this two-man mountain tent which withstands strong winds and low temperatures. *Courtesy of Alaska Sleeping Bag Co.*

water and dampness; the mosquito-proof curtains backing door and ventilator turn away insects.

The door shutter of the cruiser tent has batwing flaps to seal out beating rain and wind, and there is a 6-inch sill across the bottom to which the shutter can be tied to safeguard equipment and supplies from rodents when camp is left unattended. This feature also makes the shelter snakeproof. A small, hood-protected peak ventilator in the rear admits fresh air whenever it is necessary partly or completely to close the door.

The cruiser tent is erected with a short ridge tied to pole scissors. These sticks are comparatively short and, since they are placed on the outside, can be made of rough crooked timber when better material cannot be found. For hiking in treeless regions, you can purchase aluminum poles or make your own from short sections of bamboo or cane. The necessary short stakes may be available at most tent sites; if not, procure 6-inch aluminum ones which weigh only about 1 ounce each. This cruiser tent is perhaps the best two-man design for summer hiking in warm weather and during the rainy and insect seasons.

The lightweight Draw-tite tent can be erected on any kind of ground as shown on these two pages. Suspended from an aluminum framework,

the tent has no inside poles, pegs, or guy ropes. Here, a camper demonstrates steps in erecting the tent. *Courtesy of Eureka Tent Co.*

Several modified tents of the cruiser type, known by such trade names as "Hiker," "One-man," and "Mountaineer," are also stocked by dealers in camping supplies. They are slightly smaller than the cruiser and in thin fabrics weigh as little as 3¾ lbs. This reduction of weight has been accomplished in part by reducing length and width a few inches from the standard 5-by-7-foot cruiser dimensions, and in part by tapering the rear so it is slightly narrower than the front. The extreme lightness of these rainproof and bugproof tents appeals to back packers, but their narrowed rear makes use of full-sized camp beds difficult. However, any of these shelters will house two people of medium build if they use three-quarter-length air mattress pads with blankets or with the mummy type of sleeping bag. On the other hand, these tents can prove too small for a pair of really large men. And like the original cruiser model, they lack adequate head room and are awkward to heat with an outside wood fire.

NEW TENT DESIGNS

Most of the tent designs already discussed have been widely used for fifty years or more. They remain on the market because they do their particular jobs well.

But the years since World War II have seen a score of new tents designed and offered for sale. Nylon, Dacron, and other synthetic fibers have given tent makers lighter and stronger fabrics than they ever had before.

With light, strong aluminum rods available at low cost, manufacturers have worked out tents that hang suspended within a skeleton of jointed aluminum poles. Though intricate in appearance, these aluminum frames can be set up in a jiffy and taken down to form a bundle that auto or pack-horse campers can

Designed for campers on the move, the pop tent can be pitched in ninety seconds without poles, ropes, or stakes. *Courtesy of Thermos Co.*

carry easily. Some are light enough for hikers. And those frames of slender aluminum poles are more stable than they appear. Tents hung on such frames have already passed Antarctic tests conducted by the Navy.

Campers are now offered tents with aluminum or fiberglass poles rigged to pop the fabric shelter into shape about as quickly as you could open an umbrella. Auto campers can buy trailer tents that fold into the trailer box for highway travel by day and rise on factory-fitted poles to form a sleeping shelter at night. There are tents that rise in a comparable way from a luggage carrier clamped to the top of a car. Most children are delighted to climb a ladder to spend the night in a tent perched on top of the family car. Auto campers can also choose from a half a dozen tents designed to use the roof of the parked car as a support. And there are tents designed to fit over the open end of a station wagon, merging tent and station wagon space.

Summer campers bound for short outings by car are using large, diamond-shaped tarps or flies made of light cotton or synthetic fabric. These big awnings, pitched with upright poles at the ends and guy ropes at the sides, form breezy shelters from sun and gentle rain. Some are striped in bright colors, lending a holiday air to drive-in camps. Wind is the bane of these tents. They will catch wind like the boat sails they resemble, and it would take a large and active family to hold one down in a windstorm. But it is a fine fair-weather awning for campers who do not expect to weather storms.

Perhaps the newest tent is the one made of paper reinforced with strong threads of synthetic fiber. These are throw-aways, in the sense that they are designed to last through an easy summer or a hard month and then be discarded.

The paper tents are waterproofed and are tougher than they look. Prices on the early models are a bit too high, however, to tempt most campers to buy a new set each season. They sell for about half the price of a comparable cloth tent that would last for ten years or more with care.

TENT FLOORS

Some tents have sewed-in floors that are an integral part of them. This feature is considered a great asset by some experienced campers; other equally competent outdoorsmen would cut the floor out of any such tent that fell into their hands.

Men who like to tramp in and out of their outdoor shelters without removing or cleaning muddy boots are seldom happy with floored tents—unless they are camping among swarms of mosquitoes or on grounds covered by deep snow. Fabric floors can be a dirt-collecting nuisance.

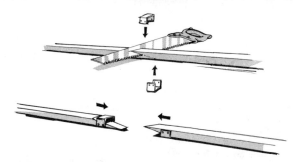

Collapsible tent poles (above) can be made at home by cutting a piece of 2" by 2" board the height of your tent, then sawing it in half at a sharp angle. Metal brackets screwed to the ends lock the two halves firmly together. Factory pole (below) has a sliding metal sleeve to lock the joint.

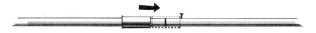

Most women are floor fanciers, mostly because they are concerned about sharing their beds with prowling snakes or bugs. Despite a million stories to the contrary, the odds against a snake of any kind crawling into a bed in an occupied camp are astronomical. Snakes studiously avoid people. A tent floor is a worthwhile bug screen, however, and it cuts out some drafts in cold weather.

A canvas-tarp floor that is not sewed to the tent walls is about as tight as a sewed-in floor and much easier to clean. It can be taken along or left at home, according to the requirements of a given trip.

If you are forced to camp on wet ground or deep snow without a floored tent or separate canvas for that purpose, put down a deep carpet of evergreen boughs to prop your bed and other gear above the wet, cold earth. A floorless tent can be made mosquito-proof with proper banking at the bottom with poles, sod, or such litter as twigs and pine needles. But the floored tent is handier under such conditions.

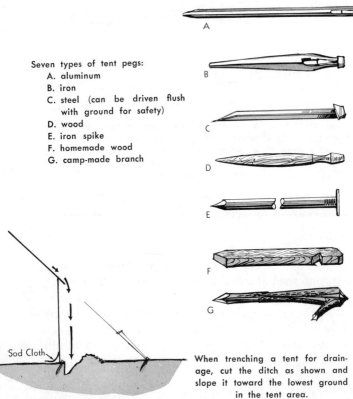

Seven types of tent pegs:
- A. aluminum
- B. iron
- C. steel (can be driven flush with ground for safety)
- D. wood
- E. iron spike
- F. homemade wood
- G. camp-made branch

Sod Cloth

When trenching a tent for drainage, cut the ditch as shown and slope it toward the lowest ground in the tent area.

The large tent used as a semipermanent camp in all kinds of weather is much more comfortable with a board floor. Rough lumber nailed over smooth poles or two-by-fours will make a floor that is appreciated more and more as the weather gets rougher and the camping days add up. Dry sand packed hard and trenched on the outside to keep out water makes a fair floor for the all-summer tent when sawed lumber is not available. A fine floor can be made of poles planed with an ax, but that is a job that takes a fair amount of skill and a lot of work.

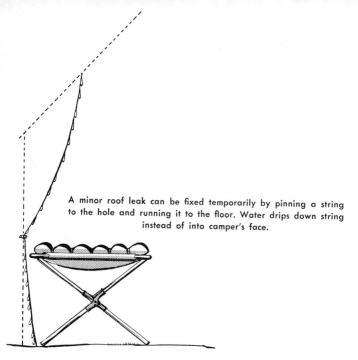

A minor roof leak can be fixed temporarily by pinning a string to the hole and running it to the floor. Water drips down string instead of into camper's face.

TENT FABRICS

Prior to World War II probably 95 per cent of all tents were made of cotton. Canvas, of course, is cotton. So is duck. Balloon silk is just a commercial name for fabric made of high-quality, long-fibered cotton. And Egyptian cotton, much used in good tents in both the past and the present, is another commercial name for a high grade of cotton that may come from Alabama or Texas.

Cotton is still a first-rate material for tents, and one much used despite competition from synthetic fibers like nylon and Dacron which are easily woven into light, strong cloth. Quality is the decisive factor in choosing a cotton tent. The cheapest cotton tents are miserable affairs which tear, leak, and deteriorate in no time. The best ones give a lifetime of service.

There are three general grades of the tent canvas often called duck: single-filled, double-filled, and the so-called "army" duck, which is the strongest and most closely woven. Judge the durability of these ducks or canvas fabrics by their weight per square foot. The heavier they are, the stronger they are—and the more expensive. A tent maker will commonly offer 8-, 10-, and 12-ounce grades.

Make your choice according to how much abuse your tent must take, how heavy you want it, and how much you are willing to pay. The 8-ounce duck will make a good hiker's tent if it is made of high-quality cotton and properly waterproofed. The 12-ounce duck would be better for a large wall tent on packhorse trips.

Good duck tents will shed water without being treated with a waterproofing solution—if they are stretched tight with a decided downslope and not touched from below. But it is a sound idea to buy waterproofed duck or canvas.

Lightness is the main virtue of the thin cotton tent fabrics of the balloon-silk type. They are also very strong in relation to their weight, however, and will stand up in rough going if made with sturdy seams and reinforced at strain points. Tents made of these thin cotton fabrics need a waterproofing solution to withstand heavy rain.

Tents made of nylon, Dacron, or cotton blended with one of these synthetic fibers are wondrously light, extremely strong and durable. Because these fibers are hard and slick, the cloth they make has some tendency to come loose at the seams if not carefully stitched, but good workmanship remedies that. Tightly woven nylon or Dacron can also be too nearly airtight. Some air needs to pass through the fabric of such tight tents as the explorer, say, to keep body vapor from making the interior of the tent wet and clammy. Good ventilation solves that problem. The best fabrics made with synthetic fibers or blends of a synthetic and cotton are comparatively expensive—costing more, perhaps, than the average camper needs to pay for a satisfactory tent.

In addition to sound design and good fabric, quality tents have double-stitched seams and extra thicknesses of fabric at peak, corners, and other points that are subject to unusual friction or strain. Grommets or eyelets that are stitched in are stronger than machine-punched eyelets. The tent's guy ropes should be of hemp, sisal, or a strong synthetic like nylon. Some cheap tents have ropes that are really nothing but twisted paper processed to look like hemp.

Be sure you get a full set of rope, poles, and stakes if they are part of a package deal. It is not uncommon for a vital fitting to be left out in factory packing or retail handling.

The factory waterproofing jobs done on tents these days are usually efficient. Some of the better waterproofing jobs make the tent fabric appear to be mottled with worn spots, but these spots are really just color differences caused by folds in the stiffened fabric during packing and handling. Water will not leak through these fold marks.

It pays to check on the inflammability of the waterproofing of a tent. Many solutions include waxes and oils that burn readily, which is a hazard in a tent heated by stove or campfire. If the tent is actually "fireproof," as the salesman says, he will not mind touching a match to one corner to clinch the sale.

Hikers and other campers who pack their tents along with food and personal gear should avoid tents with the rather greasy, sticky waterproofed surfaces produced by solutions containing boiled linseed oil. The tight, light fabrics can be waterproofed efficiently with less messy solutions.

DO-IT-YOURSELF WATERPROOFING

Most tents are treated by the manufacturer with a solution to make the fabric shed water readily. Tent makers and sporting goods stores also sell prepared waterproofing solutions which can be sprayed or painted on tents or tarps. Any reputable dealer will have two or three such solutions that will do an excellent job.

It's generally a better idea to buy a commercial solution that is painted on the tent fabric, rather than one that is sprayed on from a pressure can. The paint-on solutions soak the fabric thoroughly. The pressure cans, though marvelously quick and easy to use, are not quite so reliable. The average person also has a tendency to use about twice as many cans of spray as directions call for. There's an almost irresistible temptation to give each seam an extra blast of spray for good measure. This leads to extra trips to the store for additional spray cans, and they are comparatively expensive.

There are several good home recipes for waterproofing tents and other woven cotton fabrics used in camp equipment.

Paraffin

One simple and generally satisfactory waterproofing ingredient is paraffin, which is sold in inexpensive blocks at hardware, drug, or grocery stores in every village.

You can waterproof a tent simply by spreading it on a flat surface and rubbing a film of paraffin evenly over the fabric, then pressing it in with a warm iron.

A paint-on solution can be made by dissolving paraffin in turpentine or benzine. Warm the turpentine or benzine in hot water (they are too dangerously inflammable to heat on a stove), and shave in the blocks of paraffin. Use a pound of paraffin for each gallon of turpentine or benzine. Stir the mixture thoroughly, and while it is warm, paint it on the tent with a stiff brush. Two pounds of paraffin in two gallons of turpentine or benzine will waterproof the average 9-by-7-foot wall tent. Turpentine has a slight advantage over benzine, if both are readily available, because it makes the tent fabric a little less stiff than does a mixture of paraffin and benzine.

Perhaps the best way to apply a paraffin solution is to set up the tent tight and trim in the back yard on a sunny day and paint it like a house. Let it stand there until dry.

The paraffin formula has some weaknesses. It stiffens the tent fabric, especially in cold weather, and makes it highly inflammable. Paraffin should be chosen to treat tents and tarps made of thin fabrics like muslin and balloon silk which need its filling property. It is especially recommended for sealing tent floors that come in contact with damp ground and may at times lie in surface water.

Alum and Lead Acetate

Before using this waterproofing solution, wash the tent in a tub to remove the sizing of the fabric. Then, in a sizeable tub or container, dissolve alum in hot, soft water at the rate of $\frac{1}{4}$ pound to 1 gallon. In a second tub mix hot, soft water with lead acetate in the same proportions—$\frac{1}{4}$ pound to 1 gallon. Let the lead-acetate solution settle for about four hours, and then pour all but the settled dregs into the water and alum mixture in the first tub. Soak the tent overnight in this final mixture; then rinse it in clear water and hang up to dry. This treatment will make the fabric almost immune to campfire sparks, as well as showerproof. It makes the individual threads of a fabric water-repellent but leaves tiny spaces in between for ventilation. Thus, the tent will shed rain adequately, but it will not bar water the way rubber boots do. Expect some shrinkage when treating mill-run canvas with an alum and lead solution.

This solution is most satisfactory for medium- and heavy-weight canvas with a tight, close weave. It is less satisfactory for thin, lightweight fabrics and for tent floors or ground cloths that may have to be spread over muddy places containing shallow puddles of water.

Linseed Waterpoofing

A cheap and easy way to waterproof tarps, ground cloths, and other heavy-duty camping canvas is to paint them with boiled linseed oil. Use a good grade and be sure it is the boiled oil, which is available from paint dealers. Just spread the cloth to be treated, and paint it generously enough that the oil soaks all the way through. Hang the canvas in a shaded place to dry for about a week. An additional day or two in strong sunlight will set the oil more firmly in the canvas.

There are other home-waterproofing recipes for canvas that do a fair job, but they involve so much time and so many complicated collections of chemicals that they can hardly be recommended. Most of them are just home-brewed versions of products made better and cheaper by firms in the business of mass-producing waterproofing solutions.

3 - Camp Bedding

It should be established at once that it is the ignoramus, not the expert, who says that he will merely roll up in a blanket and spend the night under the stars. You will never hear such talk from men who know.

The experienced camper knows that, to get a good night's sleep that will keep him healthy and efficient, he must have a bed that is warm, dry, level, and reasonably well padded.

Youngsters and other novice campers get misleading ideas about outdoor sleeping from many Hollywood movies. Movie cowboys, for example, often doze off on the bare ground, their heads on their saddles. They sleep in their clothes, with a slicker or a saddle blanket as their only covering. At dawn they stand up refreshed and virile—ready to wrestle steers or bad men. But—make no mistake about it—such sleeping habits work only in the movies.

Such professional outdoorsmen as forest rangers, big-game guides, and western sheepherders use air mattresses, down-filled sleeping bags, and canvas ground cloths. They make their beds under a tent or some kind of waterproof roof when there is the slightest chance of rain or snow. Many of the wiser and more grizzled heads rest on pillows plump with waterfowl down. They are as finicky as rich brides about each item of the camp bedding.

Good bedding has saved the lives of a host of travelers caught in arctic storms. The average camper will not be sleeping out in arctic cold, of course, but he is likely to be in a few fall cold snaps in the hunting camps of Maine, Michigan, and Montana. And the brief blizzards that frequently hit October deer-hunting camps are enough to make men rear up shivering from the damp blankets and declare that death, if it be soft and warm, would be welcome.

Those are the nights when the camper with poor bedding sits up feeding the fire in hollow-eyed misery. If he hunts at all next day, it will be with red eyes, dripping nose, and aching muscles. All the pleasures of the outing will be reserved for the boys who pulled up their down-filled comforters or wiggled deeper into sleeping bags plump with wool or Dacron when the snow started to rattle on the tent roof.

Basically a good camp bed consists of an effective insulating material that is neatly packaged or held together. If waterfowl down is chosen, a sleeping bag makes a compact and sturdy package for it. Those who like wool blankets usually package them in a large square of heavy canvas (a tarp) which is folded to serve as both a cover and a ground cloth at night. On the trail the tarp is a tough, weatherproof cover for the rolled blankets and any such accessories as an air mattress, flannel sheet, or pillow.

Another good and popular camp bed is a unit made up of two blanket-sized comforters and a tarp large enough to fold under and over them with a foot to spare around the edges.

There are intricate canvas back packs that unfold to form camp beds. The U.S. Army at one time used such a pack bed. Arctic travelers have for centuries experimented with fur bags and blankets made from woven strips of fur. Hammock beds, some with tent-like roofs and side screens, have a general appeal to campers in rainy, bug-infested tropic regions. There have been many experiments, particularly in the early nineteen-hundreds, with canvas covers designed to fit over two poles in stretcher fashion.

The foundation of another style of camp bed common in those days was a mattress made of slender sticks about 3 feet long. The sticks were strung together much like the slats of a venetian blind. Unrolled over hollows dug for the camper's hips and shoulders, the stick bed formed a flat and somewhat springy mattress. Indians of several Plains tribes used the stick bed.

Each year manufacturers ask campers to try some new bedding that is advertised as a triumph of modern design. Many of the new camp beds utilize plastics, synthetic fabrics, and synthetic insulation materials. You can even buy a sleeping bag made of treated paper.

INSULATING MATERIALS

The efficiency of your camp bed, whether it be a blanket roll, sleeping bag, or mattress and comforter, depends mainly on the type of insulating material it contains.

The insulating materials that make up a good camp bed vary surprisingly little in bivouacs ranging from sunny Mexico to Alaska. A sleeping bag or a comforter filled with pure waterfowl down, for instance, is a prize in either place. The difference is merely in the amount of down needed. In regions where nights are merely cool, a sleeping bag holding 2 pounds of fluffy down will warm the sleeper without sweating him up, while 6 pounds of down in a good bag will cope with most of Alaska's weather.

Waterfowl Down

Though waterfowl down is expensive, nobody has ever proved to practical campers that any new synthetic fiber or insulating material is as satisfactory ounce for ounce in camp bedding. Down is marvelously light and warm and is springy enough to resist lumping or matting. It holds body heat without trapping body moisture, which will make the bed clammy and cold. With routine protection from dampness, moths, and vermin, down-filled camp bedding will last a lifetime and more.

Probably the finest of all waterfowl down—and the most expensive—comes from the eider ducks of arctic regions. All down from northern waterfowl is excellent. Mixtures of crushed feathers and down or feathers alone are less efficient than pure down, but they are substantially cheaper. The stems of coarse feathers require fine-woven ticking to keep them from working through.

Dacron and Other Synthetic Fibers

Dacron fibers are a new and highly efficient insulating material for camp bedding. In fact, the better Dacron stuffings are second only to down and fine feathers for warmth, lightness, and all-round suitability. Dacron is durable and immune to moths and mildew. Sleeping bags and comforters insulated with Dacron are a good deal cheaper than those filled with down.

Reputable manufacturers of both down- and Dacron-insulated bags will, however, readily point out that down is the best insulator for rough use in extremely cold weather. Batts of Dacron insulation collect and hold moisture much more readily than down (thus, tags on many good Dacron bags warn that they must be aired frequently and kept completely dry). Dacron is less resilient than down, which means that it will lose more of its warming fluffiness as the sleeper's weight packs it flat and that it will be slower to spring back when the weight is removed. Quite a lot of Dacron is needed to insulate a bag for zero weather, and manufacturers have difficulty sewing through thick batts of it. Thus, most Dacron bags have 4 pounds or less of insulation—plenty for freezing weather, but not for zero temperatures.

There are other synthetic fibers related to Dacron that are good insulators for outdoor sleeping. Trade names vary, with new versions and new claims popping up each year. Don't expect too much of the bargain-price offerings. The better synthetic bedding must be made and tested with enough care to command a fairly high price.

Wool

As it has been for centuries, wool is a fine choice for camp blankets, and it is a satisfactory filler for sleeping bags and comforters. Although good blankets are woven of synthetic fibers today, it is impossible to persuade seasoned woodsmen that they are equal to wool blankets. Virgin wool is the material in Hudson's Bay Company point blankets, the most famous camp blankets in North America. Wool is the blanket material used by the Forest Service and the field forces of all branches of our armed services.

Wool efficiently retains a sleeper's body heat. It allows body vapor to escape without dampening the bedding and holds in a lot of warmth when dampened by rain or dew. At present, wool bedding is inexpensive enough to hold its own in price wars with the new synthetic fibers, though these may one day crowd wool into a secondary role.

A few campers well endowed with both money and curiosity have experimented with sleeping bags and blankets insulated with the wool of such alpine animals as the llama and vicuña of the South American Andes, whose wool is decidedly superior to sheep wool. One experimenter claims his sleeping bag holding 3½ pounds of llama wool was warm at 34 degrees below zero. Prices of such exotic wools are high, so that they are far out of the range of most campers.

Kapok

Kapok, a natural silky fiber, which comes from the seed pods of trees native to Java, is used to pad and insulate sleeping bags. It is a fair insulator, rating below down, Dacron, and wool, but it keeps a place in the market because it is cheaper. Kapok bags are fairly bulky in relation to their warmth, and the material will mat and eventually break up with age and hard use. Inexpensive kapok-filled bags are satisfactory for knock-about use in camps where nights won't be colder than 40° F.

Forest Service workers toss kapok-filled bags from planes to firefighting crews who have hiked or parachuted to a fire in a remote area. Kapok is amply warm for fire-season weather. It withstands quite a lot of use and abuse, and it is so cheap that there is no great loss if a bag lands on the hot side of the fire line.

As kapok is also used in life-preservers, a kapok-filled bag is a good bet for the canoe camper in case of upset.

Cotton

Dry cotton is a better insulating material than wool —but it must be bone dry to be effective. Cotton has such a tendency to collect and hold moisture that it must be rated the worst possible choice as a material for camp blankets or bag filler. It holds body moisture, attracts dew, sops up rain. It dries slowly and holds the chill of death in its fibers until they are completely dry.

Waterproofed cotton makes good ground cloths and tents. A cotton sheet can be used inside a sleeping bag or a bedroll by a person whose skin is irritated by wool or other rough fabrics. Cotton blankets or cotton-filled sleeping bags will do in a pinch in camps where the night air is warm and dry. Beyond that, there is not much to be said in favor of cotton as a material for camp bedding.

Boys of Scout age who are buying their first sleeping bags are often tempted by the low price and plumpness of cotton-filled sleeping bags. Their continued interest in such bags speaks well only for the vitality of youth and the hospitality of summer nights. Cotton is the last bedding material to choose for general camping.

THE SLEEPING BAG

Harsh things have been said of sleeping bags by many old-time camping experts, who have had a wealth of experience with good blanket rolls and a few brief encounters with inferior sleeping bags. And in fact, they were right to condemn the sleeping bags of the early nineteen-hundreds.

The quality sleeping bags available today, however, are the best camp bedding of all for most climates and purposes. Filled with a good insulator and properly

Oblong sleeping bag insulated with Dacron is comfortable at 30 to 60 degrees above zero. *Courtesy of Eddie Bauer.*

made, the sleeping bag is lighter than any other style of camp bed. It is also warmer in proportion to its weight, more durable, and much easier to carry and use.

The initial cost of a top-grade sleeping bag will be more than that of a bedroll of blankets and canvas, but your grandson will be using your sleeping bag fifty years from now if it is handled with reasonable care.

Insulation

Pure waterfowl down is the insulation material in the finest sleeping bags. It is held in overlapping tubes of tough, closely woven ticking. These tubes keep the down from shifting, and they are overlapped to prevent cold strips from developing along the seams and chilling the sleeper.

Sleeping bags filled with Dacron, wool, or kapok should also be examined to determine that the insulation is firmly, evenly confined by fabric tubes or ticking stitched in a close and regular quilting pattern. Otherwise the weight of the sleeper's body will crowd the insulation aside at such pressure points as hip and shoulder.

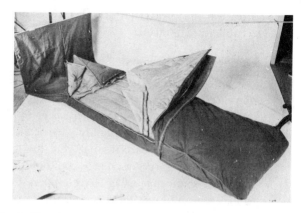

Down-insulated oblong bag with a wool liner and parka hood is warm at 60 below zero. *Courtesy of Alaska Sleeping Bag Co.*

Outside Covers

The best outside covers for sleeping bags are made of long-fibered cotton or similar light, tough sheeting woven from synthetic fibers or blends of synthetic fiber and cotton. Duck or other tent-weight cotton fabrics are fine if weight is of no great consequence.

The camper should *never,* for any purpose, buy a sleeping bag covered top and bottom with rubber, plastic, or any other material that is completely waterproof. Such a cover will be so nearly airtight that the sleeper will soak in his own sweat during the night. Body vapor will be trapped under a waterproof cover no matter how warm or cold the weather. At best, it will result in a damp and clammy bed, while in arctic cold, trapped body moisture could freeze an outdoor sleeper. The top cover of a sleeping bag must be porous enough for vapor-laden air to escape.

Some sleeping bags are made with rubberized or plastic bottoms that are waterproof. These won't trap body vapor, which rises, but they are skimpy substitutes for the protection afforded by a large tarp or a rubberized poncho.

Zippers and Fasteners

A sleeping bag with a zipper that runs all along one side and across the bottom, allowing the bag to be opened and spread flat, is much easier to air out and clean than one that opens only part or all of the way down one side. Be sure the bag you buy has a sturdy, smooth-working zipper. The good ones are dependable, but some cheap bags have zippers that are sure to lock you in or out at the wrong time—and a wilderness camp is no place to replace or repair a zipper.

Some bags have snap fasteners. These are slower than a zipper, but well-made snaps give excellent service otherwise. Snap fasteners are standard equipment on some of the more expensive bags. The gaps between snaps may yawn wide in the eyes of a salesman who wants to sell a zippered bag, but they will not bother the sleeper in actual practice—not if the bag is suitable otherwise. Some wilderness campers insist on snap fasteners, considering them more reliable than zippers.

Mattress Pockets

The built-in air mattress pocket on some sleeping bags is considered an unnecessary gimmick by most discerning outdoorsman. A mattress in such a pocket is difficult to inflate and troublesome to insert and remove. The pocket can collect dirt and moisture.

A better system is to place the air mattress on a ground cloth or directly on smooth ground and spread the sleeping bag on top of it. The bag will not roll off if the site is reasonably level—as it must be to serve its purpose—and if the mattress is not overinflated. This system also makes it a simple matter to spread a folded blanket over the air mattress for extra insulation on a cold night. Blankets used inside a bag with a pocketed air mattress have a way of getting wrinkled and wadded as the camper twists and turns in his sleep.

Canopy

The canopy at the head of a sleeping bag is also of doubtful value. It can be useful as a protective cover for the rolled bag or as a cloth panel to hold such odds and ends as flashlight and glasses while you sleep, but do not think of it as a substitute for a tent. The canopy looks effective in advertising pictures, in which the camper usually has it stretched with poles and ropes to form an awning over the head of his sleeping bag. But the rig works better in theory than in practice. It will ward off light rain or gentle snow, but a real storm with high winds will soon have the camper in an exposed sleeping bag yearning for home. There is no way to stay dry while getting in and out of such a sleeping bag in a storm, and the top covers of good bags are never completely waterproof.

Oblong Bags

The most common design for a sleeping bag is the oblong shape—the finished bag being about 6 feet long and 3 feet wide. Some of these oblong bags have zippers or snaps that allow them to be joined to a second bag of the same design to form a double bed.

The oblong shape is entirely satisfactory for most camping. Big men—and everyone who likes foot and elbow room—should get oblong bags in the largest standard size, which is 90 inches long and 45 inches wide. (The common "90-by-90" designation for this bag refers to its size opened and spread flat.) Any six-footer needs a bag at least 78 inches long. Shorter bags tend to expose the sleeper's head and shoulders as he turns in his sleep. Extra roominess is always an advantage as far as sleeping warmth and comfort are concerned. Campers accustomed to beds will feel strait-jacketed in a skimpy bag. Tight-fitting bags also wear out faster due to strain on seams and concentrated pressure on insulation.

Some manufacturers advertise their bags according to the "cut" size, which refers to the dimensions of a bag before it is hemmed and finished. The finished bag will be several inches smaller. Look for "finished" measurements to avoid getting a small bag.

Mummy Bags

The mummy bag, so named because of its shape, is designed to save the last ounce of weight. A typical

Down-filled mummy bag, which weighs under 4 pounds, is suitable for summer hikers and is comfortable at 25 to 60 degrees above zero. Courtesy of Eddie Bauer.

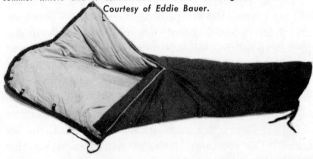

Mountain climbers sleep warm at 10 degrees below zero in 7-pound mummy bag insulated with down. Courtesy of Alaska Sleeping Bag Co.

model tapers from a width of about 36 inches at the
sleeper's shoulders to 24 inches or less at the feet.
Some models have a hood that fits the head and neck
as snugly as a parka hood.

This economy of material makes it possible to produce an adult-size mummy bag that weighs only 3 or
4 pounds and compresses into a roll about the size of
a football. Stuffed with high-grade waterfowl down,
such a bag is warm enough in temperatures below
freezing.

The mummy bag is good for hikers or other campers
who must watch every ounce of pack weight. It will tie
behind a saddle or fit into a compact emergency kit in
a plane used for bush flying.

The mummy bag has several drawbacks. Lacking the
tough outer covers of the heavy-duty oblong bag, it is
somewhat more vulnerable to rips, stains, campfire
sparks, and water. Its tight fit takes some getting used
to. Some outdoorsmen never get over the feeling of
being tied and bound in such a bag.

There is, however, an easy way to turn over in a
tight-fitting sleeping bag without having the whole bag
roll with you. Anchor the bottom of the bag by pressing down on either side of your body with the palms of
your hands. Keep your weight on your palms as you
roll. The arm that pivots under you can be straight-
ened after you have completed the turn and have let
your body down on the bottom of the bag. It sounds
awkward, but try it: there's no faster way to turn over
in a body-hugging sleeping bag. Some practiced
mummy-bag campers can do it in their sleep.

Robe Bags

"Sleeping robes" are simply roomy oblong sleeping
bags without the tough outer covers of the conven-

tional oblong bags. The usual robe is made of two sheets of tightly woven ticking material which are quilted or stitched together to form tubes or squares that hold the insulation material. The large quilt or comforter that results is folded to cover the sleeper top and bottom and is fitted with zipper or snaps to hold it in sleeping-bag shape.

Some robe bags open all the way down one side and across the bottom. Some are sewed shut from waist level down. Some have zippers up the middle of the top. Those that can be opened fully with side zippers or snaps suit most campers best. They are easier to clean and air. They can be turned inside out or top side down to distribute wear evenly. (The bottom layer of any sleeping bag takes most of the punishment.)

The robe style of sleeping bag, like the mummy version, is light and compact. A tarp or other tough outer cover is needed to protect it from gritty ground, moisture, and snags.

Liners

Sleeping bags fitted with separate liners are easier to keep clean and have a far greater comfort range than those used without a sheet or blanket liner.

In cold weather the separate liner snugly fills the drafty gaps that can occur where the sleeper's head props the top of the bag open. The soft and flexible liner helps seal the vulnerable strip where the bag is closed by a zipper or snap fasteners.

A folded sheet made of cotton flannel or light wool will add enough warmth to a warm-weather sleeping bag to see a camper through the crisp weather of early fall. With a blanket-weight liner, the summer bag will do for nights that leave a skin of ice on the water pail.

By juggling liners, most campers can be comfortable in all weathers with one sleeping bag. The basic bag should be chosen to suit the *warmest* weather it will be most used in. Add liners as the weather gets colder.

As far as temperature control is concerned, a liner has the additional advantage of letting the camper adjust his warmth during the night. He can go to sleep with both layers of the folded liner underneath him, acting as a mattress pad. As the night gets colder, he can sleep between the layers of liner or under both. The liner, unlike the bag's sewed-in insulation, can be quickly shifted to work where it is needed most. It can be slipped out of the bag at a trip's end and cleaned or laundered. In the woods it protects the bag's hard-to-clean permanent insulation from soiling.

Cleaning the Sleeping Bag

Any sleeping bag is rather awkward to clean once it has become thoroughly dirty. Postpone the cleaning job as long as possible by using a liner, airing the bag regularly when in camp, and keeping it in dustproof storage during the off season. A plastic bag of the kind dry-cleaning firms use to protect suits and dresses makes a fine storage sack for a rolled-up sleeping bag. With the ends tied tight, the plastic sack is waterproof, dustproof, and mothproof.

Many dry-cleaning firms will do a good job of cleaning soiled sleeping bags, but a professional cleaning job will ordinarily cost about one eighth of the original price of the bag.

The camper himself can clean a bag fairly well by sponging soiled surfaces with cleaning fluid or one of the quick-drying upholstery-cleaning fluids now on the market. Dry the bag thoroughly in the open air, preferably on a sunny day. Sunshine, though it doesn't remove dirt, is a potent natural force in destroying germs and odors.

Most well-made sleeping bags can be washed in a laundry tub with soap and water. We know of one down-filled bag that has been tub-washed half a dozen times with good results. The hazards in washing a bag are matted insulation, fading colors, and shrinkage, but if the bag is made of quality material and is washed carefully with mild soap and lukewarm water, you should have no trouble.

THE BLANKET ROLL

If weight and bulk are of no particular importance, a blanket roll with a tough canvas tarp for cover and ground cloth makes a splendid outdoor bed.

A camper can even use blankets and comforters from beds at home to make a good blanket roll. If they are enclosed in an oversized tarp, they will come home clean with only a whiff of the woodsy odor that inevitably penetrates outdoor bedding. A few hours of airing in sun and wind will remove most of the smell of smoke and wood.

So a bedroll, in that the bedding is already available, can be the cheapest outfit of all. It is flexible, too, since the camper can take or leave extra blankets according to the weather. And a blanket bed on a good air mattress or pine boughs under a ground cloth provides more of the familiar home-bed freedom of movement than a sleeping bag. There is also the advantage of being able to pull up a discarded blanket for extra warmth in those chill hours before dawn.

Many old-timers who refuse to give sleeping bags a fair trial keep blanket rolls just for camping. Probably the best wool blanket for such a bedroll is the justly famous Hudson's Bay blanket, the type known as the "point blanket." The name dates back to the fur-trading days of the late sixteen-hundreds, when the number of stripes, or points, woven like a brand into Hudson's Bay blankets indicated the number of prime beaver pelts needed to trade for a blanket of a particular weight. Today the number of points designates only a difference in size. A four-point blanket measures 72 by 90 inches. All sizes have the same weave, texture, and fine workmanship.

The Hudson's Bay Company, a British firm incorporated May 2, 1670, still sells its blankets through major supply houses throughout North America. These blankets are superb—and expensive. One Hudson's Bay blanket currently costs as much as a medium-priced sleeping bag.

Army-style wool blankets make a good and inexpensive bedroll. They lack the warm fluff of finer wool blankets, but their hard, close weave sheds dirt better and makes them very durable.

Comforters filled with down, wool batting, or Dacron are fine in a bedroll.

Cotton blankets or quilts should be used only when nothing else is available or in any extremely dry and warm climate. They are clammy moisture traps in cold or wet weather.

The tarp used to enclose a blanket roll should be made of Army-weight duck or similar heavy-duty canvas. Such fabric will shed rain and at the same time "breathe" well enough to let body vapor escape from the sleeper without sweating up his bed. It will also protect the bedding while it is riding on a pack horse or bouncing in the back of a jeep or truck.

Blanket Pins

Some outdoor writers have suggested that blankets in this sort of bed be fastened together with blanket pins (king-size safety pins). In actual practice, however, these pins can restrict the sleeper's movements, tear blankets, or tie them down so that warmth adjustments are difficult. In short, they rob the blanket roll of several of its virtues.

AIR MATTRESS

The air mattress is by all odds the best outdoor bed pad available. Here is a mattress that weighs about 2 pounds and folds into a package small enough to fit in any back pack. In five minutes or less it can be inflated to form a pad that is about as comfortable as the innerspring or foam rubber mattress on your bed at home.

That similarity to a household mattress is tremendously important, because it saves the restless hours most persons need to adjust to an unfamiliar bed. Healthy young people can learn to sleep soundly in blankets or sleeping bags spread on the hard ground, as long as they are warm and dry, in two or three nights. The average adult needs a week to persuade his mattress-pampered muscles to relax in an unpadded bed. An air mattress will prevent that many nights of tossing and turning.

Sizes

Men six feet tall or more need an air mattress of the greatest standard length (75 inches) and at least 32 inches wide. A width of only 25 inches leaves little elbow room, even for a very thin camper. A man who is tall, husky, and restless will be more comfortable on a mattress measuring 75 by 48 inches, which is a standard size with several makers.

There are three-quarter-length air mattresses available for those who want to save pack weight. They pad the sleeper from head to knees on the assumption that the legs can be either cushioned with some improvised padding or left to dangle. Some hardy outdoorsmen swear by these mattresses, but more campers swear at them, as the feeling of dangling is difficult to adjust to.

Keep in mind that most styles of air mattress are slightly shorter and decidedly narrower when inflated than when lying flat on a counter. Allow for this when ordering one by mail. Many dealers give the larger, deflated size rather than the measurements of the mattress filled with air.

Most air mattresses are so designed that the air is held in six tubes running the length of the mattress. This system is fine for most campers. But do not blow up such a mattress so tight that the tubes act as rollers under you. Put in just enough air to keep the points of your hips and shoulders a fraction of an inch off the ground.

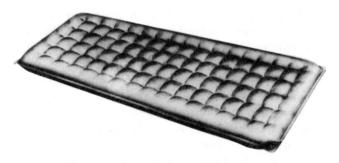

The best air mattress is the tufted style with air-tight rubber piles reinforced with a cloth covering. *Courtesy of Morsan Tents.*

A second type of air mattress is the tufted design, which forms a flat surface with dimples at the tuft connections when inflated. This is the best design of all, in that it is more like a good bedroom mattress. It is also the most expensive design.

Materials

The toughest and most reliable of the materials used to make air mattresses is a woven fabric of cotton or nylon impregnated with rubber. Mattresses are also made of plain rubber, synthetic rubber, and plastics. These are generally much easier to puncture than the fabric-and-rubber models. Some of the cheaper plastic mattresses are so fragile that they can be punctured by the sharp twigs or needles in a bough bed. Do not rely on a mattress of unprotected plastic for rough woods use. Cautious campers carry tire-tube patches to repair air mattress leaks.

Check the valves of any air mattress you buy. The most reliable are the metal tire-tube type with screw tops. The push-in plastic valves will do for backyard or close-to-home camping, but they are not designed to stand up under hard use and abuse.

Most campers blow up their air mattresses like balloons, with their own lung power. This ordinarily takes five or ten minutes. Small hand- or foot-operated pumps do the same job. Whether the pump is worth its cost and pack weight is a matter for individual decision. Pumps are fairly popular with car campers, especially family groups with a lot of air mattresses to inflate. A pump is seldom seen in the duffel of a veteran wilderness camper.

The best way to store an air mattress is to blow it up and stand it in a cool closet. Tight folds cause rubber and many synthetics to crack prematurely.

BROWSE TICK MATTRESS

A camper headed for the woods at a season when dry leaves, grass, or moss are plentiful can improvise a suitable mattress by carrying a light "tick" or mattress cover to be stuffed with woods-grown material, or browse, at the campsite. If it is made of high-grade cotton, nylon, or Dacron, a browse bag large enough to form a mattress for one person will weigh about 1 pound and take little more room in the pack than a spare shirt. The weight and bulk of such a browse tick will be substantially less than that of a full-sized air mattress.

Suitable natural stuffing will be hard to come by in wet weather or on winter and spring outings—after the dry browse of summer and fall is packed and soaked by winter snow and rain. The tips of evergreen boughs are fair browse-bag insulation in late summer, fall, or winter, but in spring they sprout new needles that are sticky and damp with sap.

Be sure the dead grass or leaves you stuff in your mattress tick is free of ants, chiggers, and similar small insects. Be wary of the browse-bag mattress stuffed with random weeds if you suffer from hay fever or some similar allergy. A ticking of fine, tightly woven threads is needed to seal in woods browse effectively.

HOME-STYLE MATTRESSES

Campers who can haul a lot of weight and bulk conveniently can use a home-style mattress filled with ka-

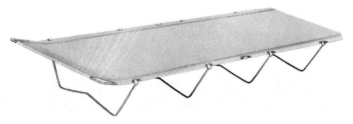

Folding canvas cot is insulated underneath with Dacron or down and is supported by spring steel braces.
Courtesy of Eddie Bauer.

pok, wool, feathers, or even cotton. Several such models are made for camp use.

Also available—and superb for its purpose—is a folding camp cot of metal and canvas with a thick layer of insulation stitched to the underside of the canvas sleeping surface. These cots, which fold into neat packages weighing only 10 or 12 pounds, are only 6 or 8 inches off the ground when set up. They are astonishingly sturdy and easy to set up, and they are ideal for tent sleeping in extremely cold weather. They are even comfortable enough to double as stowaway guest beds at home.

BOUGH MATTRESSES

Shed a tear for the young camper who has never bedded down in the deep woods on a springy, clean-smelling mattress of evergreen boughs. It is a milestone of outdoor experience. To miss it is to have a void in your life comparable to never having seen a wilderness sunrise or heard wild geese call at night.

A good bough bed takes up to an hour to assemble,

To build a bough bed, gather enough evergeen branches 18 to 20 inches long and prop them with the cut ends toward the ground in overlapping rows (above). Framed with logs to keep it in shape (below), the springy mattress will last a week with proper care.

but no particular skill is needed. Just gather enough evergreen branches of the proper size—no more than 18 or 20 inches long—and lean them together with stub ends down, soft tops tipped against one another like a duck's body feathers, to form a deep, dense mattress. The edges and ends of a bough bed will stay in place better if the bed is made inside a rough frame of small logs, poles, or rocks. You sleep inside this frame, not on it. Spread a sturdy ground cloth over the top to keep pitch from the cut ends off your sleeping bag or blankets.

Young fir trees provide the best bed boughs, and hemlock, spruce, or pine will do. The boughs of many spruce trees have particularly sharp needles, however, and require a very tough ground cloth to cover them.

All evergreen boughs will pack down after a night or two of use as a mattress. Fluff them up and add as many new boughs as needed for additional nights. Cut boughs will start to shed needles and dry up in a week or so.

The main trouble with bough beds, in addition to the time they take to construct, is that laws in most established camping areas forbid the cutting or defacing of green trees. This limits the bough bed to wilderness areas where evergreen trees are plentiful and campers comparatively scarce.

CAMP PILLOWS

A camp pillow is an unnecessary luxury in one sense, but it also will be sorely missed by a person accustomed to sleeping with a soft pillow at home. Folded coats or duffel bags are poor substitutes.

Down-filled pillows of sleeping-bag size weigh less than a pound, and they would be worth their weight in comfort if they weighed 5 pounds, especially in cold weather. A pillow blocks those drafts that otherwise creep into the top of a sleeping bag.

Air-filled pillows weighing only a few ounces are available. They are fine for warm weather and satisfactory down to freezing when tucked under blankets or the lower insulation of a sleeping bag. They can double as soft, waterproof camp cushions. Some deer hunters prize them as deer-stand seats in cold, wet weather.

The pillow you use at home is a fine choice for quick, clean camping trips when there is no particular load limit on duffel. Actually a pillow is far more welcome for outdoor sleeping than it is on a bed at home.

4 - Clothing for Campers

ONE THING SHOULD BE PUT STRAIGHT AT ONCE: it is no crime to go camping in work clothes or in camp clothing that, although it is not the best available, is what you already own or can afford to buy. A coat insulated with eiderdown, for instance, would be a marvel of weightless warmth for dawn vigils in duck blinds or deer stands in Maine or Minnesota. Yet outdoorsmen of modest means, including the authors of this book, can also be happy in less efficient cold-weather coats.

The main principles to follow in choosing camp clothes are that they are reasonably sturdy and comfortable and suit the weather you expect. Beyond these requirements, wear whatever suits your taste and pocketbook. Good outdoor clothing is much the same for both sexes.

The following evaluation of camp clothing is designed to call attention to items that have real merit and to warn against those that are inefficient, needlessly expensive, or otherwise impractical.

UNDERWEAR

Warm Weather

For camping in warm weather, the best general advice is to wear what you customarily wear at home and at work in warm weather. Women who commonly wear girdles or other tight foundation garments are an obvious exception to this rule, but most men's regular summer underwear will be comfortable, inexpensive, and durable enough to survive rough use and primitive camp laundering.

Two pairs of cotton underpants and two cotton undershirts will suit most campers on summer outings lasting less than a week. Take three pairs for a longer trip if pack weight is of no great importance. Otherwise it is usually best to take no more than one change and wash the dirty ones as needed. A small camp laundry is no great chore in warm weather, and such skimpy items as shorts and undershirts will dry in two hours of sunlight or while you sleep.

For summer underwear, cotton is as good a material as any and usually the best of all. Although wool is less clammy when wet and more efficient at dispelling perspiration, it is unnecessarily warm for summer in most climates and many people find it scratchy and ir- ritating next to perspiring skin. Good wool undergar- ments are much more expensive than cotton.

Although shorts and undershirts made of nylon, Dacron, or similar synthetic fibers are exceedingly light, strong, and fast-drying, they have a drawback for camp use. The coarser strands of these man-made fibers are often woven into a fabric that is almost as abrasive as fine sandpaper. This can be a painful nuisance when pack straps are rubbing an undershirt against bare skin for mile after mile. The friction of underwear woven from synthetics can give you a hot seat when rowing a boat, and some of this underwear is brutally abrasive to the camper on horseback. Thus, underclothes made of smooth cotton or fine wool are best for activities that involve a lot of friction.

Fall Weather

Typical fall weather or summer trips to high altitudes call for longer and heavier underwear than the shorts and T-shirts or sleeveless undershirts that suffice in summer. One- or two-piece cotton underwear with long legs and sleeves is comfortable in temperatures down to freezing, if the weather is reasonably dry and calm. More body heat is drained off in wet coastal areas with strong winds and temperatures of 40° or 50° F. than in dry, windless regions with temperatures as low as 20° F.

The cotton "thermal" underwear that is currently advertised as a scientific discovery for outdoor clothing serves very well in fall and mild winter weather. The "thermal" element is simply a method of weaving that forms a waffle pattern of protrusions and hollows in the cloth. These hollow pockets in the fabric next to the skin do, in fact, trap air and form a barrier against the rapid escape of body heat. It is an efficient idea for outdoor clothing. The basic principle is as old as the hills, however, and it is a mistake to assume that cotton underwear of routine weight and quality will be miraculously warm because of this "thermal" weave. Such cotton underwear is warmer and better ventilated than the same weight of cotton in a tight, flat weave.

The same thing is true of the fishnet type of underwear that is being widely publicized. These undershirts and pants are made of soft cords woven together in a fishnet pattern with spacious gaps between cords. Pockets of insulating air are formed when outer garments cover these holes. These net undergarments are warm, which surprises most people who try them for the first time. They are obviously light and ventilated so they will not readily trap body moisture. They must be given good marks on the basis of field tests in both fall and winter weather.

Fishnet underwear is comfortable in a great range of temperatures. A net undershirt one of the authors wore with satisfaction on a November deer hunt in Maine was later given to a friend who works and lives on the tropical island of Puerto Rico. The new owner of this T-shirt considers it ideal for fishing and golfing in hot weather. Worn without an outer garment, the fishnet shirt admits enough sun to let a winter-bleached tourist get an even tan without spending a lot of time sprawled out in the sun.

The fishnet underwear, like the "thermal" weave, is new only in the sense that it has recently been advertised extensively in this country. Scandinavian fishermen, however, have worn net undershirts for centuries, and many of the Swedish and Norwegian settlers in this country have worn homemade net underwear for cold weather outdoor activities for generations. The Scandinavians will tell you that fishnet undergarments are sound and sensible for both mild and cold weather, but they will not claim that net underwear in itself will keep a person comfortable in a heat wave or a blizzard.

The two-layer underwear that is in fact a light wool suit with a cotton liner is particularly good for both fall and winter camping. The thin inner layer of cotton is soft and smooth against the skin, which is a great blessing for the multitude of outdoorsmen who are irritated by wool. The wool outer layer and the film of air between the two layers make these garments very warm in relation to their weight and bulk. Body moisture can escape without becoming clammy. Duofold is no doubt the most famous trade name for this two-layer underwear.

For Extreme Cold

With warm outer garments, the fall-weather underwear already mentioned will be entirely satisfactory for ordinary winter weather. Actually, campers not accustomed to cold weather are more likely to wear too much than too little. This is a particular hazard with underwear, because there is no efficient way to remove or unbutton it when the exertion of snowshoeing or a steep climb makes it uncomfortably hot. Wet with sweat, the too warm underwear will be miserably cold when the hiker stops to rest.

The best combination for the man doing hard work in cold weather is fairly light wool, cotton net, or two-layer underwear with warm and windproof outer garments that can be quickly removed or unbuttoned before sweat forms. The outer garments are replaced or closed during stops, keeping the outdoorsman comfortable and efficient all the way.

But there are times and places for two suits of long wool underwear or long johns insulated with down, Dacron, Acrilàn, or some other synthetic fiber. A wind-swept duck blind is one of those places, if the temperature is freezing or below and the hunter remains motionless for long periods of time. Hunters sitting quietly on deer stands in freezing weather can seldom wear too much underwear. Anyone out in temperatures of zero and below can use extra warm undergarments, and he will need them badly when it is 30 below and windy.

Insulated Underwear

We use the term "insulated underwear" to describe suits that have fluffy insulation quilted between two layers of thin woven fabric. In most of the insulated underwear currently made for outdoorsmen, Dacron, Acrilan, or some similar synthetic fiber is the insulating material. Two or three manufacturers make expensive suits stuffed with waterfowl down.

Insulated suits of long underwear are exceedingly warm, particularly those stuffed with waterfowl down or the more expensive synthetics. Though bulky in appearance, they are actually very light. Quality underwear of this type is warm enough to reduce substantially the need for bulky outer garments. A suit of down- or Dacron-insulated underwear can be worn inconspicuously under sports or business clothes at football games or other outdoor events that are both cold and social.

Insulated underwear is the best of all for such activities as ice fishing or winter boating, where the sportsman is exposed to extreme cold for long periods without moving about much. Any outdoorsman who has ridden a plodding horse on a long mountain trail in winter will understand how valuable insulated underwear can be on any outing that involves hours of patient submission to crackling cold.

The greatest risk with insulated underwear is that it will be needlessly warm for outdoor activities involving a good deal of exertion. Sweat is far more of a menace to health and comfort in subzero cold than a slight chill is, and sweaty underwear is the most awkward garment of all to remove or dry on the trail or in a primitive camp. A lot of stove or campfire heat is required to dry any damp garment when outside temperatures are far below zero—and any garment is a frost trap until it is dry.

Observe the following three precautions when shopping for insulated underwear.

1. Be sure you actually need such warm underwear.

2. Avoid—or at least be wary of and inspect carefully—quilted suits offered at extremely low prices and advertised as containing some wondrous synthetic insulation that is "warmer than waterfowl down" or "cozy at 30 below." Insulated underwear with sturdy stitching, sound outer fabric, and insulation material that will stand wear and washing without lumping, matting, or working out of loose seams is fairly expensive.

3. Examine the outside and inside surfaces of any suit of insulated underwear you consider buying. Some of the synthetic fabrics that enclose the insulating material have a slick, hard finish which is clammy against the skin and abrasive enough to cause trouble in such an activity as horseback riding. The outer cover and lining should be of a soft synthetic or of high-grade cotton.

SOCKS

Wool

Although wool has some shortcomings, socks made of fine wool are undoubtedly the best choice for all-round camp wear. Top-grade wool socks are warm in winter, cooler than thin, sweat-trapping fabrics in summer. They dry quickly when wet. The good ones have a soft and springy texture which is the finest protection against the blisters and raw spots that afflict the tenderfoot. There are other socks that will stand more wear and abuse, but high-quality wool is tough enough to survive the routine ordeals of outdoor footwear.

The thing some shoppers ignore is that it is as easy to make a cheap and shoddy sock out of wool as out of anything else, and the terms "all wool" and "pure wool" are no guarantee against skimpy knitting or brittle, short-fibered, or reprocessed wool. The cheapest wool socks wear out in a hurry—one day of mountain hiking will ruin the heels—and they are not particularly satisfactory even before the holes appear.

Top-grade wool socks, on the other hand, will last through months of hard wear, withstand a hundred primitive washings, and remain soft and comfortable all the way. A top-grade sock is made of fine, long-fibered virgin wool. The knit or weave is close enough that the threads do not stretch wide apart when the sock is pulled over the foot. Natural or bleached white wool is better than colored wool, for while most of the dyes used to color socks are safe enough, in a hiking sock they might cause an allergy, infect a broken blister, or fade and discolor other clothing in a catch-all camp laundry pail.

The quality of any sock is wasted, of course, if the sock does not fit reasonably well. Proper fit means that it is snug enough to prevent bunching at toe or heel, yet roomy enough to overcome the tendency of tight socks to work down into the shoe or boot. The top should reach about 3 inches above the ankle if the socks are to be worn with low shoes. Socks for higher shoes or boots should be long enough to reach 2 inches above the boot top.

Synthetic-Wool Blends

Socks made of wool reinforced with threads of such a sturdy synthetic as Dacron or nylon are probably the best bargain for rough outdoor wear. The fine all-wool socks ranked in first place for sheer comfort and general practicality are more expensive than the blends of wool and synthetic, and there is no question about the blends lasting longer. They do. As a rule, the higher the percentage of synthetic thread, the more indestructible the sock. This durability ceases to be a favorable factor when the softness, warmth, and efficient ventilation of the all-wool sock is lost. Weekend hikers, who tend to plan trips that are a bit tougher than their feet, will be wise to choose walking socks with a low percentage of synthetic thread—no more than 40 per cent. On mild-weather outings where less walking is involved, socks with 60 per cent nylon or Dacron and 40 per cent good-grade wool are entirely satisfactory.

Synthetic Socks

Camp socks made entirely of synthetic fibers have two general advantages: they are usually cheaper than high-grade wool or wool and synthetic stockings, and they will stand more abuse. Those made of long, fine fibers have much the same appearance and feel as good wool. They are fine for all trips that do not involve hours of hiking or extremely cold weather. The synthetics used in socks and all other camping equipment are constantly being improved. Each year we are offered synthetic fabrics that are softer, less slick and shiny, and more efficient at dispelling moisture. A little more progress with these last three factors will produce socks of nylon, Dacron, Orlon, or a similar synthetic that will challenge socks of fine wool for first place.

Cotton

The faults of cotton socks—mainly their tendency to collect and hold moisture—are well known. Yet a great many outdoorsmen wear heavy cotton socks all their lives. The low price of cotton socks accounts for much of their popularity. But there is more to it than that. Cotton socks are very comfortable unless they are soaked with sweat or water in cool or cold weather, and the people who commonly wear cotton socks in mild climates are perfectly content with them for the simple reason that they keep them dry. Hobby campers who write a lot on the subject usually draw word pictures of campers who are endlessly hiking, wading, and battling freezing weather—activities that call for wool socks, sure enough—but the vast majority of recreational campers seldom subject themselves to such conditions.

Thus, cotton socks are fine for summer vacation trips where most of the travel is by car, boat, or horses. What difference does a wet sock, be it wool or cotton, make to a member of a family group in an auto camp on the lakeshore in July? For such summer camping trips most parents put inexpensive cotton or synthetic socks on their youngsters, reasoning correctly that there is no sense in providing fine wool socks for wading through briars and bog holes.

Socks for Cold Weather

The choice of socks becomes more important when a trip involves temperatures below freezing. At zero or colder, sound socks can mean the difference between comfort and frostbite, which in extreme cases can result in the loss of toes, feet, and even life.

Two pairs of wool or of wool and synthetic socks inside a leather boot or a rubber-bottomed shoepack are a good choice down to zero for the outdoorsman who is hiking or at least moving enough to keep good circulation in the feet. The inner pair of socks should be all or mostly high-grade wool, soft and fluffy. The outer pair, exposed to more wear and tear by friction against the boot, can be of a sturdier weave. An outer boot sock with 40 to 60 per cent of nylon or Dacron thread will wear much longer than one of pure wool. This advantage will show up in a hurry at the heels, where most friction occurs. Ankle height is enough for the inner pair of socks in this combination, whether or not the shoe top is higher than the ankle. They will not slide down if they fit properly—snug but not binding tight—and are worn in a boot or shoe that fits the same way. The outer socks should be long enough to reach about 2 inches above the top of shoe or boot.

A third pair of wool socks may be worn for additional warmth if it does not make the outer shoe or boot too tight. If it binds the foot enough to retard circulation, the third sock will be much more hindrance than help. The third sock will be most useful to the ice fisherman, the hunter on a winter deer stand, or any other outdoorsman who has to sit still in extreme cold.

Insulated Socks

A recent development in cold-weather socks is the type with loose insulating material quilted between two layers of thin fabric. The result is a rather bulky but very warm sock—usually ankle high—that may be worn inside any roomy shoe or boot in extremely cold weather. Insulated socks are excellent foot warmers when stuffed with down, high-grade wool, or quality synthetic fibers. They are particularly suited to the roomy, calf-high rubber boots that are increasingly popular with sportsmen out in cold weather. Most shoepacks also have plenty of room for bulky insulated socks. They are generally too bulky for the snug-fitting leather shoes or boots worn in fall weather.

Those insulated socks with a fabric shell of slick synthetic cloth are much more comfortable when worn over thin wool socks. Light inner socks are nearly always a good idea with insulated socks, for that matter. They fill the gaps at the top of the bulky quilted socks and improve their fit.

Rubber Socks

You can buy several kinds of cold-weather sock made of thick, porous rubber shaped to fit the foot snugly. They do hold in body heat, as claimed, but they also trap every drop of sweat created in hiking. They will do for the man whose cold-weather outing does not involve the generation of much body heat, but they are clammy, stuffy rigs for hiking.

Below-Zero Socks

Crackling cold keeps snow so dry that the only moisture the outdoorsman has to fear is sweat. Thus he can comfortably wear footgear that would quickly be soaked by the wet snow of higher temperatures.

A dandy combination for snowshoeing in below-zero weather is two pairs of thick, fleecy wool socks inside a leather moccasin with a fairly snug top reaching 4 or 5 inches above the ankle. The rig is light, warm, and entirely weatherproof in powder-dry snow. It wears well on soft snow trails.

Blanket socks, which are simply squares of blanket-weight wool fabric big enough to fold over the foot and ankle, are a cheap and easy way to insulate the feet when they are enclosed in such light and flexible outer gear as moccasins, fur boots, or mukluks. Blanket socks, common in the far North, fit better when worn over a regular sock, but they will shape to the foot surprisingly well—considering their bulk and edges—after the wearer has taken a few steps in soft moccasins or fur boots.

Thick wool socks worn with calf-high felt boots and ankle-high rubbers make fine footgear for extreme cold. The airtight and waterproof rubbers in this combination are neither high enough nor tight enough at the top to trap moisture the way high boots will. This outfit is very light, warm as toast, and comfortably ventilated. With a sturdy work-shoe rubber over the foot, the rig will stand the abrasion of a snow-shoe harness or of hiking over rocky ridges the wind has swept bare of snow.

Outer boots lined with wool fleece or made of such good insulators as fur or thick felt do much of a sock's job in extremely cold weather. Cold-weather boots are covered in the chapter on shoes and boots.

TROUSERS

All good camp trousers have several things in common, no matter for what climate or special use they are intended. First, they must fit properly—a seemingly obvious requirement which actually requires some special attention in trousers to be used specifically for camping. Many women, for example, have to be restrained from buying trousers or slacks that are too tight to allow freedom of motion or even unrestricted breathing. Most men buying their first camp clothing get trousers that are too short-waisted and far too long at the cuff.

Problems of fit for both men and women can be solved by keeping the following requirements in mind. The waist of camp trousers should be an inch larger than you usually wear at home. This allows for heavier camp shirts, thicker underwear, or tucked-in sweaters. A belt or suspenders will take up slack if the waist is a bit loose; there is no quick way to fix a too tight waist in camp.

An extra inch or so of length from crotch to trouser top is a sound idea for two reasons: (1) outdoor activities involve long steps over logs and other mild gymnastics that require more freedom than dress clothes allow; and (2) many camp trips call for thicker shirts and undergarments which need room, and many campers take up still more slack by carrying an unusual number of things in their pockets.

Long cuffs serve no useful purpose and are the final error campers commonly make as far as the fit of outdoor pants is concerned. Loggers and other professional woodsmen like their pants cuffs fairly high—at the top of the ankle, or even higher when worn with boots that have 8- or 10-inch tops. Cuffs at the shoe heel get muddy and damp in wet weather and provide an extra 3 or 4 inches of fabric that can only catch on snags and get underfoot. Turned-up cuffs should never be worn on camp pants, by the way. They can trip a hiker on brush or snags, and they are useless collectors of trash and water.

Durability is an important consideration with any pants bought for woods wear. Seams should be reinforced at strain points with cross-stitching. Be sure you have a sturdy zipper or flap buttons sewed on with tough thread. (A flimsy zipper that fails in the brush is maddening to work on and almost impossible to repair.) Get pants with deep, roomy pockets. Factory-installed suspender buttons are a good idea if you tend to fill those pockets, for suspenders hold up weight much more efficiently than belts. Unless you spend a lot of time wading through brier patches, avoid pants with legs faced with leather or plastic. They are costly to clean and maintain and needlessly heavy and complicated for most camping.

The best bet for rough going is a conservative slack design that does not have pleats, turned-up cuffs, built-in belts, or other useless trimmings. The seat and legs should be just loose enough to allow plenty of freedom of action, but not so loose that they wrinkle or flop around. Wear a strong leather belt at least 1 inch wide, suspenders, or both belt and suspenders if you carry a lot of equipment in your pockets or on the belt. Cuffs should reach to just above the shoe tops. This simple design for outdoor pants is equally suitable in hot or cold weather, the only difference being that cold or wet weather calls for heavier and warmer fabric.

Slacks with Knitted Cuffs

Camp pants with ankle-hugging cuffs are inferior to loose cuffs worn outside the boot. If they fit properly (loose enough to allow good circulation, snug enough to prevent chafing wrinkles), the knit-cuff pants will do for cold-weather outings that involve little walking. They are stuffy in hot weather, however, and cause needless friction in hiking. They funnel rain or water from wet brush into the boots rather than spill it harmlessly outside as loose cuffs do. They fill the boots with weed seeds and trash in the same way, and their fuzzy sock tops exposed at the boot tops collect burrs, snow, dust, or water which overhanging cuffs would ward off.

Ted Trueblood, who is both an outdoor writer and an outdoorsman, has one kind thought about pants tucked inside the boots: they do a service for the man with a hole in his pocket. The tucked-in pants will channel his change into the boot, where the pain it causes will lead to its recovery.

Tight Denims

The form-fitting blue denims are excellent for horseback riding in hot or moderate weather. Sturdy knock-about pants, they are fine for anyone slim and short-waisted enough to wear them comfortably. The good ones (Levi and Lee are well-known brand names) are as tough as boarding-house steak. Western denims are made of cotton, however, which makes them a poor choice for climates that are consistently wet or extremely cold. They have tight, hard-to-get-into pockets which annoy some people. Finally their snug fit is not particularly good for hiking.

Riding Breeches

The riding breeches that flare wide along the thigh and fit tight below the knee are suitable for park riding or other rather formal horseback trips where style is an important consideration. There are good campers, mainly crotchety old-timers, who wear such pants for a variety of outdoor ventures. They would not be as happy in better-designed camp pants—but you will. Formal riding breeches worn on a western or Canadian pack trip will be glaringly out of place among the blue denim and work-slacks crowd, and guides and wranglers are about as ready as any other group to mistrust the person who is different.

Overalls and Coveralls

A host of farmers and other outdoor workers do most of their hunting, fishing, and camping in bib overalls or coveralls. Those common work garments deserve to be mentioned along with other camping pants because they are entirely satisfactory for many kinds of camping. They are not stylish, of course, but they are practical, durable outdoor pants for mild climates. Some stores specializing in outdoor clothing sell rather fashionable versions of these overalls and coveralls, and many of them are designed for women and children.

Fabrics for Camp Trousers

The time has passed when wool could be confidently prescribed as best for a pair of all-round camping trousers. It is not that wool has lost any of its admirable qualities; but synthetic fibers have been developed and improved at such a pace that they have surpassed wool in several respects. The good synthetics are already more durable. Competition among the various trade-name synthetic fabrics is making them less expensive than wool.

Wool is still a fine choice for very cold weather, and lightweight wool pants are good for summer outings, too. The softness of wool pants makes them ideal for stalking deer or other game that will be spooked by the scraping noises made by duck or denim pants when the hunter moves through brush.

The blends of wool and synthetic threads make excellent outdoor pants as long as they are not marred by inferior quality or poor workmanship. Some of the pants made entirely of synthetic fiber are quite satisfactory.

Such sturdy cotton fabrics as denim and duck make splendid camp pants for summer and mild spring or fall weather. The awkward stiffness they have when new can be remedied by running them through a washing machine before wearing them. The fabric of some of the cheaper grades is thickened and stiffened with pastelike sizing which will wash out. And nearly all cotton pants shrink somewhat in their first washing. Shrink them as much as possible and check to be sure they still fit before you leave home.

Corduroy cotton pants cannot be recommended for

general outdoor wear. That ribbed weave is too noisy for a hunter stalking game. It blots up moisture of all kinds and dries slowly. It is neither as warm nor as sturdy as its bulk suggests. "Cords" are just for picnics or auto outings where style and availability are as important as anything else.

Leather outdoor shorts or pants, though rarely seen in this country, are common in the alpine regions of Europe. Mountaineers in Germany wear leather shorts with high wool stockings in all but the coldest weather. Leather pants are extremely tough, reasonably pliable, windproof, and quite warm as long as they are dry. Soaking wet, leather is clammy and cold. It blots up moisture readily and is slow to dry. Leather garments of good quality are expensive to buy and difficult to clean properly. The buckskin pants common among North American frontiersmen vanished from the scene because good wool and cotton fabrics became increasingly available at low prices, while good buckskin became scarce and expensive. Except for fur pants bought at outposts for arctic ventures, leather pants are now just expensive oddities for North American outdoorsmen. And many arctic travelers now wear quilted pants insulated with down or synthetic fiber instead of native fur garments. The latter are uneven in quality and craftsmanship and very expensive and difficult to obtain outside of the arctic regions where they are used. The fur pants are made by natives, who are indifferent to their animal odors.

SHIRTS

There are a few special considerations in choosing shirts for camping. Here is a check list of things that are generally desirable:

Roomy shoulders and sleeves, and a long tail to

allow freedom of motion. A short tail that keeps popping out of the trousers is a particular nuisance and a common fault with skimpy shirts.

Long sleeves are nearly always a better choice than short ones. They are warmer in cold weather, and they protect against insects and sunburn in hot weather. You can roll up a long sleeves if you wish, while with a short one, you are simply stuck when the mosquitoes move in or you notice the first flush of what may be a painful sunburn.

Roomy breast pockets with button or snap closings are particularly useful. The closed tops keep the odds and ends stored in the pockets and keep out twigs, trash, rain, or snow.

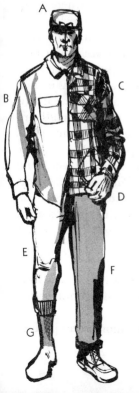

Clothing for cold-weather camping: A. wool hat, B. medium-weight wool shirt, C. heavy wool outer shirt, D. gloves or mittens, E. underwear of wool and/or cotton silk synthetics, F. pants of heavy wool, water repellent, G. socks of wool and/or nylon.

Pick a shirt with strong, fairly large buttons sewed on tight. Zippers are all right, but they are never as foolproof and easy to repair as buttons. Big buttons are easier to handle with fingers stiff from cold, and they hold better than tiny, dressy ones.

Give some thought to color. White shows dirt easily. Black absorbs heat in summer. Many residents of mosquito-infested Canadian regions are persuaded that the color blue is especially attractive to mosquitoes. (Their tests are not "proven" or "scientific," but they have observed that mosquitoes invariably chase the guy in the blue shirt, which is proof enough for a woodsman.) Large squares of white in a plaid or checked shirt will be discolored by crude laundering unless the dye is particularly fast. Unless they are hunting where there is danger of being shot for a deer by some witless gunner, most deep-woods outdoorsmen avoid shirts with a lot of flash and sheen. Mild plaids or soft solid colors are less startling to fish and animals. A fisherman wading in shallow water will actually scare fish with a gaudy, light-reflecting shirt. There is substantial evidence that fish, birds, and many game animals are color-blind or at least color-confused by human standards, yet most of them seem to spot gaudy colors far more readily than drab ones, particularly when the colored object is in motion. A bright yellow shirt on a fisherman may appear to be a certain shade of gray to a wary trout in clear water, but it is a gray that alarms him much more than the shade of a soft green or tan shirt.

Shirt Materials

Cotton in a sturdy weave makes good camp shirts for warm weather.

The synthetic fibers are fine for summer camp shirts

as long as the fabric is reasonably soft and pliable. Avoid stiff, shiny fabrics. Most of the old school of camping experts advocated light wool shirts for summer. Actually wool has only one advantage for summer wear: it will remain fairly warm and dry quickly if you are caught in a sudden shower. But a top-grade wool shirt costs at least twice as much as one made of a good cotton or synthetic fabric. It will not take as much wear and tear, and it is more difficult to clean. Wool is also rather scratchy and irritating to many people in hot weather. Summer campers do not need wool shirts, unless they are in northern regions, misty coastal regions, or mountains where altitude makes nights and cloudy days uncomfortably cool for wearing cotton shirts.

When the weather gets cold, fine wool shirts are unsurpassed for general camp and outdoor wear. There is a tremendous difference in quality—and cost—of wool shirts. There are bargains to be had in surplus Army and Navy wool shirts. The colors are not stylish, of course, and some Army shirts are made of wool woven into a rather hard, harsh fabric. The price is usually low, however, and genuine Army and Navy wool shirts are warm and durable. Look out for the cheap wool shirts of navy blue or khaki that are not service-surplus at all but just shoddy fakes offered at a low price. They are uncomfortable when worn against the skin, and will not last very long.

The wool shirts made by Pendleton deserve mention. You can pay more and get better wool shirts than the standard Pendletons in luxury stores in large cities, and stores across the nation offer pretty good shirts for less money. But a Pendleton shirt is one of the quality items the average outdoorsman can afford, and it is usually available in his home-town store.

SWEATERS

The main thing to know about sweaters for camping is that they are extremely useful. A loose, long-sleeved sweater of soft wool in the top of the pack or duffel bag saves the day when your shirt or coat is not quite warm enough. It is ideal for camp loafing. You can sleep in it comfortably when caught out with inadequate bedding. It is a good makeshift pillow. Indeed, the sweater makes so many contributions to body comfort that it deserves a place on every list of outdoor clothing.

A pullover cashmere sweater with long sleeves and a fairly tight neck is a gem for camping. This fine, soft wool is very expensive, however, and the same style of sweater in good domestic wool will do three-fourths as well for half the price.

The heavy jacket style of sweater knit from raw wool whose fibers still have their water-shedding oil is superb for wilderness camping. Indians in the Pacific Northwest knit sweaters of this kind that will last a lifetime with care. The natural wool oil (refined and sold as lanolin) makes these thick sweaters shed much of the water that would soak into factory-processed wool. The distinctive Indian sweaters with one-of-a-kind color designs are costly. They can be ordered by mail through Norm Thompson, 1805 N.W. Thurman, Portland, Oregon, a firm that handles a good many outdoor items of unusual quality.

Inexpensive factory-knit sweaters of wool or soft Dacron are entirely suitable for routine camping. They are sturdy work-horse garments.

Cotton sweaters of the sweatshirt type, least expensive of all, will do for mild weather and are fairly good supplementary garments in weather down to freezing as long as they are kept dry. Cotton sweatshirts are a dismally bad choice where the weather is consistently cold and wet or extremely cold.

JACKETS AND COATS

Army Field Jackets

Let's start at the bottom of the heap with the least expensive camp coat that is at all satisfactory. That qualified honor goes to the cotton field jacket of Army design, available all over the country in war surplus and sporting goods stores. It sells for a few dollars and makes a good knock-about jacket for cool, dry weather, but rain, snow, or freezing cold put it out of the running as a suitable outdoor coat. Water soon soaks through it, and it is too thin to hold much body heat.

Canvas Hunting Coats

Hunting coats made of canvas or duck-weight cotton rate much the same as the cotton Army surplus field jackets: they are all right until the weather gets really rough. The good ones, particularly those designed for duck hunters, will shed a lot of rain and block wind efficiently, but they are not all warm by themselves. That is no hardship, however, for the man with insulated underwear and a wool shirt and sweater under his canvas hunting coat.

The canvas coats have the advantage of shedding water and at the same time letting body vapor seep through the fabric instead of being trapped inside to sweat up the wearer. Those with a double thickness of fabric over the shoulders and sleeves are about as dry, in terms of inside comfort, as airtight raincoats that shut out all the rain and seal in all the sweat.

Precautions: Many canvas "hunting coats" have too

many game pockets, cartridge loops, recoil pads, and similar trimmings. Never buy more accessories than you will actually need. Don't expect to stalk wary game in brush with these coats. They rattle and screak when branches hit them. Be sure to get a canvas shooting coat that is loose and roomy in the shoulders and sleeves. They are somewhat stiff in the salesroom but they are twice as stiff in freezing cold.

Leather Coats and Jackets

The leather coat is becoming more and more a town and country garment—worn by people concerned as much with fashion as with utility. There is nothing wrong with leather jackets or coats for wear in the wilds, but top-grade ones are very expensive, especially in comparison with fabric coats, which are much cheaper and just as efficient in terms of warmth and protection from wind and water.

Mackinaws and Cruisers

The thick wool coats widely known as "mackinaws" are so common in many cold regions that they are almost a uniform for outdoorsmen. They are warm, sturdy, and softly textured to allow a deer hunter to slip quietly through brush. The thick fabric holds in body heat even when wet with rain or snow and at the same time breathes enough to let body moisture escape. The mackinaws and West Coast cruiser coats with a double thickness of fabric over the shoulders and midway down front and back will cope with rain and wet snow about as well as any truly waterproof coat. They are better for an active man out in wet weather. Though they get damp, they remain warm and comfortable, and they dry quickly.

The fingertip length and the roomy cut of the mackinaw and cruiser coats of the Pacific Northwest are ideal for the active outdoorsman. The coat is enough to protect all of the main trunk of the body and short enough to allow plenty of leg freedom and to keep its tail from dragging in the mud when the wearer crouches, stoops, or sits on a log. Longer coats are a knee-binding, mud-dragging nuisance for a man on the move. Not even the Eskimos will put up with parkas that reach below their knees. They keep them at mackinaw length, cut off at about the point of the fingertips reach when a man stands with his arms dangling at his sides.

The one drawback of mackinaw and cruiser coats is their weight and bulk. They are heavy, especially when rain-soaked, and they are always bulky. Quilted coats of the same general design and filled with down or fluffy synthetic fiber are much warmer for their weight and just as good in wet weather. Another lighter and less bulky rig is a combination of insulated underwear, fleecy wool shirt or sweater, and a thin outer parka or jacket of tough cotton, wool, or synthetic fabric. A parka or long jacket of tight-woven nylon or Dacron is an ideal outer cover for such a light, warm combination as insulated underwear, wool shirt, and sweater. The synthetic outer garment sheds snow and rain reasonably well, is windproof and tough as shark hide, and has little more weight and bulk than a large bandanna. You can actually fold it into a roomy pants pocket.

But because of the price difference, mackinaws and cruiser coats will survive in spite of competition from quilted insulation and combinations of light, warm garments. A down-insulated coat of mackinaw design costs twice as much as a good wool mackinaw. And the combination of insulated underwear, wool shirt, sweater, and parka will add up to much more than the bill for one thick mackinaw.

For Extreme Cold

The king of the coats for extreme cold is the quilted garment insulated with waterfowl down: it is tops in both performance and cost. A top-grade coat insulated with a fluffy synthetic is about two-thirds as efficient as down and priced accordingly. Coats lined with sheep fleece or alpaca pile are warm and durable but very bulky. Fur coats in use in the Arctic score high in warmth—too high for all but the most frigid weather. They are quite heavy, very bulky, and costly when bought through a chain of middlemen. Clean and decorative fur garments are for sale in such Alaska towns as Fairbanks, where retail stores handle them. Some of the native village products hold a persistently gamy smell to which a visiting sportsman may be slow to adjust. Many Eskimos now wear thin parkas of tough cotton over their fur parkas to protect the fur and in some cases to provide better camouflage for hunting in snow. The white G.I. parka sold for a few dollars as war surplus is one of their favorites.

Vests

There is one vest that deserves special attention—the down-insulated vest. Because of its size and simplicity, the price is not too high. It is extremely light, wondrously warm, and just the thing for weather that changes quickly from pleasantly cool to freezing cold. With the front open, a down vest is not uncomfortably hot on a warm Indian summer day. With the front closed, it is comfortable on ridges swept with chill winds. Combined with a light coat, a down vest takes the sting out of a blizzard. Few garments do so many things so well.

HATS AND CAPS

Billed Caps

The baseball style of hat in all its variations is a good and extremely popular headpiece for hot and mild weather. Wool models with earflaps are warm down to zero. Cheap, sturdy, simple, providing good eye shade, the billed cap has only one strike against it: it lets water trickle down the wearer's neck when the rain hits. A hooded parka over the bill cap puts a stop to that.

Brimmed Hats

As western cowboys have demonstrated for a century, a wide-brimmed felt hat will serve in summer heat and, with a bandanna rigged as an earmuff, in winter weather far below freezing. The high crown of the cowboy style of felt hat forms an efficient barrier of confined air to protect against blazing sun. The wide brim sheds rain like an umbrella. With the crown pushed in to form a deep hollow, the rugged felt hat is an emergency water bucket or oat bag for a hungry saddle horse which would waste most of the grain if it ate off the ground.

Woven straw replicas of the wide-brimmed felt hat are good in hot, dry weather. Their one shortcoming is their tendency to blow off in high wind. A chin strap will stop that.

Wet-Weather Hats

For outings where rain is the rule rather than the exception, the fisherman's oilskin or rubberized hat with elongated brim behind is hard to beat. That long brim spills water far out over the collar, rather than down the back of the neck. Get the model with earflaps and a chin strap for rough weather. The combination of billed wool cap and parka hood is equally good in gusty rain.

Zero-Weather Headgear

Down to zero, the outdoorsman will get by with a wool bill cap with earflaps, but weather much below zero calls for something warmer. The trooper style of hat with fold-up earflaps and forehead piece is a good choice. Trooper hats are made of fur and fabric, down-filled fabric, or sometimes of solid fur. The war surplus types with an alpaca lining are cheap and serviceable. The combination of hooded parka and wool stocking or bill cap will be as warm in subzero cold.

Most of the masks designed to protect the face in extreme cold collect so much frost from the wearer's breath that they are of doubtful value unless it is a high wind, rather than subzero temperatures, that is causing the facial discomfort. A wool face mask is good in biting wind. The body heat that collects in the front of a parka hood is the best defense against cold and frost from frozen breath in arctic cold. Natives like parka hoods trimmed with wolf or wolverine fur because these furs shed frost efficiently.

Overrated Headgear

The thick sun helmets designed for desert and tropic heat deserve a mention for lack of real merit. Thousands of soldiers and twentieth-century travelers in hot desert regions have proven that cloth caps with sun visors are cheaper, lighter, and less awkward than the pith or cork helmets that were once thought essential in torrid climates. The lighter headgear is protection enough from any sun the rest of a man's body can stand.

Underrated Headgear

The beret, first cousin of the skull-hugging wool stocking cap, is a masterpiece of rugged simplicity which has never caught on in this country. Europeans have worn light wool berets for centuries. The soldiers of half a dozen nations have worn berets. They are common headgear in some parts of Canada. Perhaps Americans believe that only an eccentric artist or musician wears a beret. It is, however, a light and jaunty cap that is cool enough for summer, warm enough for all but arctic weather, and compact enough to fit in a hip pocket. It will not blow off in wind. It sheds snow, keeps the head warm when wet with rain, can be worn with a forward fold to shade the eyes. A beret is soft enough that a bald man sleeping out will find it a comfortable nightcap. A top-grade beret can sell for a dollar or less and will last for years.

GLOVES AND MITTENS

Most novice campers will think of gloves only for cold-weather camping, but they are also useful to many summer campers. Women and men with soft hands will welcome a pair of cheap cotton gloves for campfire cooking; they will save some burns and scrapes and protect the skin from soot and smoke. Where mosquitoes or other biting insects are troublesome, gloves are better protection than insect repellents, which quickly rub off the hands when you are working.

Vacation campers who seldom do rough work with their hands on their jobs can head off blisters, cuts, and scrapes by wearing light cotton work gloves while gathering wood, hauling on ropes, or rowing with rough oars. That may sound like a sissy approach, but it takes about ten days for a desk worker to toughen his hands to the point where protective calluses substitute for gloves in rough work. With gloves available, it is no more sensible to cut and blister soft hands the first day out than it is to peel off your shirt for half a day and get a painful sunburn. Tough hands, like suntans, have to be built up gradually.

Cotton or unlined leather gloves will be fine for summer camping. Thick wool gloves, which remain fairly warm even when wet, are fine down to freezing. Wool-lined leather gloves will do down to zero. Mittens are a better choice than gloves for weather colder than zero. A mitten, though it makes work with the hands more awkward, is always warmer than a glove with separate fingers. In a mitten the fingers warm one another to a great extent.

The combination of horsehide mittens and separate liner mittens of thick, knitted wool is good for zero cold. The leather shells are tough and windproof. The soft wool liners can be slipped out and washed to restore their fluff. A spare pair of wool liners can be slipped into the leather covers in a minute if the original liners get wet by accident. Country stores in cold states sell the leather mittens and wool liners at reasonable prices. They are known as "chopper" mittens in some regions, and they reach an inch or so above the wrist joint.

Fur- or down-insulated mittens are needed in arctic cold. They should be tied to coat or parka cuffs or linked to a stout cord or strap looped around the wearer's neck. Though it sounds somewhat melodramatic as you read it in a warm room, the loss of a mitten in 50-below cold can easily mean the loss of the hand, which in turn might mean loss of life in a climate that deals so harshly with handicapped men.

A special-purpose mitten worth mentioning is the gunner's mitten with a slit in the palm to allow instant use of a bare trigger finger without removing the mitten. This mitten is particularly good for the excitable deer hunter who will otherwise drop his mitten to run after his game.

A tight-fitting glove of thin Dacron or cotton worn inside a loose leather glove or mitten is another good rig for hunters out in freezing weather. The outer glove provides warmth and protection during the long waits between shots, and it strips off quickly to allow sensitive handling of the weapon with the thin inner glove.

Outdoorsmen tempted to buy rubber or rubber-coated gloves to cope with rain or such wet and cold jobs as putting out duck decoys will usually regret their small investment. Rubber gloves are cold and clammy, and the wearer is almost certain to ship some water over the cuffs. Sturdy wool gloves are usually better for outdoor work in rain or water. They get wet, of course, but they are a great help in keeping the hands warm even when they are soaked. For jobs that wet the hands only a few times a day, like handling duck decoys or tending beaver traps, carry two pairs of wool gloves. Squeezed as dry as possible and tucked in an open pocket, the wet pair will be fairly comfortable by the time it is needed again.

BELTS

Reliability is the main thing to look for in choosing a belt for outdoor wear. Leather is the best material, all in all, although the "web" or woven-cord belts used in the military services rank high for durability. Most sportsmen, particularly those who have been in the armed forces, dislike the drab appearance of the web belts. That prejudice helps to keep leather belts in first place.

The leather belt should be of top-grade leather at least 1 inch wide but no wider than $1\frac{1}{2}$ inches. A belt narrower than 1 inch is a poor support for such things as sheath knives and is too thin to fill belt loops and support the pants properly. A belt wider than $1\frac{1}{2}$ inches is too wide for the belt loops on many good outdoor pants—and anything wider than $1\frac{1}{2}$ inches is just surplus leather anyway.

Pick a belt with a strong buckle of solid brass, stainless steel, or some other durable and rustproof alloy. Avoid tricky belt mechanisms. Tooled or stamped designs do nothing to damage a leather belt and may or may not improve its appearance, depending on personal notions of what looks well. Nickel-plated studs, imitation jewels, and the like will weaken a belt.

SUSPENDERS

Here is another piece of camp clothing that suffers from a foolish prejudice. Many fledgling outdoorsmen, particularly the younger ones, have the notion that suspenders are somehow lacking in style, bravado, or up-to-dateness. Actually, they are much better than a belt for holding up outdoor pants, which are a bit heavy to begin with and are further burdened with full pockets and various items hung on the belt. Suspenders keep the shirt neatly confined and put the weight of the pants on the shoulders, which are far better designed than the waist to support it. Suspenders also allow a looser pants waist, with an appreciable increase in comfort and freedom.

Buy the wide suspenders policemen and working woodsmen wear. If you carry a sheath knife or other things on your belt, wear both suspenders and belt, the belt a notch looser than it would need to be without suspenders. The suspenders alone work fine if you have nothing to hang on a belt.

SCARF OR BANDANNA

A light scarf or bandanna has enough uses to justify its presence in any camp pack or duffel bag. A scarf knotted around the neck in cool or cold weather seals in much of the body heat that ordinarily escapes through an open collar. For its weight and bulk, a scarf worn that way brings about a surprising increase in warmth. In hot weather a light bandanna worn the same way mops up sweat and helps to keep dust and trash from trickling down an open collar. The bandanna can be rigged over the mouth and nose to form a fairly efficient mask against clouds of dust or insects. It has a great many auxiliary uses: a potholder for hot cooking pans; an emergency tourniquet, sling, or bandage; a makeshift belt; an earmuff rig with a brimmed felt hat.

A light wool scarf is tops for cold weather. Cotton or almost any other thin, light material will do for summer. The big red or blue cotton handkerchiefs workmen use make fine summer bandannas. Silk is fine, too, though more expensive and dressier than the camper requires.

RAIN GEAR

Outdoor clothing chosen specifically for wet weather needs to be considered from two angles: the rain suit that is ideal for sitting quietly in an open boat, on a horse, or in a duck blind is not much good for strenuous work or hiking, where ventilation for body heat and moisture is as important as protection from the rain.

Tops for non-strenuous outings in rain are the two-piece suits—hooded parka and high-waisted pants. A wide-brimmed rain hat is needed if the jacket has no hood. A hoodless parka worn with a rain hat allows slightly better ventilation but is more vulnerable to slanting, wind-driven rain and mist. Take your choice. The jacket and pants combinations keep you dry in any posture—sitting, kneeling, even sprawled on the ground. A poncho or raincoat alone lets the legs get wet when the wearer does anything more than stand erect or sit with his legs tucked under.

But waterproof two-piece suits (the canvas cruiser coat and matching double-thickness pants are only water-repellent) are steamy sweat traps for the man on the move.

The poncho, which is little more than a square of waterproof fabric with a hole for the head, is hard to beat for hiking in the rain. It flares wide enough to protect the legs a great deal, and that same wide flare, coupled with rather open sides, lets in ventilating air. A poncho does not restrict the arms much, although it is a poor choice for a gunner or a woodchopper. It makes a good ground cloth, and a big one will make an emergency pup tent or a lean-to shelter. The best bet for the most active wet-weather outdoorsman, the fellow who will be climbing, chopping, rowing, and shooting, is a raincoat that has long, full sleeves and flares loosely over the lower body and reaches no lower than the knees. A hoodless model worn with a rain hat will allow a substantial improvement in collar ventilation, and the man working up a lot of body heat will not mind the few drops of rain that slip down the loose collar.

Rainwear Fabrics

Nylon fabric coated with Neoprene is a first-rate choice for waterproof jackets and pants. It is completely waterproof, tough, and light and does not stiffen much when cold. Nylon suits coated with Neoprene or a similar material are comparatively expensive.

Cheaper and proportionately less satisfactory for all-round use are the suits made of rubberized cotton fabric. They are stiff and noisy in cold weather and heavier and easier to tear than Neoprene nylon. Yet they are inexpensive workaday rain suits. They are probably used more (war surplus stores handle thousands) than all other rain suits combined.

The yellow oilskins offshore fishermen often wear are stiff, fairly heavy, sticky with softened oil when warm, and inclined to leak where creases in the fabric cause extra wear. Low cost and tradition keep them going.

Plastic rainwear, though dirt cheap, is easily snagged, readily split at the seams, and stiff as cardboard when cold. The very thinnest and lightest plastic raincoats, which sell at throw-away prices and fold almost as small as a handkerchief, are worth packing to cope with the summer shower you *don't* really expect. Plastic is not for long continuous use on trips where rain is routine.

Pure gum rubber is a good material for a heavy-duty raincoat where the outdoorsman is not bothered by its substantial weight. However, the bulky raincoats that are all or mostly gum rubber are more at home on city policemen than on a woodsman traveling far and fast.

5 - Outdoor Footwear

THE "RIGHT" FOOTWEAR FOR CAMPING CAN range from canvas sneakers (a fine choice for auto-camping youngsters) to rubber hip boots, which are worn as a matter of course by outdoorsmen along the cold and wet Alaska coast.

CONSIDER THE MATERIAL

Your first thought should be of the main material in the shoes or boots, rather than of their style. Not counting soles and heels, outdoor shoes and boots are made of three basic materials—leather, rubber, and canvas. Rubber is the best choice where there is water to cope with constantly. Canvas makes the lightest and cheapest footwear. Leather has the greatest all-round utility.

Here are some basic truths about those three general classes (leather, canvas, rubber) of outdoor footwear.

Let us start with leather, the most common material for outdoor footwear. Pay no attention to such terms as "elk" leather, "deer-tanned," or "bullhide." Those are just trade or process names. The hides of stockyard cattle make the leather for nearly all outdoor boots, and there is nothing about a bull's hide that will make a better shoe or boot than the skin of a heifer. There is a small trickle of business in slippers or moccasins made from genuine deer, elk, or moose hides, but these are mainly novelty items made by small firms which process hides taken by big-game hunters. Most so-called "elk" and "deer" leather are the hides of stockyard animals—usually cattle—which have been tanned to make outdoor shoes. The trivial deceit in those terms is difficult to explain, because cowhide makes excellent shoe and boot leather.

Do not worry needlessly about how a boot is tanned as long as the leather in the finished product is pliable and uniform in texture—free of spots that are hard, thin, or conspicuously more slick or more rough than the rest of the leather. Chemists may debate the advantages of oil, vegetable, or chemical tanning systems, but the sportsman trying to buy boots on that basis will merely be bewildered by trade terms. Better guides for the shopper are price, a brand name of known quality, a reputable store, and the visible quality and workmanship in the finished boot or shoe. It is worth mentioning that outdoor shoes dyed black or a very dark brown are often made of flawed or inferior leather which is partly disguised by dark dye. You can see the quality in good leather that is not darkly dyed: it is smooth, toughly pliable, slightly moist with oil when new. Shy away from any with the thin, hard, or shiny look of a polished dress shoe.

Head for the counter with leather boots if you do a lot of hiking or want a sturdy all-round boot that will cope with everything but water. Resistance to water is not among leather's strong points. Some of the new processes that attempt to make leather boots completely waterproof are successful in a limited way. Waterproofed leather is never as sure a shield against water as a rubber boot, and leather whose pores are tightly sealed loses the important advantage of "breathing" enough to pass off the body heat and moisture that is trapped as sweat inside any completely waterproof boot.

Rubber is the material for wet going, and insulated rubber boots are good barriers against cold.

Canvas shoes—such as sneakers or tennis or basketball shoes—are cheap, light, airy, good grippers where footing is slick or precarious. They are neither waterproof, warm, nor particularly sturdy. Their low cost and general utility for casual summer outings make them a fine choice for children, who would outgrow an expensive leather boot in a year.

SOLE MATERIALS

Never buy outdoor shoes or boots with all-leather soles and heels unless they are specialized logger boots with caulks or mountaineering boots with hobnails. Leather soles become glassy slick on dry grass or pine needles. They also slip on smooth rocks. They soak up moisture, wear out in a hurry.

Rubber or one of the tough synthetics akin to rubber (Neolite, say) is the stuff for the soles and heels of boots or shoes for hiking and general outdoor wear. The cord sole (rubber with stringlike cords of fabric embedded in it) is good. All these soles are tough, long-lasting, comfortably flexible, good grippers on any surface where routine shoes will hold. They are less vulnerable to heat than leather, which can be ruined by careless exposure to stove or campfire heat, and they will not soak up water. Rubber or composition soles and heels are also much better at absorbing the shock of walking on hard surfaces.

HOOKS, BUCKLES, ZIPPERS, AND SUCH

The most foolproof system of securing an outdoor boot to the foot is with sturdy rawhide or nylon strings laced through open eyes. Hooks speed the job of lacing high-top boots, but they are never as secure as eyes. Cheap hooks rust, bend, and break. The big ones catch on twigs. If you buy a boot with hooks, they should be the thick-based brass type found on many top-grade logger boots.

The zipper is a quick and easy way to open and close a shoe or boot as long as it is working properly. It is accident-prone, however, and almost impossible to fix in a wilderness camp.

Buckles over the top of the foot work well only with loose-fitting boots, which are not to be worn for strenuous walking or climbing.

Ankle-fit rubber boots (they stretch enough to allow the foot to be pushed in, then contract snugly at the ankle) work fine in the lighter weights. They are far better for walking than the wide-ankled hip and calf-high rubber boots. The latter are easier to slip on and off and good for the sportsman who is not moving much, but they are rough on the heels when a lot of walking or climbing is involved. The heavy rubber boots of the insulated, calf-high types are too stiff to provide a good ankle fit with elasticity alone. Get the type with laces.

TYPES AND STYLES

Although there is no such thing as a satisfactory all-purpose outdoor shoe or boot, perhaps the closest thing to it is an unlined leather shoe with a non-skid sole of rubber or a similar tough plastic. The top of this all-round shoe would be no more than 7 inches high. It would have rawhide or nylon laces run through brass or other rustproof eye rings (no lace hooks to bend or snag in brush). This boot would be of middle-weight, oil-tanned leather (not waterproofed or insulated by any new process) . It would be made in either the light "birdshooter" style—a moccasin type of shoe with a top reaching above the ankle and a medium-thick sole and low heel—or on the Munson last—the roomy-toed last used to shape the homely G.I. marching shoe of World War II. This boot would be fitted to take an extra pair of wool or wool and Dacron athletic socks without binding in cold weather. With one pair of the same socks, it would be light and cool enough for hiking in hot weather. Coated with a good boot grease or oil, this low leather boot or shoe would stay dry through light showers or short stretches of marsh. A pair of low rubbers of the heavy-duty type worn over leather work shoes can be pulled over these all-purpose camping boots to make them warm and dry in any kind of mud, slush, or water that does not reach above the 2- or 3-inch tops of the rubbers. The rubbers can be left at home in consistently dry weather or tossed in your duffel bag to be used as needed on outings where there is likely to be wet footing. They are cheap and have little weight or bulk. Coupled with the leather shoes or boots, they provide a choice of footwear to suit changing weather. The man who takes specialized boots— say, a pair of 10-inch insulated rubber boots designed for cold, wet terrain—will be stuck with heavy, steamy footwear if he gets Indian summer instead of early storms on his fall trip.

The combination just mentioned will not suit everybody. Nothing will. But it is a sound compromise for the camper who wants to get by winter and summer in different regions with one pair of boots or shoes. The supplementary rubbers which cope with rain and slush are as much everyday items as a camping expenditure.

Now to the special-purpose footwear—the shoes and boots with specific strengths and weaknesses.

Moccasins

Rare indeed is the modern camper with feet tough enough to wear Indian-style moccasins for anything but campfire loafing, where they are luxuriously light, airy, and comfortable. The Indian moccasin is also light and comfortable for hiking in dry woods, but a person not accustomed to them (that includes nearly all modern Indians) would need about ten days to condition his feet to these thin and flexible leather socks—and they are more socks than shoes, even with the double thickness on the sole that some authentic ones have.

The native style of moccasin is quickly soaked in wet woods and treacherously slick when wet. It wears out quickly on gritty trails. The white man has far better footwear for anything but picnics and after-hours wear. Factory-made moccasins with soles and heels (including the style called "loafers") are fit only for loafing. On the trail they wear out sock heels, fill up with debris, and offer neither ankle support nor protection against hostile weather.

Moccasin

Sneakers and Tennis Shoes

The low, canvas-topped, rubber-soled shoes called "sneakers" are all right for weekend auto camping or any casual fair-weather trip that does not entail a lot of hiking through swamps or really rough country. They are ideal for boating—light, quiet, sure-footed.

The canvas and rubber tennis or basketball shoes worn with thick socks are practical, though somewhat unorthodox, footwear for rough outdoor travel in mild weather. Lots of Westerners, tired of hauling the logger type of boot up and down mountains on fall deer hunts, have wisely turned to the light, rock-gripping tennis or basketball shoes. If they are big enough for two pairs of fluffy athletic socks, these canvas shoes are warm down to freezing or lower. They will walk dry without discomfort when wet in a creek or by a brief shower. They are inexpensive. There is no better choice for boys with growing feet who will need new camp shoes each summer.

Army or G.I. Shoes

These drab and ugly shoes are made according to specifications set up years ago by Surgeon-Major Munson to provide a rugged but comfortable shoe for our Army. They do their job extremely well. The ample room in front allows for a natural spread of the toes. The flat, low heel provides good balance. The rubber soles grip securely. Unlined and only ankle high, the G.I. shoes are well ventilated for hot weather.

Ugliest and best of the two or three G.I. styles is the one with the smooth grain of the leather turned *in* and

Two styles of birdshooter boot.

a plain toe. War surplus G.I. shoes are cheap. The discharged serviceman who can steel himself to forgive these shoes for the unpleasant memories they may evoke will be amazed at how suitable they are when he is marching through the woods or climbing mountains for fun. They need rubber overshoes to cope with water or freezing cold weather.

Pass up the G. I. shoes with hard, box-style toes. This awkward, foot-rubbing toe will take a shine more readily than the seamless-toe G. I. shoe, but although shoe shines are at times important to the military, they are of no consequence to the camper.

The combat boot with a high top cluttered with buckles is no bargain either. It is surplus baggage for the camper, who seldom, if ever, needs leather boots with tops higher than 8 inches and never needs such weighty hardware as top buckles. Why the G. I. needed it is a question for which we have no adequate answer.

The Birdshooter Style

These leather boots are excellent for nearly all camping, hunting, and hiking. Light, sturdy, comfortable—the birdshooters have few faults. One fault, however, is the tendency of the seam on the top and front of the toe to wear badly as the camper hikes through snagging underbrush. Another drawback about birdshooter styles—and this is the fault of customers who want it—is that they are often made with needlessly high tops, ten-inchers being common. Tops of 7 or 8 inches are far better, unless you are wearing tuck-in pants—a style of outdoor trouser difficult to defend with logical argument. Get birdshooters with 7- or 8-inch tops, rubber or composition soles, eyelets rather than lace hooks. Avoid hybrid styles with high heels. The heel with an up-sloping front edge is good:

the tapered front sheds mud and does not catch on rocks or protrusions as readily as a square-front heel. The platform sole, which forms one flat surface from toe to heel, is also a good choice.

High-Laced and Engineer-Style Boots

Laced leather boots with tops reaching to a point just below the knee were for some unfathomable reason very popular with campers in the early nine-teen-hundreds. Their many faults have gradually thinned their ranks in modern sporting goods stores. Their extra height serves no useful purpose, unless it is to tuck in the tight legs of outdated and inefficient riding breeches. Tight-laced leather around the calf merely impairs circulation and constricts muscles. High leather tops often sag down on the heel and ankle, resulting in rubbing and chafing. It is a formidable job to lace knee-high boots.

The high-topped leather boots of the "field boot" or "engineer" style, with strap and buckle over the top of the foot, are too heavy and loose for outdoorsmen who cover a lot of ground on foot. Boots of this general style are all right (but by no means essential) for horse-back trips. The high heels on some models are a distinct disadvantage, unless it is important to the owner to appear an inch or so taller. Actually the swaggering cavalier appearance of the high-topped field boots probably accounts for their continued popularity. And it *is* a good feeling to be shod in tall and sturdy boots which suggest that they will help you wade through formidable obstacles. Many snake-shy outdoorsmen like these high, laceless field boots for rattlesnake coun-try. One superbly made and well-known boot of this snakeproof type is the Gokey Botte Sauvage, (spelled just that way) made by the Gokey Company of St. Paul,

Minnesota. Gokey boots are not cheap—in either sense of the word. Actually the man wearing 8-inch boots of the birdshooter style under loose-legged pants of any tough fabric is fairly well protected from a rattler on the ground, because it would take a big snake making a perfect hit high and hard to get much venom through that protection. But Gokey's snakeproof boots offer sure, rather than probable, protection up to knee level. And while we are on the subject of rattlesnake protection, wire-mesh, buckle-on leggings are popular with bird hunters and other outdoorsmen who range such dangerous rattlesnake ranges as the palmetto flats of Florida. The larger sporting goods stores in such snake country sell them.

Shoepacs

Since the term "shoepac" will mean different things to different people, it is here used to describe the shoe or boot with a rubber bottom sewed to a leather top; the rubber bottom is similar to the separate rubber suggested for wet-weather wear with the all-purpose

Shoepac

leather boot. L. L. Bean of Freeport, Maine, who makes a fine line of this footwear, calls them "Maine hunting shoes." The Bean company even makes shoepacs in heights and weights ranging from a moccasin to a model with a leather top 18 inches high. A dozen other firms make similar shoepacs—good ones and bad ones, depending mainly on price. There are few good outdoor shoes available at "the sensationally low prices" of the come-on ads.

Shoepacs are excellent for wet and cold weather. With the leather tops greased, they are just about as waterproof as all-rubber boots for hiking in wet brush or slushy snow. Those with tops no higher than 8 inches let in enough air for fairly comfortable hiking in warm weather, since they let sweat escape far more efficiently than do airtight rubber boots; they may actually keep the feet dryer in warm, wet weather. Shoepacs worn with two pairs of socks (say, a soft wool athletic sock under a heavy boot sock) are warm at zero and below for a man on the move. Shoepacs are comparatively inexpensive, and good ones last a long time.

Shoepac precautions: Do not buy them with needlessly high tops. The high tops tend to sag down on the ankle and take forever to lace and unlace. If you plan to use felt or sheepskin innersoles in cold weather, as many shoepac wearers do, be sure to test the fit with an innersole before buying the shoepac. The innersole takes up a lot of room. Grease or oil the leather uppers with some preparation that will not harm rubber. L. L. Bean and several other companies make boot grease that will not weaken rubber. Many veteran campers would vote for the shoepac as all-purpose footwear, but the tendency of rubber to sweat up feet in hot weather, coupled with the rather loose and

wobbly ankle fit of most shoepacs, makes them inferior to the leather boot for all-round wear.

Cowboy Boots

The so-called "cowboy boots," with high, sloping
heels and loose-fitting tops reaching about halfway
up the calf, are good for riding with western saddles
and long, open-cuffed pants. They are makeshift footwear for any other purpose. The cowboy boot is a sort
of glamour boot to some people as the result of Wild
West publicity, but the standard cowboy boot was
(and is) worn regularly only by ranchers and wranglers with a strong aversion to walking. Many Westerners now do most of their riding in jeeps or pickups,
where cowboy boots are comfortable enough, but they
will risk tires and oil pans to drive that vehicle to
within a few steps of where they are going.

Cowboy boots and modified copies of them are just
expensive mistakes for any camper who plans to do
some hiking. And they are by no means essential for
western horseback trips. A lace-on leather boot with
8-inch top will be as good on horseback for the average camper—and a thousand times better once he dismounts.

Corked Boots

Sharp steel pegs in the soles and heels of the timber-
country logger's boots are "corks," not "caulks," to the
man who makes his living in those boots. If you use
the dictionary word "caulk," he'll laugh at your igno-
rance or frown and say, "What?"

The spiked boots, in any event, are only for the
camper who does a lot of cross-country prowling
through steep and heavily timbered country with many
fallen trees and crisscrossed "down" timber. A tall-

timber woodsman accustomed to sauntering along logs or around steep ridges with "corked" boots will feel helpless as a sheep on rollerskates without them.

There was a time when the writer and other young workers in a camp on Idaho's Priest Lake made a foot race of the cross-country trip to camp each day when work was done. There were bets to be won in this daily contest, and it was also against the safety rules, which added the spice of rebellion to it. The fastest and most favored route was over the drifted and fallen timber that roofed and clogged the water of Soldier Creek, a mountain stream that led to the cook shack. Wearing corked logger boots, a boy with more exuberance than sense could run down that log-roofed creek at a pace that would turn a camp boss ghostly pale. With the sure bite of those spiked soles, a 10-foot gap in logs high over the creek was just another long stride. Thanks to the corked boots, the race did not cripple a runner all summer long. Without the spiked boots, the cocky kids in those races would have gone down like lemmings rushing to a cliff above the sea.

But caulked boots are expensive and possibly dangerous toys for either boys or adults in routine camping activities, and they have countless weaknesses for all-round camping. They will cut up a boat or canoe or any wooden floor. They stick dangerously in wooden stirrups. Wet snow balls up on the soles unless they are greased regularly. The boots are heavy and awkward outside of the big woods.

Caulked boots are painstakingly made in logging-country towns such as Spokane and Seattle for working loggers and woodsmen. The soles must be made of hard and durable leather specially treated to hold the caulks. (Caulks driven into boots with ordinary leather soles will twist and work loose the first time the soles get wet.) Top-grade logger boots have uppers of premium leather 8 inches or higher, depending on regional preferences. If they have hooks rather than eyes for laces, the hooks are made of brass with solid bases and are curved so that the leather laces fill them with no brush-catching gaps. Most have false tongues to ease lace pressure on top of the foot and to keep brush out of the gap at the bottom of the laces.

If you *think* you need such boots, wait until you are in logger-boot country to buy them. Not one outside cobbler or shoe salesman in a thousand has any notion what a good logger boot is, and a makeshift boot with something like golf spikes hammered in the sole is useless where real corked boots are needed. Fifty dollars is probably a fair average price for the legitimate caulked boot, as prices go when this is written.

Hobnailed Boots

Hobnails keep a leather-soled shoe or boot from slipping precariously on grassy hillsides, rocks, or logs, and they prolong the life of the sole. Hobnails are mainly used these days in mountaineering boots worn in steep and rocky country—often by the persons who scale peaks with equipment and techniques that originated in Europe's Alps. Most campers are better off with all-rubber, cord, or synthetic rubber soles.

Hobnailed boots have the floor-mangling roughness of caulked logging boots—to a lesser extent but enough to gouge up a canoe. With soles thick enough to anchor the hobnails properly, the boots are rather heavy. Hobnailed boots are still widely recommended for hunters and campers in mountain regions by outdoorsmen who formed their strong prejudices in the early nineteen-hundreds, but sturdy leather boots with thick rubber soles are more and more the choice of present-day sportsmen heading for the high country on hunting, fishing, and camping trips.

A good hobnail pattern has no more than ten hobs in the sole, five in the heel. A sole or a heel completely studded with hobs will be needlessly heavy and much less sure-footed on rocks. Gaps between hobs give them a chance to catch and bite in, whereas close-spaced hobs quickly wear down to a slick surface.

Insulated Boots

There are two types of insulated boot that at this writing are being vigorously promoted by manufacturers. One is the high-topped rubber boot with sole and foot thickly insulated with such materials as felt or foam rubber. The other is made of leather—usually a laced boot about 8 inches high—and has insulation material between the outer shell of leather and the lining.

The calf-high insulated boots made of rubber are excellent for both cold and cold, wet weather—especially for such activities as ice fishing or deer hunting from stands, where there is no steady and strenuous walking. The lighter versions of the insulated rubber boot are fairly comfortable to walk in when the weather is cold enough that the feet have little tendency to sweat. The Army style of rubber insulated boot, known to many as the "Korean boot" from its use in that war, is awkwardly heavy and bulky. A lighter version made specifically for outdoorsmen will suit the sportsman better for anything but sit-down outings in extremely cold weather. These rubber boots are water- and snowproof, of course, and the thick insulation makes them very warm. Though the feet may get uncomfortably damp and clammy in them during a long uphill hike, there is little chance of frosting toes in these boots in anything short of arctic cold. One or two pairs of wool socks worn inside them will add to their warmth in extreme cold and help a great deal in absorbing and dispelling moisture in mild weather or when the feet are hot from exertion. Check any insulated boots you consider buying to be sure they have a fairly thick and tough layer of rubber on the outside. Once that outer shell of rubber is punctured—by something like a pointed limb or a rough cake of ice— water that gets inside and saturates the insulation is discouragingly difficult to get out. Felt insulation inside these rubber boots is notoriously difficult to dry out once it is soaked by an outside leak. Never patch a hole in such a boot (a tire-tube patch does the job) until the insulation is thoroughly dried out—a job that requires hours, even with the boot hanging near a stove.

Leather boots with built-in insulation are suitable only for conditions that seldom exist in outdoor life. They are all right for sitting or casual travel afoot in weather that is both freezing cold and bone dry. Insulated rubber boots are as good in that respect and far, far better when there is snow, ice, or water.

The specific shortcomings of insulated leather shoes and boots follow. It is a long list.

The insulation, which is no more effective as a cold barrier than a top-grade wool sock, is impossible to remove for cleaning or drying, and it cannot be adjusted to suit temperature changes, which is a simple matter when socks of various weights are used for insulation. A leather boot with built-in insulation is heavy, hot, and stuffy when the feet are heated by warm weather or exercise. Unlike insulated rubber boots, which keep the insulation bone dry unless they are punctured, the leather boot is sure to be soaked through when worn long in slush or heavy rain. Then it is a cold, sodden lump until it is dry. Wet socks in an unlined leather boot can be changed or dried easily; built-in insulation is there to stay for better or for worse, and in a leather boot it's for worse. In short, insulated boots made of leather are a frightfully bad choice for all-round outdoor wear. A pair of humble G. I. shoes and two or three changes of socks of various weights would be a vastly better choice.

Ski Boots

Ski boots are for skiing. Period. The camper not traveling with skis will find them impossibly stiff, heavy, and awkward, despite what war surplus salesmen say about the left-over Army ski boots that are being pushed as all-round shoes for hunters and campers.

Wading Boots and Waist Waders

These are for outdoorsmen who plan to spend considerable time in water while duck hunting or fishing or traveling in marshes.

Hip boots are the thing if the outing involves a lot of walking and water no more than knee deep. Ankle-fitting styles are better for climbing—say the rough places encountered by bear hunters on the wet Alaska coast and offshore islands. Wide-ankle models slip on and off more easily, but tend to rub the heels and let socks work down and wad in the boot foot.

A new type of hip boot, with the standard heavy-rubber foot welded to a top of tough fabric with a thin inner bond of waterproof rubber, is appreciably lighter and more flexible than the hip boot with uppers of rubber-coated fabric. The price of the lighter hip boot, which is just about as sturdy, is only slightly higher.

For situations where hip boots are needed in extremely cold weather or water, there are two styles that will keep the feet much warmer than the routine models. One of the cold-weather hip boots has a wide ankle and roomy foot that allows it to be slipped over a light work shoe or sheepskin slipper. An ankle strap makes this over-shoe hip boot fit well enough for anything but long-distance hiking, and the combination is very warm and comfortable. The second good cold-weather hip boot is the one with a core of insulation material built into its shoe and ankle. This model, like all regular hip boots, is worn over stocking-covered feet. The boots with insulated feet are a bit heavier, a little more expensive than those without the internal padding. There are special boot socks, by the way, which make ordinary hip boots warm down to 20 degrees or lower. These foot warmers are ankle high, with either waterfowl down or Dacron stuffing quilted between their two layers of tough cotton or synthetic fabric. They appear very bulky when seen on the store shelf, but that soft bulk just fills a roomy boot foot comfortably. With both quilted ankle-high and calf-high wool boot socks, the man who takes a few steps now and then can comfortably wear routine hip boots in zero weather.

Fishermen wading streams full of slick rocks may want hip boots with felt soles, which are available through a few of the better-stocked outdoor goods stores. Felt soles are comparatively fragile and expensive, but they are unequaled when it comes to providing quiet, sure footing on slick rocks. Both these qualities are important to the fly fisherman. Standard rubber-cleat soles are fine for any of the routine hip-boot uses, and most stream-wading fishermen are satisfied with them.

Waist-high waders, which are basically hip boots with waterproof tops extending trouser-fashion up the waist, are for deep-water wading. Most fly fishermen who do a lot of stream wading will eventually discard hip boots in favor of waist-high waders. Those tall waders take a man to those pools just out of reach of hip boots, and they save the frequent wettings that occur when hip-booted anglers pressing their luck in deep water stumble slightly or step in a shallow hole. When the trout are rising out in water an inch too deep for hip boots, you can bet that 90 per cent of the hip-booted anglers on the stream will have their boots full of cold water. They are also dandy for duck hunting—for putting out decoys in shallows, retrieving ducks, handling boats in marsh, keeping the legs warm and dry while sitting in a blind swept by cold rain.

Waist waders are sold in two general styles: those with welded-on feet of hip-boot style, and stocking-foot models which need outer shoes of canvas or leather to protect the thin covering of waterproof material that forms the foot of the wader. The styles with the welded-on boot foot are much quicker and easier to put on and take off. There is no chance, with them, of arriving at a stream a hundred miles from home and learning that a wading shoe is missing. On the deficit side, they tend to be a bit heavier than stocking-foot waders, some find them less comfortable to walk in, and they cost more than the bargain-price combinations of stocking-foot waders and canvas shoes. The light waders worn with separate shoes are now being made of light (often flimsy) plastics and rubber-coated fabrics at very low prices. Even with the added cost of tennis shoes, such a rig will be appreciably less expensive than boot-foot waders made in one piece. The very cheap and light combinations are no bargain, however. One trip around the bank through a brier patch will ventilate many of them. They tend to split at the seams and wear out quickly at friction points and they are difficult to patch.

The top-grade stocking-foot waders, worn with hob-nailed or felt-soled wading shoes, are excellent. That rig is both comfortable and durable. The combination is also expensive. The gentleman fly fishermen of England seem to be mainly responsible for the promotion of the separate-shoe wading outfit, and wealthy Englishmen in pre-war days waded in leather shoes the average American would save for church and holidays.

All in all, most sportsmen of modest means will be better satisfied with the one-piece, boot-foot waders. Hodgman is a brand name of proven merit. Get the type with built-in chest pocket, which holds a dozen odds and ends in a handy position. Look for reinforced seams, sturdy suspenders and suspender buttons. A drawstring or belted top keeps out rain and the spray that flies over surf fishermen. The all-rubber models are good, if well made otherwise. So are those with upper legs and tops made of tough fabric bonded to rubber. The latter style is somewhat lighter and more flexible.

The outdoorsman buying waders by brand name can hardly go wrong by asking for Hodgman waders. There are cheaper waders than these, and there are more expensive ones, but the Hodgman Rubber Company (Framingham, Mass.) gives the buyer his money's worth.

6 - Camp Stoves

PORTABLE STOVES BURNING SOME TYPE OF GAS OR commercial fuel have replaced the open wood fire at most of the busy roadside campgrounds across the nation. The wood fire is ruled out for two reasons that are hard to argue with:

1. Auto campers, especially women unfamiliar with campfire cooking, prefer the home kitchen efficiency of cooking with the clean and orderly camp stoves that burn white gasoline, propane, Sterno, or some other canned fuel.

2. Campfires are against the law in many areas because of the danger of forest fires or as a guard against the careless cutting of trees for fuel.

The open fire also has some shortcomings that cannot be overcome by a skillful outdoorsman with lots of good wood and the legal right to cut and burn all he pleases. A wood fire is a sweaty thing to cook over during the sultry summer weather. It blackens cooking utensils more than a stove does. Good wood and woodcraft are needed to avoid eye-watering smoke and hot sparks. An open fire is a trial in a driving rainstorm or in a gusty snowstorm of late fall. And even in mild weather a strong wind can scatter enough smoke and ashes to blight romantic notions about the joys of life by the open campfire.

These are the troubles you avoid with a suitable camp stove. A stove fire is legal in camps where open fires are ruled out. With a light Primus type of stove burning alcohol or kerosene, the camper can carry enough fuel in a back pack to get by for days in a region barren of firewood. In wintry weather the camp stove can be used inside a tent, where the camper is shielded from wind, rain, or snow as he cooks, dries wet clothes, or loafs by its warmth. A small wood-burning stove is usually the most efficient choice for drying clothes, and it is certainly the most cheerful before which to loaf.

A two- or three-burner cooking stove fired with gasoline or canned fuel will immediately win the loyalty of women and other campers who like to rough it comfortably. The burners of these stoves form hot, steady circles of blue flame that are as easily managed as the gas range at home. There is neither smoke, nor odor, nor soot to discolor pots and pans, nor excessive heat to roast the cook during hot weather. This stove may rest on legs or on a table to be at a comfortable height for stand-up cooking. Ordinarily a novice cooking over a campfire is a tragic figure—crouching, jabbing, circling like a boxer heavily favored to lose the bout by a knockout. However, the same novice may cook like a dream on a gas camp stove.

Let's examine the various types of camp stove one at a time, starting with the wood-burner.

WOOD STOVES

The wood-burning camp stoves made of sheet metal are heavier and more awkward to pack than gasoline or canned fuel stoves, but they have several solid advantages for trips to cold regions where wood is plentiful. Fuel for the wood stove is free for the gathering, and you don't have to haul it to the campsite, as you do with camp stoves using liquid fuel. A roomy wood stove also heats a tent better. A few sticks of wood in a sheet-metal camp stove will keep a 12-by-14-foot wall tent snugly warm when the forest outside is wrapped in zero cold and streams of drifting powder snow.

Tent ventilation is not so vital with a wood stove as it is with a liquid fuel one that has no stovepipe to carry dangerous gases out of the tent.

A wood stove large enough for two pots or pans will do the cooking for a party of five or six. Some models—the famous Sheepherder, for example—have a small oven for baking. You can also buy a compact oven that attaches to a section of stovepipe about 18 inches above the fuel box of any wood stove. There is plenty of heat from the pipe to bake biscuits or other camp breads. If the pipe oven is not needed on a particular trip, it can be left at home, and the stove can be fitted with a joint of plain pipe as a tent heater or for cooking.

A good all-round wood-burning camp stove should be an oblong box 10 to 12 inches high, about 15 inches wide, and 24 inches long. It should be made of sheet metal heavy enough not to buckle with heat or to deteriorate quickly from rust and the routine hard knocks any camp stove takes. The door should be large enough—say 8 by 10 inches—to take good-sized sticks of wood, and it should have an adjustable draft opening in front. The stove should weigh about 25 pounds, including four or five sections of pipe.

There are a dozen variations of this typical wood stove, including lighter and heavier ones. Choose the lightest stove you can get by with. Some are designed to fold flat for less bulk in packing, a convenience that adds to cost. The built-in oven is another feature the

buyer can take or leave according to his personal needs
or whims. Some stoves have legs, which are convenient
for campers who do not have to worry about bulk and
weight. The simplest stoves do not even have bottoms;
they are to be set on beds of sand or trash-free dirt.
Some packhorse campers have their wood stove sized
to balance with the kitchen box, so that the stove can

The wood-burning Sheepherder stove is made of sheet metal and serves
as a tent heater and cooking range. Wood is fed through the door
at left; pot or fry pan rests on top, and door at right is a baking
oven. *Courtesy of Smilie Co.*

Compact stove 14 inches long for cooking and heating
burns charcoal or wood. When the stove is used in a
tent, the chimney hood can be removed and a pipe
added to funnel off smoke. *Courtesy of Morsan Tents.*

ride on one side of the pack horse and the kitchen box on the other.

Stovepipes for wood-burners range from plain cylinders of tin to aluminum sections that fold flat or telescope to fit inside each other. The telescoping and folding types are easier to pack, but they cost more. Choose a pipe rig with the fewest possible elbow joints; as the elbows will not fold or telescope, they take up extra space.

In addition to pipes, which are sometimes bought extra, the wood stove requires a fireproof collar which is fitted in the tent fabric at the pipe's outlet. Tin collars will do the job, but they are rough on the tent fabric and produce annoying squeaks and rattles when wind jostles them against the metal stovepipe. Fireproof asbestos collars fit better and are less likely to damage the fabric when the tent is folded.

Safety Hints

There are a few things to keep in mind in managing any wood-burning stove inside a tent. First, be careful not to set the stove closer than 2 or 3 feet to the tent wall. Intense stove heat will set the fabric ablaze as surely as will an open flame, particularly if the tent is waterproofed with some inflammable wax. Be sure the metal or asbestos shield that channels the stovepipe through the tent roof or wall is fitted to keep the fabric away from the hot pipe. This is a common source of tent fires.

If the tent has a canvas floor, a box or a frame containing 4 inches of sand will save the floor from the heat of a legless wood stove. Make the sandbox large enough to allow a 6-inch border all around the stove.

Feed in wood sparingly, and adjust the stove dampers so as to let in no more air than is needed

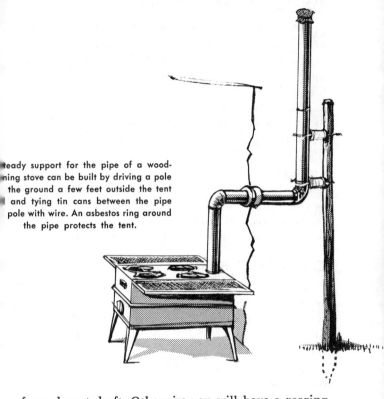

Steady support for the pipe of a wood-burning stove can be built by driving a pole in the ground a few feet outside the tent and tying tin cans between the pipe and pole with wire. An asbestos ring around the pipe protects the tent.

for a decent draft. Otherwise you will have a roaring fire that is too hot to cook on, dangerous to the tent, and likely to warp the metal of a thin stove. The bottom of the fire box of a metal camp stove will last longer if 1 inch of insulating sand or dirt is spread evenly over it before the wood is put in.

Fit a square of wire screen or some other spark stopper over the top of the stovepipe to keep flying sparks off your tent and to avoid the danger of starting a forest fire.

Take down the stovepipe and knock or brush out the excess soot when the stove has been used for a long period. Some quick-burning fuels—sagebrush, for one—will keep excess soot from forming.

The wood-burning stove is at its best in fairly remote camps where cold weather makes its heat a blessing. Canadian and Alaskan trappers and prospectors have often spent the winter in large wall tents fitted with wood stoves, and Indians in the far North live throughout the year in sturdy tents with such stoves.

But the wood stove is far too heavy and awkward for hikers, canoe campers with a lot of portages to make, or auto campers making quick and casual stops at busy roadside areas. It is also a terrible choice as a cook stove for any campers in hot summer weather.

CANNED FUEL STOVES

A stove burning some type of canned fuel is far better than a wood-burning stove for cooking in warm weather and for trips where weight must be kept to a minimum, as in the case of hikers, cyclists, and mountain climbers. Campers with featherweight packs can buy tiny folding stoves burning alcohol, kerosene, or a solid fuel such as Sterno. These weigh only a pound or so and fit in a coat pocket. A two- or three-burner stove requiring gasoline or propane is the ideal cooking rig for a family with a lot of mouths to feed at summer campsites reached by car.

Gasoline Stoves

Portable stoves burning gasoline range from 20-ounce midgets which will fit in a large coat pocket up to three-burner models which will cook for six or eight people.

The small one-burner gasoline stoves are good for hikers, mountaineers, or any solitary outdoor prowler who travels and cooks light. A typical one-burner model weighs 2½ pounds and holds 2 pints of fuel, which will normally keep it burning about 3½ hours. The intense heat from this stove will boil a quart of water in three minutes.

Single-burner stove is only 7 inches high, burns white gasoline, and is suitable for one-dish meals. *Courtesy of Laacke's.*

Tiny Primus stove stands 5¾ inches high, burns white gasoline, benzine, or naphtha. *Courtesy of Sandvik Co.*

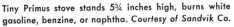

The larger gasoline stoves, with two and three burners, weigh up to 25 pounds. They fold into compact cases, however, and are easily handled. They are cool enough to rest on a table, and some have folding legs that bring them up to waist level, so that campers can avoid kneeling or crouching over a stove on the ground.

The newer models of gas stove will burn either stove (white) gasoline or the leaded kind used in automobiles. White gas is still recommended by most manufacturers, for it does not leave a clogging deposit on the vaporizer or generator, as leaded gas does after about fifty hours of use. Some stoves come with a tool for removing this deposit. Other stoves have inexpensive replacement vaporizers which can be installed

Aluminum camp stove weighs one-third less than steel models, folds flat with the fuel tank inside.
Courtesy of Coleman Co.

quickly. Carry an extra vaporizer on a wilderness trip.

Fuel consumption of gasoline camp stoves varies according to the stove and the flame adjustment while cooking, but you can figure on using about half a pint of gasoline an hour for each burner in operation. Thus, a pint of fuel will fire a two-burner model for an hour. Two gallons of gasoline should last two or three campers a week, unless they brew a lot of coffee between meals. Most campers use their cooking stoves about two hours each day.

Folding shields to keep wind off the burners are standard equipment on most stoves burning any kind of liquid or propane fuel. They are important for without them, a brisk breeze can blow out the flame or make it flicker inefficiently.

Bottled Gas

Comparatively new and increasingly popular are the camp cooking stoves that use propane, which comes in sealed containers that are easily attached to the stove. No pumping, priming, or pouring of fuel is involved. Just screw on the tank of bottled fuel, open the valve, and light the stove. Empty tanks are discarded.

This type of stove is somewhat more expensive to operate than one burning white gasoline or kerosene, but most campers find it so convenient that they do not mind the slight extra cost.

A typical single-burner stove using bottled propane weighs about 5 pounds with a full tank of fuel attached. The fuel in the tank will cook three meals a day for five days for one camper. A double-burner stove of the same type weighs about 12 pounds and holds fuel enough to last two people about ten days. Several sizes and models are available.

A bottled-gas stove is ideal for a picnic or casual roadside camping. It is also fine for a wilderness trip where it and an adequate supply of fuel can be carried easily by boat, plane, or pack horse. Do not count on being able to get propane or some other pressure-bottled fuel at outpost stores. Gasoline and kerosene, on the other hand, are sold in village stores all over the world.

Bottled propane in disposable tanks provides the fuel for this portable camp stove. *Courtesy of Hudson's.*

Canned Heat

The most common form of canned heat is the jelly-like substance with the trade name Sterno. Sold in metal cans with pry-off tops, Sterno has a rich mixture of alcohol which burns with a hot, clear flame at the touch of a match. A 5-ounce can of Sterno or a similar canned heat costs only a few cents and will burn for about forty-five minutes. Larger cans are available.

The camp stove using canned heat is nothing more than a light metal frame that holds the can in position and provides a level surface for the pot or pan. The simplest Sterno stove is a stamped metal rack which sells for about fifty cents—perhaps less in a bargain store—for a one-burner, or one-can, model. Multiple-burner models are available at very low cost.

A canned heat stove is as simple and as sure as a candle. Take the lid off the can, light the surface with a match, and put your pot on the frame above. Move either heat or pan to adjust temperature. There are no valves or screws to control the flame. Discard the can when it burns dry.

Canned heat is useful for campers who can easily pack enough of it or for auto campers who can pick it up as needed. Sporting goods stores, most hardware stores, and some supermarkets sell it. Housewives often use the small cans to heat chafing dishes.

REFLECTOR OVEN

A reflector oven is not a stove as such, but it can be a biscuit-baking wonder in the hands of a camp cook working with either a stove or an open wood fire. A pan of biscuits or camp bread set on a tray in a reflector oven is baked by heat from the campfire or stove. There is little to the oven itself but two square sheets of polished metal which are hinged to prop open at an angle that directs the heat to the baking tray in the middle. Put the food to be baked or roasted on the tray, and move the oven as close to the open fire or stove as necessary for the desired degree of heat. The oven's open front lets you keep an eye on the food as it cooks. This is a starkly simple gadget that works marvelously well.

KEROSENE SHELTER WARMERS

A good portable heater for any temporary shelter is the kerosene-burning one that somewhat resembles a tall water bucket with screened windows around it. A pail handle allows this heater to be moved as easily as a lantern.

This heater is a natural for auto campers who want to warm their tents for an hour or two on chill summer nights. It will provide quick heat for a chill woods cabin, a boat cabin, a duck blind, or an ice-fishing shanty. With the cover off, it will boil coffee or heat one cooking pot. A typical model holds a quart of kerosene, which will last as long as twelve hours with careful valve adjustment.

Like all liquid fuel stoves, this heater can be dangerous when burned steadily in a tight closed shelter. Provide enough ventilation to keep the inside air fresh.

IMPROVISED STOVES

There are many times when a camper must forget about what's best and make do with what he has on hand. A stove is one of the things that can be improvised from odds and ends.

A crude outdoor stove can be made by placing a sheet of iron or heavy tin on top of a foot-high wall of rocks arranged roughly in a square, with an opening at one end for feeding in wood. A gap left at the top of the opposite end will funnel the smoke out. The draft can be regulated by using a loose rock to close or partly close the open side where the wood is pushed in.

Such a stove can even be fitted with a pipe and used inside a tent if the rocks are fitted neatly and chinked with mud or clay. The rock walls will hold considerable heat long after the fire dies out. However, this rock-wall stove serves mainly to confine and control a campfire for heating and cooking, and its natural place is outside or under the awning of the tent.

Note that most attempts to use a large, flat rock, rather than a sheet of metal, for the top of such a stove will end in tragedy. A flat rock will usually function perfectly until the pots of stew and coffee start to simmer. Then the rock snaps like a scalded glass and dumps the meal in the fire. Few thin, flat rocks will take campfie heat without cracking, and shale and sandstone are notoriously weak in this respect. Thick slabs of fieldstone or dense igneous rock will usually work satisfactorily.

Trappers have made many a useful tent stove by cutting a hole in the top or side of a tin tub or large pail and inserting a stovepipe made of tin cans opened at each end. The draft is regulated by opening or closing a small tunnel in the loose earth or sand on which the upturned tub or bucket rests.

A tin can two-thirds filled with dirt or sand saturated with gasoline, kerosene, or cigarette-lighter fluid, makes a fair one-pot cooking stove. Punch a few holes about halfway down the sides of the can to provide draft. Do not try to add fuel while the fire is going, for it might flash back into the container you are holding, and explode or burn you badly.

A thick candle in a tin can will boil coffee and heat

short rations. The candle can even be poked into the ground and surrounded by a tight circle of stones to support a pot. A couple of thick candles, incidentally, will do enough lighting, heating, and fire starting to pay their freight in any camper's pack.

Auto campers making one-night stands can do a lot of cooking with an old bucket holding a dozen lumps of commercially prepared charcoal. Nail holes in the bottom of the pail furnish draft. The top of the pail can be covered with nail-punched tin, heavy wire, or some such improvised grid as a discarded refrigerator shelf.

There are also, of course, at least a dozen commercial models of charcoal grill. The lighter ones are extremely useful for car campers who want merely to broil a few steaks or hamburgers and make a pot of coffee. Some commercial charcoal grills have folding legs that reduce them to neat packages weighing less than 10 pounds.

CARE OF STOVES

Any camp stove should be cleaned and, if subject to rust, lightly greased at the end of each trip. Before storing them, empty and dry the tanks of stoves using liquid fuel.

7 - Camp Lighting

A GASOLINE LANTERN IS BY FAR THE BEST LIGHT-
ing device for large tents, cabins, or any back-country
camp where a lot of bright and reliable light is needed.
Such gas lanterns as the justly famous Coleman models
are almost as efficient as the light bulbs in your living
room, yet a gas lantern and fuel for a two-week trip can
be done up in a compact package weighing less than 10
pounds.

Hikers and others who must count every ounce of
pack weight can get by with firelight, two-cell flashlights, improvised candle lanterns, or even torches
made of woodland materials.

LANTERNS

The gasoline lantern mentioned above is the type
that burns white or unleaded gasoline which is fed
from a pressure tank to fabric mantles. Gas vapor collecting in the mantles is lighted with a match. It burns
with a brilliant white light which remains steady and
even as long as pressure in the gas tank is kept up.
This pressure is created by a built-in tank pump. A
few strokes of the plunger handle will pump up the
lantern before it is lighted. A few more pump strokes
midway in the evening will keep up the pressure until
bedtime. Then there is a bonus feature: When the last

man ready for bed turns off the lantern fuel valve, the last of the vapor in the mantles burns out slowly enough to light his way to bed. That minute of after-glow saves a lot of barked shins and gets you into bed without fumbling in darkness for snaps or zipper.

The newer gasoline lanterns light instantly when a match flame touches the mantle. (Some older models need a few seconds of steady match flame to get them going.) Wind will not blow out a pressure-gas lantern. It also sheds rain or snow. Insects can not get into the screened lighting unit.

The shortcomings of the gasoline lantern are few. Weight and bulk rule it out for go-light hikers. Though the typical lantern weighs less than 5 pounds, there is the added weight of fuel and a carrying case to protect the Pyrex globe. The whole package will add up to 10 pounds, perhaps a little more.

Specifications for a good gasoline lantern: It will be made of stainless steel and brass with a porcelain reflector. The globe will be of clear, heat-resistant Pyrex glass. There are one-mantle and two-mantle models: both work fine, but the one-mantle version is that much simpler. Fuel-tank capacity should be about 2 pints, which will give ten to twelve hours of steady light that rates close to 300 candlepower. Weight—about 5 pounds. Height—about 15 inches. Cost—about $15.00.

Standard fuel for these lanterns is white gasoline. (Leaded gas clogs the lantern generator.) Special lantern fuel very similar to white gas is sold by companies making gas lanterns. Some lanterns of this same type are designed to burn kerosene. As fuel must be clean, strain it through cloth or a strainer sold for that purpose, and head off trouble.

Inverted lantern hangs from a branch or ce●
or stands on the ground. It burns any type of gase●
Courtesy of Thermos Co.

Two-mantle camp lantern burning white gasoline
throws a lot of light in a large tent or a cabin.
Courtesy of Coleman Co.

Though a gasoline lantern will stand rough use and
abuse, it is a good idea to carry spare mantles and an
extra globe and generator for extended stays in country
far from stores. A tough fiberboard or plywood lantern
case is a good investment for the camper who wants a
lantern for packhorse or canoe trips.

KEROSENE LANTERNS

The old-style kerosene lanterns have a fabric wick
that feeds down into a tank of kerosene and burns at
its exposed end much like the wick of a cigarette
lighter. A glass globe fits over the flaming wick to protect it from rain and wind and to aid illumination.

This is the type of lantern that according to legend
was kicked over by Mrs. O'Leary's cow, starting the
great Chicago fire. Unlike the modern gasoline lantern,
which will extinguish itself harmlessly when tipped

over, the old kerosene lanterns with flaming wicks are a fire hazard unless handled with care. They also smoke and blacken globes unless the wick is trimmed and adjusted properly. Their last fault is that they throw only a fraction as much light as do gasoline lanterns and lanterns burning kerosene fed to mantles under pressure.

The old kerosene burners with wicks are inexpensive, and their soft yellow light has a certain romantic appeal to campers who are monotonously modern-lighted at home and on the job. Those who want a good working and emergency light on their outdoor trips will be wise to buy a modern gasoline lantern instead of a kerosene burner with wick.

PRESSURE-CAN LANTERNS

Newest of all are the camp lamps and lanterns that have mantles that are fed gas from throw-away pressure cans. Instead of filling a permanent fuel tank, the camper just unscrews the empty fuel tank and replaces it with a full one. Replacement cans are sold like bulk lantern fuel, though at higher prices.

The pressure-can lanterns have the advantage of being clean and easy to use. There is no pouring or straining of fuel. Cans will not leak and contaminate

Pressure-can lantern has a disposable container which feeds fuel to the mantle. *Courtesy of Morsan Tents.*

food or create a fire hazard, as carelessly stored gasoline or kerosene will. Pressure-can gas lights instantly and burns with bright, steady light. A typical 12-ounce can gives six or seven hours of light. It costs about 75¢.

Faults of the pressure-can lanterns: They don't work well at temperatures below freezing. Some have to be heated (with body heat or warm water, as fire is dangerous) before they will light in weather no colder than 40° or 45° F.; it often gets that cold at lantern-lighting time in midsummer camps in the high country of the western states, Canada, or Alaska. Replacement cans of fuel for these new lanterns are not stocked by most crossroads or outpost stores. Replacement cans are quite expensive, compared with gasoline or kerosene.

The pressure-can lanterns are fine for auto campers during warm or mild weather. They are also a good bet for boatmen, especially those with cabin boats that dock where canned fuel is easily available. The safe and simple refueling is a big advantage on a boat where fire is particularly dangerous and storage space limited.

FLASHLIGHTS

The dry-cell flashlight is one of the most useful of all camp tools. It is hard to imagine how any camper, even the most rabid student of the go-light school, could justify leaving a small flashlight out of his pack. There is no quicker, handier all-weather source of light. You can unravel a tricky trail at night by a flashlight beam. It is a splendid device for emergency signals if a camper is hurt or lost at night. The instant beam of light from a flashlight will quickly turn up the hundred and one things that are in the dark bottom of a duffel bag or a tent corner—and without the fire risk that goes with a match or a candle. Any trip from camp out into the dark calls for a flashlight.

The compact two-cell flashlights are powerful enough for all routine camp use. As a rule, the three- or four-cell types will only be extra weight to carry. They throw more light, true, but four cells going at once burn out as fast as two. And there is seldom need for more than a two-cell beam. The light-pack hiker can get by with one of the miniature two-cell flashlights which are not much larger than a fountain pen. Most of us are so accustomed to floods of electric light that we underestimate the effectiveness of a tiny flashlight in cutting a swath through total darkness.

There are some features the good camp flashlight should have. First, it should have extra durability. It will—and should—withstand a lot of rough use. It should be waterproof or at least sealed well enough that rain or a quick dunking will not bother it. It should have a bright or shiny finish (some have a band of luminous paint) so it will show up in the dark. The olive-drab color of many flashlights sold for camp use is useful camouflage for soldiers in combat, but the camper wants to be able to see his flashlight.

A good choice for campers is a two-cell flashlight with a hinged or socket head that will pivot so the beam can be thrown at an angle to either side. This can be hung on the belt, so that the beam lights the path ahead while the long battery-storage portion of the flashlight hangs in a vertical position. This pivot-head flashlight (or one with a fixed head set at a right angle) can be hung from a tree, so that its beam lights an area on the ground where the camper has work to do. It is difficult to prop or hang up a straight-tube flashlight in such a way that it will shine just where you want it to. The camper's flashlight should have a hang-up ring that folds into the rear end of the battery-holding tube, or a belt clasp that will serve the same purpose. The plastic lens fitted on many flashlights sold for camp use is harder to break than a glass one but easier to scratch and stain.

A solidly mounted glass lens, slightly recessed, is just about as breakproof as a plastic one. The protruding lips of the flashlight head protect it. A rubber-coated flashlight made in that way is difficult to put out of commission even if you set out to break it on purpose. Any flashlight that does not have a pivoting or right-angle head should have enough flat or squared surfaces at ends or sides to keep it from falling off a table top or other flat surface.

Bulbs are far more likely to break and burn out than batteries. Always carry a spare bulb when you leave stores behind you. A pair of spare batteries is a good idea for a trip of a week or longer. Flashlight batteries always last longer when burned intermittently than when the light is turned on and left on. Warm batteries work better than cold ones. Cold decreases dry-cell efficiency to the point where fresh flashlight batteries dim a great deal at zero. At 20 below, a flashlight has to be warmed by the camper's hands or body to throw any worth-while light. One carried in an inside pocket will stay warm enough to work fine during short exposures to subzero cold.

In an emergency you can get a little extra light from dead batteries by giving them a crude recharging with heat and water. Warm them slowly by the fire. Then punch holes in the sides, and add as much water as they will hold. Tape the holes, and slip the batteries back in the flashlight. But do not expect too much: as a rule you will gain only a few minutes of rather feeble light.

Carry your flashlight where you can get at it quickly. The best spot for it after you turn in is under the pillow edge or a fold of your sleeping bag. You may need it to spook a raccoon or a porcupine away from your grub box or for a midnight toilet trip.

DRY-CELL LANTERNS

Battery-powered lanterns are an excellent choice for campers who stay fairly close to the roads and make most trips in mild weather. A six-volt battery lantern will throw a good light for forty or fifty hours in warm or mild weather. (Spotlight bulbs and steady use will cut down battery life sharply; small bulbs and rest periods extend battery power.)

Get the wide-beam electric lantern, not the searchlight type, for general camp use. It costs about $8.00 and weighs about 5 pounds with six-volt battery in place. A replacement battery will cost about $1.00, but one battery will light a lot of summer camping trips.

A battery lantern goes on or off at the flick of a switch. There is no chance of fire, smoke, or fuel leakage. Weight is no problem. Weaknesses of the battery lantern: Comparatively short life with continuous use, particularly with a big bulb, and loss of power in cold weather. Many summer nights high in the Rockies are cold enough to sap the strength of a battery lantern.

Battery lantern weighs little and is suitable for all-round camp use. *Courtesy Burgess Co.*

PRIMITIVE LIGHTING

In real wilderness, where the law allows the camper who uses care and good judgment to cut and burn all the wood he needs, firelight alone will handle nearly all lighting problems. A blazing campfire or even a bed of glowing coals will throw as much light as one hundred candles. Built in front of a white tent or a rock ledge, the fire will be reflected enough to light all the working space a camper reasonably needs for cooking, bed making, or small repair jobs. A reflector made of logs stacked against green stakes reflects a fair amount of heat, but not enough light to be worth the effort of cutting and stacking the logs for that reason alone. The logs—dull in the beginning —soon blacken and lose most of the light-reflecting potential.

TORCHES

By wedging strips of highly inflammable birch bark in the split end of a stick, a person lost, stranded, or otherwise in need of an emergency light can make a torch that will burn brightly for a long time. Cedar bark will do the same job, though not as well. Where pines, spruce, fir, or other evergreens are plentiful, look for the big tree that has fallen and rotted away

Battery lantern with a searchlight and a small safety light is a handy camp item. *Courtesy of Burgess Co.*

so much that the heavy knobs at the base of broken limbs can be cut or broken loose. Pitch collects in the base of these limbs (and in the yanked-out roots) of many wind-toppled evergreens. Lighted over a fire, these pitch knots or roots will burn for an hour or more with a bright flame that throws a great deal of light. The limb knots often have ready-made handles. Other pitch slabs can be wedged in and held by green saplings split at one end. Needless to say, these torches are a considerable fire hazard in dry woods. They are good primitive lights in wild country too damp to burn. A lost man who hoists such a torch in a closely supervised forest is very likely to be located promptly by irate rangers or fire wardens.

CANDLES

In addition to being fine fire starters, candles are first-rate emergency and auxiliary lights. One candle in the middle of a tent with light or white walls will illuminate the whole interior enough that occupants can see what they are doing. A tin can and a candle will make a fairly good lantern, which will work in light rain and wind. Nothing can go wrong with a candle. Light it and it burns. You can make one by dipping string or a rolled strip of cloth in hot tallow or the grease gained by cooking animal fat. Candle wax has such extra uses as waterproofing a tent leak or—rubbed on the sock heel—easing a spot rubbed raw by friction between sock and shoe heel.

OIL LAMP

A crude lighting fixture can be made by filling a can or a bowl with almost any kind of animal fat and lighting a cloth wick that has one end submerged in this animal fat.

It is extremely difficult to set up an experimental oil lamp that does not smoke and stink out of proportion to the feeble light it creates.

Eskimos, who have used such primitive oil lamps for untold centuries, no doubt know some tricks with them that modern campers will not hit on immediately. The Twentieth-Century camper who has to contrive a light flare or heater will be much better off with a can of sand and gasoline or kerosene. Split half the rim of the can in banana-peel fashion, and clamp the split sections down over the two prongs of a forked stick, which forms a heatproof handle. The upright half of the can will be a crude reflector of light from the flame of gas-soaked sand in the bottom.

8 - The Vital Ax

IF YOU WERE ALL ALONE IN THE WOODS WITH only one tool, what tool would you select? To this question the wise woodsman would answer an ax—for the ax is *the* basic wilderness tool.

With only an ax, a skillful woodsman can build a sturdy shelter—a permanent cabin if need be. The steel head of an ax will spark a flint to start a fire. An ax will cut materials to build traps for fish and game. A man with an ax can build a raft, a dugout, or a canoe. The cutting edge of an ax can be used to butcher a moose that weighs a half a ton or to clean a 1-pound fish.

An ax is a formidable weapon in itself, and it will shape the materials needed for a spear or a bow and arrows. A rifle is just an elaborate club when a vital spring breaks or its cartridges are gone. Although ax handles break, the steel head can be used to cut and shape a new handle, and the head will last indefinitely.

Although modern campers head for the fringes of civilization to have fun, not to struggle for survival, the ax is still a vital camping tool. In choosing an ax to suit your particular camping needs, you will be fairly well guided by this rule: The wilder the country and the longer your trip, the bigger your ax should be.

HATCHETS

A hatchet weighing a pound or less will do well for people who drive to established camping areas for short stays in summer. It is suitable for warm-weather campers who carry factory-made tent poles and gasoline stoves. Hikers who must keep their packs as light as possible can usually get by with a hatchet.

The camper who relies on a hatchet for all his chopping jobs, however, needs a good one. There is neither satisfaction nor economy in the typical bargain-price hatchet. The person who starts by buying a cheap hatchet will usually end up buying a second and better one. The first one will probably have too soft or too brittle a head and a handle that keeps working loose. After abandoning it in disgust, the camper will cheerfully pay a premium price for a hatchet with a skillfully tempered head and a sturdy handle neatly fitted and balanced.

Though hatchets look much the same, the quality

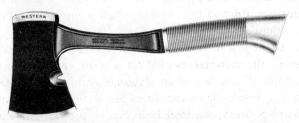

Hatchet with the head and handle forged from one piece of steel is a safe, handy camper's tool. *Courtesy of Western Cutlery Co.*

of their steel varies as much as does the steel of razors and butter knives. The camper who has to do all his chopping jobs with a light hatchet needs one with razor-quality steel.

The size and the style of a hatchet depends on a

camper's preference and needs. One good combination would be a 12-inch hardwood handle and a 1-pound head with ample cutting edge and square pounding surface. The heads and handles of some models are forged from the same piece of steel, and the grip of the steel handle is covered with leather washers or composition. The steel handles will not break or loosen. Properly balanced and tempered, these one-piece steel hatchets are fine camping tools. The narrow-bladed, thin-headed tomahawk styles and others unusual patterns are poor choices for such routine camp chores as chopping firewood and pounding tent stakes.

The hatchet should have a sturdy leather sheath that has rivets or a tough leather buffer strip facing the cutting edge. If you plan to carry the hatchet on your belt, see that the sheath has belt loops. Many big-game hunters who need a light hatchet to dress out such large animals as elk or moose like a combination hatchet-and-knife sheath. Some of these sheaths also have a small pocket for a whetstone. They have the important virtue of keeping all the essential tools in one package.

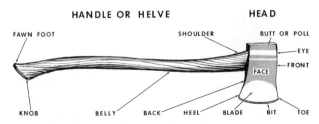

HANDLE OR HELVE   HEAD

FAWN FOOT   SHOULDER   BUTT OR POLL   EYE   FRONT   FACE   KNOB   BELLY   BACK   HEEL   BLADE   BIT   TOE

FULL-SIZED AXES

The camper with a little more room for equipment or with more chopping to do will be wise to carry something more substantial than a hatchet—an ax of the size commonly sold as the boys' or house ax. This would be a single-bit model with a square pounding head. The handle would be from 14 to 16 inches long, and the head would weigh from $1\frac{1}{4}$ to $1\frac{1}{2}$ pounds.

Discard something to make room for a full-size ax when you head into remote woods to stay for a week or more. Then you need an ax with a 28- to 30-inch handle and a $2\frac{1}{2}$- to 3-pound head.

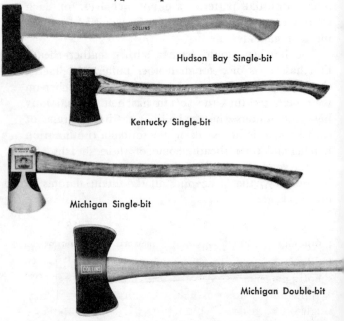

Hudson Bay Single-bit

Kentucky Single-bit

Michigan Single-bit

Michigan Double-bit

The Hudson Bay style of ax is justly famous. It is heavy enough and has a long enough handle to fell trees, split logs, cut a week's firewood. The squared end of the steel head will drive stakes or nails. The fine balance and proportion of this ax makes it seem heavier than it is. The total weight of the typical Hudson Bay ax is about 4 pounds.

The Michigan pattern of single-bit ax is another good choice for all-round camping use, as are the New England, Dayton, and Kentucky patterns.

The double-bit ax is a more specialized tool. With cutting blades on each side of the head, it allows the chopper to grind one blade thin and hone it to a fine edge which will slice deep to fell trees or chop through substantial logs. The other blade can be thicker, which will make it more useful for splitting wood. It can be used for those risky swings that might nick gravel under the log.

A double-bit ax with a 3-foot handle and a 3-pound head is the tool for the man who has a great deal of chopping to do. There are fewer pauses for sharpening, and the thin, heavy head at the end of that long handle is a supreme timber carver. But this type of ax has no pounding head, which is one of the camper's routine needs, and it can be dangerous in the hands of a careless or an unskilled chopper.

The handle of any ax, large or small, should be made of seasoned hardwood with a fine, straight grain. Be sure it is straight and has the proper "hang," which means that the center of the handle should be in line with the cutting edge of the blade when you hold the ax in front of you and sight down it as if shooting a rifle.

A handle as long as 3 feet is suitable for a heavy single-bit or a double-bit felling ax. This is the sort of ax that will whack up cabin-size logs and fell large trees. A 2-foot handle provides leverage enough for the chopping jobs in a temporary camp.

The ax handle should fit the eye of the steel ax head perfectly. Don't buy an ax that shows the smallest gap between handle and head. Such a handle is very likely to work loose under the continued impact of chopping and pounding.

The handle should be wedged at the top of the eye to expand that part of the wood and anchor it firmly to the head. Wedges of seasoned hardwood are good. The camper can replace them in the woods if need be, or swell them tight by soaking the ax head in water overnight. Metal wedges with wood-gripping side grooves are satisfactory. Some manufacturers now seal their ax handles to the heads with a plastic material that seems to be very durable and dependable.

A coat of bright red or yellow paint brushed over the sides and top of the ax head will make the ax easier to see if it is dropped in the brush or in a potentially dangerous place around camp. (The upright blade of a double-bit ax stuck in a log or a low stump is a real hazard.) This coat of paint will also serve to signal a loosening ax head, because it will crack over the eye if there is any play between wood and metal.

A properly tempered and ground ax blade is the result of a dozen painstaking steps by skilled steelworkers. It deserves the best of care. It will open a can of beans if necessary or serve as a powerful screwdriver to loosen a screw in a lantern, but do not extend its uses too far. Never cut into the ground—to chop a root, say—with an ax you value. Never use it to poke up the fire: that can ruin its temper. Needless to say, an ax is not designed to cut nails, wire, or any tough metal.

CARE OF THE AX

The camp ax needs little maintenance. A few drops of machine oil are required now and then to keep the steel free of rust. Moisture and acids in wood sap will rust an ax blade. Sand the handle with fine emery cloth or sandpaper if it becomes rough. Rub in linseed oil to protect the raw wood. Do not paint or varnish it, as those finishes will chip with rough use, and they are slick and unsatisfactory from the beginning. Also, a roughened hand grip can be useful on a hatchet or an ax small enough to be swung with one hand. Some woodsmen drill a hole ¼ inch in diameter and 3 or 4 inches deep in the butt of an ax handle. Filled with linseed oil and plugged with a neat wooden stopper, this well of oil will keep the handle in shape indefinitely.

Remember that extremely cold weather makes steel brittle. Warm a thin-bladed ax before you whip it into hardwood logs in zero weather. Friction will keep it warm as you chop.

The best axes are tempered so that the blade is harder than the steel in the rest of the head. That hard—but not brittle—blade is needed to hold a sharp edge. The steel in the rest of the ax head is tempered to be softer and more flexible so that it will do such jobs as driving stakes or wedges without breaking.

You can damage the temper of an ax head by grinding it on a fast power-driven wheel unless you use plenty of cooling oil or water to control friction heat. A slow, fine-grained grinding wheel is safer.

File and hone the blade by hand to get the best cutting edge. A vise to hold the cutting edge upright is a great aid in filing. Lacking a vise, as you will in camp, extend the blade over the edge of a stump or a log end to hold it steady. Or, if it is a double-bit ax, merely sink one edge in the log. Use an 8- or a 10-inch file held flat and stroked from the ax eye out to the cutting edge. File both sides evenly this way. Finish the job with a fine emery stone.

Some new axes are sold with surplus metal on the fore part of the blades, so that the blades can be ground and filed to suit a particular woodsman's whims or requirements. To grind such an ax, draw a chalk mark ¼ inch back of the cutting edge and parallel to it. Then draw a second chalk line 2 inches behind the first one. The surplus metal to be ground down will lie between those chalk lines. These distances are for a standard, full-sized ax head, of course. Adjust them to suit unusually large or small blades.

Some choppers like an ax that is very thin for an inch or more back from the cutting edge. Such blades cut fast but are more likely to stick in a cut and are more fragile. A bit of bevel ½ inch back from the edge will flip out chips better.

To sharpen a double-bit ax, first drive it into a and file the cutting edge, stroking downward File well back from the edge, gradually thin down the blade. The file marks should describe a like pattern.

Buy or make a sturdy sheath to cover the head of your camp ax. It is dangerous to carry without one, and the sheath also protects the well-honed edge from nicks. Leather sewed and reinforced with copper rivets makes a good sheath for the full-sized ax. A workable sheath can be made from a strip of heavy rubberized hose. Split it to fit over the ax edge, and secure it by leather straps.

Keep your ax sheathed and in the tent when it is not in use. An ax left outside is hard to locate or gets underfoot. It may also tempt a night-prowling porcupine to make a meal of its sweat-salted handle.

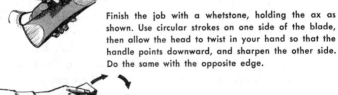

Finish the job with a whetstone, holding the ax as shown. Use circular strokes on one side of the blade, then allow the head to twist in your hand so that the handle points downward, and sharpen the other side. Do the same with the opposite edge.

9 - The Camper's Knife

THE IDEAL KNIFE FOR THE CAMPER HAS LITTLE in common with the long, thick-bladed weapons called hunting knives.

The camper needs a small, keen blade for whittling. He needs a slim, pointed blade for cleaning fish —mostly small ones. The vacationing outdoorsman will want a knife to drill the new hole that will take up his leather belt a notch. A broken fingernail will need trimming to prevent further splitting. There are onions and potatoes to peel.

Note that all of these jobs are comparatively small and delicate, and so is the good camp knife.

A regular jackknife with two sharp, slim blades is a dandy all-round camping knife. And the short, thin-bladed, wood-handled paring knife the camper's wife brings from her kitchen is very close to what the weekend outdoorsman needs. If that paring knife had a leather sheath and a blade with a little extra strength and a sharper point, it would be perfect.

James Bowie, who designed the famous Bowie sheath knife, died in the battle for the Alamo on March 6, 1836. In the century and a quarter since then, a million ill-advised campers have been cut, confused, and frustrated by knives patterned after Bowie's. That knife is admirably suited for such tasks as stabbing thick-chested men and small bears, or skinning and quartering a buffalo. But it is a sad tool for regular camping chores. The camper with a Bowie knife will always be wishing he had either an ax or a razorblade.

The worst of the Bowie-style knives weigh as much as 2 pounds and have wide blades 10 or 11 inches long. The camper needs a sheath knife one third that size —and this applies to the big-game hunter as well as to the weekend camper.

A sturdy jackknife with blades of high-carbon steel is ideal for most camp chores. It will do a better job of dressing a deer than most of the thick-bladed, too long hunting knives.

Pocket knife for all-round camp use has punch blade, screwdriver, cap-lifter, and can opener as well as a regular cutting blade. *Courtesy of Western Cutlery Co.*

The folding knives that have a blade or a tool for a dozen specialized jobs are useful to the camper. They will cut, open bottles, loosen screws, bore holes. The best of these, which are expensive, will do all these jobs quite well. Cheap all-purpose knives can be painfully inefficient at all the tasks they propose to do. If you plan to rely on an all-purpose knife, buy a good one.

The ideal all-purpose sheath knife should have a blade no longer than 6 inches. A 4-inch blade will be more suitable for all but a few heavy-duty jobs. And the blade should be thin—about half the thickness of the typical Bowie style of hunting knife. Bone, leather washers, wood, or durable plastic will make a satisfactory handle. The steel of the blade should extend all the way through the handle, so that blade and handle core are one piece of high-quality steel.

A straight-edged blade with the cutting edge curving upward at the tip is better than most of the more elaborate designs. Blades with "blood grooves" and other such hollows and indentations may please the eye, but they will not cut any better.

For skinning fish and game, and for heavier camp use, a sheath knife with a 3-inch blade (top) or a 4⅜-inch blade (bottom) meets the camper's needs. *Courtesy of Western Cutlery Co.*

Carry a small whetstone to keep the blade sharp. You can buy a leather knife sheath with a separate pocket for a sharpening stone, so that you will be sure to have the stone with you when you need it.

The belt knife should have a sheath of durable leather with copper rivets or a leather buffer strip to keep the sharp point or edge of the blade from cutting through.

10 - The Camp Saw

A SAW, AS WELL AS AN AX, SHOULD GO INTO THE pack of the camper who needs to cut a lot of wood. This applies to the camper who has to provide wood for a hungry tent stove or feed a warming fire in front of an open tent in cold weather. A light saw is well worth its weight if a lot of poles have to be cut for camp fixtures, and it is essential for building a cabin.

The saw has many substantial advantages over an ax when you have to work up large logs or a quantity of small ones. The saw is faster—about twice as fast as an ax wielded by the average camper. Unlike the ax, which requires a good deal of skill, the saw can be use efficiently by a novice.

The saw is much safer to use, too. It will not fly out of your hands to injure a bystander. There is no danger of its glancing off a log and slicing into the user's feet. Sticks will not fly up and hit the amateur sawyer in the face, as they sometimes do when cut by an untrained axman.

Veteran guides with eager but inexperienced clients who want to help with camp chores like to put them to work sawing logs into firewood. Given a sharp, light saw and a few minutes' instruction, the palest tenderfoot will immediately be buzzing through substantial logs with satisfying efficiency.

Women and youngsters who could not handle an ax safely can whack off logs with a saw. It is an easy, rhythmic job which is fun if you don't have to do it for a living.

The thin bade of a saw also makes neater cuts and wastes less wood than an ax, which turns a 1-foot length of firelog into chips each time you cut through it.

LIGHT CAMP SAWS

Half a dozen good camp saws are available now that are light and compact enough to win a place in the packs of hikers and other campers who travel light. One of these has an aluminum frame that is hinged to fold flat like a sheath over the saw's blade when the tool is packed. Folded, this saw forms a flat package 2 feet long and no wider than a playing card, and weighs about 2 pounds. Opened, it forms a buck type of saw with a thin, narrow blade which will do heavy woodcutting jobs.

Bow Saws

The Swede, or bow, saws are ideal for light-pack campers. Their thin, narrow blades of flexible steel are held taut by tubular metal frames that curve above them much as an archer's bow holds a bowstring taut. The frames of some of these bow saws are jointed, so that they can quickly be taken apart and slipped into a case only 12 to 18 inches long. The flexible blade can be curled like a watch spring and tied in a neat roll for packing with the two- or three-piece handle. The bulk and weight of such a saw are negligible, and the 2-pound package can be quickly assembled to zip through foot-thick logs.

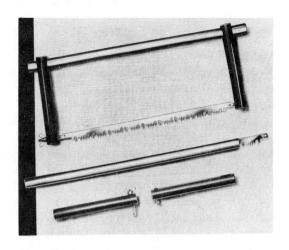

General cutting chores can be handled with a collapsible bow saw which fits easily in hiker's pack. *Courtesy of Hudson's.*

Campers able to carry more gear can buy good bow saws with one-piece handles for five dollars or less. Those with longer blades and deeper bows are more efficient. A blade 20 to 24 inches long is fine for average camp use. A bow saw with such a blade will handle logs up to 8 or 10 inches thick. Get a bow saw with a 30- or 36-inch blade for thicker logs or if you plan a lot of heavy-duty cutting.

Steel-framed buck saw with a 30-inch blade weighs only 2 pounds, will take care of logs 14 inches thick. *Courtesy of Sandvik Steel, Inc.*

Some woodsmen going to far places where every ounce of pack weight and bulk counts take only the blade of a bow saw and improvise a frame from a sapling or tree limb when they get there. Such a handle can be made by cutting a tough, springy sapling or limb about 20 inches longer than the saw blade and 1½ to 2 inches thick. Make 2-inch splits in the ends of the sapling, and in them insert the ends of the saw blade. Drill holes in the sapling ends with a knife point or nail, and wire or nails inserted through both of these holes and matching ones in the blade will anchor the blade in place. String, fishing line, or rawhide will substitute for wire or nails in a pinch, but the tension of the bowed handle exerts a steady strain that will soon wear through fragile lashings if the saw is used much.

A good medium-weight saw for camp use is the type shaped much like a carpenter's hand saw, but with a thicker blade and longer teeth which have more "set"; this means that the points of the teeth slant outwards at a sharper angle to each side to cut a groove that is about twice as wide as the thickness of the saw blade itself above the teeth. A saw with teeth whose set is as little as that of the average carpenter's saw will bind in the cut when used on green wood or splintery logs.

A camp saw should always have teeth at least twice as long as those of the saw with which most householders are familiar, for the camper is concerned not with making precise cuts in clean, seasoned wood—the job for which the carpenter's hand saw is designed—but with ripping through a random assortment of green, bark-covered, or pitch-pocketed wood in as short a time and with as little effort as possible.

Featherweight Saws

There are three saws weighing next to nothing that are useful to campers. One of them has a pistol-grip frame made of light metal which is notched to hold replaceable blades that will cut either wood or metal. Like most dual-purpose tools, it does not cut either one with remarkable efficiency, but it is the sort of tool that will pay its way by doing a lot of the trivial jobs that are almost impossible if you are forty miles from the proper tool. This little saw is about 10 inches long, weighs a few ounces, and sells for less than a dollar.

Campers can buy a similar saw with a thin blade that folds into its own handle like a jackknife. Some hunters carry these to saw through bones when dressing big game animals. They are inexpensive and will fit into the pocket of a hunting coat.

The lightest odd-job saw of all is a rig that is really a barbed steel cable about 18 inches long with steel rings on either end. With a finger through each of the end rings, the camper pulls the sharp-barbed cable back and forth across the material to be cut. He can also fit a sapling handle in the rings to make a crude bow saw.

Pocket-size folding saw (top), which measures 10 inches closed, and wire cable saw (bottom) are suitable for light odd jobs around camp.

The little cable saw eats through wood neither as fast as a power saw nor as slowly as a termite. It is a featherweight, low-cost saw which comes close to being a toy. Yet it is better than no saw at all.

HEAVY-DUTY SAWS

The two-handled crosscut saw is much too heavy for hikers or campers making short trips in mild weather, but it is a woodcutting demon for cabin building, felling large trees, or cutting a big supply of firewood. Many packers who take hunters to Rocky Mountain base camps for big-game hunts curve one of these two-man saws over the top of the pack horse's load as a matter of course. With a sheath made of split fire hose or leather, the 4- or 5-foot blade of a two-man crosscut can be safely lashed to a pack horse, hauled in a car, or even curved in horseshoe fashion around a hiker's back pack.

The larger versions of the wood-frame buck saw qualify for heavy duty if the job is limited to cutting poles to length or lopping firewood blocks off the end of small logs. They are inefficient for felling trees, however, and are heavy and awkward to carry. Except for a permanent cabin camp or some job reached by car, a large Swede or bow saw will be better than a wood-framed buck saw. It will do all a buck saw does and more.

Loggers and other professional woodcutters have just about abandoned hand saws in favor of power-driven saws. Power saws, driven by small gasoline engines, are hardly camping tools, but they can be great timesavers for the outdoorsman who is building a cabin, a pole corral, or a pole boat dock. They replace hand saws much as the outboard motor replaces the rowboat's oars—with the same roaring efficiency but the same increase in cost, weight, and mechanical problems.

CARE OF THE SAW

Aside from cutting into rocky earth or metal, pinching the saw blade in a cut while working through a thick log or tree is the main hazard to a saw. Pinching takes the set out of the teeth, and they need set to cut efficiently.

Pinched saw blades are easily avoided. A log extended over the end of a sawhorse cannot pinch when cut off from the top; its weight widens the cut as the blade goes through. On the other hand, a cut made in the center of a log that is sagging across a depression in the ground will certainly pinch the saw blade. Therefore, improvise a sawhorse support with stumps or other logs, and drag light poles or logs to it for cutting. If you are felling a small dead tree for firewood, use its own stump as a sawhorse. The limbs that drive into the ground as the tree falls may hold other large limbs in good sawing position.

Wedges will keep a standing tree or a large log from pinching the saw blade. Lacking metal wedges, you can

Avoid binding the blade of the bow saw by sawing on the outside of the support so the weight of the piece being cut off keeps the saw cut open and the blade slides freely.

cut wooden ones with your ax, or use the ax blade itself as a wedge.

Saw Sheaths

A sheath is needed to keep the needle-sharp teeth of a camp saw covered when the saw is not in use. This protects the cutting edges from dulling bumps against rock or metal and simultaneously shields the clothing and skins of campers from those edges.

Old hoses, particularly large fire hoses, can be split to make good sheaths. Leather sheaths are fine. Two or more thicknesses of heavy canvas strapped or tied over the teeth will make a good sheath. A burlap bag folded lengthwise does a good hurry-up job of padding saw teeth.

Sharpening

The word has been out for years that saw sharpening should be attempted only by experts, but that is only partly true. It does take a great deal of slow and precise work to sharpen a saw with a hand file, but there is no great mystery about the process.

The camper who finds himself in the woods with a hopelessly dull saw does not need to wait until he gets back to town to fix it—if he has a sharp file with him. Any man with a reasonable amount of manual skill can study the cutting angles of the teeth on a simple camp saw and see the dulled edges that need to be sharpened. By filing slowly and carefully, he can remarkably improve their cutting efficiency. Naturally the professional saw filer in your home town would do the job better and faster, but as he is not in camp, your own sharpening job, if you are at all competent and careful, will help you to cut a lot of wood in the meantime. Let the professional touch up your minor mistakes after the trip. You will not ruin the saw unless you do a lot of deep, careless filing.

Lubrication

If the wood being cut is full of pitch or sap that binds the saw blade, pour kerosene on the blade to lubricate it.

As rust makes blades drag and dulls saw teeth, oil saw blades before storing them or after using them on sappy or wet woods.

Finally, do not leave your ax or hatchet at home just because you have a saw. A good saw is a marvelous camp tool, but it will not drive a tent stake, blaze a tree, or split wood for kindling.

11 - Personal Items—The War Bag

A "WAR BAG" IS ONE OF THE TERMS TO DESCRIBE a sack, pack, or bundle holding personal equipment. The hobo, master of light camping, can carry all he requires in a knotted bandanna. Most recreational campers need a small duffel bag.

Many standard things belong in the modern camper's war bag, but it may also include a few that are of no use or consequence to anyone but the owner. Thus a small boy may insist on hauling three marbles for the profound reason that he doesn't want to be caught without them. A Maine guide's war bag holds an 8-inch length of deer antler that is just what he will need some day. Among the vital items in the saddle bags of a Wyoming cowboy is a pocket-sized tobacco tin holding a dozen porcupine quills. "Cain't tell," he says, "when them quills will come in mighty handy."

No camper should yield to the shallow argument that these whimsical things are a foolish burden, but he should also remember that they are just the icing, not the cake. Basic tools, however, should take up most of the space in the war bag. Every outdoorsman needs some or all of the following items:

POCKETKNIFE

A folding knife of the Boy Scout or Swiss army type

will handle all sorts of jobs. A typical model has two cutting blades, a leather punch, screwdriver, bottle opener, corkscrew, and perhaps a small scissors blade. These knife-blade tools are frustrating substitutes for the real thing if you must use them often. They are invaluable, however, when you lack the full-sized tool and have one small job to do.

A Scout knife is a war-bag knife, rather than a standard tool for dressing game or for heavy cutting. Rely on a sheath or a high-quality folding knife for big jobs and keep the Scout knife in reserve.

MATCHES

Matches are too cheap and too common in our country to command much attention from anyone but the man who has just failed to light his fire or his cigarette with his last one. Thus, no war bag is complete without a reserve supply of matches in a waterproof tube or box.

Do not rely on books of paper matches as a reserve supply. A little moisture will put them out of order, and they have too feeble a flame to be reliable fire starters when a camper must cope with high wind, rain, or wet wood.

Wooden kitchen matches are the thing for the war-bag supply. Some campers who have to build fires under tough conditions go a step farther and buy wind matches, which are extra large wooden matches that burn for a minute or more with a large, hot flame.

A waterproof tube especially designed to hold a reserve supply of matches can be bought for about fifty cents in a sporting goods store. Any household has half a dozen tubes and boxes that will do about as well. The plastic tubes that encase new toothbrushes make good match cases. Modern drug and hardware stores sell dozens of small items in light plastic bottles that make fine match containers.

Check any match container you choose to be sure the lid will come off easily. A metal container with screw threads may work fine while new and when tested with warm, supple fingers in the store, but sand or rust can seal it shut by the time you really need it. Choose a container you can open quickly in pitch darkness with gloves on or with fingers stiff and numb with cold. Under such conditions a match is vitally important.

There are two quick and easy ways to waterproof wooden matches so that they can be carried indefinitely without damage. Dip the head and front inch of the matches in melted paraffin or fingernail polish. Prop them up separately until they are dry (five minutes or less) and pack them *loosely* in the container. Tightly packed matches are hard to get out in an emergency.

Do not coat the entire match with wax or fingernail polish. That will cause the flame to spread quickly up the entire length of the match. Leave about an inch of the wood end uncoated so you can hold the fierce flame without burning your fingers while you are starting your fire.

A cigarette lighter by itself is no substitute for a reserve container of matches. Ordinary fluid will evaporate from an unused lighter in a few weeks. Spare fuel and flints are needed to keep a lighter going. Mechanical failures are few with a good lighter, but the man deep in the woods will find it difficult to replace or repair a broken screw or spring. The lighter is fine as an extra fire starter, especially if the camper smokes, but matches are more reliable in the long run. Don't leave them home.

CANDLE

A quick list of the things a candle can do in a camp will establish its place in the war bag. Lighted with a match, it will burn long enough to dry out and ignite the most stubborn campfire fuel. It will light the inside of a tent enough to allow the occupants to make beds and do routine chores efficiently. Propped under a can or a pan, a thick candle will cook food or boil coffee water when no other fuel is available. The same thick candle burning inside a tin can is a tiny heater that will substantially raise the inside temperature of a small tent. Melted candle wax rubbed into the fabric will stop a minor tent leak or seal the seams of a leather hunting boot.

A candle costs a few cents and is so light and compact any hiker can carry a couple. It can be dropped, drenched, and battered without losing a bit of its utility. Lanterns break and run out of fuel. Flashlights depend on bulbs and batteries that fail. Touch a match to a candle, and it will light and burn. "Foolproof" is a good word for the candle.

COMPASS

The compass belongs in your pocket once you get into the woods, but the war bag is an excellent place to keep it between trips. The compass is the sort of small but important item that may be left at home if it is not kept with a kit of the things that you automatically take with you.

FIRST-AID KIT

If the truth be known, few seasoned outdoorsmen carry a standard first-aid kit. Probably the best explanation is that trained woodsmen avoid accidents so efficiently that it would be surplus baggage. The average camper, however, should carry a standard first-aid kit or else include the following in his war bag:

A small bottle of iodine, merthiolate, or similar disinfectant recommended by your doctor. Most cuts and scratches acquired in the woods will quickly heal when cleaned with soap and water and exposed to sun and air, but a few drops of merthiolate will head off trouble with a seemingly minor cut. Use it as a matter of routine.

Carry a good-sized roll of adhesive tape and a large roll of sterile cotton or gauze for bandages. The tape will most often be used to bind a cracked ax handle or temporarily seal a small leak in a canoe or an air mattress. And if you need it for medical purposes, it is there.

The bandage material belongs in a small sack or tightly tied square of waterproof, dustproof plastic. Keep it clean and sterile to bandage wounds. As in the case of accident insurance, you should not be without it, but do your best to avoid using it.

A bottle of aspirin has a place in any war bag. It is one drug that almost any camper can take with the assurance that it will not hurt him and it may help him. Doctors all over the world advise patients complaining of minor and undefined ills to take a couple of aspirins and get a good night's sleep. More potent drugs may be carried if they have been prescribed by a doctor to treat a specific illness of a particular camper. But the person gulping pills and medicines at random is likely to create more maladies than he cures.

A tube or stick of ointment to sooth burns and relieve chapped lips and hands is worth more in the war bag than such complicated first-aid items as factory-made tourniquets. A shirt tail or shoestring will make a tourniquet—which is a hazardous tool needed once in a blue moon, while burns and skin irritations are everyday hazards.

A bottle of insect repellent has the same practical utility. While it is hardly possible that black flies, no-see-ums, or mosquitoes will endanger a camper's life, they can make existence an ordeal when they have unprotected skin to feed on. There is hardly a campsite in North America that is not occupied by some type of biting fly in spring and summer. A good liquid repellent applied regularly will keep them at bay.

The camper bound for strange country will do well to ask about insect repellents at the store nearest his camping area. Local stores keep the potions that are most effective on local bugs. Some insects are impervious to all-purpose repellents sold in city drug stores. Finally, the camper should carry a book of first-aid rules. (See Chapter 30)

FOR SMOKERS

An extra pipe, a tin of tobacco, or a reserve supply of cigarettes belongs in the steady smoker's war bag. The trip is ruined thereafter for the smoker who drops his pipe in the lake or runs out of cigarettes. Equally pathetic is the smoker with tobacco but no matches. He, too, needs a reserve supply.

READING AND WRITING

The outdoorsman who is addicted to reading or taking notes can avoid forgetting his books or pencil and paper if he keeps them in a sack he always takes with him on outdoor trips.

GLASSES

The person who wears prescription eyeglasses needs an extra pair in the war bag for any trip far afield. Many outdoorsmen like to have both binoculars and sunglasses in their bag of personal equipment. Many old-timers think of sunglasses as dude trappings, but they can save the camper from a painful headache or major eye trouble caused by bright sun reflecting off water or snow.

Arctic Eskimos, who are as tough and efficient as any outdoorsmen the world has known, are ready customers for sunglasses. They use them to replace the crude wooden or bone goggles with narrow slits which for centuries were their protection against snow-blindness caused by bright sun reflecting off white snow. Too much exposure to the brilliant light of sun reflecting off snow can literally blind a person, causing a painful inflammation that will last for days.

Binoculars of 6 to 10 power are invaluable to the big-game hunter in open country, and they are useful to almost any camper. With binoculars the canoe camper crossing an unfamiliar lake can see which of the distant coves is the lake outlet or the campsite he wants to steer for. Binoculars will bring the dangerous rapids downriver into sharp focus long before the unaided eye can see them. The hiker can use them to spot a distant landmark that may save him from taking a wrong turn. Binoculars are valuable just for looking at distant objects out of the curiosity all outdoorsmen have for the world about them.

REPAIR KIT

A couple of sturdy needles with large eyes and a few yards of strong nylon or Dacron thread will repair a dozen things the camper could not fix otherwise. If you have the needles and thread, you can stitch up a split seam in a leather boot, fix a torn tent or pack, repair a saddle or a vital strap on a pack-horse harness, or sew on that button that keeps your coat collar closed in stormy weather. Those small jobs can be urgent and important in the woods, and there is no easy way to do them without needle and thread.

The thin fishing lines made of braided nylon or Dacron make fine camp thread. They are thin enough to stitch on a button without undue bulk and strong enough so that a dozen stitches will secure a saddle or harness strap that must hold 100 pounds or more.

A small roll of copper wire also has a host of practical uses. It has enough stiffness to repair mechanical things that cannot be fixed with fishing line, and it will not burn when used to repair the handle of a campfire coffee pot or to support a stovepipe. It is soft enough to work with bare hands, but a pair of pliers—handy for a dozen other things—will speed any wire work and do a better job.

The light, soft aluminum wire now sold in small coils at hardware counters is as good for camp use as copper wire. Both copper and aluminum wire are cheap enough on camper-size coils that a quarter's worth should last through a dozen outings.

Steel wire is too stiff and springy for the mending and lashing jobs where the camper ordinarily uses short lengths of wire. A large roll of steel "baling" or "hay" wire gets a lot of use around a cabin or by packers using horses, but it is not a war-bag item. The same applies to rope. A 100-yard spool of braided fishing line, which weighs a few ounces, will lash a raft or bind tent poles as well as rope, often better. Just take a few extra turns to get the necessary strength.

TOILET KIT

There is no excuse or need for the camper to look like a recluse or a grizzly bear after several weeks in camp or on the trail. Only a few small items are necessary to keep clean and neatly groomed. They weigh little and occupy hardly any space in your pack. A kit along the lines of the one listed below will add to your health and morale and its inclusion in your outfit is recommended strongly. On very long trips add a pair of hair clippers.

> Toothbrush and paste
> Razor and shaving soap
> Comb
> Nail file
> Toilet soap and towels
> Steel mirror

MAPS

The war bag is the place for maps that should never be left behind. Take your map along even if you know the country well; it will help you to show others in your party where they are or to put some stranger on the right trail.

WHIMSY ITEMS

Though the idea of the war bag is to get all the essentials into a light and portable bundle, do not be afraid to add something that will lighten your mind, if not your load. Snake-shy campers need snake-bite kits, whether or not there are poisonous snakes in the region.

12 - The Grub List

IF YOU HAVE A GRUB LIST OF YOUR OWN THAT
has fed you well through the years, stick to it. Few
things vary so much as individual notions about what
constitutes a good diet. But beginners planning trips
of a week or longer are frequently at a loss for a starting point in planning their grub supply. Lacking a
standard list, they forget some such vital item as
salt. And how much of each item is needed for a
two-week stay?

Here is one good, standard grub list which has been
tested and revised through years of camp cooking.
The quantities specified will supply two men for two
weeks. Simple arithmetic will adjust the list to suit
any number of campers. One man on a two-week trip
needs half the amount listed here, for example, and
four would need to double the quantity of each item.

Substitutions or additions can be made in any category. Many of the miscellaneous items can be pruned
off the list if pack weight is a problem, but variety
has as much appeal in camp life as it does at home.

Grub List for Two Men for Two Weeks

Meats and Fats
1½ pounds steak or fresh meat (for first day out)

10 pounds bacon
2½ pounds butter (canned is best)
1 pound Crisco or similar shortening
1 pound dried beef
2 pounds dry sausage
1½ pounds cheese
2 cans corned beef

Breadstuffs

1 loaf ready-baked bread (for first day)
3 pounds Ry-Krisp or similar long-lasting wafers
2½ pounds cornmeal or corn-muffin mix
2 pounds rice
1½ pounds quick-cooking oats
5 pounds pancake flour
2 pounds plain flour
4 pounds biscuit mix
1 pound gingerbread mix
1 pound macaroni
¼ pound baking powder

Condensed Foods

3 pounds dried milk
2 pounds dehydrated potatoes
¼ pound dehydrated onions
¼ pound dehydrated carrots
½ pound dried eggs
1 pound dehydrated soup
¼ pound split dried peas

Beverages

2 pounds coffee
¼ pound tea
½ pound cocoa

Sweets

6 pounds white sugar
2 pounds brown sugar
4 packages pudding mix

2 pounds jam or jelly
4 pounds candy bars

Miscellaneous

3 pounds dry beans
1 pound salt
1 bottle pickles
4 cans tomatoes
1 pound powdered lemon juice
5 pounds dried fruit
1½ ounce pepper
1 bottle catchup
2 ounces cinnamon
2 ounces baking soda

FURTHER GRUB LIST CONSIDERATIONS

Steer clear of the outdated grub lists in many of the old-time reference books. They were good for their day, but modern developments in dehydrated and ready-mixed foods make the old lists needlessly heavy and troublesome. A good brand of prepared biscuit mix, for example, will with one third of the effort make biscuits two-thirds better than those the average camp cook will produce by following his own recipe. Go-light campers can now get good dehydrated foods which save the burden of packing great loads of food that, like raw potatoes, are mainly water.

Do not rely heavily on catching fish or game to fill a substantial part of the grub list. Stricter laws and shorter open seasons rule out the live-off-the-land plans that were once possible, if not actually practical. The bird in the bush or the trout in the pool is always an uncertain prospect. It is not always the big one that gets away, as fishermen commonly report; sometime you cannot catch the little ones either.

BALANCING THE GRUB LIST

Since individual tastes and appetites vary so much, check your final list to see how it suits the known habits of various members of your party. If there is one who drains pots of coffee, tally up his daily consumption in cups. Each pound of ground coffee will yield fifty cups of average strength. Pack extra coffee accordingly. In proportion to its bulk, tea goes much farther than coffee. One ordinary tea bag will make three cups of medium-strength tea.

Sliced bacon runs about twenty slices to the pound. If each adult has four slices for breakfast, he will consume a pound in five days. Slab bacon, by the way, is easier to keep for long periods and can be sliced to suit heartier appetites.

A SPECIAL-PURPOSE GRUB LIST

The best way to plan a special-purpose grub list— one to fit a light pack or a prescribed diet—is to write down a sample menu for one day. Then multiply to figure the amounts needed for two days, two weeks, or whatever time the trip will take. This will establish a sound basic list that can be quickly altered to allow a certain amount of variety. Where to start—that is the common problem with inexperienced campers— and this simple system solves it far better than random browsing through a supermarket.

WHERE TO GET DEHYDRATED FOODS

Many of the dried or dehydrated foods that serve light-pack campers so well are difficult or impossible to obtain in neighborhood stores. The following firms do mail-order business and will furnish lists and specifications of such camp foods on request.

Bernard Food Industries, 217 N. Jefferson Street, Chicago 6, Illinois

Trail Feeding Specialties, Box 441, Summit, New Jersey

DriLite Foods, 8716 Santa Fe, South Gate, California

Ad Seidel, 42 Lispenard Street, New York 13, New York

Hilker and Bletsch, 614 W. Hubbard Street, Chicago 10, Illinois

J. B. Kisky, 1829 N. E. Alberta Street, Portland 11, Oregon

13 - Cooking Equipment

CAMP COOKING UTENSILS ARE SO ESSENTIAL THAT no one who has ever camped without them will do so more than once. Do not skimp on cooking utensils unless you are on a trip where every extra ounce of pack load is a burden.

BASIC KITCHEN KIT

Here is a check list of utensils any party of four persons will ordinarily need for the full cycle of camp feeding—cooking, eating, and dishwashing. A lone camper can pare down the list to suit a lighter pack and more Spartan standards. Expanding the kit to suit a large party is mainly a matter of adding a suitable number of plates, cups, and such, and perhaps an extra or a larger pot.

1 8-quart bucket or stew kettle
1 4-quart kettle
1 2-quart kettle
1 2-quart coffeepot
2 10-inch frying pans
4 plates
4 cups
4 knife, fork, spoon sets

With soap, dishrags, and towels, this basic kit will do all your kitchen jobs. Some things serve a double purpose, however. The big bucket or kettle, for example, may start out as a water pail at the beginning of the meal and end up on the fire full of hot water for dishwashing. And somebody has to eat with the fork or the spoon that stirs the cooking food or flips the frying fish. Some campers think this is a sensible economy of utensils. Others want more equipment.

Aluminum nesting cooking kit for four. *Courtesy of Morsan Tents.*

Extras

Here are some additions that will add substantially to the ease and productivity of camp cooking with the four-person kit. Pack them if you can.

First, and perhaps most valuable, is a cast-iron or thick aluminum Dutch oven, which has a raised rim on the lid to hold hot coals and three stubby legs to let heat under the oven. This Dutch oven, which is really just a thick-walled pot with a tight-fitting lid, will do a fine job of frying, boiling, baking. It warms slowly, cools slowly, cooks with steady and even heat.

A stew put in a Dutch oven and buried in coals will cook to perfection with little or no attention. Just dig out the oven in a couple of hours, and pass out the plates. The Dutch oven will bake bread or biscuits to a golden brown without burning. It makes an admirable frying pan. It has only one weakness: It is discouragingly heavy. Even the lighter cast-aluminum Dutch oven weighs 7½ pounds in the size 4 inches deep and 12 inches wide. The cast-iron model is about 2 pounds heavier. Thinner, lighter models lack the ovenlike heat that makes a heavy Dutch oven worth packing despite its awkward weight and bulk.

An oversized frying pan of Dutch oven thickness is also worth its weight on most trips. The cast-iron models are tops. Thick aluminum is about as good, if it is thick enough. Most aluminum frying pans and all the light-gauge steel or tin frying pans are too thin for efficient cooking. First they are too hot, then too cold: unless fire and cooking are tended meticulously, the food is first scorched, then chilled. The thick and roomy cast-iron frying pan gives working room and holds the steady heat that makes for good cooking.

An oversized griddle of the generous thickness of a Dutch oven or cast-iron frying pan is a tremendous asset to the camp cook who has a lot of fried eggs or pancakes to serve each morning. Get one 10 by 12 inches, or even larger. It will cook eggs or hotcakes to a turn as fast as four or five hungry campers can eat them. A small frying pan will not keep up with the crowd, and pushing it with extra heat only burns the food. Two small, thin pans are not the answer. One is scorching or getting cold while the cook tends to the other.

A folding aluminum reflector oven is a fine addition to the basic cooking kit. A typical model folds into a package about 1 foot square and 1 inch thick and weighs about 3 pounds. It will bake bread and biscuits and broil meat. It is easy to handle. Just prop it up near a campfire, and move it a little closer to or away from the heat as needed. The cooking food is always in sight and can be checked by a glance at the open front of the oven.

A good spatula turns pancakes, eggs, and many frying foods better than a fork, a hunting knife, or any routine substitute for a spatula. And a thin-bladed kitchen knife beats a heavy sheath knife for most slicing jobs.

A separate water bucket—a folding canvas model, if pack room is scarce—is worth its weight. So is a separate dishpan.

A pair of cotton gloves will be valued by the woman pressed into service as campfire cook. Gloves save burns, cuts, ground-in soot and grime.

And do not forget such homely items as soap, towels, and dishrags. Scouring pads made of plastic, copper wire, or steel wool do a far quicker and easier job of cleaning stubborn pots and pans than such wilderness tricks as rubbing them with grass and sand. Where water is at a premium—in a desert camp, say—dishes that have not been rinsed with hot water can be sterilized with fire heat or by being put out in bright sunshine. Slipshod dishwashing can produce some impressive gastric upsets among campers.

MATERIALS IN CAMP COOKING GEAR

Stamped aluminum makes fine pots, pans, plates, forks, and spoons for camp use. Cast aluminum, thicker and heavier, makes good griddles, Dutch ovens, frying pans. Aluminum knives will not hold a sharp edge and are inferior to steel where a cutting edge is needed. Aluminum plates and cups tend to be too hot to hold at first, then let food or beverage cool too fast.

Cups and plates made of a thick, tough plastic are better. Cups with full-loop handles will not stack as compactly as those with handles that hook down like a crooked finger, with a gap between cup and handle at the bottom.

Stainless steel, another fairly common material in camp cooking kits, is tougher than aluminum, a bit easier to keep clean. It is heavier than aluminum, but not enough so that the extra weight will overburden the camper. Thin plates, cups, or frying pans made of stainless steel have the common weakness of getting too hot or too cold.

Plastic is good for plates, cups, or dishpans that will not be put on campfire or stove. No ordinary plastic will withstand that kind of heat. A plastic water bucket will do, though a folding canvas one will haul and hold as much water and fold into a much neater package for travel.

Cast iron or cast aluminum is the stuff for Dutch ovens, frying pans, and griddles. Nearly all camp-kit frying pans are made of stamped aluminum or stainless steel that is too thin to hold steady and even heat. Substitute an oversized cast-iron or cast-aluminum pan unless there is some compelling reason to cut pack weight down to the last ounce.

Glass is a poor choice for any camp cooking or eating utensil that will be involved in rough travel. It is heavy, easily broken, and impossible to repair, and it will not stand direct stove or campfire heat.

PACKING THE COOKING KIT

The cooking kit should be packed as a unit, with all the essential items in one neat box or bag. Factory kits are designed just for camping so that all the pots and pans fit inside the largest container. Knives, forks, and spoons are usually in a rattleproof canvas bag that goes into the smallest container—the one in the core of the packed kit.

The factory-made cooking kit slipped into a sturdy canvas bag is entirely satisfactory at first. But most campers who use such a kit for long will make some substitutions (a thicker and larger frying pan) and additions (a spacious griddle) that will not fit into that neat nest of matched utensils. The answer is a larger pack, such as a heavy duffel bag or a wooden grub box. Fill the gaps in the roomier container with towels and dishrags. Use a few clean burlap bags to muffle the rattles if you plan to haul the rig on a horse, as rattling hardware spooks pack animals. Burlap bags have a dozen spur-of-the-moment uses in a pack-trip camp.

Use the cooking-kit box or bag just for cooking utensils. This saves general disorder in camp and also lessens the chances of contaminating the utensils with such potent fluids as insect spray or lantern fuel.

ALUMINUM FOIL COOKING

A big roll of aluminum foil will do a lot of odd jobs for the camp cook, but those who have been persuaded that aluminum foil is a substitute for a cooking kit have been oversold. A roll of foil is a worthwhile supplementary item, not the whole answer to campfire cooking.

You can rig a frame of green sticks and cover it

with aluminum foil to contrive an efficient reflector oven. It is rather precarious, however, and involves quite a lot of cutting, lashing, and draping. It is not portable—at least not in the sense that it is worth the effort. And the expenditure of foil and time involved in setting up such a reflector oven will soon pay for a factory-made one.

Heavy aluminum foil folded over the fork of a green stick will form a makeshift frying pan, but one that has the faults already mentioned.

Foil can, however, be very useful. It makes a fine pot liner for cooking foods that would otherwise gum up the pot and make it difficult to wash. Potatoes wrapped in foil can be baked in hot ashes or in a camp oven with little danger of burning. Fish or fowl wrapped in foil for baking in coals or oven or broiling near open flames will cook evenly and without charring. Leave enough gaps to let part of the steam escape, unless you like the boiled-food taste and texture that results from cooking foot tightly sealed in foil.

WOODS-GROWN UTENSILS

Anyone who has participated in a weiner or marshmallow roast has used one of the simplest and best of the woods-grown cooking utensils: a green stick sharpened on one end. The food is speared on one end; the camper holds the other. If he tires of holding it, he can prop it over a rock or forked stake or stick one end in the ground. Then he has a dingle stick. It will hold a kettle to boil, broil a steak or a slab of fresh ribs, cook a fish or fowl. There is no rig so uncomplicated that does so many things so well.

For campfire broiling of large fish or fowl, a split stick holds the food better than a pointed one. Choose a green limb about 4 feet long and about 1½ inches thick. (Avoid evergreen limbs, which are full of resin, and willow, which imparts a bitter taste to food.) Split the limb about 18 inches down from one end, and wedge in the fish or fowl, which should be split and spread flat to present a thinner slab for broiling. Push a few twigs about 8 inches long (cut off the same limb) into the split on either side of the fish or fowl to help support it. Squeeze the split ends of the limb close together and tie them with string or a strip of bark from the limb itself. Hold or prop up this woodland grill so that the meat has hot, even heat from the fire burned down to red coals.

EMERGENCY MEASURES

Dressed fish, birds, or small animals can be coated with an inch-thick layer of wet clay or mud and baked right in the coals of an open fire. The fire-dried mud will peel off easily when the cooking is done, exposing food that is cooked well enough to suit a person who is either ravenously hungry or dedicated to survival experiments.

Small stones heated piping hot in a campfire can be used to boil water, soup, or coffee in crude bowls made of folded bark or trench bowls chopped in green logs. If the stones are hot enough, they will shed most of their soot and grime. Needless to say, that heat also kills any germs. The hot rocks will boil water in containers that cannot be suspended over a fire in any practical way. They will even work in a fresh animal hide cupped hair side down in a hole dug in the ground. Soup or stew made in this fashion is notable more for its warmth and unique flavor than for its appetizing appearance.

PART **2**

On the Move

14 - Auto Camping

PLANNING AND PACKING

FIRST, WHERE DO YOU WANT TO GO ON YOUR auto-camping vacation? Spread your maps and travel folders at least a month in advance of the trip, and reach a solid decision about your destination and general travel route. You should start to plan early to allow time for letters of inquiry to be answered and for assembling the equipment needed for a long trip.

With the destination and general route decided, you are ready to get down to details. For a trip into unfamiliar territory, nothing supplies more detailed information than a few letters of inquiry mailed well in advance. In the appendix you will find the addresses of state, national, and private agencies that will supply maps and camping information free of charge.

A good letter of inquiry states specifically where you are going and what you want to know. For example, a letter to the Government Travel Bureau, Ottawa, Ontario, Canada, will be largely wasted if it merely asks, "Where is a good place for auto camping in Canada?" It would take a five hundred-page letter to answer such a question properly. Choose a definite destination or travel route, and ask for information about that one route or area. Such a letter can be easily answered in detail.

For precise advance mapping of an auto trip in the mainland states of the United States, there is no better reference book than the *Family Camping Directory*— 168 pages of maps and campground listings, published by Barcam Publishing Company, Inglewood, California. This book costs $2.00, but it offers a lot for the money. California alone has 52 public campgrounds in state parks and 668 public sites in national parks and forests within the state's boundaries. This directory tells all about each one—how to find it, what facilities it offers. All states are covered in the same way.

VEHICLE CHECK-UP

Give your car, station wagon, or trailer a mechanical check-up a week or so in advance, so that any necessary mechanical repairs or adjustments can be tested on routine driving near home, where mistakes can be corrected quickly and conveniently. This is a good time to get the car freshly greased, change the oil and the oil filter, replace worn sparkplugs or tires. Anyone driving from a warm climate into northern regions or high mountains may need radiator antifreeze in the car. Brakes, lights, and windshield wipers must be in good order for safe or even for legal driving.

CHECK-LIST OF GRUB AND EQUIPMENT

Draw up a check list of the grub and equipment you will need and tick off each item as it is packed. Lacking a written list, not one person in a thousand can load for a family without forgetting two or three important items.

Separate boxes and bags simplify the packing, the unloading, and the camp use of all grub and equipment. Canvas duffel bags generally work better than wooden or cardboard boxes. They will bend to fit into odd corners. They are light and tough, are reasonably water- and dustproof, and they are cheap. It is better to pack in half a dozen bags of modest size than in two or three that make heavy, bulky loads. Label each bag as to contents in order not to waste time later looking for things. If there are young children on the trip, it saves squabbles if each one has a labeled duffel bag for his or her personal clothing and equipment.

If you have an extra storage box and room for it, by all means take it along. Most campers collect enough souvenirs and such to make the coming-home load heavier than the going-away one.

For a long trip with a large group, it pays to make a trial loading of the vehicle to be sure all the basic equipment is going to fit in. There is *not* always room for one more.

ROOF RACK

If test loading makes it clear that the vehicle's ordinary passenger and storage space is going to be swamped, a roof rack will solve a minor overloading problem. The roof rack is a good place for the tent, cooking kit, stove, ax or saw, and rolled-up sleeping bags. The idea is to load it with durable, compact equipment that will not be used on the road.

A tarp or the unfolded tent lashed over the roof rack will protect the load from rain and dust. Lash this cover down tight, for a gale wind tugs at a roof rack when a car is going 50 or 60 miles an hour. Be sure the rack itself is cinched down tight, for if it is not, a sudden braking may cause the load to move forward. Good racks have strong metal hooks to grip the vehicle's rain gutter above the doors and four or more broad suction cups to grip the roof. They will safely hold 200 to 300 pounds of equipment.

The auto-top rack is a good choice for the motorist who wants to haul a canoe or a small boat. There are several roof racks made just for this purpose.

Rack Covers

Car campers who buy the simple racks that are designed only to hold extra baggage can save the trouble of lashing down the load by choosing one of several models with a fitted canvas cover. Some have slide-fastener ports for loading and unloading. Another style of cover is held tight over the rack with elastic cords. Some rather expensive racks have stream-lined canopies made of aluminum. They open and close as simply as trunk lids.

All of these ready-made covers allow the camper to take out a single item without tying and untying

Top rack with water-resistant canvas cover.
Courtesy of Morsan Tents.

the knots and hitches that would be needed to lash a tent or tarp over a car-rack load. The factory covers go on and off in a jiffy. They require no skill with knots or lashings. They cost extra, however, and they cannot be adjusted to hold oversized packages or withstand unusual strains. The man with a tarp or a tent and a lot of lash rope can rig a cover to suit any reasonable load and take extra wraps of rope for extra security.

SMALL AND LARGE TRAILERS

One- and Two-Wheelers

The best trailer for auto campers who want more hauling capacity without the imposing bulk and driving complications of a house trailer is the one-wheel model which clamps solidly to the rear bumper or bumper braces. The light one-wheeler so hitched can be backed or steered as if it were part of the car. It requires no overload springs on the car and will not overload a standard sedan or station wagon. The one-wheelers trail straight and, even at high speeds, carry all the surplus equipment any family group will ordinarily need.

Small one-wheel and two-wheel trailers are available with built-in bunks, slide-out cabinets for cooking and storage, and fold-down canvas covers that blossom out on hinged frames to form a tent over the trailer. Some of the trailer tents are big enough to enclose all of the trailer and a good-sized area beside it. Supporting legs at the four corners of the trailer fold or slide down to make it stand steady, even though it is unhitched from the car or station wagon. These small trailers with built-in tents and shelves are quite expensive—in the $500 bracket.

A small trailer with two wheels will handle better on dirt or gravel roads than will the little one-wheelers. Campers often drive on roads that are a pair of smooth tracks with a rough, high center. The tire of a one-wheel trailer has to bump along this rough center strip, while a two-wheeler will follow the car along the tracks on either side.

House Trailers

Some of the so-called "house trailers" are light and maneuverable enough to travel most of the woods roads auto campers use. Any good sedan or station wagon will pull one of the light 12- or 14-foot trailers over the better mountain roads. Such a trailer will offer built-in beds for two adults, stove, refrigerator, wardrobe, food cupboards, and enough space to move around in comfortably.

A 16- or 17-foot house trailer will hold two double beds, two wardrobes, heater, four-burner cooking stove, sink, refrigerator, dinette table and seats, possibly a small bathroom. This is the general size limit for travel off the paved roads with standard sedans or station wagons. A 17-footer made mainly of aluminum or a similar light and tough material will not overheat the engine or overload the springs of a full-size sedan or station wagon. It will back and turn easily. A pickup truck or a similar extra-power vehicle is needed to handle a trailer larger than 17 feet on mountain roads or over rough flatlands.

Rental Trailers

It will often pay the camper to rent a small trailer rather than to buy one that will not be used often. All United States towns of any size now have trailer rental agencies, which can be located through the classified section of a telephone book or your local newspaper. The rental trailers are licensed, insured, and equipped with required lights or reflectors.

The Pickup Coach

The coach living units that fit into the beds of pickup trucks are a popular compromise for campers who like the comforts of home but not the inconvenience of parking, backing, and towing a trailer. The larger pickup coaches will sleep three adults in built-in beds. They are offered with stoves, sink, closet, storage lockers. Some even have a shower and toilet. The whole unit can be fitted on the pickup or taken off with little time or effort. It makes a snug mobile home for one or two campers.

The price of a pickup coach unit is fairly steep. The more elaborate models run from about $600.00 up.

Remember that a pickup coach is both car and camp. When two or three campers are using one for the first time, one member of the party may thought-

Detachable cab converts a pick-up truck into a rolling bedroom. Courtesy of *Highway Cruisers.*

lessly drive it off on a short side trip without stopping to think that he is taking the whole camp with him.

But this is a lesson quickly learned when the driver returns to find his partners standing in the rain eagerly, if not angrily, awaiting him.

Station Wagon Sleeping

Several firms make canvas "boots" that fit over the open rear doors of station wagons and enclose extra feet of sleeping and storage space. Some boots or canvas awnings are designed to connect a pitched tent to the rear of a parked station wagon.

Mattresses designed to fit station wagons can be had in either inflatable or fiber-filled models. There are double-bed models contoured to curve around the rear-wheel wells of wagons that bulge inward at those points.

Curtains (you can buy or make them) will give station-wagon sleepers more privacy in a crowded campground. They also keep sunlight from arousing campers who want to sleep after sun-up.

Nets like those hanging above the berths of Pullman cars can be swung like small hammocks under the roof of a station wagon to hold odds and ends. When not in use, they roll up into tiny, nearly weightless bundles.

In insect time there is an easy and efficient way to keep out bugs without rolling up all the windows and robbing the interior of the station wagon of needed ventilation. Carry one or more panels of mosquito netting a foot wider and longer than the door opening. Open the door, drape the netting over it, and then close the door so that the edges of the netting are sealed between the door and the body of the wagon. This makes a tight, bugproof seal. The window can be opened in advance or cranked to the desired height later by leaving a little slack in the panel of netting.

There is an easy way to rig the rear compartment of a station wagon so that it provides both sleeping room and storage space at the same time. The key to the system is a sleeping platform of three-quarter-inch plywood mounted on four iron-pipe legs threaded into flat bases. You sleep on the platform, store gear under it. Gale Siegal, a Wilbur, Washington, schoolteacher, designed the model that first came to our attention. His station wagon allows a plywood sleeping platform wide enough for two adults and nearly 7 feet long. The 13-inch legs leave enough space under the platform for wooden foot lockers which hold grub and gear.

The storage lockers will slide in and out while the platform is in place. Thus, the camper can slide the grub and gear boxes out onto the tailgate to do camp chores and cooking, then push them back under his ready-made bed and close the tailgate for warmth at night. On a long haul one man can sleep on this platform while the other drives.

A similar platform can be made with little effort or expense to fit any standard station wagon.

TENTS FOR CAR CAMPERS

Many traditional tents, such as the wall tent, require too many poles, stakes, and guy ropes to suit impatient auto campers. Manufacturers, however, offer dozens of tents that pop up from trailers, fold out from car racks, connect with station-wagon boots, or drape over joined frames requiring few or no stakes and guy ropes. Though the good tents of this type are comparatively expensive, they provide quick and efficient shelter in the strictly governed campgrounds where there are rules against cutting tent poles, digging tent trenches, and rigging ropes to trees. Hundreds of busy campgrounds are forced to draw up such

Aluminum trailer (above) opens into a luxurious tent
with a sewn-in floor and foam rubber mattress (below).
Courtesy of Vesely Co.

Family tent packs on top of any car and can be erected in five minutes.
Courtesy of Kar Kamp.

Car-top tent sleeps two adults or four children off the ground on an inner-spring mattress. *Courtesy of Sky-Vue Sleeper.*

Porch enclosure converts a station-wagon interior into a sleeping area for two or three people. *Courtesy of Morsan Tents.*

Four adults sleep comfortably in this tent trailer which can be erected in five minutes without any tools.
Courtesy of Morsan Tents.

rules to protect ground and growth from a steady assault with ax and trenching tools.

The umbrella tent is the best of the traditional tents for summertime auto campers. It goes up quickly, either with one factory-jointed center pole or on a frame of corner poles joined to a peak support. A peg at each corner will hold it steady in any normal wind. It sheds rain or snow efficiently and has plenty of head room.

Roadside and state park campers are also taking to the new pop tents which open like umbrellas to form an inside shelter space 7 feet in diameter. They set up and take down in minutes, folding into light, compact packages.

Cottage tents roomy as small apartments are also in vogue with car campers, particularly those with large families. They require a good many factory-fitted side and ridge poles, but the good ones properly pitched give a fine combination of room and utility with their separate dining porches and bedrooms.

Pup tents and the smaller sizes of umbrella tent are ideal auxiliary tents for car campers with children old enough to manage simple shelters of their own. These are inexpensive and easy to erect. The youngster who is put in charge of such a tent will soon learn some valuable lessons in self-reliance.

The auto camper can buy car-top racks that are factory fitted to hold a double-bed mattress and a fold-out tent. On the road the whole unit is neatly packaged, with a portion of the folding tent serving as a waterproof, dustproof cover. In camp the tent opens and swings out to form a roomy shelter over the car-top bed alongside the vehicle to accommodate six people. Two people can sleep on top of the car, in the rack bed, and there is room for two more in the fold-out tent that roofs the top of the car and a two-man sleeping area beside the vehicle. The whole rig can be opened or packed in minutes.

There are many variations of this basic car-top tent-and-bed rig. The Heilite model is one of the better ones. The good ones work fine, but price is their drawback: they cost around $300.00.

ACCESSORIES

Front-Seat Box

A small box or basket placed on the front seat between driver and passenger will hold a dozen odds and ends that auto campers need on the road. (Most of the glove compartments built into dashboards are small and overcrowded.) This box or basket will hold road maps (the accordion-pleated style is easiest to fold and unfold), sunglasses, cigarettes, flashlights, camera, binoculars, travel folders, and turnpike cards in one neat package within easy reach. (Where, by the way, are your automobile registration and insurance papers? They need to be in some safe and convenient place.)

Inside Rack for Clothing

Some extra room for clothing can be gained by installing a clothes-hanger bar that fits up against the roof over the rear seat. It is anchored to the tops of the windows on either side of the rear seat. This bar, which has a screw adjustment to fit it to any standard car, will hold pressed clothes on hangers without a wrinkle. If the back seat is not loaded with passengers, it provides a wide, closet style of rod to hold all manner of camp clothing that would otherwise have to be stored in the trunk or another space more in demand than the space below the roof. A side-mounted rear-view mirror is needed when the rear window is blocked by clothes on a roof bar.

INSULATED CHESTS

If you plan to make a brief roadside stop for lunch or eat snacks while driving, a fine container for such foods is an insulated chest of the sort used to hold ice and perishable foods. Such a chest will keep hot things hot as well as it keeps cold things cold. A big one with a good ice supply allows auto campers to carry a good supply of fresh milk or perishable food.

A handy place to store an insulated chest in a station wagon is right behind the front seat. This keeps it out of the sun in hot weather and makes it easy to reach when you want a snack.

Water frozen inside waxed-cardboard milk containers will do a neater job of cooling an insulated chest than cakes of bare ice. The exposed ice will soon flood the bottom of a chest in hot weather, while melted in a milk carton, it becomes cool drinking water. Sporting goods and hardware stores also sell sealed cans of a chemical which can be frozen in a refrigerator and used as dripless cooling units in an insulated chest. Such a can holds its chill longer than a piece of ice of the same size, and it can be used over and over again. Just refreeze it when it thaws out.

Insulated chests for cooling food and vacuum bottles for both hot and cold foods are particularly useful to auto campers, who have the means to carry them easily. A cup of coffee (in winter) or cold water (in desert heat) is a luxury few other campers can enjoy while they are on the move. Adequate size and durability are the main considerations in buying either insulated chests or vacuum bottles. Most customers buy them too small the first time, then head to the store to get a larger model after a trip or two. Hot-weather fishermen buy small chests to keep their fish on ice and end up with grub and beverages crowding the fish. A pint vacuum bottle of hot coffee can hardly be large enough to suit three or four men on a long winter day. Get the quart, half gallon, or gallon size.

Fishing Tackle and Firearms

Many auto campers are dedicated fishermen who will find it difficult to pass up roadside pools in the back country without stopping for a few trial casts. They will get more fishing done—and fewer complaints from non-fishing passengers—if they pack their tackle in easy reach on top of the load.

Firearms cannot be handled so casually in cars on public roads. A loaded firearm in a car is both dangerous and illegal. Uncased guns carried in cars are illegal in many regions, and firearms of any kind are ruled out in such wildlife preserves as Yellowstone National Park. In general, a solid citizen with a hunting license or a target-gun permit will have no trouble carrying a cased and unloaded firearm on autocamping trips. But he will be rigidly restricted in how he can use it in most public campgrounds.

Check on the laws where you are going before you set out with your guns. Western, southwestern, and southern states as a rule have more lenient firearms laws than do eastern states. Canada has stern rules about Americans crossing the border with pistols in their possession. So does Mexico. Save trouble by writing for advance information. Carry with you a complete set of credentials—license, permit, registration, and so forth.

FINAL PACKING

Start by putting aside space for the spare tire, jack, signal light, and other tools that will be needed if you have tire or mechanical trouble on the road. Be sure all these items are present and accounted for, and plan the loading so that they can be reached quickly. A canvas bag of water hanging on front or rear bumper is a comfortable precaution for travel through desert or arid regions. There are still lots of side roads where lack of radiator or drinking water can become a serious problem.

An extra gallon of motor oil stored in cans will get a vehicle out of rough country after it has lost its oil through a cracked oil pan. The break can be caulked temporarily with a wooden peg or a rag driven into the gap. Tire chains are needed where there is a good chance the car will be driven through mud or snow. A tow rope, a short-handled shovel, and a light block and tackle are worth their freight if the trip involves back roads in rough country. All this emergency gear should be packaged in a corner where it can be reached without unloading everything in the car trunk or station wagon.

The bottom load, which will be difficult to get at on the road, should be made up of things that will be used in camp: tent, sleeping bags, stove, cooking utensils, the bulk of the grub.

ON THE ROAD

We have no wish to cast gloom over an auto-camping crew that is packed and ready to drive, but there are two or three things you can do in your own driveway that could head off a death on the road. One of the simplest of these is to see that all the car doors are locked. Researchers studying automobile accidents can prove that the flick of a finger needed to lock each door is a substantial help in preventing fatalities in car wrecks. The inside lock may keep the door from flying open on impact and throwing out a passenger. It also keeps doors from being opened by accident, particularly by children.

Saftey belts, though the motoring public has been slow to accept them, would save hundreds of lives each year. That is an established fact. Act on it as you will.

Good rear vision is another safety factor, so adjust your rear-vision mirrors properly.

The Navigator System

A sharp-eyed passenger in the front seat, supplied with maps of the travel route, is a far better navigator on unfamiliar roads than the driver. The driver frequently needs to focus all his attention on other cars at the busy intersections where most road signs are posted. On country roads the driver trying to read dim road signs or steer while glancing from road to map has far less chance of dodging a deer bolting across the road or of spotting a mud-spattered car coming into an unmarked intersection. When possible, pick a good navigator to keep track of maps and road signs and let the driver drive without distraction.

Children old enough to read maps and signs confidently make good navigators if you make a game of it and let them take turns. They will like to have a compass and perhaps a pair of binoculars, as well as road maps. Instruments add importance to their job. A car compass is not often useful, but it can save driving a lot of miles in the wrong direction after a wrong turn in open country. It is not difficult to make such wrong turns on dim, poorly marked roads at night.

Signs of Car Trouble

Every driver should know the standard danger signs that are registered on the dashboard gauges of an automobile. The most important is the fuel gauge. Do not gamble that you have enough gas to reach the next service station. It costs no more to keep the top half of your gas tank full than it does to fill the lower half repeatedly.

Check the heat gauge from time to time, particularly when climbing steadily in mountain country. If the gauge shows a reading hotter than normal, it is very likely that either the radiator water (or anti-freeze) or the motor oil supply is too low. A serious shortage of either will quickly send the heat gauge needle into the danger zone. No water-cooled car can run far without radiator fluid (water or antifreeze) and motor oil. A broken fan belt will also cause a car to overheat.

The third gauge you should check regularly is the one showing the performance of the car's electrical system. One side of the dial is ordinarily marked "Charge"; the other, "Discharge." If the needle swings to the "Discharge" side and stays there, your car has electrical trouble—a faulty generator, say, or a short circuit—that needs immediate attention.

Other mechanical troubles, which do not register on gauges, can often be heard. Stop for a check at garage or service station if there is persistent grinding or knocking which seems to tie in with the rhythm of the engine. A tire that is conspicuously low will cause the car to veer gradually toward the side the low tire is on when the steering wheel is released. A very low front tire will exert a strong pull on the steering wheel. Tires nearly flat will thump audibly.

All of these are danger signals which can be recognized by any driver. You do not have to be a mechanic. You may need one, however, if you ignore such warnings.

Driving Pace

The fact that speeding is a major cause of traffic deaths is well known to all drivers—or should be by now. For the car camper, such foolish urgency can also be the slow way to his destination. It leads to running out of gas on a lonely road, losing the way, and all sorts of other delaying troubles. One of the more common of these may be the village policeman who pays his own salary out of the money collected from tourists exceeding the local speed limit. This is a racket of sorts in hamlets across the nation. The auto camper, whether actually guilty or not, has little choice when hailed into traffic court in such a situation: he can plead guilty, pay a fine, and go on; or he can spend his vacation fighting the case. Do not tempt the village police by exceeding their speed limits, no matter how clear and wide the road and how small the settlement.

Sunglasses are invaluable when the summer sun is bright on the road and the car hood. Tip them up for tunnels; otherwise the sudden change will leave you in a hazy gloom.

Brief stops to stretch and have a sandwich or coffee slow your progress only slightly, and they make long roads *seem* shorter in the end. Change drivers each two hours when possible. A mediocre driver rested and alert is safer than an expert nodding over the wheel.

How far can the car camper on a long trip plan to travel each day? A great deal depends on roads and geography, but 500 miles is the absolute maximum, even for a powerful new car on roads running monotonously straight as they do in Kansas and Nebraska. That 500 miles requires a solid ten hours of driving at an average speed of 50 miles an hour. Owing, however, to the necessity of slowing down for villages and to miscellaneous short stops, maintaining this average will require a lot of driving much faster than 50 miles an hour. A daily quota of 300 miles is plenty in mountain country or in crowded Eastern states.

The miles driven very early in the morning—just after good daylight—are usually the easier ones, although most tourists are inclined to sleep late and drive late to make up for it. The air and the roads will be cooler in summer, the traffic lighter, and visibility far better early in the day than during dusk or early dark. The early bird also has a better choice of campsites, motels, or other overnight accommodations, since he finishes his daily driving quota while the late riser is still intent on piling up mileage rather than settling down for the night.

Breakdowns

There is comparatively little chance that a good automobile thoroughly checked before a long trip will break down on the road. But it happens. And it sometimes happens in unsettled country where drivers will waste their time waiting for patrol cars and tow trucks—so quick to appear on turnpikes—to rush to the rescue.

Wherever you are, try to get a disabled car off the road and onto some firm and safe roadside area. On both busy highways and backwoods roads a raised hood is a routine distress sign which will announce your trouble to a passing patrol car or to other travelers. After dark, put out flares or other signal lights to warn approaching cars and attract attention. As a rule, it is better to stay with the disabled car, no matter how deserted the road and region. If there are two or more adults in the party and a farmhouse or a settlement is known to be fairly close, chances for quick help are better if one hikes toward the house or settlement to seek help while the others stay with the car. Happily, people in sparsely settled regions are not so indifferent to the plight of a stranded motorist as are those who stream by on busy highways. They know what it means to be stranded on an out-of-the-way road. They often baffle stranded city dwellers by refusing pay for rescue efforts that involve considerable time and energy. The outsider will not offend them by offering to pay, however.

IN CAMP

Since the auto camper is always camping at sites owned and managed by someone—state, Federal Government, or private owner—the first consideration in setting up camp is to be sure you have a right to locate there. The fellow who drives past "Keep Out," "Closed," or "Private" signs to pitch camp is likely to pitch and break camp in rapid sequence, with a troublesome squabble in the middle.

Get permission before you settle on private land. Be sure the state or Federal land you choose is open to campers during summer forest-fire seasons.

Parking

Pick a solid and well-drained parking place as close to the actual campsite as possible, but do not try to drive over jagged rocks or through a bog to get your car right beside the spot where you want to pitch your tent. As mentioned in the chapter on pitching camp, that short drive off the regular road can damage a car as much as a thousand miles of driving on a highway.

Leave the car at the nearest good parking site, and carry your gear the short distance to your tent site. Back the car into the parking place so that it is facing the road and is easy to get out if rain or snow falls while you are there.

Drain the radiator if it has no antifreeze in it and night temperatures are likely to drop below freezing. Roll up all windows tight in cool weather, but leave at least one open a crack in hot summer weather. Hot sun on a tightly sealed modern car can heat inside air enough to crack windows as the air expands. This is by no means unusual in such hot and arid regions as Arizona and New Mexico.

Do not park the car in reach of tall dead trees that might blow over or drop heavy branches in a windstorm. The shade and shelter of a live tree firmly rooted is worth-while protection.

Camp Ground Rules

Because public campgrounds are used by so many people, they have to set up strict rules. Busy auto-camping areas usually forbid the following: digging tent trenches (a waterproof ground cloth or tent floor is the answer) ; cutting green trees or limbs (you need factory tent poles and stakes, air mattresses instead of bough beds) ; wood fires, except in stoves provided by the campground (use those stoves or your own gas stove).

In other words, there is far more use for factory-made equipment in a campground than in the wilderness, where common sense mainly prescribes what you can and cannot do with nature's materials. Thus, the car camper is the camper who most needs the portable rigs that stand on their own mechanical feet and operate on factory fuels: the gas stove and the kerosene heater, the gas lantern, the air mattress, tents that pop up or fold up from car-top racks or trailers, folding camp stools and tables. Many car camps have established toilet and garbage facilities, piped drinking and cooking water, and stores where you can buy food.

Cleanliness is no less a virtue around a campground than it is at home. Keep your camping area clean by using the receptacles usually provided for garbage and paper. If such receptacles are not provided, always bury trash or burn it. A clean camp area deserves to be left the same way; dirt breeds insects and rodents which will be there to greet future campers.

Camp Courtesy

Courtesy is essential to life in a busy, crowded auto campground. Tents are often close together, and so are the people.

If you carry a portable radio, see that it is turned low. Escape from radios is one of the dreams of most campers. Keep down other noise at night, so other campers can sleep.

Restrict neighborly visits to those campers who want to be visited. Advise only those who specifically ask for information about, for instance, how lanterns should most effectively be adjusted and placed. This one restriction—withholding unsolicited advice—is the toughest of all for most campers.

15 - Back Packing

    THERE ARE AT LEAST FIFTY DIFFERENT DEVICES made in this country alone for the hauling of camp equipment on the human back, but we can narrow our discussion to the following half a dozen models that have real utility.

1. The light rucksack, which is basically a sack of canvas or other sturdy fabric fitted with shoulder straps.

2. The Duluth or Poirier packsack—a heavy-duty rucksack with both shoulder straps and head strap to support its weight.

3. The pack basket made of woven splints of wood—a device used for centuries by woodsmen in the Adirondack Mountains of New York and throughout the New England states.

4. The Bergans or Norwegian framed packsack—the type of metal-frame alpine pack the U.S. Army used for heavy-load packing in World War II.

5. The wood or metal packboard—a frame to which a sack, a bundle, or heavy equipment is lashed.

6. The tumpline—a wide leather headband with trailing leather straps which can be looped around almost any man-sized load. A strong and experienced tumpline packer (Canadians portaging canoe cargo are tumpline specialists) can loop his tumpline straps

around a stack of boxes and bags that will total two or three hundred pounds and walk off with the whole load.

Those are the six basic packing devices for the camper who carries his gear on his back all or part of the time. There are versions of each of the six, varying in quality of material and craftsmanship.

The type the individual camper needs depends on the load he expects to carry and the distance he needs to carry it. The tumpline, unsurpassed for moving huge loads over short portages, would be useless to the Rocky Mountain hunter who wants to back-pack only such small items as lunch, camera, rope, sheath knife, hatchet, and spare ammunition while he roams the big-game country near his car or base camp.

FOR LIGHT LOADS—THE RUCKSACK

Let's start with the rucksack or packsack, which is the ideal package for hikers, hunters, or campers who carry a lot of odds and ends as they prowl the woods on one-day jaunts.

The whole point of the rucksack is to get all these awkward odds and ends into a single neat, compact package, which is held on the back by straps that leave the arms free. Many campers—big-game hunters are the worst offenders—prowl the woods all day with twenty pounds of equipment bulging their pockets and hanging every which way from belt and shoulder straps.

Consider the Montana elk hunter, for example. He leaves base camp at daylight, planning to spend the whole day scouting the ridges and basins, hoping to down a bull elk, which will take a fair amount of labor and equipment to dress out. If the kill is made close to nightfall and miles from base camp, the hunter may wisely choose to spend the night near his kill and unravel the trail to camp in good daylight next morning.

This elk hunter is a man who needs a rucksack. He has good reason to pack any or all of the following: sheath knife; hatchet or light folding saw to quarter that big bull; 30 feet of light but strong rope; four cotton meat sacks to cover the elk quarters; sandwiches and quick-energy rations to hold off hunger through two or three mealtimes; a poncho or light plastic sheet which can be rigged as a rain shelter; dry socks and an extra wool shirt or sweater for cold snaps; flashlight; compass; container of waterproof matches; binoculars; camera; light meter; regional map; spare box of rifle ammunition; elk tag; hunting license. He might have a hand warmer, spare eyeglasses, a compact first-aid kit, a light mess kit, a pocket-size block and tackle to hang his game, an elk whistle to call up a bull during the rutting season. He has a pipe or cigarettes if he smokes. He can also be trusted to carry a couple of items—a folding cup, say, or an air cushion for wet-log sitting—that would escape a routine listing.

All these easily make a twenty pound load, which probably seemed outlandishly heavy when it was first

The rucksack, a simple canvas bag with side pockets and shoulder straps, is designed for short outings.
Courtesy of Laacke's.

mentioned. Actually it's only outlandish when the separate items are bulging the hunter's pockets, dangling from his belt, and swinging on two or three neck loops and shoulder straps. Tucked into a rucksack, all this gear will ride neat and easy. The hunter has his hands free to handle his rifle. His gear won't catch in brush, rattle against rocks, or get soaked with rain. While the hunter sits watching a ridge gap where elk cross or when he stops for lunch, his rucksack is slipped off, leaving him completely unencumbered. If he wishes to make a one-night stand in some basin far from base camp, he can carry a little extra grub and a light sleeping bag with his rucksack. An ordinary sleeping bag will be too bulky to fit inside the rucksack, but it can be rolled short and lashed to the top or rolled long and curved in a horseshoe shape to fit over the top and down the sides of the rucksack. Most rucksacks have outside rings to allow such bulky items to be lashed to them. Roll the sleeping bag inside a poncho or waterproof shelter sheet to keep it dry on the trail. The poncho or shelter sheet becomes a waterproof lean-to roof in the overnight camp.

Selecting a Rucksack

In choosing a rucksack, the first thing to be sure of is that this type of lightweight, light-load pack will hold all you ordinarily carry. It is an inadequate pack for the camper who hopes to carry food and equipment for two or three days. The rucksack is also a poor choice for backpacking steel traps, canned goods, or any other hardware heavy enough to bite into the packer's back. A thick canvas sack protects the back as long as the rough load is limited to a few light things such as binoculars, camera, hatchet.

Be sure your rucksack has web or leather shoulder straps at least 2 inches wide and thick enough that they won't curl into narrow bands as the pack weight works on them. Thin, cheap straps quickly roll into narrow, shoulder-cutting ropes. If the pack is satisfactory otherwise, the shoulder straps can be reinforced with strips of thick leather about 10 inches long and 2 inches wide. Rig these on sliding loops so they can be adjusted to fit the shoulders properly.

Look for a rucksack with sturdy buckles, snaps, and rings made of brass, bronze, or rustproof steel. Lots of rucksacks have junky hardware, which makes the whole pack a bad buy. Avoid those with a surplus of zippers, buckles, and tricky snaps. What you want is sturdy simplicity.

Heavy canvas is still as good as any material for a rucksack bag. Nylon or Dacron is lighter and stronger for its weight, but the stiffness of heavy-duty duck or canvas helps to pad the back and holds the pack in shape. The few ounces of extra weight won't be noticed. A canvas pack is easier to waterproof and to keep waterproof than one made of synthetic fibers. The paint-on waterproofing solutions which work so well with the cotton threads in canvas won't hold for long on the hard, slick, synthetic fibers.

A good average size for the bag is 14 by 16 inches, measuring the flat front or back surface of the bag. Look for a long top flap, which will easily drape over the top of the bag when it is full. Many rucksacks have a skimpy flap which fits properly only when the pack is lying empty on the store counter. A model with one or two small outside pockets may be handy if you carry a lot of small items, but shy away from one covered with outside pockets. Chances are you'll have to search all those pockets to find the one small thing you're looking for, and the whole point of the rucksack is to keep incidental tools and equipment in one big pocket.

THE DULUTH OR POIRIER PACKSACK

This pack, originated years ago by the Poirier Tent and Awning Company in Duluth, Minnesota, has both shoulder straps and a headband or tumpline rig which puts part of the pack weight on the packer's forehead. This distribution of weight lets a camper move a heavy load with the Duluth packsack, which except for the head strap is just an overgrown rucksack.

The head strap brings into play the neck muscles, which are powerful beyond the belief of the person who never carries anything heavier on his head than a hat. The head strap also balances a heavy load and keeps the pack weight lined up with the body. With a

Equipped with a tumpline rig, the Duluth pack is recommended for packing heavy loads on canoe portages. *Courtesy of Laacke's*

Duluth pack a strong novice can move one hundred
pounds across a short canoe portage with no dangerous risk of sprains or strains. Once his neck muscles
are conditioned to the strain, he can handle the same
load over portages of a mile or more.

The Duluth pack has two notable weaknesses for
the camper whose trip involves steady backpacking
with food and equipment for several days. The first
shortcoming concerns hiking posture. The head-
strapped pack, if it is heavily loaded, keeps the hiker
slightly bowed and facing straight ahead. He is far
more a working packer than a vacationing tourist, and
he is too firmly harnessed to do any sightseeing along
the trail. If his hat is on top of the head strap, the
strap will keep knocking it off. Bareheaded, the hiker
gets more sun than he wants or needs. A soft felt hat
or a billed cap worn under the head strap is a fair
compromise.

The other weakness of the Duluth pack for steady
hiking is that the person whose muscles are untrained
will soon have a painfully stiff and sore neck. These
muscles toughen up after three or four days, but that
is little consolation for the person on a two- or three-
day jaunt.

Use the Duluth pack for short hauls with fairly
heavy loads—canoe portages, say—or for longer hauls
when there is time to toughen the neck muscles gradually and to get some worth-while use out of their
hard-won toughness.

THE PACK BASKET

The pack basket, sometimes called the Adirondack
pack basket because it is used so often in that range of
upstate New York mountains, has several things to
recommend it. The stiffness of the woven wood splints

makes it a good package for steel traps, canned goods, all the hardware outdoorsmen carry. The pack basket is light, strong, and roomy. With a canvas cover, it is waterproof. Loaded, it will flex enough to fit the packer's back and at the same time protect him from sharp or rough objects inside. Lots of New England trappers use this roomy basket because tools and equipment can be tossed in and hauled away with no special lashing or packing. A good basket will haul a heavy load. The basket doubles as a storage box for outdoor gear at home or in camp.

The main disadvantage of the wooden basket is its inflexible capacity. The load has to be sized to fit the basket; there is no way to adjust the basket to fit a larger or smaller load. As a result a couple of small items will rattle around in the bottom unless the space is padded in. Bulky sleeping bags or bedrolls just won't go in, and the basket itself is so bulky that it is often awkward to tie them on the outside, though a sleeping bag neatly rolled will fit on top. An empty pack basket has the same bulk as a full one.

The woven wooden sides of the pack basket protect the hiker's back when he carries sharp objects.

You can't fold it up neatly for the trip home after you have used up the groceries in it.

A pack basket is a sturdy, inexpensive rig for the person who carries fairly heavy but compact loads. It is too bulky for the hiker or hunter who packs lunch, camera, raincoat, and binoculars for a one-day trip, and it is no good at all for such bulky freight as an outboard motor or a quarter of elk meat.

Give your new pack basket a coat of high-grade spar varnish if the wood splints are untreated when you buy it. Varnished and used with reasonable care, a well-made basket will last a lifetime. Get a basket with thick web or leather shoulder straps 2 inches wide. Many store-counter models have skimpy shoulder straps and basket harness which will need to be altered or replaced for lasting satisfaction.

Some outdoorsmen buy pack baskets without the straps and slip them inside large rucksacks fitted with sturdy shoulder straps. This is a good combination. The basket protects the packer's back, and the rucksack closes and waterproofs the basket. For canoe travel the rig may be fitted with a basket liner of plastic or other light waterproof material that can be tied tight at the top. This outfit will float high and dry in a spill unless it is crammed with something as heavy as ore samples or canned goods.

NORWEGIAN OR BERGANS FRAMED RUCKSACK

This pack is essentially a large rucksack fitted on a frame of light, tubular metal. Cross straps—mainly one broad one at hip level—hold the pack away from the body, which allows cooling air between back and load. Shoulder straps hold the pack in place. Most models have one large storage pocket and two or more small outside pockets. These hold lunch or other small items which can be reached on the trail without fishing through the main pocket.

The metal-frame pack, used by the Army for much of its heavy-duty back packing, is a fine choice for hikers heading into the hills for a week to ten days. This pack looks fairly heavy and formidable when empty (a typical model weighs about six pounds empty), but that frame pays dividends to the man carrying a heavy load on his back. Rough objects in the load will not touch his back. There is no sweaty friction between the pack and the packer's back. The broad strap across the hips puts a lot of the weight straight down on the powerful leg muscles and keeps the center of gravity low—a great aid in keeping your balance in rough country. The notion that heavy packs must be carried high on the shoulders is wrong. Riding high, they make the packer top-heavy and force him to lean forward to compensate for the backward pull. That puts a steady strain on the back and cramps the abdomen enough to impair breathing slightly. The low pack exerts more of a straight down pull on the shoulders, allowing the packer to walk more upright.

Unlike the wood-splint pack basket, the Norwegian framed pack will neatly hold a bedroll, tent, or duffel bag lashed to the top of the frame. All the camper

Web frame on alpine rucksack allows free passage of air between pack and wearer's back. Courtesy of Himalayan Pak Co.

Adult hikers wearing pack frames fitted with packsacks carry enough gear for a family camping trip. *Courtesy of Himalayan Pak Co.*

needs for a week-long trip will go in and on this pack. It is a fine big-load pack.

THE PACKBOARDS

Packboards easily beat all other devices for backpacking heavy loads of irregular shapes. A quarter of a moose can be lashed to a packboard and carried with

Aluminum pack frame weighs only 30 ounces, but it will comfortably support heavy loads. *Courtesy of Himalayan Pak Co.*

a minimum of effort and discomfort. A packboard
will move an outboard motor or two heavy, sharp-
cornered cases of dynamite. An injured camper or
mountain climber can be lashed to a packboard and
hauled out on a companion's back.

Although packboards vary quite a lot in material
and details of construction, their basic form is standardized; a long list of regional and trade names for the
slightly different models is unnecessary. Packboards

Wooden Alaska packboard has a specially fitted packsack
attached to frame. *Courtesy of Eddie Bauer.*

Aluminum pack frame can also be used as a camp chair. *Courtesy
of Himalayan Pak Co.*

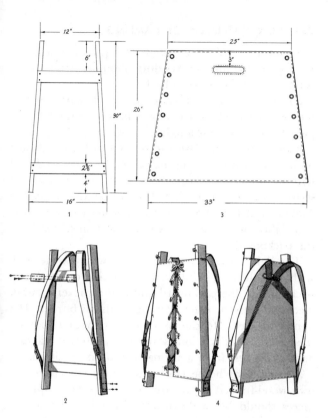

The Alaska packboard frame can be made of 1-by-3-inch stock. 1. Join the crosspieces to the uprights with lap joints and screws. 2. Cut the canvas to size and grommet the holes. 3. Secure web or leather straps to the top crosspiece with a strip of aluminum and screws, and screw the ends of the straps to the bottom side of each upright. 4. Wrap the canvas around the frame and lace it tight with a leather thong. Install eye screws on each upright for lashing the load.

have a frame of hardwood or light metal such as aluminum which is shaped much like the back of a cross-slatted kitchen chair. The frame is covered with heavy fabric cords, close laced, which keep the hard frame away from the packer's back. The strong side pieces of the pack frame have strong hooks or eyescrews which hold the lash rope used to attach the load to the frame. Heavy-duty shoulder straps keep the frame on the packer's back.

Alaskans are great users of the packboard; in fact one popular model is commonly known as the "Alaska packboard." A sourdough can wrap a dozen steel traps in canvas and lash the bundle to his packboard on his outward trip from the cabin. Ax, rifle, or shovel will fit under the lash ropes and ride neatly and securely on the same load. Having set the traps, the Alaskan can haul home a frozen wolf, a cabin stove, or a brace of ptarmigan. All can be lashed neatly to the packboard.

The light frame is comfortable to wear on the back with a small load. Unlike the tumpline or headstrap packing rigs, the packboard allows the packer to walk erect and scan the country as he hauls his burden. His hands are free. He can use a rifle without removing the packboard. For a long shot, the packboard makes a dandy rifle rest from a sitting or a prone position.

A competent home craftsman can easily make his own wood-framed packboard. The two side or upright pieces should be made of straight-grained spruce or hardwood 1 inch thick, $2\frac{1}{2}$ inches wide, and from 25 to 30 inches long. Use two cross pieces of the same material or three made of hardwood $\frac{1}{4}$ inch thick. Cross pieces should be fitted flush with the edges of the two uprights on the side away from the packer's back. The top cross piece should be about 6 inches below the tips of the upright side pieces, the lower cross piece 3 or 4 inches above their lower ends. Vary the length of the cross pieces so that the packboard will be about 1 foot wide at the top and flare to 16 inches wide at the bottom. Details of canvas cover and anchoring of shoulder straps and eyescrews can be seen from the illustration. A metalworker can make an aluminum model just as easily.

Easy to make, inexpensive to buy, the packboard is a back-packing rig worth owning. It is as good as the Norwegian frame pack for a trip on foot with food and equipment for several days. If the trip involves heavy loads of widely assorted sizes, the packboard is tops for long hauls.

As a rule, packboard loads are either bundled in canvas and lashed to the board with strong cord or rope or else (as with an outboard motor) tied directly to the board. A packsack of heavy canvas can be hooked to the board in a more or less permanent way if that seems more convenient. Lash smooth loads to the board with a crisscross or shoelace weave of the rope through hooks or eyescrews.

THE TUMPLINE

A tumpline is a long, strong strap, rather than a

The tumpline requires strong neck muscles, but with it a rugged camper can carry huge loads for short distances.

proper pack. It is used to haul duffel bags, crates, trunks, luggage—all manner of gear that is already packaged in some fashion. A strong tumpline packer can haul an incredible load—as much as four hundred pounds—for a short distance. A typical tumpline has a center strap about 20 inches long made of heavy leather 2 to 3 inches wide. Running out from either side of this wide headband are leather straps about 1 inch wide and 7 or 8 feet long. These long straps are looped around a stack of duffel bags or other neatly piled gear and tied with a square knot—sometimes buckled. Then the packer kneels to fit the head strap over his forehead, tips the load forward onto his back, and straightens his legs to hoist the whole works off the ground. Since he is tipped slightly forward a companion may add an extra bag of duffel to the top of the load, where it will be held by its own weight and friction. As a rule the tumpline straps are cinched only to the bulky bundle at the bottom of the load. The top bundles are stacked on loose.

The domain of the tumpline is the canoe country of Canada, where big loads must be moved over short trails between lakes or rivers. Since light loads mean several trips back and forth to complete the portage, a great deal of time is saved by hauling all the gear in one or two big loads and getting back quickly to the relative speed and ease of canoe travel. Canoe-country Indians and experienced guides can carry tumpline loads over short portages that would cripple a western pack horse on a long trip.

The world's record tumpline carry would be impossible to verify. The device is used in most parts of the world where men commonly haul heavy loads on their backs. Weights carried by packers in informal contests are seldom published and authenticated. But one published report of a tumpline contest between Cree and Chippewa Indians at Pelican Narrows, Manitoba, establishes a Cree named Joe Morin as champion. The contest load was flour, which was to be tumplined over a hundred-yard course. Joe Morin's winning carry was 620 pounds.

To keep muscular vacation campers from becoming intoxicated with the notion of tumplining 620-pound loads, it should be noted here that 80 to 100 pounds is a big load for the novice. And that's for a short haul. Forty pounds is a heavy load for a camper on an all-day hike with packboard, Duluth packsack, or Norwegian frame packsack.

The man with neck muscles toughened to handle tumpline loads can no doubt haul more freight with that simple rig than with any other routine backpacking device. The hands steady and help support the load, and the combination of legs, back, neck, and arms gets all a man's power under the load. If he should trip or lose balance, the load will fall free, rather than drag the packer down heavily as a shoulder-strapped pack would. Loading and unloading is starkly simple. A tumpline is the cheapest of all packing rigs. Indians commonly use a leather headband with short lengths of scrap rope fixed to either end of it. It is easy to improvise a tumpline in the woods with a belt or a strip of folded canvas and rope ends. A good leather tumpline can be made at home in thirty minutes by anyone who has the little skill needed to sew or rivet leather straps together.

But don't be oversold on the tumpline. It takes a little practice and a fair amount of conditioning to use it efficiently. The rig is only good for short hauls with heavy loads. And the packer is a staggering drudge every step of the way. His head is bowed to the trail, all his thoughts as well as his muscles committed to the task of getting the load to the new canoe-launching point. All the fun of a wilderness trip comes before and after the tumpline sessions.

16 · Canoes and Canoe Handling

ALTHOUGH A CANOE CAN BE USED ON ALMOST any lake or river in North America, it is most at home in the states bordering Canada and in the Canadian provinces of Quebec and Ontario. Much of this region, especially the great sweep of central Canada, is wild and unspoiled and perfect for canoe camping. Indeed, there are so many lakes and streams in this heart land of the continent that all the canoes in the world could cruise uncrowded there.

With all the opportunities for canoeing, sooner or later most campers will try it. The first step for beginners planning to buy or rent a canoe is choosing a suitable design and material. Here is what to look for:

CANOE MATERIALS

Aluminum

Aluminum rates top honors among materials currently used to build canoes. The aluminum canoe is substantially lighter than a similar craft made of wood, wood and canvas, plastic, or fiberglass.

Light weight is extremely important in the allround canoe, because a typical canoe trip includes portages across necks of land where the camper back-

Lightweight 16-foot aluminum canoe weighs only 72 pounds, yet has a load capacity of 435. *Courtesy of Aluma Craft Boat Co.*

packs the craft, and easy portability keeps the canoe going in country where bulky boats bog down.

The aluminum canoe is like the cow pony: it is light, tough, inexpensive, and able to function despite neglect and rough use. The better fiberglass and plastic canoes are not far behind in this respect.

There is a certain amount of unpleasant rattle and metallic roughness about an aluminum canoe. (Rubber deck mats and rubber sleeves over gunwales at paddling stations will cut down noise.) Other canoes are more pleasing to the eye than aluminum ones, which always have the harsh, bare look of stamped, riveted, and welded metal. Unpainted, the aluminum canoe has a reflector-oven look which would seem to make it a poor choice for travel under hot summer sun. Actually, the water keeps the whole craft cool to the touch. Paint will put an end to objectionable shine or reflections that may be bothersome while the aluminum still has its factory finish.

Sun and weather soon dull the gloss of new aluminum if it is left unpainted.

In the end, the virtues of aluminum far outweigh its faults as a canoe material. It is best for the craft that will be portaged and handled in a rough and ready way in all kinds of weather and water. Canadian Indians, who give wilderness canoes their most exacting tests, are buying aluminum canoes.

Plastic and Fiberglass

Good canoes are already being made of these relatively new materials, and better ones seem sure to follow. The light and incredibly strong fiberglass or a similar plastic material may one day steal the show from aluminum. But the current fiberglass models usually have a lot of heavy plastic filler molded into their hulls along with the fiberglass. The resulting canoe is trim and durable, but it is heavier than an aluminum canoe of similar size and ordinarily more expensive. Heavy weight and high price are the common shortcomings of the present crop of canoes with hulls made of synthetic materials, but these faults are likely to be corrected soon.

All-wood and Wood and Canvas Canoes

The all-wood canoe—wooden ribs covered with thin planking— has just about become an expensive antique. Meticulously made by a skilled craftsman, the all-wood canoe is a delight to the man who likes fine things that are visibly valuable. But the all-wood canoe is rather fragile, no matter how well it is made. It is also relatively heavy and far too expensive to compete economically with aluminum, plastic, or plastic-fiberglass canoes.

The wood and canvas canoe will take more abuse and is easier to repair than the aristocratic all-wood

Traditionally popular in the north woods, the carefully crafted wood and canvas canoe is still popular. *Courtesy of Old Town Canoe Co.*

one. Yet any canoe made of wood or wood and canvas requires paint, varnish, and regular maintenance. The hulls always absorb a certain amount of water in continued use—sometimes enough to add 10 pounds to the craft's portage weight.

No doubt our lakes and rivers will continue to float such superb canoes as the wooden Peterborough and the Old Town. Like thoroughbred horses, they are magnificent performers which need and deserve special care.

SIZE AND DESIGN

Let's start with the general lines and features of a soundly constructed canoe. There are several things all serviceable canoes have in common.

Though all craft that fall in the canoe category are similar in design, there are important differences. The canoe with bow and stern curving high above the gunwales, for example, is difficult to manage on waters where stiff winds are common. Those needlessly high ends catch wind like sails, and it takes extra paddling and planning to keep the light craft on course. The high bow has some advantage for riding rough water or bucking waves head on, but the high flare of bow and stern is far more a hindrance than a help in routine situations. Get a canoe with a low bow and stern for all-round lake and river travel.

Seats

Many of the canoes sold for workaday use by Canadian guides and trappers have no seats. Their owners prefer to paddle from a kneeling position, which keeps their weight lower in the canoe and thus makes the craft more stable. Most campers and recreational canoers will prefer a canoe with seats near bow and stern, as steady kneeling troubles untrained muscles. The seats should be fitted low, however, to allow a good compromise of comfort and stability. Some of the early aluminum canoes seated the paddlers nearly as high as the gunwales, but that fault has been corrected in most of the more modern models. Campers stuck with a high-seated canoe—a rented one, say—can gain stability to ride waves or rapids by loading all heavy cargo as low as possible and kneeling next to the seats while paddling.

Flat or Round Bottom

The canoe with a hull to form a wide, rather flat bottom is generally more useful than the narrow, round-bottomed one. The flat-bottom design is more stable, responds quicker to steering, and does not draw so much water when loaded. Thus, it is less likely to drag bottom when running down shallow, rock-strewn rapids. The round-bottom has only two points in its favor: it is easier to keep straight on a wind-tossed lake, and it may be slightly faster than the flat-bottom craft.

Keels

Some canoes have a keel; others are made with the bottom smooth as a glass jar. The model with a shallow keel is a good compromise. The craft with no keel at all will turn more quickly to dodge a rock in white water or rapids, but a sturdy keel will frequently bounce the canoe over a rock or snag that would rupture a canoe without a keel. A keel is a great help in fighting wind and waves on big water. It saves wear and tear on the thin canoe bottom when the craft is beached roughly or bumped on the bottom by an awkward launching in shallow water.

Capacity

The camper or sportsman will ordinarily shop for a canoe to carry from one to three persons and a reasonable load of equipment for each person. The lone traveler can get by with the 13-foot aluminum alloy canoe which weighs about 40 pounds. At the other end of the practical size range for recreational trips is a 20-foot aluminum craft which weighs a little more than 100 pounds. With a 40½-inch beam and 14-inch depth, this canoe has a load capacity of 1,600 pounds—enough to accommodate a small family and its equipment. Anything heavier than this twenty-footer will be too much of a portage load for the average crew touring canoe country for fun.

The load capacity of a canoe naturally involves depth and width as well as length, and different models vary slightly, depending on construction material and the presence or absence of such features as air chambers filled with buoyant Styrofoam. The following table is a general guide to one load capacity of standard canoes.

Length	Depth	Width	Capacity
16 ft.	13 in.	36 in.	1,000 lbs.
16 ft.	15 in.	38 in.	1,200 lbs.
17 ft.	14 in.	36 in.	1,200 lbs.
18 ft.	13 in.	36 in.	1,250 lbs.
19 ft.	14 in.	36 in.	1,350 lbs.

Note that the second sixteen-footer listed, with 2 extra inches of depth and width, has the same capacity as the seventeen-footer which is 1 inch shallower and 2 inches narrower. Length alone is a poor guide.

A depth of at least 13 inches is needed for use that will include runs through splashing rapids and windy lakes. A canoe 14 inches deep is an even greater comfort when the load is heavy and the waves are high.

The all-round canoe for two or three people and their gear should have a beam, or width, of at least 36 inches to go with the 13- or 14-inch depth. The length of the craft would be 17 or 18 feet. There is room, stability, and safe freeboard in such a canoe. Yet it will weigh a bit less than 75 pounds when made of aluminum. A husky tourist can carry it easily on portage trails.

Float Chambers

Since a water-filled metal boat will sink like a stone without some flotation system, aluminum canoes and those made of alloys such as Dow metal need air chambers or built-in blocks of Styrofoam. These floats are standard on all good metal canoes. They are usually built into the covered portion of bow and stern, and any canoe made of a material that will not float should have them. All-wood or wood and canvas canoes are natural floaters and will not go to the lake or river bottom in an upset unless they are heavily weighted with some quick-sinking cargo.

PROPELLING THE CANOE

The paddle is the best-known, and in many ways the best, tool for moving a canoe through the water. There are places, though, where long push poles are far better than paddles. A small outboard motor mounted on a side bracket near the stern takes all the sweat—and some of the romance—out of canoe travel between portages. When the wind is favorable, an improvised sail will whisk a canoe over miles of water with no more work than a little steering on the part of the paddlers. Tracking lines (lead ropes from canoe to handlers walking the shoreline) will occasionally be the best canoe movers on rivers broken by stretches of shallow rapids. The canoe traveler should have a basic knowledge of all these methods.

Paddles and Paddling

Though experts vary in their preferences, a paddle can be chosen according to a set of sound rules. First, proper paddle lengths. The most comfortable and efficient stern, or steerman's, paddle will be long enough to reach to the user's eyes when both paddle and paddler are vertical. The bow paddle should be about 3 inches shorter—reaching to the paddler's chin. Paddles a little shorter or longer than these ideal lengths will do the job well enough in a pinch. Any canoe country has skillful eccentrics who swear by paddles longer or shorter than those considered standard for a person's height. The novice who is not told in advance will usually dig in happily with any paddle he gets his hands on. Head winds and long lakes, however, will inspire him to obtain a paddle that fits perfectly.

White ash is hard to beat as a wood for canoe paddles. Ash is springy and strong, and strikes a good compromise on weight: it is heavy enough to slice into the water without a push and at the same time light enough not to tire the paddler needlessly. Hard maple paddles are attractive in appearance, but they tend to be a bit heavy and are easier to break than ash. Spruce, which is light and fairly strong, will make a good paddle for the person who is content to do things gradually. A strong and explosive paddler will break thin-handled spruce paddles.

A paddle broken far from the nearest supply point can be replaced in 30 minutes by a camper who can handle a sharp ax skillfully. It is just a matter of chopping a new one from the first suitable tree. Pick a green pine or spruce if possible. Both have soft wood that can be shaped quickly with an ax, yet they are strong enough to make a paddle that will see you through to a supply post. Choose a tree with a straight, even trunk slightly thicker than the width of the paddle blade you have in mind. Fell this tree, and prop a 12-foot section of the smooth trunk over a log or low windfall notched to hold it securely in place. The idea is to get a paddle length of the green spruce or pine anchored securely at a good chopping height, and the surplus length is needed to hold the paddle portion in place while you use both hands to chop the free end to shape.

Start at the high end of the propped-up paddle log and chip it down to a core of wood a little thicker than the finished handle of a paddle. Then rough out the blade portion without cutting through the log. The surplus length will still be needed to hold the paddle portion firmly in place. Work handle and

Kneeling position, which can be alternated with sitting, helps keep the center of gravity low to avoid upsets.

paddle blade as smooth as required with a sheath or pocketknife. Then use your ax to cut the blade end loose from the supporting trunk and trim as needed with a knife.

A patient novice can chop out such a paddle about as well as a professional chopper. He just needs more time. In neither case will the finished product be the finest paddle ever dipped in the lake, but it will keep the canoe going with little waste of time and effort.

Perhaps the most helpful thing a beginner can learn from reading about canoe paddling is that it is just a matter of pushing or pulling against the water. Paddling motions are as natural and as obvious as those used to sweep a room or rake leaves. The right way is the easy, natural way. Much of the stylish instruction involving "proper form" is based on the foolish assumption that humans are standard in size, shape, and strength. The straight-elbow school of paddling instructors, for example, are mainly teaching their students to do a natural thing in an awkward way. *Basic Power Stroke.* A basic paddle stroke is about this simple: If the paddler is paddling on the right side of the canoe the knob at the top of the paddle handle fits naturally into the palm of the paddler's left, or upper, hand; the right or lower, hand grips the handle

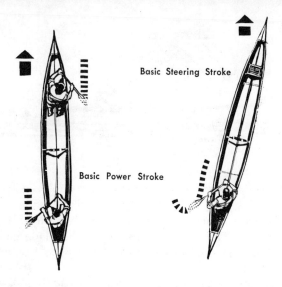

Basic Steering Stroke

Basic Power Stroke

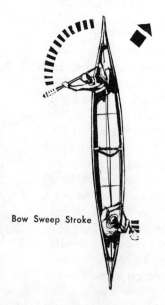

Bow Sweep Stroke

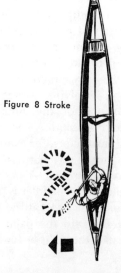

Figure 8 Stroke

at the point that gives the paddle the best leverage. The paddler—either seated or kneeling according to his craft and personal whim—thrusts the paddle blade forward, dips it deep enough to get a suitable pull against the water, and makes that pull by hauling back with his lower arm and pressing forward with the upper one .The lower hand, gripping the paddle handle about halfway down, acts as a fulcrum as the upper end of the paddle is pushed forward. The result is a powerful lever action that will drive a light canoe ahead with a smooth surge. Keep the paddle handle as close to the canoe as possible without scraping your hand or paddle handle.

Basic Steering Stroke.   With bow and stern paddlers working on opposite sides of the canoe, the basic power stroke will keep the craft on a generally straight line. A lone paddler needs to add a steering twist to his paddling to keep a straight course.

The best steering stroke for the lone paddler in the stern position is a power stroke that is completed by twisting the paddle so that the flat of the blade is pushed out, away from the canoe, just before the paddle is lifted to start the new stroke. The twisting of the paddle blade and the slight outward push will become part of one smooth, even motion with a little practice. This steering stroke can be used on either side of the canoe. It is often useful to the bow as well as to the stern paddler.

Sharp Turns.   A strong outward push from the basic steering stroke will produce a decided change of course, but other strokes do the job more abruptly.

One quick and simple way to turn quickly is with a reaching sweep of the paddle from the bow position.

The bow paddler simply reaches ahead as far as he comfortably can and makes a wide outward sweep through the water with the flat of the blade. This turns the bow of the canoe away from the paddle pressure, so that a sweep from the right produces a strong turn to the left and a sweep stroke on the left turns the canoe to the right.

Either the bow or the stern paddler can turn the canoe by reaching out to sink the flat of the canoe blade in the water and pulling as if raking leaves. The end of the canoe where the paddler sits will be drawn toward the point where the reaching paddle bites into the water.

Braking or Backwater Stroke. A decrease in speed or a turn in gentle rapids is easily accomplished with a braking, or backwater, stroke that is just the reverse of the basic power or steering stroke used for forward progress. The backwater stroke starts with the paddle dipped in as far *back* as the paddler can comfortably reach. Then the paddle is powered forward to slow the canoe's motion. An outward push at the end of the backwater stroke will alter the canoe's course if that is necessary.

Figure 8 or Sculling Draw. This figure 8 is the most sure and powerful of the strokes a paddler can use to slow and turn a canoe when dodging obstructions in fast water. A smooth performance of this stroke takes practice, for it is most valuable in fast-water situations where there is no time to stop and think. Practice in calm water will soon teach a paddler to apply this stroke with the same reflex motion with which a driver presses his break pedal at sight of an obstacle in the road.

The figure-8 stroke allows a continuous sweep of the paddle, with the blade angle changing to exert a constant pull against the water. This steady, powerful pressure pulls the end of the canoe in that direction. There is no pause for a new dip or grip.

Outboard Motors for Canoes

The three most important features of a good out-board motor for a canoe are: light weight, reliability, and fuel economy. Standard American-made motors between 1 and 3 horsepower generally meet these requirements. Square-sterned freighting canoes can be powered with larger motors, but anything larger than 3 horsepower dangerously overpowers the ordinary cruising canoe on the water and badly overburdens it on portages. Large motors also use more fuel, which is heavy and troublesome to carry in quantity in wilderness canoe country.

Several foreign firms, less concerned with the horsepower race than American makers of outboard motors, turn out small kickers that are excellent for canoes. Possibly the best of these is the British-made Seagull, a starkly simple and extremely reliable little motor made in 1½- to 2½-horse sizes. It weighs only 28 pounds and runs at cruising speed for more than five hours on a gallon of fuel. It is a tough little mule of a motor, with no flashy hoods, cowlings, or surplus gadgets. All it does is push a canoe day after day with a minimum of fuss, fuel, and portage weight. Abercrombie & Fitch, in New York City, is one of the firms that handle this English motor. It currently sells for a little less than $150.

Mounting the Motor. A bracket holding the small outboard close to the side of the canoe near the stern works fine with the canoe that is sometimes paddled, sometimes powered with the outboard. There is no need to buy a square-sterned canoe with a built-in motor mount unless the craft is to be used mainly for heavy freighting, which calls for a larger canoe than the camper usually uses.

With the small motor mounted on a side bracket, the camper can either steer with the motor or set it to run straight and steer with a paddle held as a rudder. The paddle used as a rudder allows quicker turns.

An outboard motor can be mounted at the stern of canoe on a simple side-bracket mount.

Two canoes can be rigged side by side with joining boards or poles to gain carrying capacity or extra stability on wind-tossed lakes. With this set-up, an outboard up to 10 horsepower can be mounted on the frame between the two canoes. The resulting outfit is both fast and seaworthy. Lumber or other bulky loads can be hauled on the frame joining the two canoes. Position the connecting boards or poles so that the bows of the two canoes are slightly closer together than the sterns. This keeps water from piling up between the two hulls.

Carry waterproof canvas or plastic cases for the outboard and fuel cans on trips involving portages to keep oil and gas off your clothing during overland hauls and protect your grub sacks from accidental contamination.

Makeshift Sails

An improvised sail will speed canoe travel along a broad river or across a lake when the wind is right. The sail itself can be a poncho, a tent fly, a tarp—any large square of tough fabric. Most canoe country has plenty of saplings ashore that can be cut and lashed to seats or thwarts to support the sail. Paddles will do as masts in a pinch.

Never tie a sail solidly in position when rigging it on a canoe to take advantage of strong winds. Hold the lower edges of the sail or the connecting ropes by hand, so they can be released instantly to spill a powerful gust of wind. A fixed sail can easily capsize the craft. When both hands are needed to handle the paddle used as a steering rudder, sit on the rope or ropes holding the sail. Your weight will hold the sail lines tight enough, and a shift in weight will release them to spill a too strong blast of wind.

Two canoes lashed together are ideal for open-water sailing. The sail is spread between them, and steering can be done from one or both canoes. The two-canoe rig is a real wave-buster. It will safely cross a lake that is so rough a lone canoe would be swamped at once.

Tracking Lines

A pair of strong ropes or lines, each about 50 feet long, will "line" a canoe quickly and safely through rapids too rough or shallow to run while riding in the craft. The canoe travelers step ashore at the head or tail of the rapids and use the long lines attached to bow and stern to guide the canoe through the dangerous water.

By shortening or lengthening the two lines, the canoe can be angled in the current so that it is steered as well as powered by the ropes. In traveling upstream, for example, a longer bow line will let the current push against the side of the bow and steer the craft away from the man holding the bow line. A shortened bow line will steer the canoe toward the man handling it. The system works in either upstream towing or when lining the craft downstream. One man can line a canoe, but it is much easier with two.

Most canoes have a bow ring for a tow line. The stern line is tied to the stern thwart. Coil the lines and leave them attached for routine travel. They double as anchor or mooring lines.

Poling a Canoe

One or two men with poles 10 or 12 feet long can stand up in a canoe and pole it through rapids that would defeat a motor or paddles. Poles are sure brakes when running downstream in shallow rapids, and they are far more powerful than paddles for upstream travel through rock-studded shallows. They can be handled to lift the craft over submerged obstacles—the downward thrust of the poles easing the weight on the canoe bottom.

There are no special grips or moves involved in poling a canoe. A good poler maintains a wide stance for balance, reaches for bottom, and shoves—that's all. A sitting or kneeling posture, though it may keep the beginner dry, takes most of the efficiency out of poling. The balance that is the key to safe and efficient poling is obviously best learned in warm, shallow water. A few spills are part of the learning process.

BALANCING CANOE LOADS

The primary consideration in loading a canoe is to keep passengers and cargo low and centered. The bow as a rule should ride slightly higher than the stern; this is accomplished by loading duffel a bit back of center.

All routine cargo should be encased in waterproof bags. Loose items such as rifles or cameras will be much safer if they are anchored to the canoe by straps or slings. Otherwise they will be on the lake bottom at the first slip or spill.

Some experienced canoe campers like to have all cargo tied to the canoe. They reason that the whole outfit will thus stick together in an upset and can be salvaged as a unit. The drawbacks of that system are the bother of lashing all gear down after each portage and the outside chance that the whole outfit will be lost, rather than salvaged, in some wild-water mishap.

Other equally competent canoemen package their gear in separate watertight bags and stack them loose in the canoe bottom. They save time on portages and get at small items needed en route with less trouble. Loose cargo is quickly shifted for better balance if a sudden breeze makes it advantageous to sink the bow lower in the water for easier steering. In a spill the advocates of loose-cargo loading count on picking up floating cargo bags one at a time. Upsets are rare among experienced canoe campers. The craft is more stable than its reputation suggests.

PORTAGING THE CANOE

Yokes

Where one man is carrying the canoe over portages, the job will be much easier with a carrying yoke to fit his shoulders. Commercial yokes are sold for this purpose, and some canoemen make their own, fitting them across the gunwales so that they act as thwarts on the water and balance the canoe properly on the shoulders for overland treks.

For short hauls a pair of paddles lashed to the thwarts will serve well enough as a portage yoke. The blades of the paddles are positioned so that the packer has one flat blade on each shoulder close to his neck, the paddle handles pointing in the direction the packer is facing as he shoulders the canoe.

Simplest Yoke Pad

A regular or paddle yoke can be padded most simply by rolling a sweater, jacket, or spare shirt and tying or buttoning the sleeves so that the loosely rolled garment rides the top of the shoulders like a back pack. The tied sleeves run over the shoulders and behind the back to hold the shirt in place like packstraps.

Two-Man Carry

When two men team up on one canoe, the lead man should rest the narrow part of the bow on one shoulder, balancing it there with one hand. His head leans against the outside of the bow, allowing him good straight-ahead vision on a tricky trail. The second man supports his half of the load with a paddle yoke on the rear thwart, where he has enough freedom of motion and vision to follow the leader without difficulty.

Shouldering the Canoe

Any strong man can pick up a light aluminum canoe and hoist it overhead as easily as dumping a trash can. That no-system method needlessly invites strained muscles, however. A simpler way is to ease the craft ashore, tip it on one side, and lift it onto the knees. Then the knees help the arms boost the craft to shoulder height. The first knee lift is started with the

For a one-man portage, paddles should be lashed to thwart and seat to form a yoke to rest on the carrier's shoulders. Canoe is lifted to the knees, then hefted to shoulder position.

canoeman's knees against the center of the bottom of the on-edge craft. The canoeman reaches over the canoe to grip the far gunwale, then rolls the craft onto his flexed knees with a rhythmic heave. An upward thrust of the knee makes the final boost to shoulder height an easy matter.

A second shouldering method for a lone packer is the walk-up system. With the canoe upside down on beach or shore, the canoeman hoists the bow to shoulder height and holds it overhead as he works his hands toward its center with a grip on each rail or gunwale. The canoe, balanced on the point of the stern at first, will be easily lifted free of the ground and settled on the shoulders when the packer gets to the center. This system works fine on soft ground or sand. It chews up the grounded end of the craft when used on rough gravel or sharp rocks.

It is a good idea to break up long portages into 200-yard or quarter-mile relays. Start out with part of the load, travel the short distance, drop the gear, and go back for more. In this manner all the equipment can be gradually moved forward in small bunches, which is less taxing than trying to portage part of the load the entire distance. Also, the gear left behind does not remain unguarded for as long a period in case of a storm or foraging animals.

EMERGENCY REPAIRS

Adhesive tape pressed firmly in place will effectively seal pinpoint or hairline leaks in any type of canoe—canvas, wood, metal, or plastic. There is no better temporary repair. The tape, which is a standard item in any camp kit, is quickly and easily applied. It is astonishingly tough and waterproof, and the seal is neat and smooth.

A square of cloth saturated with waterproof glue will seal larger leaks. The clear all-purpose cement sold in dime stores is good for this purpose.

A liquid aluminum compound sold by hardware stores will do a fair job of repairing small leaks in aluminum canoes. It takes an hour or so to dry. Pound out the dent with a sock or bag full of sand to smooth the aluminum surface and close the crack in the metal as much as possible. Scrape or sand the metal clean before smoothing on the patching compound.

The resin or pitch from evergreen trees makes a fair glue. Heat the resin and mix in 1 part of cooking fat to 6 parts or resin for a more workable mixture. Pure resin applied hot will do in a pinch, but it tends to harden and crack when exposed to cold water.

Plain chewing gum warmed and pressed into a small canoe leak will seal the hole better than many of the intricate repair jobs a novice might try in an emergency.

Carry a coil of soft and flexible copper wire and a simple drill or awl on a wilderness trip with a wooden or wood-framed canoe. Copper wire laced through drilled holes will pull most minor fractures together.

It can even be used to lace in a new rib or panel cut from a tree ashore and axed and whittled to size.

Rawhide thongs laced in place when wet will form extremely strong bonds. Split strands from spruce roots will also substitute for wire.

17 - Pack and Saddle Trips

WITH THE POSSIBLE EXCEPTION OF A WILDER-
ness canoe trip, a long jaunt into wild mountain country with pack and saddle horses is the finest camping
adventure in North America—our continent's answer
to the African safari. Horses allow campers to carry
food and equipment to last for a month or more into
mountain basins where the only trail is the tracks the
horses leave behind them. The saddle and pack animals do the hard trail work, while the rider sits his
saddle and watches the scenery go by.

Horses and their equipment are bugaboos for most
first-timers on a pack trip. Some beginners are unrea-
sonably afraid of horses and needlessly dismayed at
the prospect of dealing with saddles, cinches, and packing hitches. Others have the foolhardy notion that
they can pet and fondle any range horse or pack mule
they approach with a smile and lump of sugar. Both
those extremes are wrong.

Probably the best way to cover the basic rules for
handling camp-trip horses and their trappings is to
start where the typical beginner does—at a corral or
hitching rack—and deal with the questions as they
crop up in actual practice. Let's assume that our mythi-
cal novice knows very little about horses but wants to
learn enough to become reasonably self-reliant, per-

haps make future trips without the help of professional wranglers and packers.

RIDING CLOTHES

Before we start saddling horses, a word about suitable riding clothes for pack trips. Many first-timers have the idea that they will need a special cowboy costume—chaps, boot, spurs, ten-gallon hat, and the like. Nonsense! All those things are useful to professional cowboys or other workaday riders, but a vacation camper does not ordinarily need them. Any sturdy camp clothing that suits the climate will do for pack-trip riding.

A billed cap is about as good as a sombrero. Regular pants made of wool, synthetic fibers, or tough cotton will usually suit the pack-trip rider as well as any cowboy style of pants he might buy. Chaps are an expensive and rather pretentious extra for the vacation rider. Spurs are useless, dangerous toys for the novice, who is likely to be shot into orbit by the first mountain horse he goads with them. Low-heeled hiking boots have far more all-round utility on a pack trip than high-heeled cowboy boots, which are good for nothing but western-saddle riding when the rider rarely dismounts to walk. Eastern riding outfits—pants tapered to tuck into high boots at the knee—are as out of place as a tuxedo at a barn dance in the pack-trip regions of the West, Mexico, and Canada—so forget about them.

Show up for your pack trip wearing the sturdy outdoor clothes in which you plan to hunt, fish, or hike after you reach your destination. If you already own and are comfortable in some of the cowboy style of clothing, wear them. The point is that it is not necessary to buy a special costume.

DUDE MEETS HORSE

Now let's hike out to the corral or hitching rack and meet the horses that will be ridden and packed. There are a few things the beginner needs to know before he approaches pack-string stock. Though no reliable outfitter or wrangler will knowingly allow a novice to work with an outlaw horse or a wild pack mule, there are some rough customers among the animals in a typical pack string. The stranger cannot tell by looking whether he is approaching a gentle saddle horse or a half-broken pack horse that will kick, bite, and paw with little provocation. The safe and sensible rule is to stay away from pack-string animals unless you have reason to be working among them and know what you are doing. A kicking horse or mule is not the joke it appears to be in cartoons and movie comedies. One kick to head or chest can easily kill a man.

Speak calmly and move slowly as you approach any horse. Sudden motions and sneak-up appearances startle the animal and the frightened horse is the dangerous horse. A "mean" horse or a calculating "man-killer" is extremely rare, usually the result of some man's ignorant or brutal handling, but any horse can be dangerous when frightened, and some horses spook easily.

Never wave a blanket, canvas, or rope close to a horse. Loud noises scare horses. So do rustling papers and rattling and scraping sounds. Some scents—blood, fresh animal hides, bear—will make gentle horses act momentarily like outlaws. A range bronc accustomed to the full-bodied aroma and weathered look of wranglers in their work clothes may kick and plunge at the sudden appearance of a rider who reeks of store-fresh clothes and shaving lotion.

Take your time about approaching any nervous horse. Give it a minute to look you over. Yelling "Whoa!" or any such routine command will only add to its alarm. Soft talk helps. It is the calm, even tone of voice that soothes the animal. Loving words in English are no better than Spanish profanity spoken with soft assurance. Ease up to the horse's left side, and stroke it on the neck or back once you are close to it. Stay away from its heels. Move your hands slowly when working around its head. Lots of rough-broken western horses have been hit in the head by men and will mistake a sudden move for another punishing blow.

Saddle horses are accustomed to left-side handling. The bridle or the halter is put on from the left, or near, side of the horse's head. The saddle is swung on and cinched from the left. The rider mounts and dismounts from the left. Experienced horsemen working with familiar animals often break that left-side rule, but the novice dealing with strange stock is wise to be more conservative.

Choosing a Pack-Trip Horse

Many novices given the chance to choose their own mount from a string of gentle saddle horses make the mistake of selecting by color. Fiction of one kind and another has spread the belief that a white horse, for example, will be of pure and dauntless spirit and of gentler nature than the coal-black steed. The strawberry roan is supposed to be wild and woolly. A buckskin horse is tough and durable. The palomino and the pinto are thought to have special virtue because of their unusual color.

All this is pure fancy. Color by itself is no indication of a horse's speed, temperament, or any other ability.

Disregard color, and choose a compact, short-backed horse with clean-cut legs and head. An excess of speed and spirit can be a hazard in a horse that will be ridden at a walk over rough, narrow trails with steep drop-offs. Leave the jumpy, highstrung mounts for flatland riders, and choose a horse that is alert but calm. Pass up the round-backed, big-bellied horse. It is awkward to straddle and possibly soft and lazy, and a saddle turns too easily on that balloon-shaped torso. The gaunt, long-legged horse is also a poor choice as a rule. It may be a poor rustler of feed in mountain meadows and is likely to be nervous and jumpy, lacking the steady power and stamina a trail horse needs.

The quarterhorse is the mount for tough mountain trails. This horse has a neat, rather small head and a compact and solidly muscled body on clean, muscular legs. Its back is short and straight, with enough ridge over its deep chest to keep a riding or a pack saddle from turning. It is agile and surefooted and has the power to climb mountains and ford streams all day with a sizable pack or a heavy rider.

If you see rodeos, pay attention to the horses ridden in roping and bulldogging events. They are the ideal type of saddle horse for hard riding in western mountains and meadows. Hollywood, astonishingly, has also started to mount its Wild West heroes on good horses in recent films. You do not want the showy white or palomino stallions fancy movie cowboys rode for years, but the ranch foreman's bay gelding or the cavalry officer's roan mare will probably be a superb mount.

Though no inexperienced horseman will ever be offered a stallion by any pack-trip outfitter in his right mind, it is worth mentioning that not even one stallion should be taken on a trip with a bunch of mares and geldings. Unless he is ridden by a tough wrangler by day and tied up securely at night, the stallion is a sure bet to turn the trip into an endless Donnybrook. He will fight the geldings, the mares will fight him, and any mules in the string will join in for the sheer joy of violence. When one fight is broken up and the broken straps and ropes are repaired, the animals will remain nervous and treacherous in anticipation of the new encounter which will not be long in coming.

Thus, stallions have no place in strings of pack-trip horses. Mares and geldings are one hundred times safer and more reliable.

Catching and Haltering

The first chore in outfitting a corral, or holding pen, full of loose horses is to catch each horse and hitch him by a halter and a short rope to a strong hitching rack or tree. Wranglers ordinarily do this job for dudes, but here is how it is done.

With a gentle or fairly tame horse, a calm approach and a little smooth talk will allow you to walk up on its left side and slip on the halter. Step back if the horse whirls or turns its heels toward you. Speak to it calmly, and again angle in toward its left shoulder. Keep the halter and its lead rope down by your side until you have a grip on the horse's mane. Even a gentle horse may shy away from a halter if you thrust it out in front of you as if you were reaching out to net a fish.

A handful of oats or a sugar cube prominently displayed will often bring a halter-shy horse to you. Animals that know about such treats find them hard to resist.

Roping is a last-resort measure. The minute you throw a rope in a corral you are going to spook every horse in it. Then you will probably have to rope them all, including the tame and gentle ones. Worse, you will have the same rodeo to contend with next time, whereas a horse coaxed to the halter with oats one time will be crowding the fence to get them after a few haltering sessions.

Bring out the lariat only when there is a renegade left that will not be caught calmly and when time is too short to allow continued attempts by more constructive methods. Walk toward the horse with a 3- or 4-foot loop dangling beside you. A roper twirls the loop around his head only when roping from horseback. Slowly crowd the horse toward the fence until it makes a running break either left or right along the fence. Then toss your loop in one smooth motion to hang it open in the air in front of the running horse's head. It will poke its head into the noose if it is on the move. Momentum makes it hard for it to duck and dodge, as it likely would if you tossed the loop while it was standing still watching you. Tighten the loop and bring the horse to you quietly. Pet it and offer it a bait of oats if you want to avoid future roping contests.

Efficient roping takes a good deal of skill gained by practice. The average amateur trying to rope a horse will have enough trouble so that he will become an easy convert to milder horse-catching methods. Roping a horse is likely to start a cycle of trouble. A greenhorn flailing away with a lariat may catch his horse eventually, but he will make the animal so rope-shy that two real cowboys will be needed to halter it next morning.

Sometimes a first-timer on a horse trip feels a strong urge to play with a lariat after he is on his saddle horse. Maybe a pack horse is running loose, and the dude thinks he will help out by roping the errant animal and snubbing it up short with a hitch around his saddle horn the way calf ropers do in rodeos. A coroner's jury of western horsemen would have to call it "death by suicide" if a novice killed himself while roping a loose bronc with a lariat snubbed to his own saddle horn. Two excited horses on opposite ends of a strong rope are a dangerous combination even for a rodeo cowboy. The best the beginner could hope for would be to get tossed quickly into some crevice where he would be out of the way while the plunging horses tore up terrain and equipment.

All this is to emphasize the point that a lariat is a horse-handling tool to be used sparingly, even by experts.

Hitching

Once the horse is caught and haltered, it should be tied to a strong hitching rack or tree before bridle and saddle are put on. Tie the horse with no more than 2 or 3 feet of slack rope between halter and hitch knot, at least 4 feet above the ground. Otherwise the horse can step over the slack rope and get in some formidable tangles. Never hitch horses to dead trees or limbs that might be broken or uprooted. Two gentle horses hitched to the same dead sapling will go wild if they uproot it or break it off and have the broken snag flopping around between them. Any good knot will do as a hitching tie. The three important things in hitching are to tie to something solid, to tie high, and to tie short between halter and hitching knot.

Gentle horses can be bridled without a halter and hitched with the bridle reins, of course, but the halter and halter rope is a far stronger, safer rig. Pack horses do not wear bridles. Saddle horses on pack trips commonly wear halters under their bridles, the halter and halter rope being used for all hitching.

Putting on the Bridle

The first step in putting on a conventional bridle is to slip the bit between the horse's teeth. Warm the bit with your bare hand or by fire in freezing weather to take the sting out of the frosty metal. Pull down the animal's lower jaw with gentle force if it grits its teeth. With the bit in place, raise the headstall over the horse's ears, tipping them forward to get it over them. Buckle the throat strap if the bridle has one. That is all there is to bridling a horse. Any novice can do it after one two-minute demonstration. The reins can either dangle loose or loop over the horse's neck while the saddle is put on.

Saddling

Western pack-trip horses are hardy beasts unaccustomed to the careful brushing and currying that precedes the saddling of more sophisticated mounts. If the horse's back is already clean and sleek, the saddle blanket can be placed without further ado. Use brush, currycomb, or rough cloth to clean the animal's back of dirt or twigs or to smooth and partly dry a rain-rumpled coat. A rub with a burlap bag does a good job of smoothing and drying the back of a horse bedraggled by rain.

A saddle blanket made of wool, hair, or a similar resilient, well-ventilated fabric goes on before the saddle. Get it even on the horse's back, far enough forward to protrude a couple of inches in front of the saddle, and be sure major wrinkles are smoothed out. That done, you are ready to toss on the saddle.

The western saddle, with saddle horn and high pommel, is the type used for nearly all pack trips and rough-country riding. The western saddle is heavier, stronger, better adapted for tie-on loads and rope work than the light eastern saddle with no horn. The hornless eastern saddles are standard for bridle paths and all kinds of work and pleasure riding in eastern

The latigo hitch is for tying the cinch strap to the ring on the loose end of the cinch. First, pass the strap through the cinch ring, then pass it back through its own ring, and finish off as shown.

and southern states. They are seldom seen in the western regions where horses are commonly used for hunting, fishing, and camping trips.

Hook the right stirrup over the horn of the western saddle and pull the cinch over the saddle seat before swinging the saddle onto the horse's back. Otherwise the stirrup and the cinch will flop and swing during the saddling, possibly ending up under the saddle. Swing the saddle onto the horse's back, and rock it a couple of times to settle it in place. Check to be sure the blanket has not been wrinkled or pushed out of position. Next push the cinch over the saddle seat, and reach under the horse's belly to catch the dangling end. Loop latigo, or cinch strap, through the ring on the loose end of the cinch twice, and tie with the latigo hitch. Some western saddles have a second cinch to the rear of the first. It ordinarily buckles like a belt. Unlike the primary cinch, which is pulled as tight as possible, the rear cinch is buckled snug but not tight.

And that is about all there is to saddling. Ten minutes of demonstrated instruction should teach any novice to saddle his own horse.

Loading the Saddle Horse

A pair of leather saddlebags makes it easy to pack such things as lunch, camera, and binoculars on a saddle horse. The saddlebags are draped over the saddle skirts behind the cantle and are held in place with saddlestrings. If you have saddlebags, tie them on just before you hit the trail.

A slicker or a poncho should be rolled neatly and tied behind the cantle. Sudden showers are common in pack-trip mountains, and there is no time on the trail to stop the whole string and dig into a pack mule's load for rain gear.

A rifle to be carried on a horse for a hunting trip needs to be in a saddle scabbard of thick, stiff leather. There are two satisfactory positions for the rifle scabbard. One is to loop a heavy scabbard strap through the pommel gap and hang the rifle with the butt end high and forward, the rifle barrel slanting down about 45 degrees and aiming toward the rear. Some horsemen reverse that scabbard position, carrying the rifle with the butt high and to the rear, the barrel angling down and forward. Some carry the rifle under the right stirrup; others like it under the left one.

The best scabbard position is the one that works best for you, of course, but if you are new to the game, try the scabbard under the right stirrup with the butt high and forward. Keeping the extra weight on the right side makes the saddle less likely to turn when a rider mounts from the left. With the rifle butt *high* —right up by the pommel—the barrel end of the scabbard can be angled down so that it is not an uncomfortable lump under the rider's leg. A scabbard positioned to carry the rifle high and butt forward on the right will not let it slip out when the horse rears or climbs a steep hill. That can happen with an open-ended scabbard tied on with the rifle butt to the rear.

The best saddle scabbard for a rifle is the full-length job that has a flap or jointed boot that fits over the butt of the rifle. True, it takes a little longer to get a rifle out of such a full-length scabbard if game pops up along the trail, but quick-draw shooting in the middle of a pack string is foolhardy conduct anyhow. If the horses are jammed together on a steep and narrow trail, a hunter who excitedly yanks out a rifle and fires at game on the hillside is dangerous to himself and his companions. The shot is likely to stampede the whole string, and it will be a minor miracle if all the horses and riders are still on the trail and in one piece when the show is over.

Easy does it with any shooting that involves horses. Signal the other riders and give them time to control their horses. Dismount and tie your horse or hand the reins to a helper. Time lost opening a full-length scabbard is of no consequence. On the trail the full-length scabbard protects a fine gunstock from scratches, keeps dust and rain out of the scabbard. Scoped rifles need scabbards with a built-in hump to accommodate the contour of the scope.

A good horseman on a gentle horse can carry a rifle slung across his back or even uncased and resting across his lap as long as he is traveling on a wide trail or through open country. A back-slung or hand-held rifle is an awful nuisance where the rider has to dodge low limbs, ledges, and trees—all common on a typical pack trail. A rifle dropped off a horse onto rocky ground is likely to be damaged. Having the heavy butt end of a scabbard break loose and drop a rifle under the horse's iron-shod feet is even worse. A spooky horse may kick the expensive weapon into junk before you can control it. Do not trust staddlestrings to hold the heavy butt end of the scabbard-cased rifle. Anchor it with a heavy strap run through the pommel or around the saddle horn. Do not leave the rifle on an unattended horse, as it may be whacked against a ledge or snagged on a tree.

The leadman of a pack string may carry an ax on his saddle to clear windfallen trees off the trail. The ax should be cased in a sturdy scabbard and firmly strapped to the saddle like a rifle scabbard.

Do not drape a lot of loose, rattling equipment on a riding saddle. It makes mounting and dismounting awkward, snags on brush and trees, and frightens horses with its rattle and commotion. Carry small items in saddlebags or rolled inside the slicker tied tightly behind the cantle.

The average amateur has no business packing a lariat on his saddle for the purpose of roping anything, but a similar rope (half-inch manila, sisal, or nylon 40 feet long) is handy for other things. It can be used to picket a horse, pitch a tent, tow a deer to camp over a snow-covered meadow or sage flat, substitute for a lost or broken pack-horse lash rope, or form a link in a rope corral. Tie the coiled rope on the right side of the saddle near the pommel unless there is a rifle or ax on that side. If the right side is already weighted, tie the rope on the left to help balance the saddle weight.

A good all-round saddle rope for pack trips is of lariat size and length with a snap hook on one end that hooks to the horse's halter ring. On the trail the slack is coiled and tied to saddlestrings. This elongated halter rope can be used to hitch the horse close or to picket him long in good grass. Unsnapped from the halter, it will do all the long-rope chores already mentioned.

So much for the saddle horse. Keep him hitched close with the halter rope while the pack horses are saddled and loaded.

LOADING PACK BOXES

The first chore in loading pack horses is to get the food, tools, and camping equipment neatly packaged for loading inside the pack boxes and on top of the pack saddle.

Food, cooking utensils, and all small items will go in pairs of matched pack boxes which ride on either side of the pack saddle. These pack boxes average

Two types of pack boxes are the curved plywood box (left), which fits the side of the horse, and the kind made of canvas bound with leather (right).

about 20 inches long, 20 inches deep, and 10 inches wide. They may be made of wood, fiberglass, canvas and leather, rawhide over wooden frames, or hemp or pliant strips of wood in a basket style. Some boxes are curved and tapered to fit the horse. Depending on the packer and the region, these pack boxes or containers may be called "kyacks," "alforjas," "panniers," or simply "packsacks." The names for pack-horse equipment are made up of a lot of local slang and blended English and Spanish.

The outdoorsman who makes a good many pack trips will endear himself to professional packers by arriving at the jump-off point with all his gear neatly stored in his own pair of pack boxes. Any fairly competent home craftsman can make a pair. Fiberglass, light and nearly indestructible, is probably the best material on the market for the man who buys his own pack boxes.

All the gear that goes into pack boxes should be packaged and padded so that it will not rattle, break, or spill when hauled all day on a horse that may buck a little and whack the box against some unyielding trees and ledges. Merely stacking nearly fragile things like eggs or glass containers will not do. They must be padded and braced with heavy cardboard, crumpled newspaper, old burlap sacks—which are handy for a lot of things in a pack-horse camp. The gear in your pack boxes is safe for the trail only when it is stowed so that you could roll the closed box down a flight of concrete steps without damaging the contents.

Since pack boxes, or panniers, ride on opposite sides of the pack saddle, they have to weigh almost the same when full to prevent the load from tipping when the horse lurches and scrambles through steep country. Experienced packers can do a fair job of guessing the weight by hefting the loaded boxes. Sometimes they load them on the horse and rock the saddle a bit to see if the weight is even, adding an item or two to a box that is noticeably light. The surest and quickest way to balance the boxes is to weigh them on a spring scale with a dangling hook. Hang the empty box on the scale and load it to the desired weight. Then fill the matching box to the same weight.

You can put 100 pounds or a little more in each box if you are packing a strong horse for a good trail and do not plan to add a heavy top pack to the load. Fifty to 75 pounds is plenty of weight per pack box for long, steep trails or when a substantial top pack will be lashed to the pack saddle above and between the pack boxes.

A husky pack horse can walk away with 400 pounds or more on his back, but a total load of 150 to 200 pounds is plenty for a long haul on up-and-down trails. That means 50 to 75 pounds in each of the two pack boxes. The extra 50 pounds is made up by such top-packed gear as tents and bedrolls. The lighter the loads, the less trouble you will have with limping, sore-backed horses.

Sleeping bags and tents should be rolled or folded into compact bundles before they are loaded on a horse. Extra clothes and personal gear should be neatly packaged in duffel bags. Ordinary suitcases are miserable things to pack on a horse, and they will take an unavoidable beating. Toilet gear and such small personal items as flashlight, compass, and camera film can be neatly padded by rolling them inside the sleeping bag.

Axes, shovels, and saws should have the cutting edges covered with sturdy sheaths. Short handles make packing easier. Be sure such items as gas lanterns and liquid fuel stoves are well padded and tightly sealed to prevent leakage. Do not put gas, kerosene, or other liquid fuel in a pack box with groceries, as food soaks up fuel odors.

Folding bathtubs, canvas chairs, and the like are awkward and cumbersome things to haul into the wilderness on a horse. Stick to basic items of camp and personal equipment.

DRESSING THE PACK HORSE

The well-dressed pack horse wears a halter with 8 or 10 feet of lead rope, one thick or two medium saddle blankets, a pack saddle with breast and breech straps. For all-purpose packing, the rig for each horse also includes a pair of pack boxes, or panniers, about 30 feet of three-eighths-inch manila or similar strong sling rope, 40 feet of half-inch manila or equally strong lash rope with a pack cinch tied to one end of it, and a canvas pack cover about 8 feet square to go over the entire pack. Many packers call these canvas covers "mantas," the Spanish word for shawl or cover, or "manties," an American corruption of the Spanish. The manta should be made of heavy-duty canvas that will shed rain and survive tough knocks.

Each saddle and pack horse in a trail string needs a pair of hobbles, and the natural leaders of the horse herd (elderly mares, as a rule) should wear bells as well as hobbles for outcamp grazing. Be sure you have enough hobbles and bells when loading up at the start of the pack trip.

The Pack Saddle

The popular sawbuck pack saddle appears to the man seeing his first one about as bare and mechanical as a sawhorse. In fact, this type of pack saddle is so named because of its similarity to a wooden sawhorse. It has upright wooden crosspieces fore and aft. The bottom prongs of these crosspieces are bolted to flat and slightly rounded slabs of wood that fit on either side of the horse's spine. Thick saddle blankets under the contoured wooden slabs protect the animal's back. The sawbuck saddle ordinarily has two cinches, or belly bands, a leather breast strap, and a breeching rig that circles the horse's rear end. All this tackle is needed on mountain trails to keep the loaded saddle from rolling, sliding forward, or tipping back.

The Decker pack saddle, second of the popular styles, looks like a thickly padded and reinforced saddle blanket with half-circle iron rings rigged to stand upright fore and aft. Cinches, breast strap, and breeching will be about the same as on a sawbuck saddle. With the sawbuck model, however, cargo is lashed to or slung from the upright crosspieces, while on the Decker one it is slung on ropes run through the upright iron rings. Loading is much the same otherwise. Which saddle is best is a matter of personal preference; both work fine when properly rigged and handled.

Sometimes you will encounter a pack saddle made from a remodeled McClellan (Army style) riding saddle or a similar wooden saddletree that allows sling ropes to be tied to it fore and aft. Such improvised saddles do the job if they are rigged with sturdy cinches and straps and fitted over good saddle blankets. A pack saddle, like a riding saddle, has to fit the back of the horse that wears it. The better the fit, the less chance of shifting packs and saddle sores on the horse.

The pack saddle goes on much the same as a riding

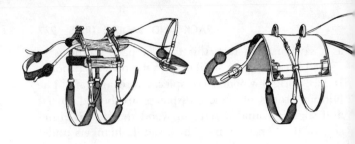

The sawbuck pack saddle (left) is built of wood and has crosspieces for hanging the pack boxes. The heavy-canvas Decker pack saddle (right) has half-circle iron rings from which the boxes are slung.

saddle—blankets first, then the cinches and buckles. Many pack saddles have two cinches, front and back. Fasten them down tight, adding an extra tug or two to thwart the cinch-smart bronc that swells up and holds his breath during your first haul on the cinch straps. Cinches loosen a bit on the trail, particularly when they are stiff and cold when first fastened down. Keep them tight. Few men are strong enough to hurt a pack horse with a too tight cinch. Breast and breech straps buckle just like a man's belt on most pack rigs. When they are buckled, the pack animal is all set for loading.

LOADING THE PACK SADDLE

Good outfits load their horses systematically. The saw that may be needed to cut windfalls off the trail is curved over the outside of the lead pack horse's load, where it is quickly available on the trail. Kitchen gear is in the pack boxes on the same lead pack horse, and tents are top-packed on the lead and second pack horses. Pack boxes are branded or colored to show what manner of food or equipment they contain. This saves searching the whole outfit for some basic item.

Any intelligent dude should be able to load the

pack saddle after one demonstration. Although pack saddles vary somewhat, they are enough alike that a man who can pack with one will have no trouble figuring out another model.

First, the pack boxes, or panniers, holding loads of equal weight, are hoisted up on either side of the pack saddle. Most panniers have built-in loops that fit over the fore and aft crosspieces of the sawbuck saddle and thus hold the box in place. If the box has no loops or if the saddle is an iron-ringed Decker model, hold the boxes in place and use the sling rope to hang them in position. Use either the basket or barrel hitch. Two men, one on each side, make the job easier, but one man can do it. Most packers like to have a box supported by a sling rope even if the box does have its own loops to fit over the sawbuck crosspiece. The rope is ordinarily a stronger rig, and it is easier to adjust.

The barrel hitch is good for regular-size packages. The basket hitch will haul quartered game; it is useful, since a great many pack trips involve big-game hunting. A pack cover, or manta, and a diamond hitch can be thrown over the meat quarters after they are secured with a sling hitch, but that is optional. The sling hitch alone will ordinarily do the job. Two front or hind quarters from the same game animal will be almost identical in weight, so they balance neatly.

After the pack boxes are slung, fill out the top and center of the load with rolled sleeping bags, flat-folded tent, or duffel bags of clothing. Balance all this gear, keeping the weight equally distributed on each side of the horse's spine. A careless top pack can ruin the balance of carefully weighted pack boxes. A top pack 12 or 18 inches above the pack saddle will ride satisfactorily unless the trail is lined with low limbs.

A lower, flatter top pack rides better.

Now cover the entire pack with the manta, draping it like a bedspread. Tuck the sides under the pack

The barrel hitch (left) is for lashing an irregular-shaped load such as a hind quarter of game. Pack boxes that are not equipped with sling ropes can be lashed to a sawbuck or a Decker pack saddle with the basket hitch (right).

boxes and push down the front and back edges to make as tight and as neat a rain and dust cover as possible.

The next and final step is the outside hitch made with lash rope and the cinch on one end of it. There are lots of good hitches to do this job—most of them variations of the diamond hitch. As good as any—and better than most—is the one-man diamond. It is easy to tie and simple to remove, and one man can do a good job with it. Double diamonds and such work much better with a man on each side of the horse.

Since the simplest knots are difficult to explain with words alone, follow the illustrated instructions to tie your one-man diamond hitch. You will find it no more complicated than tying your shoelaces if you run through it a time or two with a piece of rope. You practice with a wire coathanger as a cinch. Grab the

With their pack boxes slung and covered with a canvas manta, two packers complete the job with a diamond hitch.

coathanger's hook in one hand, the middle of the hanger in the other, and pull it into a long loop. A piece of string, and a couple of pillows propped on a chair will simulate rope and gear. Don't let it faze you—a bow tie is a trickier hitch than the one-man diamond.

Short-Cut Packing

The procedures just described are as standard as any, but pack-country guides and outfitters tend to be fierce individualists. This individuality has produced a couple of short-cut packing systems that are worth knowing about. One of these, based on the reasonable notion that it is easier to pack the complete load on the ground, does away with top packs and outside hitches like the diamond. All the gear is loaded into two panniers of equal bulk and weight. These are hung over the fore and aft forks of a sawbuck pack saddle—and the pack horse hits the trail. No tie-down. No outer cinch or outside hitch.

Actually these hanging panniers do very well on reasonably smooth and open trails. Where they work

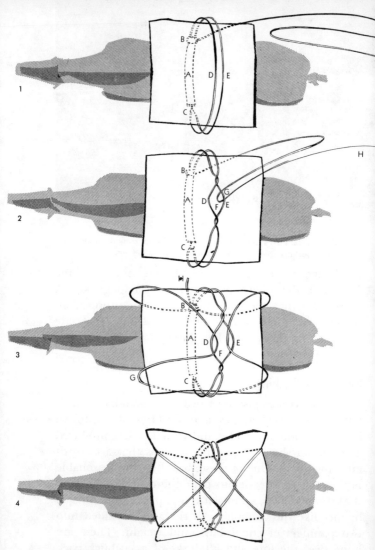

The loaded pack saddle, covered with a canvas manta, is lashed down with the diamond hitch. 1. Tie the lash rope to the lash cinch A at ring B. Pass the rope over the load, under hook C, back over the load again, and through ring B forming loops D and E. 2. Twist parts D and E to form loop F, and pass middle of rope's working end, G, through this loop. 3. Pull loop G down and under the load, and loop end H under the load and pass it through ring B. Adjust loops thus formed under the load at each corner. Pull end H, tightening the entire lash, and tie to ring B. 4. Completed diamond hitch.

at all, they save time and effort. Some people claim they are better on rough trails, arguing that a pack *should* be loose enough to fall free if a horse tumbles downhill with it. They figure that damages the pack contents less than having a horse roll with a load that sticks to him.

The second type of short-cut pack uses the slung panniers, bundles, or pack boxes and perhaps a top pack with a net or a pair of straps tossed over the top and tightened with a cinch under the horse's belly. That's all there is to it. Some panniers which have belly straps as well as top loops ride without an outer hitch thrown with a lash rope.

Like all short cuts, these packing systems are fine for the man who knows exactly where he is going. But a pack that may come off is likely to be a total loss if the pack string bumps into a bridgeless river where horses must swim and plunge. The canvas pack cover under a diamond hitch sheds rain better than other rigs. And the diamond-hitched rig is unsurpassed for moving routine camping equipment through rugged mountains on unpredictable horses.

ON THE TRAIL

Lining up Pack Horses

Once loaded, pack horses can be lined up on the trail in several ways. Many packers like to "tail" them —tying the halter rope of one horse to the tail of the horse ahead. This is a good system for fast travel on a clear trail. It keeps the string in line and makes the loafers and trail feeders hustle along. A rider at the head of the string holds the halter rope of the lead pack horse, towing the rest along like coupled cars on a train.

Tailing precautions: Do not tie together two horses that are persistent enemies, for they will find chances to kick and bite one another. Do not leave too much slack in the rope between the halter and tail, for a tailed horse can step over slack lead rope—resulting in all sorts of tangles. Make the tail hitch sure and solid so that it does not work loose and drop off half your pack horses.

A horse's tail is so strong that it can pull several hundred pounds. Thus, one tailed horse that loses its footing on a steep and narrow trail can yank other horses over. This works both ways, of course. The horse that slips may be jerked back in line by the pack animals ahead of and behind him. The point is that tailing forms too solid a string to suit many packers. They prefer to tie halter ropes to heavy twine or light rope loops attached to the pack saddles, stringing out the horses with a linkage that will break if one horse falls or causes trouble. This is a good system on steep and treacherous trails.

The third common system of trailing pack horses is to tie up their halter ropes and let each pack animal pick his own way. Riders more or less herd the string of loose pack horses. This is the best system of all with well-trained horses. Horses are gregarious, especially in wild and strange country, and the trail browsers and dawdlers will run to catch up with the string when they fall far behind.

Leading a Pack Horse

The rider who is new to the simple chore of leading one or more pack horses has a tendency to do two things that can get him in serious trouble. The first and greatest hazard is tying the lead rope tightly to the horn of the riding saddle. That means that about 1,200 pounds of unpredictable horse is ready to yank your seat out from under you the first time something spooks it. This can be more disastrous than humorous if it happens on a cliff edge or in a thicket of sharp-limbed dead snag. Keep that lead rope loose in your hand or wound just *once* around the horn. *Never* tie it solidly to yourself or to your saddle.

The second hazard arises when you let the lead rope get under the tail of the horse you are riding. There are a few horses that are calm and philosophic about this little blunder. Others go wild. Avoid putting a strange mount through this test unless you are at ease on a bucking horse.

WHEN YOU REACH CAMP

Pack strings heading into the mountains usually travel ten or fifteen miles a day, taking a short lunch break or eating a sandwich in the saddle. The idea is to reach a campsite—a place with horse feed, water, and wood—with enough daylight left to get comfortably settled for the night.

When the horses string into such a camp flat—say, a fairly dry meadow with creek water and bordering timber—tie the whole string and unload them all before you do anything else. They need feed, water, and rest. And you need to keep those horses healthy and happy. They are the key to the success of the whole operation.

If the horses have been packed systematically, they will be easy to unpack. The saw on the lead pack horse comes off first. And the cook is standing by to get the kitchen gear into action, so it is unloaded next. Tents go up at once. Each pack horse's load is dropped where it will be most handy for its job .

As soon as they are unpacked, pack horses are hobbled (leather, chain-connected handcuffs are put on their front feet) and turned loose to graze. Bells with loud chimes go around the necks of a couple of the leaders to help keep track of the grazing herd, which may wander into timber where they can be heard—thanks to the bells—but not seen. Some horsemen like to take the halters off their horses before letting them loose. Horses have a habit of scratching their heads with their hind feet, and a shod horse can hook a shoe in his halter. This can tie him up so that he falls in a creek or depression and cannot get up. A horse toppled on his back in that way after dark will be dead before the morning roundup. Tight-fitting shoes and thick halters minimize this risk, however, and lots of packers leave on the halters to make the horses easier to catch when they are needed again.

Keep a gentle saddle horse that is a good picket-rope feeder securely tied to a long rope in good grass near camp. You need it for roundup work in case the main herd decides to hit the trail toward home, as horses accustomed to hobbles can easily outrun a man afoot. Tie the picket rope to a smooth log that the horse can barely move or to a thick, green stake pounded deep in the ground. Although a horse can graze with fewer rope tangles when picketed by a hobble around one front foot than when picketed by the halter, front-foot tethering takes some training for most horses. Keep an eye on any strange horse you picket by the foot to be sure he is not going to fight the rope.

Unless natural grass is lush and plentiful, the pack outfit should have enough oats to give all the horses about a quart a day—and more for a picket horse which is handicapped in its grazing. Oats do a lot to keep the horses close to camp and to head off trouble from homesick horses trying to break for the home ranch.

A block of stock salt put out near camp is another top-notch horse anchor. With salt, oats, and plenty of water in the out camp, a wrangler seldom has to roll out in the middle of the night to chase horses that are jangling down the home trail at their top hobbled speed. Horses on sparse feed and without oats and salt act a lot like smokers out of tobacco. All their thoughts are of the luxuries at the end of the home trail—and don't think they do not know the way home. A lost camper riding a mountain-raised horse always has a good guide. All he has to do is give the horse its head long enough for the animal to discover it is in charge of navigation. The horse will prick up its ears and head for camp (if the other horses are there) or for the home ranch. He will steer a good course and a fast one. Just slacken the reins and let him go.

Care of Equipment

All the saddles, blankets, and tackle taken off the horses should be lined up on a pole or hung from tree limbs. This airs out sweaty blankets and keeps the leather off damp ground and out of reach of such leather-gnawing rodents as ground squirrels and porcupines.

Hang each horse's equipment in neat order and coil lash ropes neatly. Cover all the horse tackle with canvas pack covers. (A big outfit may carry a tent just for saddles and pack-horse tackle.) Soaked by rain or wet snow, the leather straps will stretch, the ropes shrink, the saddle blankets slump into soggy slabs. If you let the horse gear get wet and then freeze, the job of getting it cinched down on the animals again is indescribably dismal. Finally, remember that saddles and pack equipment are expensive; gear that is hung high, dry, and in neat order will last much longer.

The pack boxes are usually kept in or near the cook tent. They make good grocery racks, campfire seats, improvised tables. Those that hold personal equipment can be moved into sleeping tents, where they will be handier and stay cleaner.

Moving Camp

Except for keeping an eye on the horses, this is the end of the problems peculiar to pack trips. You are camped in remote country with loads of groceries and conveniences brought in with comparatively little effort on your part. With good grass, water, salt, and oats, the hobbled horses will be happy and healthy indefinitely.

Once a good base camp has been set up in the general area you want to explore, keep it there as long as possible, and make one-day side trips. Leapfrogging the whole outfit from lake to lake or from one hunting area to another soon gets tiresome and monotonous. If you are late getting back from a one-day side trip, somebody who chose to loaf around camp will have fire and food waiting for you. Your tent is pitched, your sleeping bag spread. It is the finest kind of homecoming after a long day of stormy hunting or high-lake fishing.

18 - Bicycle Camping

ALTHOUGH MOST BICYCLE CAMPING TRIPS IN-
volve a large crew of exuberant boys supervised by a
few perspiring adults, many adults themselves have
discovered that bicycling is an excellent form of exercise and a pleasant way to reach the camping areas in
their vicinity. Many clubs of grown-ups, equipped
with European-style, gearshift bicycles, have taken to
the road on camping expeditions or one-day outings.

BEFORE YOU ROLL

A typical bicycle camping trip covers 200 miles or
more and involves several overnight stops at forest
camps, lakes, or rivers. This calls for advance planning. Once the general route is agreed upon, it is a
good idea to drive over it in a car, particularly in the
case of a trip with a Scout troop. On the drive the
leader should plan each day's travel and inspect pro-
spective camping sites. If the camps will be made on
private land, the owner should be consulted for permission and instructions. A farmer who will offer the
warmest hospitality if given advance notice may well
be annoyed if twenty boys on bicycles swarm into his
woodlot unannounced. He has every right to order the
group to hit the road again. It will be near dark by
then, perhaps threatening rain, and the next decent

campsite miles ahead. The advance trip by car prevents such inconveniences.

Pick some alternate campsites in case storms or minor breakdowns slow the day's travel. Even when camps are to be made in national forests or on other public land, it pays to notify rangers or camp supervisors in advance. It may be necessary to reserve tent space in a busy camp. A dry season will rule out campfires in some areas for several weeks. Check these things ahead of time.

It is a good idea to select a camping area near enough to a small town so that you can make trips for food supplies during your stay in camp. Since equipment should be kept to a minimum on a bicycle trip, carry enough food for two days, and plan to buy the rest at a designated location.

PACKING THE GEAR

Camping gear should be carried on the bicycle and not on the back. A back pack makes cycling an arduous chore, putting unnecessary strain on the back and shoulders, and it should be avoided whenever possible.

Rear and Front Rack

The standard rack over the rear fender, which usually clamps to the rear stays, provides a platform for lashing bulky gear such as a tent and sleeping bag. It can be widened by bolting on a piece of quarter-inch plywood 1 foot wide and 2 feet long. Drill four half-inch holes along the outside edges of the plywood to help lash the load in place. A rack that fits over the front fender can also be obtained in bicycle supply stores. This front rack will expand packing surface that much more.

Saddle and Pannier Bags

The saddlebag is a roomy little trunk which straps to the rear of the bicycle seat and packs a lot of gear. A typical saddlebag measures 13 by 8 by 9½ inches and has two side pockets for added storage space.

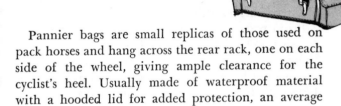

Typical cycle bag hitches on the rear of the saddle, measures 13 by 8 by 9½ inches.

Pannier bags are small replicas of those used on pack horses and hang across the rear rack, one on each side of the wheel, giving ample clearance for the cyclist's heel. Usually made of waterproof material with a hooded lid for added protection, an average pannier bag measures 12 by 4 by 14 inches.

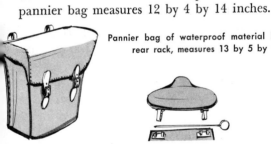

Pannier bag of waterproof material hangs from the rear rack, measures 13 by 5 by 15 inches.

Quick release rod enables cycle bag to be quickly removed, yet it is securely attached while traveling.

With saddlebag, rear rack, front rack, and pannier bags loaded, a cyclist can carry enough gear—not counting food—for a one- or two-week trip. He can also strap a fishing rod to the bottom of his crossbar and carry a thermos bottle of water or other liquid in a special holder which clips to the frame.

Equipment

Below is a list of equipment suitable for a bicycle camping trip. The entire load weighs about 35 pounds. (Courtesy of Gene Portuesi's *Cyclo-Pedia*)

Camping Equipment

1 stove
1 individual mess kit
1 battery light
1 canteen
1 waterproof matchbox
2 Brillo pads
1 dish towel
  50 feet of nylon parachute cord
1 sleeping bag

1 tent
1 first aid kit
1 sewing kit
1 tube mosquito repellent
1 small D.D.T. bomb
1 box of tissues
1 candle or wax cartridge for igniting damp wood

Tools and Cycle Equipment

1 tire patch kit
1 6-inch crescent wrench
1 pair small offset pliers
1 brass screwdriver with assorted heads
1 tube bicycle grease

2 40-inch webbed straps
1 map measurer and compass
1 bicycle cable lock
  Maps

Personal

1 toothbrush
1 tube toothpaste
1 bar soap
1 washcloth
1 hand towel
1 razor and blades
1 comb
1 stainless steel mirror
  Camera and film
2 pairs of socks

2 pairs of underwear
2 nylon sport shirts
1 light wool shirt or knit sweater
1 pair sunglasses
1 cap
1 pair woolen mittens
1 ¾-length waterproof windbreaker with hood

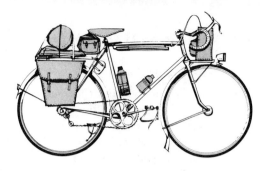

Complete outfit for a one-week bicycle trip with a partner weighs 25 pounds. Front rack supports a cycle bag; another cycle bag hangs from the saddle; the rear rack holds a shelter half, sleeping bag, and a pair of panniers; a thermos and plastic water bottle clip to the frame.

ADJUSTING THE BICYCLE

For prolonged travel along roads of varying grades, the bicycle should be adjusted to fit the rider. Improper seat and handlebar adjustment will cause fatigue before you have traveled 5 miles. First, sit on the bicycle, and adjust the height of the seat so that when your heel is on the pedal, your leg is straight without having to stretch or favor either side. You will now find that when reaching the bottom of the stroke with the ball of your foot on the pedal, your leg will have a slight bend at the knee. The seat should be horizontal, or tipped slightly up, but should never be tipped down as this causes extra pressure on the arms and wrists to keep from sliding forward. If you are especially tall, you should have long handlebar stems and will probably have to slide the seat back to avoid a cramped position.

Toe clips and straps on the pedals are excellent accessories for touring, as they hold the feet in proper position on the pedal and enable you to pull up with the feet when an extra burst of power is needed.

HOW FAR EACH DAY?

Forty miles is a good limit for each day's ride, even when roads are good and the riders are tough teenagers. Shorten that daily travel quota if the route involves slow roads—steep hills being the main obstacles. Husky kids can pedal much farther than 40 miles a day, of course, but the trip is for fun, not to test endurance. Cut the daily travel to about 20 miles a day if the trip involves a lot of one-night stands. That allows ample time for cooking, packing, fishing, and prowling as you go. The advance trip by car will show how to plan for unusual stretches. For example, there may be 30 miles of desert below the mountains which can be crossed with a hard push in the cool hours just after first daylight. With a good road running flat or slightly downhill, tough kids will pedal that distance in two hours with ease. Mountain grades take the starch out of them quickly; they will have to push their loaded bikes a lot of the way and will be ready to call it a day after 10 miles.

SERVICING THE BICYCLE

Any bicycle in good routine running order will take a camping trip of several hundred miles without special mechanical attention or spare parts. A small grease gun, oil can, and a pair of adjustable wrenches are worth carrying along, but spare parts are likely to be excess baggage. Good bikes have few mechanical failures. If some part does break, chances are the rider who packs spare parts has guessed wrong about which parts to carry. Anyway, bicycle travel is along automobile roads, where it is easy to get help for a serious breakdown.

Coasting down long hills at unusually high speeds

will toss out grease and oil at a great rate, so that oil needs to be replenished more often than on short-trip rides.

IN CAMP

If the crew is large, park the bikes in an orderly row or in neat groups, and leave them. Scattered on the ground, they are booby traps for anyone walking through the area at night. There is also a chance that a horse, a cow, or a deer will blunder into one and mangle enough spokes to put the bike out of commission.

Lacking a stand that will hold the bike upright for easy loading and unloading of gear, take a clove hitch around the top frame bar, and tie the long ends of the rope or cord to a tree or a peg. This simple hitch holds the bike steady and upright and can be tied and untied in seconds. Trying to load a wobbly bike or one flopped on the ground is a miserable chore.

The final rule—and the prime consideration—in all bicycle camping is to keep the load of grub and gear pared to essentials. The bike is a fine, light, mild-weather vehicle. It will haul what you really need and no more. Be calm but firm with the lad who shows up for the bike trip with a folding camp chair.

19 - Air Travel

CHESTER CHATFIELD, A SEATTLE OUTDOORSMAN
and writer, explains a lot about the appeal of wilderness trips by saying that they give a man a chance to swap one set of problems for another. The fastest way to make the swap is to climb aboard one of the many airliners or charter planes that now cater to sportsmen.

CHARTER FIGHTS

First, how do you arrange for a flight to that remote trout lake or game country beyond the traveled roads? There was a time when this was a troublesome matter of sending out letters to obscure stations from which bush pilots operated in a haphazard way. That time is no more. Now the airline serving your home town can line up a trip that will make connections with efficient charter service planes. Just pick up the phone and call them. A letter to the tourist service of any state or country (see appendix for addresses) will bring a list of bush pilots who make regular or charter flights in the region you want to go to. Travel agencies in larger towns will set up charter flights. Outdoor magazines regularly have advertisements offering light-plane flights to out-of-the-way hunting, fishing, and camping regions; a letter, a telegram, or a phone call to the advertiser will set up the trip. Small private and municipal airports near wilderness areas will have qualified pilots eager to serve you. Remember that reservation and advance agreements (written) on price and service will head off last-minute trouble. Some such airports have more or less standard prices based on cargo weight, flight mileage, and lay-over time; with others it is a matter of individual bargaining.

PACKING YOUR GEAR

The outdoorsman who travels by air needs to weed out surplus weight and bulk as carefully as does the back packer. The major commercial airlines have a free-baggage limit of about 40 pounds (some allow 44) for each ticket holder on domestic flights. On overseas flights the free-baggage limit is generally 66 pounds for holders of first-class tickets, 44 pounds for tourist-class tickets. Any baggage over those limits must be paid for by the pound, and the overweight charge is so high that even Texas oilmen complain about it.

The big airliners can haul heavy loads if the customer will pay for it. The small bush planes that set down on back-country lakes or improvised landing strips simply cannot get off the ground with ponderous overloads. They have to make extra trips, which cost so much that in some situations it is cheaper to abandon heavy gear than to fly it out. This can happen when a trophy hunter flies into remote game country with a maximum load of firearms and duffel. Any meat, hides, or horns he takes out will be overload. Thus, the hunter who wants to fly out with a bear skin may find it cheaper to abandon that much weight in camp gear than to pay for a return flight to pick it up.

Do not fly into wilderness regions without essentials,

but do not haul any extras unless you are willing to pay an extravagant freight rate on them. Pack your gear in light duffel bags. Suitcases, trunks, footlockers, and such are heavy and awkward when they are empty.

Ship heavy loads by truck, rail, steamship, or air freight when the trip involves flight to some jump-off point where additional travel will be by pack horse, boat, jeep, or some other means that will handle heavy baggage. Calculate how fast the baggage will travel under ideal conditions; then ship it out twice that far in advance. What with strikes, holidays, storms, breakdowns, and customs inspections at border crossings, delayed baggage is almost inevitable—so allow for it.

Major airlines offer air freight service that will move bulky gear almost as fast as regular passenger-ticket baggage and at rates substantially lower than the overweight charges. Do not confuse air *freight* with air *express,* however. Air freight is little more expensive than railway express, but air express—though fast and easy—is very costly.

RODS AND GUNS

A great many flying outdoorsmen are hunters or fishermen with rods and guns they prize greatly. Cased guns and fishing rods can be carried aboard by the passenger and stowed under his seat or turned over to the stewardess, rather than being checked and handled as routine baggage. This adds to their longevity and to the owner's peace of mind.

20 - Snowshoes and Skis

ANY OUTDOORSMAN WHO HAS HIKED FAR through snow more than 16 inches deep will quickly understand why snowshoes and skis were developed. The basic purpose of both snowshoes and skis is to allow a person to travel with comparative ease on top of deep snow, rather than flounder through it comically and inefficiently.

Skis are designed to slide over the surface of deep snow. They allow fast and easy travel on unobstructed flatlands and downhill slopes. They are slow and awkward for hill climbing or travel over flatlands obstructed by dense timber, brush, or boulders.

Webbed snowshoes are not designed to slide; as they spread the hiker's weight over a greater surface, they offer non-sink, non-skid footing for each step in deep snow. Although a snowshoe expert can sprint over a short course of packed snow as fast as the average man can run in sneakers on bare ground, the snowshoe is designed for slow, sure travel. Snowshoes are far better than skis for up-and-down travel through regions where the snow is generally studded with bush tops, close-spaced tree trunks, or protruding rocks.

A trapper in rough and rather trackless forests would surely wear snowshoes on his trapline travels. Skis would provide much faster transportation over a clear trail leading to the nearest village or trading post. Skiing, particularly downhill on slopes served by mechanical lifts, is a thrilling sport with millions of participants. Except for the wonderland views and the beginner's sense of satisfaction at surmounting the deep drifts, snowshoe travel is mainly hard work.

SNOWSHOES

Standard materials in quality snowshoes are ash frames and rawhide webbing. The rawhide webbing in factory-made snowshoes, which is as good as the general run of native-crafted webbing, is nearly always cut from the skins of stockyard cattle. There are promising experiments with aluminum and magnesium frames laced with synthetic monofilament or plastic-coated wire.

Types of Snowshoes

Despite the many trade and regional names, snowshoes break down into three basic patterns. The choice depends on snow and terrain.

One common and useful style is the bearpaw, an oval shoe with no tail. The compact bearpaw is ideal for travel in thick growth or over very rough terrain. It places first for maneuverability. Other styles are better for open trails and spaces. A typical bearpaw shoe will measure about 12 inches wide by 30 to 35 inches long. The upward curve at the toe is slight.

Bearpaw snowshoe is ideal for use in brush and across broken terrain.

Alaskan snowshoe is for fast travel on powder snow across open country.

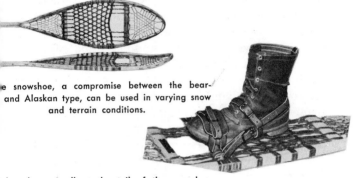

e snowshoe, a compromise between the bear- and Alaskan type, can be used in varying snow and terrain conditions.

shoe harness allows the tail of the snowshoe to drop as the front end is lifted.

Several snowshoes fill the gap between the squat bearpaw design and the slim cross-country styles. Two of these are the Michigan and the Maine patterns, which are so nearly identical that quality of material and workmanship is the only reason for choosing one over the other. A standard Maine or Michigan snowshoe will have a fairly long tail and a slight and gentle upward curve at the toe. It will be from 10 to 12 inches wide and about 4½ feet long.

All sizes given for the three common patterns of snowshoe are for the man who weighs 175 or 180 pounds when he steps on his snowshoes with clothing and pocket equipment. Big men or those hauling heavy packs need more supporting surface on soft snow. A person who weighs less or commonly travels on packed and frozen snow can get by with smaller snowshoes.

Snowshoe Harness

The rigging or harness that holds the snowshoe on the foot may or may not be sold with the shoes. Some makers sell the harness as a separate item, partly because so many of their best customers are belligerently loyal to a homemade harness of their own design.

A snowshoe harness can be quickly and efficiently improvised by taking a hitch through the webbing and around the foot with a 4-foot length of leather thong or cord. Canadian backwoodsmen use long strips of lamp wick for this purpose. Any cord or leather harness that will fit snugly over the toe and circle the heel with enough pressure to keep the foot in place will do as snowshoe rigging. The harness is attached to the snowshoe webbing just forward of the balance point, so that the tail of the snowshoe drops when the snowshoe is lifted by the harnessed foot. The slight lift and forward swing of the snowshoe stride keeps the toe of shoe or boot pressed into the toepiece of the rigging. There is no need for heavy or complicated harness. For travel over frozen, snow-covered lakes or streams where thin spots or air holes are a hazard, there is a margin of safety in a toe strap or a friction harness that can be kicked off instantly. Snowshoes, needless to say, are cumbersome for swimming.

Care of Snowshoes

Snowshoes must be kept dry to work properly. Moisture lets the webbing stretch, and webbing soaked in an accidental breakthrough at a flooded creek or spring hole will collect pounds of ice and snow which must be hoisted with every plodding step back to camp or cabin. A thorough painting with spar varnish protects and waterproofs rawhide webbing. Crusted snow soon sands varnish down, however, and it is impractical to touch up the varnish while traveling on overnight trails. Since freezing keeps raw webbing tight and dry in routine snowshoe weather, do not lose this advantage by propping the webs near a fire or taking them into a warm cabin. The harder and stiffer that rawhide is frozen, the better it will work. Heat and moisture are the pitfalls. Extra wrappings of rawhide at such friction points as the toe of the shoe will add a good many miles to the life of a snowshoe. Otherwise crusted snow will eat down that part of the webbing long before the rest is worn out.

SKIS

The ski equipment that is ideal for downhill runs on clear and packed ski slopes needs a few modifications to serve the cross-country skier or the backwoodsman who thinks of skis as a businesslike means of winter travel. Boots made for the downhill and slalom skiing that keep the ski shops open are too high and rigid for comfortable cross-country touring. Ski-slope skis are generally too short for unbroken trails, and their bindings hold the heel too tight against the ski. Some cross-country skiers prefer a binding that secures only the toe of the boot, leaving the heel free to rise off the ski at each stride.

The long and narrow ski makes a narrow path that offers little resistance in cross-country racing. The comparatively short and wide ski is easier to turn with on slalom runs over packed snow. Jumping and downhill skis are both long and wide for stability on fast downhill runs. Jumping skis commonly have three bottom grooves to give them more straight-ahead stability. A good uphill ski—though there is no demand for one—would be about 1 foot wide and 4 feet long and would have something like a tractor-tire tread in place of a smooth-grooved bottom.

So the all-purpose ski—the uphill, downhill, flat-land ski—must be a hybrid of sorts. It is 3 inches wide and about 7 feet tall for the adult weighing 170 pounds—a bit shorter for a lighter person, longer for a heavyweight. It is fitted with a sturdy cable binding that allows the heel to rise easily but holds the toe of the boot tight. The proper ski boot for the rig would come just above the ankle joint and be a bit softer and lighter than the rigid, ankle-locking slalom and downhill boot.

Ski poles (tubular steel) for the trail traveler should be elbow high on the skier as he stands erect.

The Bergans type of framed alpine pack, which rides low and snug on the hips, is a good one for the skier who plans overnight stops that require basic camping equipment. A lighter packsack with a belt loop to hold it in the same position will handle lesser loads. Any ski pack needs to be low and snug to avoid a pendulum swing that disrupts balance on turns and downhill runs.

Plain paraffin is an excellent wax for the running surface of skis that will be used uphill, downhill, and on the level in different textures of snow. Many commercial ski waxes will make the skis faster on downhill runs in very cold weather, but simple paraffin is hard to beat for most conditions. Follow this general rule for ski waxing: Use a thick, soft layer of wax for wet snow, and a thin layer of wax for cold weather and dry snow.

Any well-stocked library can supply half a dozen books treating in detail the subject of skiing techniques and specialized equipment. The purpose of this brief discussion, however, is to point out that skis can be used far beyond the narrow confines of resort slopes where crowds line up for the lift ride up the hill.

In Lapland, where skis were commonplace before America was discovered, the natives show little interest in using skis to slide down hills. Skis provide the Lapps with cross-country transportation and winter footwear for reindeer herding, wolf hunting, and the like. They take a man where he wants to go when deep snow would otherwise stop him.

PART 3

In the Woods

21 - Pitching Camp

CAMPSITE ESSENTIALS

THE THREE PRIMARY REQUIREMENTS OF ANY campsite are: water, wood, and reasonably flat ground for tent and cooking space. Established campgrounds will supply all three, but wilderness campers must look for a site that has them.

One night in a "dry" camp—one without water—is a hardship, even in cool weather. In hot weather a night without water is a genuine ordeal. It is possible to haul water for desert camping, of course, but that involves rationing water, which is an awkward restriction of camp life. A few months in a Forest Service lookout station will instill a lasting reverence for water in any outdoorsman. The typical lookout station is built on the point of a rocky peak, and every drop of water used at the station requires a round trip to a spring at the base of the peak with a canvas water bag rigged like a back pack. A lookout worker, washing his dishes in one cup of hot water, dreams of a camp near a rushing stream.

But pick a site *near* the water, not right on the edge of a lake or a stream. There is the danger of flash floods in streamside camps in desert country. And in any poorly drained campsite you run the risk of waking up at night to find your tent flooded from a sudden rainstorm. In the mountains a knoll or a low

Careful choice of a campsite is important. Heavily wooded coast-line (A) and marshy area (B) would lack good drainage and would be insect ridden. Also, the terrain would be poor for tent pitching and offer little sun. Partially shaded points (C) and (D) are good campsites, as they are near water and open enough for adequate air circulation. Island (E) is an ideal campsite, if a boat is available, as it would have wood, water, and be relatively free of insects and varmints.

bluff above the water will be better drained, have fewer insects, and be better air-conditioned—if that is the right word. Low ground, in any event, collects more frost, fog, and dew. Even the view is better with a little elevation above the water, and it is no chore to pack water a few hundred feet.

The ideal campsite has plenty of dry wood and poles for construction jobs. Gas stoves and heaters will do as well or better than wood for cooking and will warm the camp, but they will not hold up your tent, make a raft, or build a camp table. Pick the spot with plenty of wood when you have a choice.

The third major requirement—a piece of fairly flat and clear ground—seems simple and obvious enough until you look for it in rugged mountains.

Then it is not always easy to find—or not near the wood and water you want. Sometimes a spot that is not quite big enough can be enlarged to tent size by cutting out a couple of saplings or rolling aside a few large rocks. The small trees you cut off close to the ground become tent poles, say, or back logs for the fire. Roll the rocks into position for improvised seats, or use them to frame your fireplace. When the tent is set up in the middle of a large clearing, poles and rocks have to be hauled to the tent. Do it the easy way, by pitching camp close to your materials.

If you have no choice but to camp on a slope, build up the lower side of your bed with rocks or a staked-down log, and level your sleeping area with boughs. A slight downhill slope of the sleeping area is all that is needed to roll the sleeper a dozen feet downhill before the night is over.

How Are You Traveling?

There are other campsite requirements that depend on means of travel. With horse trips, a meadow or slope with good grass for the horses is an important consideration. Horses need some grazing territory to ward off that head-for-home urge, even when they have salt and a daily ration of sacked oats. On boat and canoe trips the camper needs a sheltered cove for safe anchorage or a smooth shoreline where the craft can be beached high and dry. Auto campers need a parking space, which in the woods should be a place which rain will not turn into a bog, where rocks do not menace the oil pan, and which is out of the way of other traffic. Take the good parking place 100 yards from the campsite, rather than trying to plow through mud, sand, or rocks to save steps. That urge to drive the last 100 yards creates a lot of business for rural tow trucks and mechanics.

Insects and Varmints

Scout any potential campsite for concentrations of troublesome varmints or insects. Look for ant dens and wasp nests. A camp on low, swampy meadowland invites mosquito trouble in spring or summer. In southerly regions the same sort of tall grass is likely to be full of chiggers. Bedbugs are a potential hazard in old cabins or logging shacks.

Packrats have a fondness for old buildings in mountainous regions, as do skunks and porcupines.

Look around. It may be easier to locate another campsite than to adjust to one already occupied by troublesome bugs or varmints.

Plan for Sun and Wind

Where possible, pick a campsite that will get the warmth and cheer of the rising sun early in the day and then will be shaded by trees when the sun is high and hot near noon and in the afternoon. This is accomplished by pitching the tent on the east or northeast side of shade trees. A high rock ledge or a steep hill on the southwest or west side of the tent will also let in morning sun and provide afternoon shade.

Most regions have prevailing winds that are quite predictable. In most western states, for instance, winds usually blow from west to east. In summer, when wind is wanted to cool the camp and blow away mosquitoes, position the tent in the flow of the wind.

In cool or cold weather try to pick a spot with trees or rocks that block direct wind on the tent.

METHODICAL CAMP PITCHING

System is the key to setting up a neat camp quickly. Even when all members of the party are experienced

campers, there are a great many false starts and dupli-
cated efforts unless some routine is followed. The crew
working on the tent has to wait for the ax, because
George has started to fell a dead snag for firewood
before the tent poles are cut. Fred is off somewhere
with the water bucket, and that keeps the cook from
getting a quick start. If it is after dark, Fred also has
the lantern. And where, in that dark mound of baggage, is the flashlight?

Experienced campers who often make trips together
work out orderly camp-pitching systems by trial and
error, without being much aware of the plan they
follow. Beginners, or any group thrown together for
the first time, will save a lot of effort with some advance discussion about job assignments and systems.
Settle the arguments about general methods—how to
rig the tent, say—at home or on the road to the
woods. That saves standing in the rain to debate
whether the tent should have a ridgepole or be strung
on a rope. Elect or draft a cook. That is job enough
for one man, and the others should keep him supplied
with wood and water. Dishwashing is a necessary but
dismal chore to most campers. Rotate the job or make
it a group effort after each meal. If you have a man
who is particularly good with an ax, or wants to be,
it is his job to cut tent poles and firewood.

No matter how you travel, everybody should pitch
in first to unload the grub and gear after a good
campsite has been selected. The next group effort is
to put up the tent, a job that goes much quicker with
two or three people working on it. One camper can
level the ground covered by the shelter while others
unroll the canvas and procure stakes and poles. The
third step is to gather wood, if it is to be used for
cooking, and to procure water. The cook can concen-

trate on finding some fast-burning wood to serve as kindling; his companion or companions can carry in larger, longer-lasting pieces. The cook clears a spot of ground of leaves and forest litter so his fire cannot spread. Then he starts the blaze and unpacks pots and pans.

The cook has already planned the meal and knows which bags, packages, or cans to open. He starts the items that need long cooking over the heat first, then the others in proper sequence so all will be done at about the same time. Boiled meats, for instance, should be started first; vegetables should be boiled, bread baked in a reflector oven later, with the coffee or tea last.

Note now that bad weather might dictate some change in the order of steps scheduled above. In a rain the tent is unpacked and erected first, while the other gear keeps dry under a tarp in the canoe, on the horse packs, or in the auto. When the tent is ready, beds and supplies with clothing bags and personal toilet kits are moved inside for continued protection.

There are plenty of jobs to keep the cook's companions busy while he prepares the food. They can gather more wood, pack in more water, unroll and inflate air mattresses, and spread sleeping bags or blankets. In wet weather the man working inside the tent should remove his boots at the door to keep the floor clean.

Before the cook sits down to eat, he should put a kettle of water on the fire to heat for dishwashing. He can also put water in utensils containing stuck or burned food to soak the scraps loose. Before retiring, someone should gather and store kindling where it will stay dry and be available to start the morning fire without delay.

When pack horses are used, the schedule should give priority to staking them out or hobbling them as soon as the campsite is chosen, so they have maximum time to graze.

TOILET

An outdoor toilet is one of the most important finishing touches in setting up camp. If you are not in an established campground that has a toilet, dig a trench about 200 feet from camp. A frame seat and backrest can be set up over the trench by lashing poles on either side of convenient trees or sturdy stakes or by setting up a sawbuck frame.

Prop up toilet paper on a stick thrust in the ground. A tin can dropped over the paper will keep it dry and prevent it from blowing all over the area. Cover body wastes with dirt after you use the toilet trench. This is a simple and sanitary solution to an everyday camp problem that is seldom discussed in how-to writings about camping.

Camp latrine can be built between two trees by digging a trench and lashing three poles to the trees at the proper height.

GARBAGE DISPOSAL

Whether you camp in a regulated state park or forest with posted sanitation rules or in a wilderness where your nearest neighbor may be several hundred miles away, it is still your obligation to keep the ground about your tent site attractive and clean. You owe this not only to your own health and comfort but to that of others who may travel the same trail.

Promiscuous dumping of waste and trash breeds insects, germs, and unwholesome odors. Regulated campgrounds usually supply containers for your convenience, but if they do not or if you are in real wilderness country, it is still simple and easy to police your tent site.

Small amounts of refuse like paper, food scraps, and small bones of fish and game can be burned in the campfire or wood stove. The easiest way to dispose of larger quantities is to bury them. Dig a garbage pit 100 feet behind the tent; a short-handled trench shovel is excellent for this job.

If possible, locate this pit beside a flat rock, stump, or log that will serve as a work table to clean fish and small game. As you work, scrape scales, fins, feathers, and entrails into the hole, and cover with a layer of dirt. Treat unburnable scrap materials and large bones similarly. If the hole fills up too fast or if rodents dig into it for food at night, build a fire in it daily. Also pour hot water over the working surface (rock, stump, or log) to kill odors.

Burn out tin cans in the fire to destroy bits of food and odors that might attract small animals; then flatten the cans with your ax. Then cans can be buried with a minimum of digging. If burying is not practical, pile cans some distance from camp; after the burning they will disintegrate fast. Do not throw cans or bottles in a stream, as they are a menace to waders.

Never empty dishwater close to your tent, as it makes the ground greasy, smelly, and attractive to flies. Instead, pour it in a hole or trench, and burn the place out regularly. Campers have at their command three of nature's best purifyers: fire, boiling water, and earth. Use them promptly and copiously so nobody will ever feel sorry you stopped here before him.

CAMP TABLE

A table is worth building in any camp where you expect to prepare several meals. Auto campers can buy half a dozen different folding tables that will set up in minutes.

A roll-up camp table top can be made at home by stitching a double thickness of canvas with seams 2¼ inches apart. Wooden lath-size slats slip into the pockets. When laid on a frame of saplings, it provides a rigid surface. Canvas stool top is stitched at corners, slipped over a tripod of poles lashed in camp.

Many pack-horse campers, who find folding tables awkward to carry on a packsaddle, carry a table top made of canvas and thin slats of wood. Such a table top is easy to make. A piece of canvas about 10 feet long and 3 feet wide is doubled and stitched together to form pockets for thin wooden slats (plastering lath is good), which form stiff ribs. This outfit will roll into a neat bundle that will take the hard knocks of pack travel. In camp it is unrolled on a frame of poles to form a table top.

A camp table can also be made of saplings lashed side by side to a stake frame. Clean sand or gravel spread on this pole table top will fill the gaps so that cups or other small containers will not tip over.

Food table can be built of saplings with tin cans wrapped around the legs and nailed in place to discourage varmints.

TARP CANOPY

A canvas tarp strung 7 or 8 feet high over the camp table is a great help on either rainy or sunny days. Since the table and cooking stove or fire will ordinarily be close together, a tarp hung high over the table will shield both cook and diners from rain or hot sun.

IMPROVISED COOLERS

A cool storage place for fresh vegetables, butter, eggs, and similar perishable foods can be set up easily in a camp with a good water supply. Perishable items in sealed jars or tightly tied plastic bags can be put in a wooden box or cloth sack and tied in the shallows of a lake or a stream. A wooden storage box covered with wet burlap or other heavy fabric will keep foods cool as long as the cloth cover is damp; evaporation of water is an efficient cooling method. A sturdy wooden box that can be tightly closed with a latch, a snap, or a strap makes the safest cooler. Cloth sacks or fragile boxes with fresh foods in them are likely to be raided in the night by raccoons, mink, skunks, or other night-prowling animals. A bear can break into any ordinary storage box if it wants to, but the noise it will make getting into a stout wooden box will usually wake up a camper, who can drive it off with no more than a flashlight beam and appropriate remarks in a loud voice.

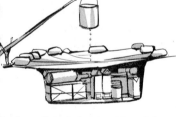

Food supplies can be stored in a hole covered with canvas or burlap that is kept moist by a dripping bucket (above). Rock circle in a brook (below) cools food wrapped in waterproof material.

Collapsible shelves can be made of squares of plywood suspended on knots tied in four pieces of rope. Ends are tied to a ring and nailed to a limb.

CAMP STOOLS

Some substitute for a chair will become increasingly valuable to the vacation camper unaccustomed to sitting on the ground or squatting on his heels. A log or a rock will do. Sawed-off chunks of log 1 foot thick and the same height are more comfortable and easier to move from place to place around the fire or in the tent. Pack boxes are usually pressed into service as seats on pack trips. Comfortable and easily carried stools can be set up by carrying three-cornered canvas seats (see illustration) and cutting three sapling legs in camp. The simpler factory-made aluminum stools are light and compact enough for many campers to carry.

DISHWASHING

Cooking utensils must be kept clean and sanitary if you are to remain healthy on the trail. Arctic explorers, among others, have reported serious illness caused by improperly washed skillets. The grease that accumulated in utensils absorbed lye from the soapy dishwater and tainted the next batch of cooked food. The result was bowel trouble that seriously affected endurance and strength.

Fortunately there are short cuts that permit the individual responsible for dishwashing to do the job with expedition and dispatch. First adopt the logging-camp rule that every man must wipe his plate clean with a piece of bread when he finishes eating. Each person should also dump uneaten scraps and bones into the fire or garbage pit. Then, and not before, he delivers the rough-cleaned plate with his cup and cutlery to the dishwasher.

The washer will save a lot of time by putting a kettle of water over the fire as soon as the food is cooked. Then it will be boiling hot and ready for use when the meal is finished. If any food has burned on or stuck to a pan or pot, fill the utensil with water to soak the debris loose while you eat. Scrape grease from the skillet while it is still warm. A rubber plate scraper will wipe a skillet almost clean. If you don't carry one, whittle a small wooden paddle at the camp site and use that. The paddle is also handy to loosen stuck cereals, bread dough, and gravy. A metal pot scraper works even faster, so carry one if you have packsack room for it.

When you camp along a waterway, dishwashing is simple. Just carry the soiled pieces to the bank and scour them with moist sand and wads of grass or leaves. Lacking sand, use plain dirt. Tufts of grass pulled from the ground with dirt sticking to the roots scour well. Rinse sand or dirt off in the lake or river, then take the utensils back to your fire and scald them in boiling water. Pour the water over the dishes after you arrange them in a compact stack, or dip them in it one at a time. Dipping is better because the water stays hotter, with more sterilizing power. Dishes now are clean and sanitary.

When water is less plentiful, heat a quantity and pour it into your two largest pails or kettles. Add soap to one, wash the dishes in it, then rinse them in the container of clear water. Have suds very hot and, to save your fingers, rub dishes with a mop made of a short stick and a wad of cloth. Plastic household cloths make good dish mops. They're cheap, don't absorb odors and dirt like regular fabric, and occupy scarcely any room in your pack. If the rinsing pan is left on the stove or fire as you work, its contents remain hot until the last piece is sterilized. Always work fast so the suds won't cool either. Dishes wash easier and dry faster when the water is very hot.

Dishes rinsed in hot water need not be wiped, especially when a detergent is used. Instead of rubbing with a towel, you simply lay them out—on a tarp or the piece of oilcloth you used for a tablecloth—to dry of their own heat. Some campers wash utensils in hot suds and wipe without a rinse. This is all right if your dish towels are above suspicion. Unfortunately, it is hard to keep them that way, and a soiled dish towel becomes smelly fast and is far from sanitary. If you use dish towels, wash them once a day or even after each meal.

Always wash the less-soiled dishes first, saving sooty, greasy ones for last. The best way to handle the skillet is to fill it partly with water, add some ashes from the wood fire, and bring to a boil. Then empty with a quick flip and the pan is practically grease-free.

Before using pots and skillets over open wood fires, it is best to coat their outside surfaces with moist clay or mud, or rub them with yellow soap; accumulated soot then comes off quite easily when the utensils are washed. At home, thick deposits of soot can be softened by rubbing the utensil surface with kerosene. Let the utensil stand for half a day, then wash it in a solution of 1 cup of detergent (or soap) and 3 cups of hot water. Use a rag swab to keep fingers from the mixture.

Soap chosen for camp use should suds well in the hard water you generally have to use. The popular household detergents are excellent because they work ably in all kinds of water, cut grease fast, and are easily rinsed off. But they may be harder to pack on rough trails than a solid cake of soap and can be spilled and lost. The aluminum food jars with screw tops sold by outfitters make good packing containers for powdered cleaning products. On a short trip you can store the stuff in a plastic bag and fasten the end wih a rubber band doubled several times. Pack soap with the cooking kit rather than in the bags of food.

WASHING CLOTHES

You don't have to spend a lot of time and effort in washing soiled garments. At night dip cotton shirts, pants, socks, and underwear in water, rub soap over the soiled areas, roll each garment up tight and leave until morning. Then unroll and work them up and down in a pail of hot (even cold) water; the dirt will float away. Now rinse and hang them out to dry. A detergent can be used in this short-cut plan, although cake soap handles easier in the rubbing operation. If you carry both soap and detergent to camp, don't mix them in the same water because neither is so effective then.

Wool garments require different handling. Don't soak them any length of time and don't rub them with soap. Instead, immerse them in lukewarm suds and work gently up and down with the hands. Wool "kills" suds faster than cotton, so use enough soap to maintain plenty of bubbles on top of the water. Rinse the soap out, squeeze the garments partly dry (never wring wool), pull each piece out into its original shape and size (this is very important to prevent shrinkage), and hang from a pole or a rope in the shade to dry.

Cotton clothing can be exposed to the sun for faster drying. Lacking a pole or a line, simply spread the garments over low bushes. Remember that frequent camp washing really saves you work because if garments are allowed to become badly soiled it is almost impossible to get them clean with the limited laundry facilities available on outdoor trails.

ESTABLISHED RULES AND REGULATIONS

Even in comparatively wild parts of the country, camp conduct is governed by a good many Federal, state, and local rulings. These rules—and many of them are enforceable laws, rather than polite requests —are needed to protect campers and campsites.

Here is a sample set of instructions published by the U.S. Forest Service. These instructions govern camping in the High Uintas Primitive Area in Ashley and Wasatch National forests in Utah—a remote and primitive region with comparatively light camper traffic.

The High Uintas instructions are as follows:

Help keep the waters pure. Boil all suspected water.

Burn or bury all garbage, papers, tin cans. Where public toilets are not available, bury all human excrement at least 1 foot deep and 200 feet from streams, lakes, or springs.

Use an air mattress instead of cutting boughs for a bed.

On horse trips, carry horse feed and stake out horses a good distance from established tent sites to keep horses from denuding and soiling the campsite.

Do not litter trails.

Hold each match you strike until it is cold. Pinch it to be sure it is out.

Crush out your cigarette, cigar, pipe ashes. Use ashtrays.

Drown your campfire, then stir and drown it again.

If you can, put out any forest fire you discover. If you cannot, report it promptly to the nearest forest officer or county sheriff.

Carry a shovel and an ax.

On trips into the wilder regions, let a responsible person know where you plan to go and when you expect to return.

Do not travel in the primitive area in parties of fewer than three persons.

22 - The Campfire

Boy scouts and adults who read similar camping manuals are familiar with about a dozen standard and stylized systems for stacking wood to make open fires for heat or cooking. There is no harm, certainly, in knowing about all those patterns, but the beginner should also be told that half of them make fires that are mainly interesting playthings. Working woodsmen, such as trappers and guides, solve all their heating and cooking problems with fires built in two or three starkly simple patterns.

BASIC FIRE BUILDING

All campfires can be started efficiently with the same three-decker combination of tinder, thin kindling sticks, and medium-size sticks of firewood, which are loosely stacked or pyramided in that order. Then a match is touched to the tinder under the two layers of coarser wood. The quick result of these few steps is a campfire. With suitable tinder and wood, nothing short of torrential rain or gale winds will prevent that basic three-decker stack of fuel from starting and burning steadily with the first match. With top-grade tinder and firewood, it is fairly easy to build a fire in the open despite strong winds or soaking rains. We will get to that in a minute. First, more about the importance of choosing highly inflammable tinder and kindling.

Tinder

Tinder is the small wad of quick-burning fuel at the bottom of the basic fire. Before you go looking for such natural tinder as birch or cedar bark, see if you have something just as good right under your fingertips. A sheet of dry paper loosely crumpled under thin kindling makes the finest kind of tinder, and nearly all campers have some scrap of paper that would be admirably disposed of in this way. The classic case of overlooking the obvious is the auto camper who tosses his papers in the trash can as he hikes into the woods to look for fire-starting tinder. All dry paper burns readily. Waxed paper and such wax-treated papers as milk cartons burn like lighter fluid.

There is no harm in dashing a little cigarette-lighter fluid, stove gas, or kerosene over kindling to substitute for woods-gathered tinder. If you have such fuel at hand, why not use it? Nothing you find in the woods will start a fierce flame faster. Just be sure to apply the liquid fuels to the kindling before you strike your match, as they are explosive. The liquid-fuel fire starters also are likely to encourage man's natural laziness, so that he tends to use more of them and less kindling and in time may defeat himself by trying to light fires with thick chunks of poor wood saturated with some liquid fuel.

Birch bark torn into strips and loosely wadded makes wonderful tinder. It has enough inflammable pitch in it to burn wet or dry. Dry cedar bark is fine tinder. Dead evergreen twigs hanging on the tree with browned needles intact burn fiercely. Sagebrush, common throughout the West, will light easily and burn whether green or dead, wet or dry. The shaggy bark of sagebrush is excellent tinder. A handful of dry, dead grass or weeds crushed into a loose wad will often furnish quick and efficient tinder.

The decayed trunks and upturned roots of pines, spruce, fir, and other evergreens usually have chunks of solid wood saturated with pitch. You can see the yellow or amber pitch in these sections. You can also tell it by the resin smell and the heavy heft of the wood as you pick it up. Slivers or shavings off such a pitch chunk light at the touch of a match and burn as if soaked with kerosene. Rain does not soak into these pitch slabs. They are superb for fire starting, wet or dry.

Dead twigs broken off the lower portions of live evergreens are fairly good tinder in wet weather, though they are a bit slow to light. Thin splints of wood split from the trunks of standing dead trees and whittled into shavings or fuzz sticks will always start a fire. Standing dead trees, exposed to wind and sun, are always a better bet for firewood than windfalls on the ground. Many woodsmen keep an eye open for a standing dead tree (one small enough to cut easily) when scouting for a campsite. They chop it down and split out kindling and firewood as soon as they get their duffel stacked at the campsite. A lot of limbs and chunks suitable for firewood will break loose as the dead tree hits the ground, saving saw or ax work in making them into suitable lengths. In most wild country it pays to fell a dead tree close to camp, rather

In wet weather, fuzz sticks whittled from dead tree wood will supply flammable tinder.

than rustling about for dead limbs and windfalls. You spend less time and effort in the long run, and the wood from the standing tree will be sounder and dryer in damp weather.

Kindling

The tinder should be loosely covered (before the match is struck) with thin sticks of dry wood criss-crossed or propped upright in teepee fashion. The best kindling is that split with an ax from sections of a dead but solid tree. Dead twigs or limbs up to half an inch thick will do if they are fired by a good supply of hot-burning tinder.

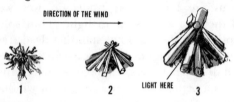

DIRECTION OF THE WIND

1   2   LIGHT HERE   3

Basic fire-building material: 1. Tinder—paper, tree bark, or twigs. 2. Kindling—small limbs, or pieces split from log, stacked in pyramid. 3. Firewood—heavier wood 3 to 4 inches thick to keep the fire going. Light on the upwind side.

Basic Firewood

With tinder and kindling in place, four or five lengths of fairly heavy firewood are stacked or leaned over the top. These lengths of heavier wood, which can be 3 or 4 inches thick, are the basic firewood. The smaller stuff underneath is there to start the fire; the larger chunks keep the fire strong and stable. Like kindling, the best firewood is made from thick branches or small logs sawed or chopped to length and split into sections up to 6 inches thick. But whole limbs or sections of small logs will burn well enough in a fire that has a hot base of coals and smaller chunks.

Lighting the Fire

With the three decks of fuel in place—tinder, kindling, heavier firewood—touch a match to the bottom of the tinder on the upwind side. The match flame will go upward and lean with the wind. By starting it at the bottom of the tinder and upwind, you direct it into the bulk of the tinder. Though these precautions may seem childishly obvious to experienced fire builders, many a city-raised beginner gingerly drops his match on top of his tinder or on the downwind side, so that what little heat and flame he starts with slants up and out instead of eating into the bulk of the fuel. Doing it the right way makes all the difference in the world.

When the tinder is blazing, the fire can be coaxed into faster action by blowing on it gently or fanning it with your hat. Some recreation campers addicted to gadgets carry 2-foot lengths of rubber hose with a few inches of metal tubing slipped in one end to do this firefanning job. The metal tube goes under the lighted tinder, and the camper blows in the attached rubber hose. The device works very well and is a great help when you are dealing with damp or inherently poor fuel. However, the camper who fans with his hat or simply blows on the tinder has one less tool to carry than the rubber-hose fan.

FIREWOOD PATTERNS

The basic fire can be rigged to serve many specific purposes: channeled between rocks or logs to confine hot coals for slow and steady cooking, bolstered with back logs to reflect heat into a lean-to, dampered with ashes or dirt to hold the heat of hot coals for hours. These systems hinge mainly on the way the firewood is arranged and whether or not it is confined by rocks, green logs, or trenches.

Dual-purpose Fire

A simple dual-purpose fire—one that will furnish bonfire heat and light and also supply hot coals for cooking—is generally best for short-time camps or when making a series of one-night stops on a canoe route or a pack trail. If rocks are plentiful, line up a few small and generally flat ones to form a corridor about 1 foot wide and 3 to 6 feet long. This is your open-fire cooking trench. Start your fire in the middle of this corridor when you first reach the campsite, and let it burn in bonfire fashion while you tend to such chores as getting the tent up, laying out bedding, and hauling in water and extra firewood. By the time you are ready to start cooking, the rocks will be hot and the trench lined with a bed of coals throwing off steady heat. Now use a stick of firewood to push all the high-blazing chunks of wood down to one end of the cooking trench—far enough so that they are not too hot for the cook and are out of the way of pots and pans. Keep enough chunks and coals going at one end of the corridor to replenish the cooking coals as needed, but keep the cooking heat low and steady. Beginners nearly always have far too much fire and flame for open-fire cooking. Nobody can cook over a blazing bonfire.

Start with pots and pans over a glowing bed of coals that throws little or no flame. Use a stick to haul up a few more coals from the fire at the end of the trench if you need more heat to keep a cooking pot simmering just right. This way you have all the heat you need, and no more. And you can control it. There is no sparring with flames or cringing from clouds of smoke. In hot weather the cook is not roasted along with his cooking. Most of the heat is confined in the corridor and under the pots and pans.

Two green logs (left), or rocks laid in a keyhole pattern (right),
provide a corridor in which the burning wood and hot coals can be
separated for warmth at one end and cooking at the other.

This fireplace is not supposed to be neat as a
mason's stone wall; in fact, that would defeat your
purpose to some extent. Gaps between the rocks let
in air which keeps the coals glowing. All fires, particularly at the start, need a lot of air to burn well. Coals
will keep their glow with very little side or end ventilation, however.

Lacking rocks for a trench fire, use two green poles
to form the same corridor. But put the poles into place
after the fire has burned into a good bed of coals,
rather than start it between them: a bonfire on top of
rocks does no damage, but it will slowly eat up green
poles. If the cooking coals lose their vigor, prop up the
ends of the cooking-trench poles enough to let some
air in along the sides.

Rock Fireplaces

Circles of rocks pushed together in a quick and casual way will support a pair of iron bars or a metal grill to provide a level surface for pots and pans. Most mountainous camping country has so many rocks and so little soft ground that rock "stoves" are much easier to set up than the combination of driven-end stakes and cross-arm pole that holds pots dangling over the fire. In some rock-strewn high country it is difficult to find suitable poles to set up a cross-bar rig for kettles hung by their bails. In established campgrounds it is often illegal to cut green poles for cross-arm cooking frames. Seldom, if ever, will a camper encounter a rule against gathering together a few rocks to frame a cooking trench. Flat rocks stacked in a wall 2 to 3 feet high will reflect as much heat as the same reflector made of logs propped against stakes. Such a fire of stacked green logs is usually more troublesome to put up, too, even where forest rules allow cutting green logs. Once the logs are cut to length, two sturdy stakes must be driven to prop them up. And that stake driving is a chore to strain patience and muscle where the ground is rocky or partly frozen. Good old gravity holds up the rock stoves and reflector walls.

A few words of caution about rocks: As mentioned elsewhere, porous rocks gathered from wet ground or streambeds may hold enough water to steam up and explode when heated in a campfire. And flat rocks are undependable tops for improvised stoves; intense heat will nearly always crack them. Heavy chunks of nonporous rock are best for fire frames.

The accompanying illustrations show a variety of fire patterns. Some, such as the dingle stick and the Indian fire, are the extremely simple and practical types wilderness woodsmen use. Others—the altar fire, for example—are mainly novelty items. The altar fire, built on a bed of dirt piled on a waist-high platform of logs, is a somewhat cooler and easier-to-reach cooking fire for hot-weather camps. Campers with time on their hands and logs for the cutting may enjoy building one.

Reflector fireplace of green logs will throw plenty of heat into a tent, or bake biscuits in a reflector oven.

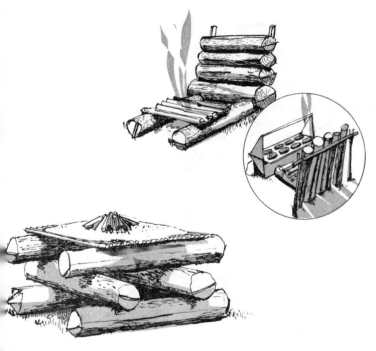

ised platform for hot-weather cooking can be built of logs, topped with branches laid side-by-side and covered with dirt.

Cooking pots can be suspended on a variety of camp-made pot holders from a crossbar supported above the fire by two forked sticks.

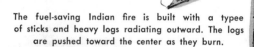

The fuel-saving Indian fire is built with a typee of sticks and heavy logs radiating outward. The logs are pushed toward the center as they burn.

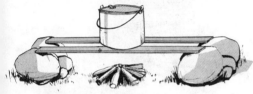

Iron bars suspended between two piles of rocks make a level cooking surface over a campfire.

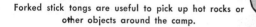

Forked stick tongs are useful to pick up hot rocks or other objects around the camp.

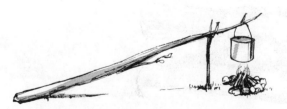

Two ways to use a dingle stick to support a single pot.

STARTING A FIRE IN RAIN OR SNOW

Fire building in rain or snow is not particularly difficult if the preparations are methodical; hurried attempts are pretty sure to fail. If the ground is literally flooded with rain, build a foundation for the fire with rocks, broken limbs, or slabs of bark. For a fire foundation that will not drown on melting snow, use thick chunks of green or wet and punky downfall, and do not build it under snow-laden trees which, in the rising heat, may dump a small avalanche of snow on it.

Standing dead trees furnish the best wood for fires you have to start in driving rain or blizzards of wet snow. The wood split from the inside of such trees will always be dry enough to burn readily, and the rain that hits it during the cutting and splitting will not spoil it. Pitch sticks from dead evergreens light and burn though soaking wet. So does birch bark. White ash split fine will light and burn even when it is both green and wet.

First, before you think of reaching for matches, gather plenty of tinder, kindling sticks, and heavier firewood at the site you have chosen. Lacking a natural overhang such as a rock ledge, set up the best overhanging shelter you can to shield the tinder and kindling from rain. A slab of bark, a flat rock, or a log propped up at an angle will create a small roof. A canvas tarp, a tent awning, or a poncho is better, if you have one.

Get tinder, kindling, and firewood stacked under the best shelter possible. Then be sure you have something dry to strike a match on. The cover of your match case should be dry. Zippers and buttons inside your clothing should be dry. The end of your thumb-

nail, wiped as dry as possible, will do. In the last resort, a kitchen match will strike on the edge of your
teeth. If you have a candle, use the match to light it;
then hold it under the wet tinder. The match alone
will do the job, however. If your improvised roof is
leaking badly, lean over the fire to shield it with
your body as you strike the match and hold it under
the tinder. Shield the fire all you can until the flames
have a good start on the heavy firewood. Once the
chunks of split wood are blazing and forming hot
coals, additional heavy pieces of wood propped up
teepee-style over the original fuel will protect it from
everything but a monsoon. No ordinary storm will put
out a fire as long as you keep leaning slabs of good
wood against the blazing pyramid.

GOOD WOODS FOR FIRES

Try to find wood that is highly inflammable like
white ash. Split fine, an ash green with spring leaves
will start a quick bonfire. You can pour water over
green ash, then split and light it with no trouble.
There are other woods—willow, for one—that are inherently poor firewood.

Hardwood trees in general burn with a hotter,
longer-lasting flame and form better beds of coals
than do the soft woods. Trees cut on breezy ridges usually burn better than those growing in swampy
land. Very few trees burn well while alive and green
(white ash burns even better when dry). Most green
trees burn better when cut in fall or winter when
there is less sap in the trunks and limbs. Evergreens,
though they burn well enough when dry, have a
strong tendency to pop and throw sparks. Resinous
evergreens are no good for smoking fish or game.

FIREWOOD RATING OF COMMON TREES

Good	Fair	Poor
Ash	Beech	Willow
Hickory	Mulberry	Alder
Oak	Buckeye	Chestnut
Holly	Sycamore	Magnolia
Dogwood	Tamarack	Tulip
Apple	Pine	Catalpa
Birch	Cedar	White elm
Maple	Juniper	Cherry
Locust	Spruce	
Mountain mahogany	Cottonwood	
	Fir	
	Aspen	

FIRE SAFETY

This has been said before, but the first and final consideration in handling any campfire is safety. Clean the fire area down to mineral earth and scrape clean a substantial buffer zone around the fire boundary. Watch for flying sparks: they are a forest-fire hazard and a threat to tent roofs, sleeping bags, and clothing near the fire. Drown your fire with buckets of water when you leave camp. Stomping it down or covering it with dirt is a dangerous gamble in summer-dry woods. Pour water on the fire and stir it in until the last wisp of steam is gone.

23 - Axmanship

IN THE NINETEEN-THIRTIES, AXMEN SUCH AS Peter McClaren of the Plumb Ax Company, were frequently seen in contests sponsored by hardware stores in country towns. In a typical show of this sort, the sponsors would put up a cash prize to support the challenge that the professional could chop through the displayed log *twice as fast* as any man in the crowd. A stack of silver dollars looked as big as a lighthouse in those depression days, and some muscular farmer would have his coat off before the pitchman finished his speech.

The professional chopper, a man no bigger or stronger than the average challenger, would win these contests with strokes that seemed arrogantly easy and unhurried. His only secret, if that is the word for it, was knowing how and where to land each stroke for maximum efficiency. He never wasted an ounce of effort or an inch of motion.

Here are the basic points the beginning axman should know. Mastery of them is a matter more of intelligent practice than of brute strength, though strong and disciplined muscles are a great help.

BEFORE YOU SWING

There are three things that must be in order before any chopping can be done efficiently.

1. The ax itself must have a sharp, relatively thin blade and enough head weight and handle length to suit the chopper and the job at hand. The chapter on axes tells how to choose and sharpen the ax.

2. The chopper must have secure footing and room to swing. Those are safety as well as efficiency requirements.

3. The axman needs to be free of slick gloves or heavy, binding clothing. It is impossible, for example, to chop safely and efficiently while wearing such a combination as wet leather gloves and a floppy poncho or a tight-shouldered raincoat.

GRIP AND SWING

The right ax grip will come instantly to anyone who has handled anything from a broom to a baseball bat. The hands are spread comfortably on the handle, one hand near the handle end, the other closer to the ax head. The spread depends on the proportions of the ax and on the size and strength of the chopper. There is no rule and no need for one. Some chop right-handed by natural inclination; others, left-handed. Start with the hand most natural to you, then practice switching. All good axmen can chop either way, for there are many times when a one-way swinger will have his stroke blocked by another tree or his footing hampered by some obstacle. Good choppers switch from left to right—whichever offers the most efficient swing—without stopping to think about it.

The important thing about the swing is to keep it smooth, easy, and on target. Beginners, especially the strong and young ones, will nearly always swing too far and too hard—as if they hope to clip off log or tree with one home-run blow. Shorter, smoother strokes which put the ax edge right on the mark cut a lot more wood with less effort.

BASIC BLADE ANGLE

An ax blade cuts wood most efficiently when driven in at about a 45-degree angle. An ax blade landed at this angle will cut five or six times as deep as the same edge landed squarely against the wood. The angle stroke also pries out chips to open a wide notch in a thick tree or log. It is hard to imagine how much a rank novice would labor in cutting down a tree 2 feet thick if he drove the blade straight into the tree each time, rather than angling his blade to open a wide notch.

STANDING TREES

It is probably a waste of time to point out that the beginner would profit by an apprenticeship on stumps or logs. The minute he has his ax sharpened and his coat off he wants to cut down a tree. Since he is going to do it anyway, here is how to do it right.

First, a word about legal rights. Unless the chopper himself owns the tree or lives in real wilderness country, he must stop to consider what tree, if any, to cut. Many managed forest areas allow campers to fell dead trees for fuel or other camp use. Some areas with more campers forbid all chopping. Green trees cannot be legally cut without a permit in most camps in state and national forests, though this rule is not rigidly enforced in the back country as long as campers limit their cutting to tent poles, firelogs, bough beds, and such. But be sure of your rights. Careless tree chopping is the thing that forced those rigid no-chopping rules in the busy summer-camp regions.

When you have chosen your tree—say, a dead pine for campfire fuel—size up its natural lean, and figure the best place to drop it. You can determine the general lean of a tree fairly closely by letting your ax dangle like a plumb line from a light grip on the handle end and comparing its vertical line with that of the tree trunk. (See illustration.) In judging lean this way, you must of course use common sense. If the tree has most of its long and heavy limbs on one side, it will tend to fall that way, despite the fact that its trunk is neatly vertical as you sight it along the ax handle.

A notch or a wedge will fell a fairly straight-standing tree in the direction you choose, although some leaners will go the way they lean, despite notch and wedge. If you want to fell the tree straight south, say, cut a wide notch on the south side of the trunk, using the basic chopping pattern shown in the illustration below. Since this notch will be cut about halfway through the tree, the top and bottom cuts that start the wide mouth of the notch should be about as far apart as half the tree thickness at that point. A tree 1 foot thick would need a notch that started 6 inches wide. A 2-foot trunk would need a notch that started 1 foot wide. A more narrow notch will gradually force the ax blade into those straight-in strokes which produce more sweat than progress.

Keep the cuts as nearly in line as possible. Most chopping is more efficient if the strokes are landed in the following general pattern: First on the near side, next on the far side, then in the middle—the third stroke cutting loose the center of the trunk previously loosened on the edges by cuts one and two. Follow this sequence on one side of the notch, then on the other—flipping out the wide, thick chip formed with a slight twist of the blade on the final stroke on the second side of the cut. Chips from dry wood usually fly loose without any deliberate blade twist. If the tree is too thick for the one-two-three cut sequence on each side of the notch, make the side cuts first and drive the final strokes into the thick center portion. This cleans chips out of the notch more efficiently, and slices through the trunk faster than cuts that land first in the middle and then on the edges.

When the first notch is about halfway through the tree, start a similar notch on the opposite side but 2 or 3 inches higher. Work this notch deeper until the tree is ready to fall. It will fall toward the first notch.

Felling a tree: determine the lean of the tree by letting the ax hang naturally like a plumb line from one hand and comparing the vertical line of the handle with the line of the tree trunk.

Cut a notch about one-half the diameter of the tree, chopping in a sequence of strokes—near side, far side, then flip out the middle chip formed by the first two cuts.

Cut a second notch a few inches higher on the opposite side of the tree. When this notch has been cut deep enough, the tree will fall in the direction of the lower notch.

PRECAUTIONS

Check to be sure you have escape space before the tree is ready to fall. Also be alert for dead branches high in the tree, which may crack loose and fall from the vibrations of chopping or the tremors of the tree as it starts to topple. These are "widow makers," and it does not take a limb of tree size to spear the chopper after a 50-foot fall. Be equally cautious about dead snags on near-by trees: they may be dislodged and tossed your way by the fall of the tree you are chopping on. Size up these dangers in advance, and plan to avoid them.

Step aside, not backward, as the tree starts to fall. The severed trunk may kick back several feet, particularly if the top hits any obstruction as it falls. This kickback is often fast and forceful enough to kill or maim a chopper. So move to one side, and stand poised and watching as the tree falls. There will be plenty of tremors and crackling to warn when the tree is about to go. Sizable trees do not go down like slammed doors. At the stump end, where the falling arc is very short, the falling seems to be taking place in slow motion. There is lots of time to step aside calmly and deliberately.

Trees 8 inches thick or smaller can be felled without notching. Just slice into the trunk at the same level with a few powerful downward strokes, and give it a push with your hand in the direction you want it to fall.

Saplings of wrist size or smaller are best cut with the ax gripped about 6 inches from the head and swung with only one hand. The free hand is used to bend the upright sapling enough to put tension on the wood at the point where the cut will be made.

Thus, one stroke of medium power from a sharp ax will cleanly lop off a sapling up to 3 inches thick. The bend given the sapling by the free hand makes much the same difference as cutting a taut, rather than a dangling, length of string: the cutting edge is about twice as efficient against tension. Forceful, two-handed ax swings at slim and springy saplings are both inefficient and dangerous. The blade will often bounce or glance off.

Cut a springy sapling by bending it with your free hand, creating tension at the chopping point so that the ax will not bounce dangerously off the wood.

When felling small trees that will be dragged to camp with limbs on them, drop them with butts toward camp to ease the towing job. Otherwise they have to be dragged against limb resistance or turned around where turning around is sure to be awkward.

LIMBING FALLEN TREES

To trim limbs off a fallen tree, start with those nearest the butt of the tree. Angle the ax cuts in the direction of the limb's growth, rather than cutting into the tight angle between tree trunk and limb. Cut off the limbs on the upper side nearest you first, stacking or tossing them aside as you go. Then work the far side of the tree. At that point the whole tree, balanced on a few supporting limbs, can often be pushed over on one side or the other. This saves reaching underneath to finish the trimming. If lengths are to be sawed off the end of the tree, leave a few supporting limbs underneath to serve as a sawhorse.

CHOPPING LOGS

A fallen log is chopped in half with notches on opposite sides which are cut much the same as those for felling a standing tree. But the notches in a log should be exactly opposite one another, and the axman uses a different chopping stance. The most efficient approach for thick logs is to stand on top of the log and chop down between your widespread feet, first notching one side of the log, then turning around to chop through the other half. This is a hazardous system, with precarious footing and the danger of a glancing stroke's sinking the blade in a foot. Good axmen, who use this stance without question, would scoff at these hazards, but they do exist for the novice. A safer system for the beginner is to stand beside the log and notch the top; then roll or pry the log over with a pole, and cut an opposite notch from the same position. This, of course, limits the beginner to logs small enough to roll and involves the extra labor of rolling them, but chopping between the feet is no task for the duffer who lets a stroke glance now and then.

THE CHOPPING BLOCK

A big and solid chopping block—a low stump or a section of log—is needed for splitting wood, sharpening pegs, or cutting limbs to firewood lengths. Hold pegs upright on the block with one hand, grip ax close to the head with the other, and sharpen with downward strokes. It does not damage the blade to slice through into the wooden chopping block, while the same stroke made on a peg held on rocky ground would ruin the cutting edge.

Good axmen can rapidly split fine sticks of kindling off a larger section of wood held upright on a chopping block with one hand. Short, light strokes of the ax held in one hand near the head will split off kindling in a steady shower. This takes a bit of skill and judgment, however, when the blade gets close to the hand holding the wood. At that point, move the holding fingers and leave the stick standing alone for a second as the ax blade comes down. Then catch the stick quickly. This can be done so fast and smoothly that it seems like a magician's sleight of hand to an onlooker who expects to see fingers in the kindling pile. Play safe, though, even if you are a good axman: one slip *will* drop a finger amid the kindling.

To split or chop off short lengths of stove wood, place them flat and solid on the chopping block so that they will not fly into the air at the impact of the ax blade. Never brace them against the side of a log or a stump and hit them in the middle, for this sends sharp-ended sticks flying fast enough to put out an eye.

SPLITTING THICK LOGS

Most straight-grained logs, even those up to 2 feet thick, are fairly easy to split with an ax and wooden wedges cut on the spot. If two axes are available, they can be used in turn: one holds the split open while the other is driven in, to become the wedge for a new blow from the first ax. With one ax, start at the top end of the log, swinging the ax to drive the blade in as deep as possible. Pull the blade free, and repeat this stroke until a decided split starts down the grain of the log. If the split comes easily, follow it with wedging ax blows. Wooden wedges will not be needed. If the wood is stubborn, cut and drive in sturdy

thick logs with two axes, driving the second ax into the split opened by the first, and moving down the log in this sequence.

Drive a wooden wedge into the first ax cut in a thick log, alternating wedge and ax cuts along the log until it splits.

wedges of hard, dry wood to aid the wedging force of the ax. There is less risk of loosening an ax head if wedges (especially steel ones) are driven in with a hammer or a heavy club rather than with the head of the ax.

FLATTENING SURFACES OF LOGS OR POLES

The quickest, neatest way to flatten poles or logs for such uses as camp tables or floors is to chop a series of notches of the proper depth along the full length of the piece of wood. Then chip off the protruding humps with short, prying ax strokes.

Flatten a log by cutting a series of notches along its length; then chip off the protrusions with short ax strokes.

24 - Camp Cookery

THERE IS NOTHING MYSTERIOUS OR DIFFICULT about cooking substantial and tasty food in camp. All camp cooking depends on a few basic rules and a good measure of common sense.

Camp cooks, particularly beginners, should avoid recipes requiring a great many ingredients or involved operations. Plain dishes adequately satisfy outdoor appetites, and they can be prepared efficiently with the limited equipment you have in a typical camp—and with less risk of failure.

COOKING METHODS

Good camp cooking involves the mastery of four simple methods—frying, broiling, baking, and boiling—and anyone who does them properly will make a competent camp chef.

Frying

The easiest and quickest way to prepare many camp foods, especially meats, is frying. The skillet is your most useful and efficient tool, so use it often. Frying entails fewer risks of failure than do some of the other popular methods. But remember that the taste of fried meat may eventually pall and prove monotonous. So alternate the three frying techniques:

plain or regular frying, sautéing, and pan-roasting. All are easy to do.

To plain-fry, put 1 rounded tablespoon of grease in the skillet, and heat until it gives off an occasional puff of smoke. When heating fat smokes steadily, it is too hot. Cut meat in serving-sized pieces—cut vegetables smaller—add salt and pepper, and, in case of the meat, dust with flour. Add pieces slowly to the grease so it does not cool. Sear both sides of meat quickly; then turn it less often. Stir frying vegetables so they cook evenly. Do not cover the skillet, as foods containing considerable moisture may then boil instead of frying.

Tender, quick-cooking cuts like steaks and chops, liver, and young game birds are suitable for plain frying. Do not slice meat too thin—about half an inch thick is usually good.

Sautéing gives meat a slightly different flavor, since almost no grease is used. Heat the pan until it smokes; then rub a piece of bacon or suet over the bottom, but do not leave it in the pan. Add the meat immediately. Sear it fast on both sides. It may stick a little and have to be loosened with a fork or a pancake turner—a drawback with sautéing, because constant attention is required. Season with salt or pepper just before the first turning; season again before turning the second time. When meat is well seared, put pan over lower heat and cook a minute or two longer. Sauté only the cuts you like rare or medium rare. This rules out pork, which requires prolonged heat to avoid the risk of trichinosis.

Tougher meats should be pan-roasted. Given enough time, they become tender enough to cut with a fork, and eat with store teeth. Being simple and practically foolproof, pan-roasting can be a lifesaver for amateur or overworked camp cooks—especially when tough game meat must be made palatable. To pan-roast, brown both sides of the cut in hot grease; then add ¼ cup hot water (it steams less than cold water), and cover pan tightly. Set over low heat so it simmers slowly but steadily. Add a little water occasionally to prevent sticking. A Dutch oven is the best utensil for pan-roasting, but you can use a regular skillet or even a kettle with a well-fitting lid.

Tough meat cooks in less time and will be less dry if you first pound dry flour into both sides of the piece with the head of your ax or a stone. The vegetable tenderizing powders sold in grocery stores are effective, too, and many big-game hunting camps keep them on hand.

Meat prepared by any frying method can be seasoned beforehand, or you may add salt and pepper as you turn it during the initial browning. Presalted food may lose a little of its natural juices as it cooks, but you will get them anyway in the gravy.

The liquor that collects in the pan as meat fries makes delicious gravy. If this is pure grease, stir in an equal amount of dry flour, and cook smooth, stirring constantly. Then add milk or water to get the thickness preferred. The usual proportion is: 1 cup of liquid to 2 tablespoons each of fat and flour. If the pot liquor is mixed grease and water, as it will be in pan-roasting, make a smooth paste of the flour and a little cold water before stirring it into the boiling residue. This keeps the gravy from being lumpy.

Cured and smoked meats require slightly different treatment. Do not sear them at the start. Bacon should be laid in a cold skillet, ham slices in a moderately hot one. Add grease to the ham, but none to bacon, which supplies its own. Put a little water in the skillet with cased sausages, and cook them slowly 15 minutes. Then increase the heat, and cook several minutes longer to boil off the water and brown the meat.

If you fry eggs over a low heat, they stick less in the pan and are easier to digest. Do not drown eggs in grease unless you really like them that way. An alternate method—and one appreciated by campers unaccustomed to very rich food—is to put a very little fat in the pan and, when it is hot, add the eggs with 2 or 3 tablespoons of water. Cover pan and steam slowly until the whites have set.

Broiling

The foods most often broiled by campers are fish and steaks, the latter from beef or big-game animals. To broil fish of some size, remove heads, split down back and spreat flat on a greased grid or grill. Sear quickly in clear flame (both sides) then move over a moderately hot bed of coals. Small fish are easily handled on sticks. Sharpen small green branches and thrust one through the mouth of each fish and down into the body. Hold over hot coals, turning steadily so all surfaces receive equal heat. Avoid over-cooking or fish will be dry and leathery. From five to ten minutes, usually suffice, depending on size; small fish obviously need less time than larger ones.

Broil only lean meat known to be tender. Cut steaks at least 1-inch thick. Venison is improved by pounding it with the ax head or similar tool to bruise the fibers. Rake a bed of bright coals from the fire but leave part of the fire intact and flaming. Sear both sides of meat quickly over the flames, then move to the coals and broil according to the time chart below. Some campers prefer to broil meat in front of the heat instead of directly over it so they can catch dripping juices in a pan set beneath.

Season broiled fish and meat just before serving. Steak is improved by dotting the surface with small chunks of butter.

BROILING TIME CHART

Thickness of cut	Rare	Medium
1-inch	5	6
1½-inch	8	10
2 inches	15	17

Minutes specified are for each side of the meat. Campers are advised against trying to broil meat well done; the result may be very poor, even uneatable.

Boiling and Stewing

Fresh meat should be boiled about 50 minutes to the pound (a 3-pound cut requires 150 minutes, or 2½ hours), cured meats are boiled about 30 minutes to the pound. Boil vigorously for 5 minutes, then gently until done. Boiled meats are seasoned just before you serve them.

The basic way to prepare camp stew is to cut the meat in small pieces, crack any bones to release their marrow, start in cold salted water, and simmer until the meat is almost done. Then add the vegetables as follows: raw carrots and onions go in first because they need 30 to 35 minutes of cooking time; potatoes a little later, as they require only about 20 minutes to become tender. These cooking periods may vary, however, with the age of the vegetables and with the altitude. In the mountains and on high mesas, food has to be boiled longer than at sea level. To shorten time for preparing a stew, the vegetables can be cooked alone in a covered pot and added when the meat is done. Adding salt to the water hurries the boiling process. To give camp stew a different and perhaps better taste, brown the chunks of meat in hot fat before you start them boiling. This browning can be done in the same pot.

Baking

You can bake meats and vegetables in camp, but it may be more convenient to save your baking equipment for breads. Loaves and biscuits can be baked in a Dutch oven, a reflector baker, or a covered skillet. Specific recipes for handling camp breads appear on page 364.

GENERAL COOKING INFORMATION

Camp cooking is often a matter of compromise. For example, when some seasoning (excepting basic salt and pepper) called for in a recipe is unavailable, go ahead and prepare the recipe with what you have. Chances are the result will be good.

The term "milk" in the recipes that follow means fresh milk, but you can substitute an equivalent amount of canned or dry milk after either is diluted with water as directed on the container. Similarly, when evaporated or dry milk is indicated, you can substitute fresh.

Ready-mix flour combinations for making breads and desserts, which require the addition of milk or water and occasionally an egg, are recommended to camp cooks because they save pack space, time, and trouble. When it is more convenient, a prepared mix can be substituted for the blend of flour, baking powder, and shortening called for in a few recipes offered here.

When fresh vegetables like potatoes and onions are

specified, equivalent amounts (according to the figures given on the package) of dehydrated ones can be substituted.

In a recipe requiring fish or meat to be rolled in cracker crumbs, you can substitute dry breadcrumbs, cornmeal, flour, or crushed breakfast cereals like corn flakes.

Lemon juice comes in both canned and powdered forms, but if it is unavailable, substitute vinegar.

Bacon fat substitutes nicely for butter in camp cookery.

Measurements

Unless the recipe states otherwise, all measurements are level. Camp service cups and spoons, however, may be smaller or larger than standard measuring cups, so check them at home and memorize any adjustments that may be required in camp.

When measuring grease or fat, pack it firmly in cup or spoon and level off with a knife. If shortening is too hard to pack solidly, use the following method to measure it: for half a cup, fill a cup half full of water, then drop in the grease until the water reaches the cup's brim; you now have half a cup of shortening. Pour off water, and put shortening with the other ingredients.

Equivalents

3 teaspoons = 1 tablespoon
4 tablespoons = 1/4 cup
16 tablespoons = 1 cup
2 cups = 1 pint
No. 1 can = 1 1/3 cups
No. 2 can = 2 1/2 cups
No. 3 can = 4 cups
No. 10 can = 12 1/2 cups

The following are cup equivalents of some foods usually packed in pound units. In some instances you may be able to add the carton or can directly to recipe without having to measure it first.

1 pound granulated sugar = 2 cups
1 pound butter   = 2 cups
1 pound cornmeal   = 3 cups
1 pound dry beans   = 2½ cups
1 pound flour   = 4 cups
1 pound raisins   = 3 cups
1 pound rice   = 2 cups
1 pound rolled oats   = 6 cups

Camp cooks sometimes worry about precise measurements, but they should not. Except for emphatic seasonings like salt and such leavening agents as baking powder, the proportions of ingredients are seldom critical. A little more or less makes no important difference. Be careful, though, in adding salt, pepper, and sugar. It is always better to use too little than too much of these seasonings in cooking, and it is easy to put on more at the table. The opposite is true of baking powder: lean to the heavy side with it to make sure the biscuits, bread or pancakes rise well and bake light. An extra teaspoon or even two will not affect the food's taste.

Fewer campers and trail men, however, carry baking powder each year. Many of them rely on the prepared mixes that contain leavening in the right proportion and everything else necessary for tasty results except liquid and sometimes an egg. These mixes are available for a large variety of foods. They are entirely practical for camp use because they save time and trouble and—what is equally important—practically guarantee success.

Oven Temperatures

Slow oven	about 300° F.
Moderate oven	about 350° F.
Hot oven	about 400-450° F.

Since camp cooks seldom have ovens with a temperature regulator or a thermometer, they must use rule-of-thumb methods for estimating heat. A cook who has done a lot of baking can probably determine approximate heat by holding his hand inside the oven or in front of an open fire where the cooking food will be. Another plan, practical for both amateur and expert cooks, is to put a pinch of flour in a pan, on a can top, or on a bit of wood and set it inside the heating oven. If flour turns light brown in 5 minutes, oven is slow; if golden-brown in the same time, oven is moderate; if dark brown in 5 minutes, oven is hot.

Liquid fuel stoves are easily regulated, and only a little experience is required to discover the correct height of flame. Wood-fire cooks should remember that bad results come most often from too much heat rather than from too little. So keep the open wood fire small and low, or let a large one you have kindled for the added purpose of supplying warmth burn down to coals before you start to cook.

When Is It Done?

It is easy to tell when cooking food is done. Boiled and baked vegetables and meat can be tested with a fork: if the tines enter easily and without real resistance, dish the food up. Rice, beans, and other cereals should cook until soft. Bread or cake is ready when a sliver of wood or a grass stem shoved into the center comes out clean with no adhering dough. Cook eggs until the yolks are as soft or as hard as you like them.

High-Altitude Cooking

Since water boils at a lower temperature at high altitudes, a longer cooking time is required. This additional time may be from half as much to twice as long.

Foods prepared in an oven require slightly higher heat in the high country. For food to be done in the specified baking or roasting time, a moderate heat of 350° F. serves up to 3,000 feet of elevation. Between 3,000 and 4,000 feet increase oven temperature to 375° F.; at 5,000 and over, to 400° F. Increase similarly for recipes citing a hot oven.

Special Seasonings

Ground cinnamon mixed with twice as much sugar and dusted lightly over warm camp bread gives it a flavor quite out of this world. Cinnamon and sugar turn plain toast into a tasty dessert—remember this when there is no other sweet to serve. The mixture can be carried in an extra salt shaker.

If you plan to cook fresh game meat or game birds in camp, include a small can of poultry seasoning (a blend of sage, powdered onion, black pepper, and other spices). Use 1 teaspoon for each 3 pounds of meat. For rough fish, fishy ducks, and coots, double this quantity to help overcome their "wild" flavor.

If you carry jars or cans of sweet pickles to camp or vacation cabin, save every drop of the vinegar in which they are packed. This liquid has an attractive sweet-sour flavor and can be used to season beans, potato salad, fried potatoes, fried or boiled fish, cooked vegetables, beets, and greens in particular. A little rubbed over domestic or game meat will make a tough cut more tender when cooked the following day.

A zesty sauce for fish, shellfood, ham, and pork can

be made simply at home. Mix 1 cup of chili sauce with ¾ cup of prepared horseradish; then pack in original containers. This quantity will last two campers about two weeks.

Cooking in Cans

Canned foods are available in great variety for the camp grub supply. They are tasty and inexpensive and can be prepared with a minimum of time, trouble, heat, and cooking utensils, and there is little risk of failure. By following the easy directions below, you can serve a well-balanced meal of meat and vegetables without soiling a single pot or pan. Canned foods are, or course, heavier than raw or dried ones, but if you can handle their extra weight on the trail, you have it made.

As canned foods are already cooked, they need only to be heated. Select the cans you want, remove labels, but leave them unopened. Place in a kettle of cold water (cans should be covered with water), and set over heat. When water boils, the contents of the cans are ready to eat.

A little care is necessary in opening hot cans. Hold with a cloth to protect your hand, and make a small puncture in one end close to the rim. When bubbling ceases, remove the entire end as usual. Save the hot water in which cans were heated to wash plates, cups, and cutlery. The kettle will dry clean from its own heat.

Do not discard the liquid from canned vegetables, as it contains wholesome food nutrients and provides flavor. When you open a can, drain liquid into a pot or a pan, and boil briskly until reduced by one half. Then add the vegetables, butter, salt, and pepper, and cook until vegetables are heated through. Or to the boiled-down liquid add ½ cup of dry milk and ¼ cup of water for a rich cream sauce in which vegetables can be boiled or baked. This sauce can be enriched with butter and/or thickened with flour.

Cream

Camp cream is a heavy, dry-milk mixture made by using one half as much water as you do when mixing the equivalent of whole milk from its dry form. It is a good substitute for real cream and is easily prepared in camp. Use in coffee and on puddings, fruits, and cereals. A dry cream, which needs only the addition of water, is also available at stores. If kept in a tight container, this cream keeps well until mixed with water.

RECIPES FOR COMMON CAMP FOODS

The number of servings specified for each recipe is only approximate, because some appetites are larger than others and the amount of any one dish eaten at a meal will vary with the number of other dishes served. Generally the number of servings is based on the usual meal of a vegetable, meat, perhaps a salad, and a dessert.

Explorer Foods

Recipes for these two dishes popular with early fur traders are included for their historical interest but are not recommended for general use.

Voyageur Dope

Canoers in the North Country used this recipe (minus the dry milk) more than one hundred years ago, and it could still be good when you need nourishing food but have only a limited variety in your pack.

It is a tasty way to utilize salt pork or bacon and makes a good substitute for syrup and butter for bannock bread and pancakes. Serves 4.

1 pound salt pork	½ cup dry milk, or 1
4 cups water	large can evapo-
½ cup flour	rated milk
½ teaspoon pepper	

Dice pork, put in frying pan with ½ cup water, and bring to a boil. Boil 1 minute, and then pour off the water; this freshens the salty meat. Now let pork fry down to a light brown color. Pick out the pieces of meat, and rub flour into the hot grease. Add pepper. When flour is lightly browned, add remaining water in which milk has been dissolved. Bring to a boil, stirring till smooth; then replace bits of pork and serve.

RUBBABOO

French-Canadian *voyageurs* lived on this sweetened meat and flour soup for days on end. History says when the big 40-foot freight canoes stopped for meals, the cook made a huge pot of rubbaboo and, scorning plates, poured each man's portion in hollowed-out places in the rocks that lined the shore. The recipe for two men was:

1 pound pemmican	1 cup flour
2 quarts water	½ cup sugar

Pemmican and water were mixed and brought to a boil; then the dissolved flour was added, and finally the sugar. The mixture was then simmered until smooth and thick. If you want to experiment with this dish, use ½ pound of chipped beef and ¼ cup of bacon fat in place of the pemmican. The old-timers' pemmican was made of the lean meat of game animals, which was dried brittle, pounded or ground fine, and mixed with melted fat.

Beverages

Cocoa

A tasty stimulating drink in any season because it can be served hot or chilled.

½ cup cocoa
½ cup sugar
1 large can evaporated milk
2 cups water

Mix cocoa and sugar with a little water. When smooth, add balance of water, and boil 3 minutes. Remove from fire, and add milk. If necessary, reheat to just below boiling point for a very hot drink.

Ready-Mixed Cocoa

You can buy this product, but if you want to prepare your own, use these proportions:

1 cup cocoa
¾ cup sugar
4 cups dry milk

Mix well, and store in waterproof sack or can. At camp use 2 to 4 teaspoons for each cup of hot water, depending on how strong you like the drink. Put cocoa mixture in cup, pour in hot water, and stir. To cook in a pot, mix with a very little cold water and stir until smooth; then add rest of cold water, and heat to just below boiling point.

Quick Camp Coffee

If you like both cream and sugar in your coffee, here is a convenient way to prepare it and still keep packing and cooking simple. It is especially recommended for light-load hikers and canoers. At home mix and pack in an airtight jar:

1 part instant coffee
1 part sugar
1 part dry milk

At camp put 3 teaspoons of the mixture in your cup, and fill with hot water. Since individuals vary in the amount of sugar they like, test the proportions at home to arrive at the most satisfactory blend.

COFFEE WITH COLD WATER

Although many campers use instant (concentrated) coffee because of its lightness and convenience, some still prefer the regular pot-brewed kind. For them this recipe produces a quality drink.

6 heaping table-spoons coffee	5 cups cold water
	Small pinch of salt

Tie coffee in a thin cloth bag, leaving room for it to swell, and put in pot with cold water. Add salt. Bring to a brisk boil. Reduce heat, and simmer 1 minute. Then set pot off fire but near heat to stay warm until you are ready to drink it. Serves 2.

NORTH WOODS TEA

Bring 8½ cups of water to a brisk boil; then empty it into an empty teapot or kettle. Half a minute later, pour water back in the first pot to reheat. Drop 4 teaspoons of dry tea on bottom of the hot kettle. When water boils again, pour it over the tea, cover, and set beside fire to steep 5 minutes. Then serve. Serves 4.

SPICED TEA

There are two ways to make this invigorating hot drink, which is popular with skiers. In the first, put a 3-inch stick of cinnamon in 4 cups of water, and bring to a boil. Pour this over 2 or 3 teaspoons of dry tea, and let steep several minutes. Then pour into four cups each of which contains 1 teaspoon sugar, 3 cloves, and a slice of lemon.

With the second recipe, make tea as usual, pour it into cups containing sugar, cloves, and lemon, and stir with a stick of cinnamon instead of a spoon.

Breads

BACON-SKILLET BREAD

This recipe produces tasty camp bread—with a delicious smoky flavor—without an oven.

6 slices bacon	4 teaspoons baking
2 cups flour	powder
2 tablespoons sugar	2 teaspoons salt

1½ cups milk

Cut bacon slices crosswise, and cook until about half done. Then arrange them like spokes of a wheel on bottom of skillet. Mix dry ingredients, add milk, and pour batter over the bacon. (You can use a prepared biscuit or pancake mix if you wish.) Skillet should be wide enough so batter or dough is not more than ¾ inch thick. Cover, and cook over moderate heat 12 minutes. Then turn the loaf bottom up, and cook another 12 minutes—longer if a wood sliver thrust in center of loaf comes out sticky. Loaf may have to be slid out on a plate for easy turning. Serves 4.

BANNOCK BREAD

In the northern canoe country this quick, rich camp bread is considered a test for camp cooks: anyone who can bake up a good bannock is in.

4 cups flour	⅓ cup cold bacon
6 tablespoons sugar	fat
1 teaspoon salt	Milk or water

4 teaspoons baking powder

Mix dry ingredients; then cream in fat with a fork. Add small amount of water or milk until dough gathers into a ball with no dry spots but not sloppy wet (too much moisture makes bread soggy). Press into a round cake not more than 1 inch thick. Dust top and bottom with dry flour. Get skillet hot, rub bottom with grease, dust with dry flour, and lay in the bread. Brown both sides. Cook about 15 minutes, or until a sliver of wood or a dry grass stem thrust into loaf's center comes out clean. Some cooks finish bread by propping skillet partly on edge before the open fire; others hold skillet above the flames the entire time. If you use the latter way, remember to turn bread over frequently. Serves 4.

CAMPAIGN BREAD

This bread keeps a long time since it contains no grease.

4 cups flour	3 teaspoons salt
4 teaspoons baking powder	3 cups water (about)

¼ cup sugar

Mix dry ingredients. Add only enough water to make a dough that will slowly level itself off in the pan. Bake about 45 minutes, depending on loaf's thickness. When done, sprinkle top with sugar, and let it melt in before eating. Cinnamon may be mixed with the sugar. Serves 4.

FRIED BREAD

If your supply of store bread becomes dry and hard in camp, this recipe makes it as tasty as hotcakes. For 4 slices, beat 1 egg lightly and add ¼ cup milk. Dip slices in this mixture, making sure each is coated. Fry in bacon fat until golden-brown. Eat with syrup or bacon gravy (bacon fat thinned with boiling water). Each camper can handle 3 or 4 slices nicely.

KETTLE BREAD

When frying pan is busy and you also lack an oven, cook your bread in a kettle. You may be surprised how good it is. Use 4 cups of biscuit mix for 4 people, and add enough milk or water to form a soft dough.

Shape in balls about ¾ inch in diameter, and drop into a kettle of boiling water. Use the largest pot you have, and add balls slowly so water never stops boiling. Then cover kettle, and boil hard for 15 minutes. Do not lift the lid during this time, or the bread will fall and be heavy. Do not crowd balls in the pot either. Better practice this at home until you get the knack; then in camp it will be easy.

CAMPFIRE TWIST BREAD

Use biscuit or pancake ready-mix flour, allowing 1 cup per camper. Mix into a siff dough, using less liquid (either milk or water) than usual. Press dough flat, cut in 1-inch strips, and wind these spirally around clubs of green wood. Clubs should be about 2 inches in diameter and 3½ feet long. Hold over a bed of coals, turning stick constantly so bread browns evenly on all sides without burning. Eat with jam, jelly, or syrup.

FRIED BISCUITS

No oven in camp? Then try this simple, almost foolproof recipe.

2 cups flour	3 teaspoons baking
1 teaspoon salt	powder
¼ cup dry milk	¼ cup shortening
⅔ cup water	

Mix dry ingredients; then mash in shortening with a fork. Add water slowly until you have a soft dough that will flatten out when dropped. Drop teaspoon-size balls in a skillet containing a little hot grease. Cook over moderate heat until biscuits are brown; then turn and brown the other side. Do not cook too fast, or biscuits will be doughy in the center. Allow 12 to 15 minutes. Makes 12 biscuits.

Shortcake Biscuits

These big biscuits are fine to serve with sugared fruit—canned, fresh, or dried. (Dried fruit must be cooked first.)

2 cups prepared bis-   ¼ cup shortening
    cuit flour   2 tablespoons sugar
          ½ cup milk

If evaporated or dry milk is used, mix first with water according to directions on the milk package. Blend sugar, flour, and shortening; then add liquid. Dough should be soft but not sticky; if sticky, add a little more flour. Knead gently, and shape in cakes ½ inch thick and about 4 inches wide. Bake 18 to 20 minutes in hot oven. Split, butter each half, and put fruit between pieces and also on top. Serves 4.

Cinnamon Pancakes

Always appreciated for camp breakfasts, they do not really require butter and syrup, so remember to make some if you run short of those delicacies.

1 egg   1 cup milk
       2 cups pancake flour

Beat egg lightly with fork; add milk and then the flour. Have hot grease about ⅛ inch deep in skillet, and cook rather thick cakes. As soon as each is browned on both sides, remove, and sprinkle the top liberally with sugar and cinnamon. Serves 2.

Oatmeal Pancakes

2 cups milk   3 teaspoons baking
2 cups quick-cooking   powder
    oats   ¼ cup shortening
2 eggs   1 teaspoon salt

Heat milk, and stir in oats. Do not let milk boil. Take

from heat, and cool. Then beat in eggs; add other ingredients. Bake on greased griddle or in skillet; at home you can use a waffle iron. Serves 4.

CORN PONE

No other camp bread is as easily made. It is tasty too, so try some if you run short of flour, baking powder, or biscuit mix.

4 cups cornmeal   1½ teaspoons salt
                3 cups hot water

Mix all together, and stir briskly (stirring makes bread lighter). Press into thin cakes less than ½ inch thick, and bake in reflector oven. Or fry with a little fat in a skillet. Baking time about 35 minutes; frying time about 15 minutes. In an emergency you can prepare corn pone without utensils. Push back part of your campfire; lay the pone cakes on the hot ground exposed; cover them with cold ashes, then with hot embers (coals). Renew embers several times to maintain a steady heat. Brush off ashes and serve. Serves 3 or 4.

CAMPFIRE TOAST

Rake out a pile of hot coals from fire, and level off. Drop a slice of bread on the coals, and lift it off quickly. Repeat with the other side, and you will have delicious toast in less than half a minute.

HUDSON'S BAY TOAST

Good cold-weather food to start the day off right. Fry about ½ pound of salt pork (or bacon) slowly until grease is extracted. Remove slices of meat, and put ½ cup of brown sugar into pan. Stir smooth, and pour most of the mixture into a cup. Lay sliced bread in the remainder, and fry brown on both sides.

Add a little of the sugar and fat mixture each time new bread is fried. Cook 3 or 4 slices per man.

TORTILLAS

Tortillas are daily food for multitudes of Southern folks. Properly baked, they are tasty and nutritious.

2 cups cornmeal   ¾ cup flour
2 teaspoons salt

Mix ingredients. Add enough water to make a stiff dough. Let stand 30 minutes; then squeeze into small balls, press each ball into a very thin cake, and bake brown on both sides in a lightly greased skillet or griddle. Use just enough grease to prevent sticking, none if you have a well broken-in aluminum griddle. Serves 3.

DUMPLINGS

Dumplings which are simply boiled biscuits are preferably made of prepared (self-rising) biscuit flour but if this product is not available and the separate ingredients are, mix as follows:

2 cups flour   4 tablespoons short-
3 teaspoons baking   ening
  powder   1 teaspoon salt
¾ cup milk or water

Add the liquid gradually; dumplings should be quite thick and you may not need all of the quantity specified. If dumpling dough drops off the end of a spoon it is too thin, you have used too much liquid.

Roll or press dough in a sheet about ½-inch thick and cut in discs using the top of a small tin can. Or squeeze the dough into balls about 1-inch in diameter. The soup or stew in which dumplings are cooked should be boiling briskly. Put in enough of them to just cover its surface; crowding dumplings makes them heavy and wet inside. Cover kettle immediately and boil 15 minutes. Don't use too much heat now because if steam in kettle lifts the lid, the dumplings will fall and taste soggy. The same thing happens if you cook dumplings in an uncovered kettle or if you lift the lid too soon or too often to peep inside. Keep kettle covered until dumplings are done.

Dumplings can be cooked on top of boiling stew, soup, beef, game, poultry or dried fruit, or even on top of salted boiling water. They make a pleasant change from baked and fried camp breads, are easier to cook, requiring less special equipment and attention.

Cereals

LEFTOVER CEREAL

Since camp grub lists are often figured on a man-meal-day basis, wasted food could cause someone to go hungry on a long trip. This means that leftovers should not be thrown away. A good way to utilize leftover cereal is to combine it with scrambled eggs. Use 1 cup of cooked rice, oatmeal, or wheat cereal to 4 eggs. Beat eggs lightly, add a little milk and seasoning, stir in cereal, and pour in a greased skillet. Cook until mixture is well set. This makes two big servings.

FRIED CORNMEAL MUSH

You can hike, fish, hunt, snowshoe, or ski for hours without feeling empty after a breakfast of this hearty food. It should be started the night before with:

1 cup cornmeal   3½ cups boiling
1 cup cold water   water
1 teaspoon salt

Mix cornmeal with cold water until smooth. Stir in salted boiling water, and cook 5 minutes, stirring steadily. Then cover, and put in top of a double boiler (you can rig one in camp with two pots of a different size, whose bottoms are separated by a coil of wiry brush or three small stones), and cook 30 minutes longer. Turn mush out in a greased pan, and let cool.

To fry next morning, cut in slices ¼ inch thick, roll in flour, and brown in hot fat. Makes a substantial meal for 2.

HOMINY GRITS

This popular item in the traditional Southern breakfast should be tried by campers in all climes. An excellent substitute for both potatoes and bread, grits can be cooked in a double boiler or in a single pot over direct heat.

If you have or can improvise a double boiler, use 1 cup grits, 4 cups water, and 1 teaspoon salt. Using the top container only, bring salted water to boil, and stir in grits. Then cover, set in the outer pot partly filled with hot water, and cook 45 minutes, stirring occasionally.

To cook in a single pot over direct heat, use 1 cup grits, 5 cups water, and 1 teaspoon salt. Bring salted water to boil, stir in grits, cover, reduce heat, and simmer 30 minutes. Stir every few minutes to prevent sticking.

When done by either method, serve like any hot breakfast cereal with syrup, milk, or cream. Or pour in a greased pan to cool, and later slice for frying. Serves 3 or 4.

BOILED MACARONI

Macaroni has a distinctive flavor, since it is made from hard durum wheat and is slightly fermented in the process. It is useful in camp, easy to pack and prepare, and substitutes well for potatoes. Put 4 quarts water and 4 teaspoons salt in a kettle, and bring to a vigorous boil. Add 8 ounces of macaroni slowly so boiling does not cease. Boil uncovered until tender, about 10 minutes; then drain. Now add 1 can of cream of tomato soup diluted with 1 can of water, and heat through.

Or add 3 or 4 cups of gravy to the plain macaroni. To make this gravy, heat 6 tablespoons bacon fat in skillet; blend in 6 tablespoons dry flour. When flour is slightly browned, stir in 3 cups of milk, and cook slowly until smooth. An 8-ounce package of macaroni serves 4.

QUICK-COOKING RICE

Rice is easy to digest and very nourishing. It substitutes well for potatoes and bread in camp meals. A quick-cooking type is available that needs less than a minute of heating: simply bring water to a boil, add this processed rice, stir briefly, then cover pot, and remove from heat. Let stand 5 minutes, when it is ready to serve. This rice is recommended highly since it saves time and stove space as well as the tedious stirring often necessary when regular rice is boiled. The package containing this rice states the proper proportions of water and rice to use.

Desserts

CAMP BAKED APPLES

Fresh apples are sometimes available at fall fishing and hunting camps as well as at vacation cabins. Wash apples but do not peel. Slice off top, and dig out core. Fill the cavity with mincemeat or brown sugar, set in a shallow pan, pour in about 1/4 inch of water, and bake at 375° F. 40 minutes. During this time add a little water to pan if it cooks dry. Allow 2 medium apples or 1 large apple per man.

CORNMEAL CUSTARD

This can be served either for dessert or as camp bread.

1 cup cornmeal	3 tablespoons melted
1 quart milk	fat
1 teaspoon salt	3 eggs, beaten
2 teaspoons baking powder	

Cook cornmeal and half the milk in a saucepan until thick; use very low heat. Remove from fire, add seasoning, milk, fat, and beaten eggs. Put in a greased pan, and bake 30 minutes in moderate oven. Serves 3.

DRIED FRUITS

Dried or evaporated fruits are easy to pack and cook: 1 pound usually equals more than a No. 2 can or 4 to 5 pounds of raw fruit. Take several varieties—peaches, apricots, apples, pears, and prunes. For a sauce to eat on bread, oatmeal, or rice, use:

2 cups dried fruit	Dash of salt
6 cups cold water	½ teaspoon cinnamon or nutmeg
½ cup sugar	

Spices can be omitted, as they are not strictly necessary. For best flavor soak fruit overnight in cold water. Next morning add sugar, salt, and spices, if available, and simmer 5 minutes. Then serve. A few drops of lemon juice improve the flavor.

FRIED PIES

The famous fried pies of fishing schooners are just as good in camp. Use dried fruit, as it is really better than fresh. Stew dried peaches, apricots, or apples with a very little water until soft. Soaking overnight hastens this step. Make a plain piecrust, using a ready-mix product, and cut in 6-inch circles or squares. Put ½ cup fruit on one side of each piece of dough; then fold the other side over. Pinch edges to hold fruit inside, and prick small vent holes in top crust with a fork. Brown in hot fat until crust is flaky. Lift pies out with a pancake turner. Unless kettle or skillet is quite large, do not fry more than two pies at one time.

BREAKFAST PRUNES

Prunes are a popular camp food because of their laxative action. They are especially tasty and effective prepared this way. Wash if necessary (some prunes do not need washing), put in a jar or a can, and cover with boiling water. Let stand overnight. Prunes will absorb most of the water and be soft and well flavored in the morning. Prunes give 5 to 6 servings per pound.

DRIED APPLE PUDDING

2 cups dried apples	¼ cup brown sugar
½ cup flour	½ cup butter

Soak apples until soft in enough water to cover; then spread them over the bottom of a greased baking pan. Mix flour, sugar, and butter, and spread over apples. Bake 40 minutes in a moderate oven. Serve hot with milk or cream. Serves 4.

CAMP BREAD PUDDING

When bread goes stale in camp, make it up into this nice dessert instead of feeding it to the birds.

1 cup dry milk	3 cups dry bread, cubed
½ cup sugar	
½ teaspoon salt	½ cup melted butter
2 eggs, beaten	1 teaspoon lemon, vanilla, or cinnamon
4 cups hot water	

Mix powdered milk, sugar, and salt together. Beat eggs and add; then pour in the hot water, stirring constantly. Drip melted butter over the bread, and add to the mixture. Add flavoring. Pour in a greased pan, and bake at low heat 40 minutes. Serves 4.

CANNED FRUIT PUDDING

For this quick, tasty dessert use any canned fruit that contains a good proportion of juice. Cherries are especially good. Use 3 tablespoons of flour for a No. 2 can of fruit, 4 tablespoons for a No. 3 can. Heat fruit, and when it begins to simmer, add flour you have previously mixed into a paste with a little cold water. Stir until fruit juice thickens. Add a dash of salt and a lump of butter. If fruit is quite tart, put in a little sugar. This pudding can be eaten hot or cold. Instead of plain flour you can use biscuit mix or any of the dry pudding mixes.

INDIAN PUDDING

This pioneer dessert still tastes good in camp or at home.

2½ cups milk	½ cup sugar
½ cup cornmeal	¼ cup molasses or
1 cup cold water	sorghum

2 eggs

1 teaspoon each cinnamon, salt, ginger, and nutmeg

Heat milk in double boiler to scalding point, mix cornmeal and cold water, and add to milk. Continue to stir and heat until thick. Remove from fire, and add sugar and molasses. When cooled to lukewarm, add beaten eggs and seasonings. Pour in a greased pan, and bake in a moderate oven 1½ hours. Or the pudding can be steamed over boiling water in a muslin bag.

RICE PUDDING

½ cup dry milk   2 cups water
3 cups cooked rice   1 cup raisins
¼ cup sugar   2 beaten eggs
Pinch of salt

Eggs are not strictly necessary, and the pudding will be good, but less nourishing, without them. Mix milk, rice, and sugar; then stir in the water, raisins, and beaten eggs. Add salt, also cinnamon or nutmeg should you have either. Lacking an oven, this pudding can be cooked on top of the stove over low heat with frequent stirring. It will require less attention, however, if baked 30 minutes in a reflector oven.

LAZY COOK'S DESSERT

Every overworked camp cook has a right to cut corners occasionally and save time, especially when by doing so he can rig up a dish this good. Grease the inside of a deep pan, and cover bottom with a layer of slices of heavily buttered bread. If bread is a little old, so much the better. Then dump in half a can of apricots, peaches, pears, or pineapple. Sprinkle fruit with sugar, and cover with more bread. Add rest of can of fruit, and cover with a third layer of bread slices. Bake covered in a moderate oven 20 minutes. A No. 2 or 2½ can of fruit with 6 slices of bread serves 4.

Eggs

HIKING TRAIL EGGS

Try this when you do not want to stop more than a few minutes to cook lunch. It is a good quick dish, too, when a hungry camper or hunter comes in after the regular mealtime. Heat 2 tablespoons of shortening in a skillet, and add 1 cup of milk. When milk is hot, break in 3 or 4 eggs, and stir. When eggs start to stiffen, add 2 cups of broken crackers or pieces of stale bread. Season with salt and pepper (lots of the latter), and cook 2 minutes more. Serves 1 or 2.

POWDERED EGGS

Popular with light-pack campers because ½ pound equals 2 dozen fresh eggs. Be sure to buy the best quality of powdered eggs for best flavor; camp outfitters usually offer them.

A good recipe for this concentrated product is:

¼ cup powdered eggs	1 teaspoon salt
2 tablespoons dry milk	½ teaspoon pepper
	1½ cups water

Mix eggs, milk, and seasoning; then add part of the water, and blend smooth. Add rest of water, beat to mix, and pour into a skillet containing a little hot grease. Cook slowly until bottom is brown; then fold over with a pancake turner, and brown the top. Serves 3 or 4.

TEXAS TRAIL EGGS

Fry several slices of bacon. When done, remove from the skillet, and pour off all but about ¼ cup of the fat. Mince 1 onion (or use 1 tablespoon dehydrated onion). drain juice from 1 can of tomatoes, and put both in the hot fat. Cook several minutes; then add 6 eggs, beaten. Season with a little salt and pepper. Simmer until eggs are set. Serve on plain or buttered toast. Serves 4.

Gravy

BACON-ONION GRAVY

When bacon is cooked, it yields a tasty grease that is very useful in camp cookery. Be sure to save it all. This fat makes excellent gravy to eat on potatoes, cereals, macaroni, and griddle cakes. Use 2 tablespoons of fat to make 1 cup of gravy.

For four campers, stir 8 tablespoons of flour into the same quantity of hot bacon fat, and cook, stirring steadily, until flour is lightly browned. Then add 4 cups of water or milk and 2 tablespoons (dry measure) of dehydrated onions that have been soaked in a little water until soft. Cook until gravy is smooth; then season with salt (sparingly) and pepper.

Plain bacon fat thinned with twice as much boiling water as you have fat makes a tasty rich gravy for griddle cakes in cold weather. You won't miss butter with it!

Chipped Beef Gravy

Chipped, or dried, beef is a convenient meat for camp and trail use. It is concentrated, keeps well, and prepares easily. The moisture-proof package prevents molding, but when it is opened, use contents without much delay.

4 ounces chipped beef	4 tablespoons flour
4 tablespoons fat or shortening	2 cups milk
	¼ teaspoon pepper

Tear beef in small pieces, and brown in the fat. Add pepper. Sprinkle flour over the meat, and stir briskly, continuing to cook. After 3 minutes add milk, cooking and stirring until smooth and sufficiently thick. If too thick, dilute with milk or water. This is excellent on camp bread, cooked potatoes, and cooked rice.

Meats

Bacon

Bacon can be eaten as meat, in sandwiches, or combined with other foods like beans as a flavoring. Bacon keeps well, is convenient to pack on difficult trips, and is easy to prepare. For these reasons it is the most popular trail and camp meat.

Buy a good grade of bacon, as it will be more lean and contain less salt. Sliced bacon keeps up to two weeks in camp; for longer periods unsliced or chunk bacon is less likely to mold. Cook slowly (bacon is frequently fried over a too high heat). If you dip the slices in cold water, they will not curl so much in the skillet. For a different taste, sprinkle them with a little brown sugar when half cooked. The flavor is improved if you pour off accumulated fat several times during the cooking.

DEVILED DRIED BEEF

A good quick breakfast dish on canoe and hiking trips.

1 cup dried beef	2 tablespoons vinegar
2 tablespoons bacon fat	2 tablespoons prepared mustard
4 eggs	Salt and pepper

Pull beef into shreds, and put in skillet containing hot fat. Cook 3 minutes; then add lightly beaten eggs and seasonings. This dish will stand plenty of pepper. Cook until eggs have set. Serves 2.

NOTE: For plain dried beef and eggs, cook as above but omit mustard and vinegar.

DRIED BEEF AND HOMINY

Heat 3 tablespoons of shortening in a skillet, and add ¼ pound of dried beef torn in small pieces. Cook 3 minutes. Add 1 can of hominy, season with a little salt and more pepper, and simmer until well heated. Serves 3 or 4.

Sausage Skillet Meal

Brown 1 pound of bulk sausage in skillet with 1 medium-size onion chopped fine. Pour off fat, and add 1 cup of cooked rice and 1 No. 2 can of tomatoes. Season with salt and pepper and prepared mustard, and cook slowly about 30 minutes. Serves 2 or 3.

Savory Tinned Meat

Canned luncheon meat like pressed ham or corned beef is delicious prepared this way. Heat 2 tablespoons of bacon fat in skillet, and add 1 sliced onion, a No. 2 can of tomatoes, and a 12-ounce tin of meat, which should be broken into small pieces with fork. After mixture has boiled up well, thicken with 3 tablespoons of flour blended smooth in a little cold water. Cook about 5 minutes more; then season to taste with salt and pepper. Serves 4.

Soups and Stews

Onion Chowder

Makes a one-dish lunch.

¾ cup dehydrated potatoes	1 cup diced salt pork
	2 cups water
¼ cup dehydrated onions	2 cups evaporated milk

Salt and pepper

Soak potatoes and onions in water as directed on their packages, several hours in advance. Brown the pork on bottom of kettle until most of the grease is fried out. Then add potatoes and onions. Cook 10 minutes. Put in water and milk. Just before chowder comes to a boil, season with salt and plenty of black pepper. Serves 2 or 3.

Split Pea Soup

This dish never lets you down and is a prime favorite with hunting and logging camp chefs.

¼ pound dry split peas

2 tablespoons dehydrated onions

¼ cup dehydrated potatoes

1 pound ham or salt pork

Salt and pepper

Soak peas, onions, and potatoes overnight in 1 quart of water. Next morning add meat and 2 quarts more water, and simmer 6 hours. Before serving, season to taste. Small dumplings made from biscuit flour can be cooked on top of this soup (be sure to cover kettle then) for the last 20 minutes; then you really have a nourishing meal. Serves 3 or 4.

Soup Stock

Sometimes called simply "stock" and required in many cook book recipes, this liquor is an excellent base for soups, stews, gravy, and other dishes. Save the water in which you have boiled a piece of any lean meat. Add scraps of meat, except fat, and the bones of game, beef, or poultry, cracking the larger ones to expose the marrow. Also put in bony pieces of game birds like necks and wings. Simmer the mixture 5 hours, strain out bones, let cool, and skim off congealing fat. If not tasty enough, heat and add a beef bouillon cube to each pint of stock. Combine stock with vegetables as desired for soup and stew. Use this stock also to moisten meat loaf and fried meat cakes and to strengthen gravy.

Canned Meat Stew

Tinned meat keeps longer in camp than any other

form of meat. The tins add a little extra weight, but campers can offset this by carrying dehydrated vegetables in place of fresh or canned ones

¼ cup dehydrated onions	1 teaspoon salt
1 cup dehydrated potatoes	1 can meat
	4 slices bacon or salt pork
¼ cup rice	1 can condensed tomato soup
2 quarts water	

½ teaspoon pepper

Soak dry vegetables and rice in water for 30 minutes. Then add meat, soup, and seasonings. Simmer over low fire 1 hour. Serves 4.

CANUCK STEW

This recipe provides a nourishing meal with only one cooking utensil. That is why it is popular with northland canoers.

4 slices bacon	1 sliced onion
3 tablespoons flour	1 cup shredded dried beef
4 cups water	

3 sliced potatoes

Cut bacon in 1-inch pieces, and fry until most of the grease is extracted. Remove bacon, and put flour in the fat. Blend smooth; then add water slowly. Stir and cook until flour thickens; then add dried beef, potatoes and onions; cover skillet and cook 20 minutes. Thin with a little hot water if too thick. Serves 2.

CORNED BEEF STEW

Besides being useful for sandwiches and potato hash, tinned corned beef makes a dandy stew.

1 small onion	1 can kidney beans
3 tablespoons bacon fat	1 can tomatoes
	1 tin corned beef

Cut onion fine and brown in hot fat; add beans and

tomatoes, and simmer 5 minutes. Break beef into small chunks, add to the mixture, and cook 5 minutes more. Season with salt and pepper. Serves 3 or 4.

Sandwiches

HIKER'S SANDWICH FILLING

A nourishing, tasty filling, which keeps well, for white or brown bread sandwiches.

1½ cups raisins, ground
¼ cup mayonnaise or butter
1 cup peanut butter
¼ teaspoon salt

Grind raisins in food chopper, add other ingredients, and mix well. Will keep about two weeks, even in summer, if stored in a tin with a tight lid.

HUNTER'S SANDWICH

To make hearty sandwiches for two hunters, canoers, or hikers, use 8 slices of bread. Spread 4 of them with butter, 4 with prepared mustard. Slice contents of a 12-ounce tin of corned beef with a sharp knife, and place between bread slices.

SALT PORK SANDWICHES

Although today's campers carry bacon instead of salt pork, the latter is still available in both city and backwoods stores. Nothing else quite equals salt pork for seasoning beans, potatoes, chowders, soups, and stews. It will also make tasty and nourishing sandwiches. Try these when a cold wave hits your fishing or hunting camp.

Cut pork in slices ¼ inch thick, and rinse in hot water to remove some of the salt. Cook slowly in skillet until almost done. Remove slices from the fat, and drain them half a minute. Dip first in milk, then in dry flour. Put back in the hot grease until a crust forms on both sides. Lay between slices of bread. The grease remaining in the skillet can be diluted with four times as much hot water, thickened with flour, and used as a gravy to pour over the sandwiches or cooked potatoes. Allow ⅓ pound of salt pork for each camper.

Vegetables

CANNED BAKED BEANS

If you think canned beans are just ordinary grub, this recipe will change your mind. Soak 2 tablespoons of dehydrated onions until soft. Cut 4 slices of bacon in small pieces, mix with the onion, and fry until moisture is gone and bacon has browned. Then add a No. 2 can of baked beans, heat thoroughly, and serve. Hearty portions for 2.

BEAN AND CHEESE ROAST

When low on meat in camp or vacation cabin, use this hearty substitute.

1 can kidney beans	2 tablespoons butter
½ pound American cheese	1½ cups soft bread-crumbs
1 small onion, chopped	2 eggs, beaten
	Salt and pepper

Drain beans; cut cheese in small chunks, and beat or mash with beans until smooth. Cook onion in butter until brown, and add to bean and cheese mixture. Fold in breadcrumbs and eggs, season, and bake 1 hour at 350° F. Serves 3 or 4.

BAKED BEANS

An excellent cure for that empty feeling amidships after a hard day on the trail.

2 pounds navy beans
1 teaspoon baking
   soda
1 minced onion
3 tablespoons pre-
   pared mustard

1 teaspoon salt
1 pound bacon
1 bottle catsup
½ cup brown sugar
   or molasses
2 cups water

Soak beans overnight. In the morning add fresh water
and soda, and bring to a boil. Pour off water and rinse.
Add all other ingredients and simmer over low heat
4 or 5 hours. Add a little more water if beans cook too
dry. These beans can also be baked in an oven or a
hole dug in the ground. Serves 8.

Roasted Sweet Corn

To roast sweet corn over a campfire, open husks
enough to remove the silks. Then close husks, and tie
the opened ends with string. Soak ears in water 5
minutes, remove and drain 1 minute, and lay on a
grate sitting several inches above hot coals. Cook about
12 minutes, turning ears often. The absorbed water
turns into steam and makes corn juicy and tender.
Lacking a grate, bury the ears in hot ashes, cover with
hot coals, and cook 20 minutes. Golden Bantam is a
popular variety of corn to roast this way. Each camper
should be able to eat four ears.

Toasted Corn

Pioneer families ate a lot of this crunchy food; primitive people in other parts of the world still do. They
call it "pinole." Pinole is completely concentrated, and
hikers find it ideal for lightweight packing.

Shell kernels from dry mature field or sweet corn,
and toast them in a heavy skillet, shaking frequently
so the grain is not burned on any one side. Do not add
water or grease. When corn is brown and can be easily

crunched with the teeth, it is done. Store in waterproof sacks or tins. To serve, warm up kernels with a little butter and salt. Or grind into meal, and eat with milk or cream.

North Woods Lima Beans

You will put more canned lima beans in the grub sack after you taste these. Fry 4 slices bacon crisp and remove from pan. Into the hot fat put 1 sliced onion, and cook 5 minutes. Then add 1 can of lima beans and 1 can of tomato soup, the concentrated kind. Stir and cook until heated through. Serves 2.

Peas and Pork

Canned black-eyed peas, cabanza beans, or red kidney beans can be cooked this way. Cut 4 slices of bacon or salt pork in small pieces, and fry until light brown. Then add a No. 2 can of peas or beans, and simmer 10 minutes. A little black pepper is the only seasoning needed. Serves 2 or 3.

Dehydrated Potatoes

Good brands taste very like fresh potatoes when properly cooked. They are popular with long-trail campers because 1 pound equals about 8 pounds of the raw vegetable. One ounce makes one serving; cook 3/4 cup for two men.

Soak dehydrated potatoes 1 hour in twice their bulk of water. Then boil in the same water 10 minutes, adding salt and more liquid if necessary. If you can cook away most of the water, you save vitamins that would be lost if the liquid is drained off. Cooked dehydrated potatoes can be browned in bacon fat to resemble the regular hash-brown product. Or mash them with bottle or club, and mix in a little hot milk and butter. Or make them into a salad.

Pail-Baked Potatoes

These are really delicious. Select large potatoes, preferably bakers; wash skins and rub with grease. Slit each potato down the center, but leave skin at back intact. Open halves, salt and pepper each, cover one side with a short slice of bacon. Close halves, and wrap each potato separately in foil. Bury them in a pail of damp sand. Potatoes must not touch bottom or sides of pail or each other. Support pail on 3 small stones or on empty tin cans filled with sand, and cook over a medium fire about 75 minutes. Potatoes can be baked this way whole, without the bacon, and will still be excellent. Prepare 1 potato for each camper.

Sour-Fried Potatoes

Campers relish this dish in both hot and cold weather.

6 slices bacon	¼ cup vinegar
1½ cups dehydrated potatoes	¼ cup sugar
1 tablespoon dehydrated onion	Salt and pepper

Fry bacon until crisp, remove slices, and add to the hot grease the potatoes and onion which have been soaked 1 hour in a little water. Add vinegar, sugar, and salt and pepper. Simmer until vegetables are done; then put bacon (broken in small pieces) back in mixture. Serves 4.

Meatless Stew

Should the hunting go sour or you run short of other

meat, try this hearty vegetable stew. It is another reason for saving bacon fat in camp.

¼ cup dehydrated onions	1 No. 2 can peas
½ to ¾ cup bacon fat	1 No. 2 can lima beans
1 No. 2 can corn	1 No. 2 can tomatoes
	2 cups water

Salt and pepper

Soak onions at least 1 hour in cold water. Heat fat in kettle (use larger amount of fat in cold weather, smaller in warm); add drained onions, and cook 3 minutes. Put in canned vegetables and water. Cook until heated well, about 15 minutes. Season to taste. Serves 4.

CAMP SAUERKRAUT

Carry a can or two of sauerkraut if possible; it satisfies cravings for both salad and vegetables. It can be eaten right from the can or cooked with meat; preferably meat with considerable fat. If sauerkraut is cooked alone, drain off most of the juice to remove excess salt, and replace with fresh water. (Omit draining when cooked with meat.) Add a little bacon fat, and boil about 15 minutes.

SUCCOTASH

Early settlers learned about this dish from the Indians. It is well suited to camp cooking, where combination dishes save time and stove room.

1 can lima beans	1 can corn
½ teaspoon salt	Dash of pepper
1 tablespoon sugar	¾ cup milk
1 tablespoon bacon fat or butter	

Mix ingredients, and simmer slowly over low fire for 15 minutes. Serves 4.

Cooked Canned Tomatoes

In hot weather canned tomatoes can be eaten cold as a salad, in cool weather stew them this way. Put contents of a No. 2 can of tomatoes in skillet, and add 2 tablespoons of sugar, 3 tablespoons of butter, 1/2 teaspoon of salt, and 1/4 teaspoon of pepper. Bring to a boil, and add 2 tablespoons of flour blended to a paste in cold water. Cook until flour thickens. Serves 2 or 3.

Salads

Wilted Green Salad

Spring campers and camping fishermen often use dandelion greens and water cress as salad. Both of these common plants can be prepared this way: Wash 2 quarts of fresh leaves. Fry 4 slices bacon until crisp, then remove from skillet. Put greens in the hot fat, and cook until wilted. Season with a little vinegar; break bacon in bits and mix with the leaves. Serves 4.

NOTE: As water cress is usually coated with slime and dirt, it should be washed thoroughly.

25 - Cooking Fish and Game

CAMPERS AND SPORTSMEN SOMETIMES THINK they need special or distinctive recipes to cook fish and game so they will be tender and tasty. This is not so. You can prepare fish and game birds and animals the same way you handle similar domestic ones, and the results will be excellent. For example, you can roast wild ducks and geese just as you do tame ones. Pheasant and grouse respond satisfactorily to recipes for chicken. Big game such as deer, elk, and moose can be cooked like beef, and bear comes through nicely if prepared by any method recommended for pork. So when you are ready to cook fish and game, just look in any standard cookbook.

GAME BIRDS AND ANIMALS

Although special recipes are not necessary to make good food out of game, a little extra treatment may be desirable somewhere along the line because of its different nature. Compared with domestic animals, game is tougher, leaner, and more fibrous because wild species lead a more active life and are not yard fed or fattened. And most animals have a characteristic gamy flavor, which may be objectionable to the unaccustomed palate and which is sometimes augmented by careless treatment in the field. Longer exposure to heat will eliminate toughness, and parboiling will reduce strong flavor. But these variations are neither complicated nor difficult, and you can still follow the cookbook.

In deciding how to cook game, consider the species, its probable age, and the type of cut. For instance, you should not try to broil or fry tough steaks from mature animals or tough breasts of old birds. If you do, they may taste like leather. Instead, use the casserole or Dutch-oven method which, like pan-roasting, consists of an initial browning in hot fat and then a long period of simmering over reduced heat in a covered utensil, with small amounts of water added at intervals to prevent burning. (In casserole or pan-roasting cooking, the best-tasting meat always results from adding very small amounts of water often, rather than from putting in a lot at greater intervals.) Very tough cuts of game can be made perfectly tender this way if you take enough time. If in a hurry, use a pressure cooker, which is quite practical for semipermanent camps and trailers. It works fast, and while food prepared in one may not taste the same, it is still delicious and easy to chew and digest.

Broil or fry only the best steaks from fairly young game animals or the breasts of young birds, and even these only if you and your companions like meat rare. Long broiling or frying makes meat tough and dry and increases its fibrous taste and texture. You can successfully broil or fry quail, young pheasants and grouse (preferably hens), young rabbits, and young squirrels. Youngish venison turns out well also from a short exposure to heat, and so do carefully chosen steaks from older animals if they have been properly and previously aged in a cooler or a freezer.

Cut broiling steaks about 1 to 1½ inches thick. Remove all fat and hair, and wipe with a damp cloth. Sprinkle both sides with a little meat tenderizer if you have it and the time; meat thus treated should set an hour before it is cooked. Then rub both sides of the steak with cooking oil or melted fat, and expose to high heat. Turn every 30 seconds the first 2 minutes, then every minute until done. Eight to 10 minutes may be enough for a rare steak. Dot liberally with chunks of butter before serving.

If you like food cooked with a nice brown crust, tenderize tough cuts by parboiling them. This is good practice for coots, old squirrels, rabbits, and pheasants as well as coons, woodchucks, and the coarser sections of mature big game. Parboiling means to boil the meat in water containing a little vinegar and baking soda for 1 to 1½ hours, or until tender. Then drain and wipe dry, season, roll in flour or crumbs, and brown quickly on both sides in hot fat. Parboiling also effectively reduces or completely eliminates the gamy flavor of many wild meats.

Another way to deal with toughness and strong flavor is by marinating. Use only lean meat, and soak it a little longer than is recommended for domestic meat, using the combination of seasonings and spices listed in any cookbook. Rabbits are especially improved when marinated, as the treatment removes some of that sensation of chewing on cotton when you eat them. But here is a tip: most marinating recipes say to save the liquid in which the meat was soaked, for use in sauce or gravy. If the game you marinated was at all strong in flavor, however, throw the liquid away.

A useful, almost indispensable utensil for hunting camps and homes which prepare considerable game meat is the ordinary food grinder. The practice of turning deer, elk, antelope, and moose meat into "gameburger" material is becoming more popular yearly, and in some instances as much as one-third of the carcass is so handled, particularly when the game is processed by experienced freezing-plant operators. Grinding is the surest way to make palatable such cuts as shank, neck, brisket, and flank and thus to prevent their being uneaten and wasted.

Ground game meat is certainly not tough, but it still may taste strong. One remedy for this is to remove all fat before grinding, because fat is usually more gamy than lean meat. Then to keep the patties or loaf from tasting dry, add some bacon fat or beef suet. (Frying gameburgers or regular hamburgers in beef suet always improves their taste.) You can also tone down a strong "wild" flavor by mixing in freshly ground beef. A good proportion is half and half, which gives very satisfactory results with mule or whitetail deer whose flesh sometimes has a muskylike taste.

Plenty of onions and some sage added to ground game meat will also camouflage an objectionable flavor. If you have a lot of gameburger material, you can add ground ham or ground liver to part of it for a different taste. Be careful not to overcook ground game meat.

Coots and fish-eating ducks are notorious for their strong flavor. No treatment yet devised will make them taste as sweet as quail, but you can improve them substantially. Always skin these birds. It saves work and time and removes two sources of poor taste—the skin itself and the thin fat lying directly beneath. Check each bird for small tainted or "soured" spots caused by contact with ruptured entrails, and cut such places away. They can usually be detected by their different color.

To fry coots and small ducks, dismember and parboil for half an hour with a little baking soda in the water—½ teaspoon soda per quart of water. Drain and dry, and finish off in the skillet with plenty of bacon fat. If you prefer roasting, which is probably the best way to prepare these less desirable birds, put a wire rack in the roasting pan to hold them an inch above the bottom. This keeps them from soaking in their own fat which, as mentioned before, is a potent source of strong flavor.

Put an apple, an onion, and a celery stalk (if available) inside each roasting duck or coot, and bake ½ hour at high heat to drive out as much of the grease as possible. Then remove from oven, empty and scour the pan, and discard the temporary stuffing. Refill body cavity with your favorite wild-fowl dressing, return birds to oven, and roast at slightly reduced heat until done.

Even game as easy to prepare as quail may taste dry when served. This is caused by the larger proportion of breast, which lacks natural juices. One remedy for dryness is to casserole the birds as described above, and then finish by simmering with a little water, sour cream, or cream of mushroom soup. If you prefer to bake quail and other small birds like grouse, doves, or pigeons, lay slices of bacon over each, and put them breast down in the pan so that part absorbs the accumulating gravy stock. If turned upward, the breast receives most of the heat and dries out too fast. Wild geese (tame ones also) should be roasted breast up.

A very important step should always be observed when handling game you plan to eat: clean it promptly. The sooner entrails are removed and the body heat has cooled, the more you will enjoy the food. This is just as true with a 600-pound elk as a 3-pound rabbit or pheasant. Most soured, bad-tasting game comes from poor handling in the field. Running a wounded animal hard has the same undesirable effect, although this is less common today with the ultra high-powered rifles hunters carry. Remember, too, that game animals of all sizes and kinds usually possess scent glands, which must be removed or covered in such a way that they and their secretions cannot contact the meat.

Aging is another factor that may determine how good game meat tastes at the table. Unless game is frozen with reasonable promptness, its strong flavor may increase with each day that passes before cooking. This is especially true of birds. A short ripening period in the refrigerator or simply hanging in a cold place is often beneficial, but don't hold unfrozen game too long—unless, of course, you want a high flavor, in which case let it wait a week or two.

FISH AND SHELLFISH

While the meat of game animals and birds is improved by cooling and a reasonable period of aging, in the case of fish, flavor and freshness go together. The sooner you cook a fish after it is caught, the better it tastes—unless, of course, it can be adequately cooled and immediately preserved with ice to prevent further deterioration.

Special steps are sometimes desirable to improve the taste of fish taken from water containing moss and rotting vegetation. Bass are an example. Since much of the disagreeable flavor lies in or on the skin, an effective remedy is to scald the fish in hot water, and then skin it. The bones of some fish also carry a taint of sorts, so cut out some of the larger bones before cooking. Removing the lining of a fish's abdominal cavity is another precaution that pays off.

When preparing a meal that consists mostly of fish, allow 1 pound whole or ¾ pound cleaned and filleted fish for each person. If you lack scales and do not trust your judgment, you can get a rough estimation of its weight like this: Put it whole or cut up in a pot or pail, and add water to fill the vessel completely. Then remove fish, and pour in more water, a cup at a time, until the container is again brimful. The fish weighs ½ pound for each cup of water you added.

FISH AND GAME RECIPES

Fish and Shellfish

FRIED FISH

Frying is the easiest, quickest, and most popular method of preparing fish. Small fish can be left whole; larger ones cook better if cut into rather thin serving-sized pieces. Dip in milk, beaten egg, or water. Sprinkle with salt and pepper, and roll in cornmeal, flour, or dry crumbs. Fat should be hot but not quite smoking; it can be bacon grease, lard, or vegetable shortening. Use enough fat to cover skillet bottom about ¼ inch deep. Butter burns easily, but a little can be put with other fats for better flavor.

Put fish in hot grease, and brown on both sides. Do not overcook. Fish are usually ready when flesh flakes easily away from bones with a fork. If pieces are thick, brown quickly; then lower heat, and cook slowly until done clear through.

With deep-fat frying, use enough fat to float the pieces of fish. Grease should be kept below smoking point. Brown fish well, remove, and drain on paper towels or a grid of twigs. Season with pepper and salt.

BAKED FISH

This is a good way to break the monotony of fried fish. Panfish like perch, sunfish, bullheads, bluegills, and crappies are left whole. Small trout, bass, and big crappies are halved. Pike, pickerel, and walleyes can be filleted. Kingfish, salmon, swordfish, and whitefish may be cut crosswise in ½-inch steaks. Rub cleaned fish with salt, sprinkle with lemon juice or vinegar, and wrap each piece separately in wax paper or foil, if available (otherwise, omit this step). Lay on a rack in baking pan (use grid of small twigs in camp) to hold fish ½ inch from pan bottom. Add ⅜ inch of hot water, and bake 20 to 25 minutes in moderate heat. Prepare ¾ to 1 pound of fish per man.

BOILED FISH

"Boiled" is actually misleading because fish cooked in water should be gently simmered; if boiled, it loses flavor and becomes stringy.

Wrap fish in cheesecloth or in greased parchment paper. Start whole fish in cold water; fillets or pieces in water already boiling. To each quart of water used, add ½ teaspoon of salt and 1 tablespoon of vinegar or lemon juice. As soon as water boils, reduce heat so it merely simmers. Allow 8 to 10 minutes per pound of whole fish, or a total of 15 to 20 minutes for pieces depending upon their thickness. Serve with a white sauce containing chopped boiled eggs, or a sauce composed of equal parts of melted butter and lemon juice. Lean-meated fish like carp, pike, perch, pickerel, and lake trout boil better than the fatty kinds. Prepare ½ to ¾ pound of boiled fish per person.

BROILED FISH

Fish weighing ½ pound and less are broiled whole; larger ones should be split in half or in fillets. Clean fish, wash in cold water, wipe dry, and rub with melted butter. Lay on an oiled broiler grid. Fish less than 1 inch thick is turned once and cooks in 8 to 10 minutes; larger sections may need several turnings and 15 minutes of broiling time. Salt when taken off fire, and serve with tartar sauce or a mixture of melted butter and vinegar.

FISH CHOWDER

A famous down-East recipe. Fry out several slices of salt pork, and add one sliced onion. When onion is brown, lower heat, and add 4 raw potatoes sliced, 1 pound of fish sliced (any eatable kind) salt, and pepper. Cover with hot water, and cook 20 minutes.

Meantime soak a dozen soda crackers in 1 quart of milk, and add to fish when it has boiled 20 minutes. Bring the whole to a low boil; remove from heat and serve. Serves 3 or 4.

STRIPED BASS

Or use a large smallmouth or bigmouth bass or any other variety with solid, flaky flesh. Cut in pieces to fit your largest frying pan, or use a Dutch oven. Roll pieces in flour. Heat bacon fat in utensil; add fish and brown on both sides. Then add a large onion sliced with 2 cups of cubed potatoes. Put in 1 cup of hot water, cover with tight lid, and simmer ½ hour. Add water if it boils away. The gravy this makes is delicious.

BAKED CARP

This is usually the most tasty way to handle these rough fish. Clean, wash, and dry the fish. Remove as many large bones as possible without mangling the body, rub inside and out with salt, and stuff with this dressing:

1 cup breadcrumbs, dry	½ cup onion, chopped
½ cup butter	Salt and pepper
Little minced parsley	Hot water to moisten

Sew up opening in stuffed fish, brush outside with

lemon juice and then with butter, and sprinkle with pepper. Dredge with dry flour, and lay on a rack in baking pan. Pour in ½ cup of hot water and 2 tablespoons of cooking oil (or use butter), and bake 1 hour in moderate heat. Baste with liquid in pan bottom every 10 minutes.

Baked Clams

Seashore campers should not miss this treat. Build a fire 2 feet high with layers of sticks laid crosswise to each other. Mix 15 or 20 stones about 3 inches thick among the sticks. When wood has burned down, cover hot stones with a thick layer of damp seaweed, lay on the clams, and cover them with more seaweed. Steam littleneck clams 20 minutes; the hard-shell kind, 40 minutes. Serve with melted butter.

Fried Eels

To dress an eel, cut off its head, split skin lengthwise and peel it off, then open body and remove entrails. Cut in 2-inch sections, and parboil 15 minutes in water containing ¼ cup vinegar. Drain, dry the pieces, salt and pepper them, dip in beaten egg, and roll in dry crumbs or cornmeal. Fry until tender in hot fat. Serve with butter or catsup. Allow 1 pound per person.

Boiled Fish Dinner

Try this recipe on the larger, coarser kinds of fresh-caught or home-frozen fish.

2 pounds fish cut in small pieces	1 cup sliced carrots
¼ cup bacon fat	1 cup diced celery
½ cup onion, chopped	¼ cup vinegar
	Salt and pepper

Brown fish in bacon fat on bottom of kettle; then add

vegetables and 3 cups hot water. Season to taste, and simmer slowly until vegetables are tender. Serves 3, perhaps 4.

Baked Fish and Chips

Crumble enough potato chips to make 2 cups crumbs. In a saucepan put 1 cup of mushroom soup (condensed), 1 cup of milk, 2 cups of flaked canned or cooked fish, and salt and pepper to taste. When mixture starts to boil, add a small lump of butter, and pour in a greased baking pan. Cover with potato chip crumbs, and bake in moderate heat 15 minutes. Serves 3 or 4.

Fried Frog Legs

You do not need the large commercially grown frogs for this recipe; legs of any size of frog, even small ones, serve nicely. Skin the legs, moisten them with lemon juice, sprinkle with salt and pepper, roll in bread or cracker crumbs, and drop in deep hot fat. About 4 minutes cooks small legs; up to 6 minutes may be required for large ones.

Mussels

Cook only selected mussels with tightly closed shells taken from unpolluted water. Scrub them very clean. Shells can be steamed open in a large kettle containing about ½ inch of water. Cover kettle, and heat 15 minutes, or until shells open. Or insert a sharp knife between shell halves, and sever the muscle holding them together. When shell opens out flat, cut out the meat and dip it in beaten egg, then in breadcrumbs or cornmeal. Fry in deep hot fat until well browned and tender. Serve with chili sauce, horseradish, or a mixture of both. Prepare 6 to 8 mussels for each camper. The medium sizes taste better than very big ones.

STEAMED OYSTERS

Campers may in some regions be able to gather the small oysters, which often have a better flavor than the bigger, commercially procured kind. Wash and scrub clean about half a bushel. Put in a deep tub or pail, pour in half a gallon of hot water, and set over heat. Lay an old towel over top of container, and wet this well to hold in the steam. Boil vigorously for 15 minutes, or until the oysters open easily. Remove from shells, usually at the table as you eat them. Serve with your favorite hot sauce.

SPICED SMELT

Here is a different way to prepare these small fish, of which truly enormous quantities are taken during their yearly runs. Soak 3 pounds of cleaned smelt in salted water for 2 hours. Wipe dry, roll in beaten egg, then in cracker crumbs, and fry in hot fat. When brown, lay fish in a deep dish and cover with:

4 slices onion	1 bay leaf
6 slices lemon	½ teaspoon dry mustard
Several whole allspice	
1 tablespoon salad oil	

Now brown ½ cup of butter in a skillet; add 1 cup of boiling water, 1 cup of beef stock (use bouillon cubes and water if more convenient), juice of 1 lemon, and a dash of red pepper. Pour this sauce over the fish, and let stand 24 hours. Serve cold as appetizers. Enough for 5 or 6.

BAKED RAINBOW TROUT

This is also good for smallmouth bass and walleyes. Clean about 3 pounds of fish, cutting off heads, tails, and fins. Dust inside and out with salt and pepper, and lay in a greased baking dish. Slice 2 lemons and 3 medium-sized onions very thin; put half the slices inside the fish, and cover them with the remainder. Dot with ¼ cup of butter or bacon fat, and bake in a moderate oven until flesh separates easily from bones, about 35 minutes. Serves 4 or 5.

TROUT WITH MUSHROOMS

8 brook trout
1 small onion, sliced
½ cup canned mush-
    rooms
½ cup boiling water

¼ cup butter
¼ cup flour
2 cups milk
1 teaspoon salt

¼ teaspoon each pepper and paprika

Clean trout, remove heads, and lay in greased pan. Drop onion and mushrooms in small pot containing the water, and boil 3 minutes. Add butter and flour, stirring steadily. Then put in milk and seasonings. When this sauce has thickened, pour it over the trout, and bake 30 minutes in a medium, 350°F. oven. Serves 4.

BAKED TURTLE

Sever junctions of the shells, remove meat, and discard all yellow fat. Cut in serving-sized pieces, and soak several hours in water containing a little salt and vinegar. Wash in clear water; drain and dip each piece in lemon juice, then in beaten egg. Salt and pepper the pieces, and roll them in a mixture of flour and cornmeal. Put in hot fat, and brown well on all sides. Then add ½ cup hot water, cover utensil (a Dutch oven is good), and cook slowly until meat is tender. Add a little more water at intervals if needed. Allow about ½ pound of turtle meat per person.

CRABS

Soft-shell crabs (usually same species as hard shell only caught in moulting season when old shell has been discarded and the new one is still soft) can be broiled or fried. Kill by dropping in boiling water or by thrusting a knife between the eyes. Open shells and remove waste material between body and shells at sides, remove tail, and clean off sand. Wipe dry, season with salt, pepper and butter, also lemon juice if available, and broil about 10 minutes, 5 minutes for each side.

To fry, dip cleaned, seasoned crabs in flour or corn meal or in beaten egg and crumbs until well coated, then fry in hot fat until browned.

Hard-shell crabs may be cooked in boiling water until they turn red, about 20 minutes. Cool and clean out the white meat. This can be mixed with a white sauce, with tartar sauce or with cream of mushroom soup, then put back in crab shells and baked 20 minutes or until tender and brown.

Game Animal

BEAR STEAK

Try this recipe for bear steaks that have been well ripened. Steaks should be cut about 1 inch thick. Into each pound of meat, hammer a mixture of $\frac{1}{2}$ cup of dry flour, $\frac{1}{4}$ teaspoon of ground ginger, 1 teaspoon of salt, and $\frac{1}{4}$ teaspoon of pepper. Get $\frac{1}{2}$ cup of fat very hot in skillet, and sear meat on both sides. Lower heat, cover pan, and cook 15 minutes more. If steak is still tough, cook longer, adding a little hot water to prevent its burning. Each pound serves 2.

WILD BOAR CHOPS

Only a few campers are fortunate enough to enjoy this delicious game meat; the rest must be content with domestic pork chops. But if you should bag a wild boar, serve it this way.

Salt and pepper 4 chops, sprinkle with flour, and brown well on both sides in 3 tablespoons of hot fat. Core (but do not peel) 2 pounds of apples, and cut in thick slices. Put a dash of paprika and 6 raisins on top of each browned chop. Then cover with the apple slices, 2 tablespoons of brown sugar, and ¼ cup of hot water. Cover skillet, and simmer until well done, about 40 minutes. Cook 1 large or 2 small chops per person.

CORNED BIG GAME MEAT

This old-time recipe makes big game meat tender and tasty. To cure a 5-pound chunk of meat, mix:

5 tablespoons brown sugar	6 tablespoons salt
	1 teaspoon saltpeter

Trim all fat off meat, mix ingredients with enough water to cover the meat, pour over the meat, and let cure 2 days. Then wash, and boil in fresh water until tender. Very good cooked with cabbage.

SMALL GAME FRICASSEE

Young woodchucks, squirrels, and rabbits are delicious cooked this way (woodchucks should first be parboiled 30 minutes) . First fry 6 slices of bacon until grease is extracted. Use about 4 pounds of dressed game for 3 or 4 people. Cut meat in serving pieces, season them with salt and pepper and lay in hot grease. Sprinkle meat with 1 teaspoon of dried onion and 1 tablespoon of dry flour mixed together. When bottom side is browned, turn and dredge with another tablespoon of flour. Then add 1 cup of hot water, cover skillet, and simmer until tender.

BIG GAME MEAT CAKES

This is a good way to prepare the tougher cuts of deer, elk, antelope, moose, and bear, which the freezing plant or processer usually grinds for hunters. To each pound of ground lean meat, add 1 teaspoon of salt, ½ teaspoon of pepper, ¼ cup of catsup, and ¼ cup of chopped onion. Mix well, shape in small flat cakes, and cook in hot greased skillet, usually about 4 minutes on each side. One pound of lean meat will serve 2.

GAME MEAT HASH

4 cups cooked lean meat	½ cup fat
1 minced onion	4 cups raw diced potatoes

Cut meat in small pieces (grind in a food chopper if one is available), and brown with onion in hot fat. Add potatoes, and cook about 25 minutes longer. Turn frequently with pancake turner so brown bottom crust is mixed through the rest. A cup of leftover gravy or canned vegetable juice can be added to advantage. Season with salt and pepper as the hash is turned. Serves 4.

FRIED GAME HEARTS

Hearts of big game are a real treat prepared like this. Clean blood clots from inside, and slice off top of heart to remove fat and blood vessels. Soak in cold salted water (1 teaspoon of salt to 1 quart of water) for 1 hour. Parboil hearts 30 minutes. Then cut in ½-inch cubes, season with salt and pepper, and fry in hot grease 15 or 20 minutes, or until tender. Cook ½ pound of cleaned hearts per person.

Ground Meat Loaf

2 pounds ground lean meat	2 teaspoons salt
1 can condensed vegetable soup	1 chopped onion
1 cup soft bread-crumbs	1 egg, lightly beaten
	¼ cup evaporated milk
	½ teaspoon pepper

2 tablespoons horseradish

Mix ingredients thoroughly, and pack in greased pan. Bake 1½ hours in medium oven. Serves 4 or 5.

Hunter Mulligan

Use about 4 pounds of the shank of any big game animal. Be sure bone is well cracked. Cover with cold water, and simmer with 4 teaspoons of salt and 1 teaspoon of pepper until tender. Then add 1 can of tomatoes, 1 can of peas, 3 slices of bacon, 4 medium-sized peeled potatoes, and 3 medium-sized onions. Potatoes and onions are quartered. Add more water if necessary, and cook slowly until raw vegetables are done. If mulligan is thin, thicken with a little flour and cold water made into a paste, and cook for a few minutes longer. Serves 5 or 6.

Baked Muskrat

Use only hams and shoulders. When skinning animal, take care not to cut into the musk glands on lower belly. Also remove white stringy tissue from inside of each leg. Parboil with 1 sliced onion 30 minutes. Drain, flour the pieces, and put in baking dish. Season with salt and pepper, and cover with 8 slices of bacon. Put ¼ cup vinegar and ¼ cup water in pan, and roast until tender. Baste frequently with liquor forming in pan. One muskrat serves 3 or 4.

Fried Rabbit

Adult rabbits should be parboiled, since their flesh is often tough and strong tasting. Clean animal, cut legs off close to body, and halve back section. Soak meat in cold water containing a little salt for 2 hours. Then put in a pot of cold water, bring to a boil, and simmer 30 minutes. Pour off water and add new water, hot this time, along with a sliced onion and 1 teaspoon of pepper. Cook slowly until meat is tender. Remove from water, drain, season with salt, roll in flour, and brown in hot grease. One rabbit usually serves 4.

Rabbit Pie

Cut a rabbit in serving-size pieces and stew in a covered pan with a sliced onion, 3 bay leaves, and 2 teaspoons of salt. Use just enough water to cover. When meat is tender, remove and take out the bones. With flour, thicken liquid left in pan. Replace the boned meat, and add pepper and Worcestershire sauce. Cover meat with ½-inch layer of cooked mashed potatoes, and bake in a hot oven 20 minutes, or until potato crust is browned. Serves 4.

Smothered Rabbit

This is also a good way to cook squirrel. Use a Dutch oven or a heavy metal skillet with a lid. Cut dressed rabbit into serving pieces, season with salt and pepper, and roll in flour. Heat ¼ cup of bacon fat in the casserole or skillet, add meat, and brown on both sides. Then cover meat with a thick layer of sliced onions; add 1 teaspoon of salt and 1 cup of sour cream. Put lid on pan, and simmer about 1½ hours, or until meat is tender.

Roast Raccoon

Coon meat is best in those months—late October through December—when the pelt is prime. Skin, dress, and remove kernel-like glands on inside of fore and hind legs. Leave carcass whole, and parboil until tender in water containing 1 tablespoon of black or red pepper. Drain. Lay in baking pan, sprinkle with flour, salt, and pepper, and roast until browned, turning carcass top and bottom for even cooking. Parboil an old coon in two waters instead of one. It helps the taste also to cut away and discard as much fat as possible when the animal is dressed.

Open-Fire Roast

Squirrels, raccoon, woodchuck, and game birds can be roasted whole this way, as can a shoulder or a ham of deer or antelope. Build a wood fire before a low wall of logs or stones, so heat is reflected forward. Suspend meat with a stout cord (or wire) from a tripod of poles or a single slanting stick so it hangs about 18 inches in front of and level with the center of the fire. Keep the cord wet so it will not burn. Set a pan below to catch drippings, which are used to baste the roast periodically. Spin meat occasionally so the cord twists up and then unwinds, turning the food for even cooking. Baste to prevent a hard crust from forming on the outside. Cooking time varies with size of cut—2 to 3½ hours. Salt and pepper meat a few minutes before serving it, and thicken the drippings with flour for gravy.

Squirrel Pie

Cut 2 squirrels in 5 pieces each—quarters and back. If old and tough, parboil for 20 minutes. If young, parboiling can be omitted. Brown the pieces in hot fat, preferably bacon or salt pork, and lay in a baking dish lined with dough made from ready-mixed biscuit flour. Slice and add 2 carrots, 2 onions, 2 potatoes, and, if available, 1 green pepper.

Brown ¼ cup of flour in the fat left in skillet, add enough water to make a thin gravy, and pour over meat and vegetables. Season with salt and pepper, 3 tablespoons of lemon juice or vinegar, and several chunks of butter. Cover with a top crust, and bake 1½ hours in medium, 350°F. oven. Serves 4.

SQUIRREL STEW

2 dressed squirrels	2 raw onions
3 quarts cold water	2 teaspoons salt
3 raw potatoes	½ teaspoon pepper

Cut squirrels in small pieces, put in a kettle with cold water, and bring to a low boil. Simmer until meat is almost tender. Add vegetables and seasonings, and continue to cook until you can stir up bones with no meat on them. Then the stew is done. A full meal for 2.

DUTCH-OVEN ROAST

Try this method with the rump or the flank of any big game animal. A heavy metal kettle with a lid will substitute for the oven if necessary.

2 pounds lean meat	1 onion
¼ cup fat	2 carrots
2 potatoes	Salt and pepper

Dust meat with flour, and brown in the hot fat. Cover and cook slowly 30 minutes. Slice vegetables and lay on top of meat; add seasonings. Cook slowly 2½ hours, or until meat is tender. Add a little hot water occasionally to prevent sticking. Serves 2 or 3.

Quick Game Steaks

Since it can be quickly prepared, this food is fine in camps where hunters may appear for meals at different hours. With a sharp knife, shave lean deer, elk, or moose meat in very thin slices. Heat butter or bacon fat ⅜ inch deep in skillet. When hot, drop in a few slices of meat (they should be nearly paper thin), and cook 15 seconds. Turn and cook another 15 seconds. Then remove to a plate, sprinkle with salt and pepper, and eat between slices of bread dipped briefly in the hot skillet fat. Prepare at least ½ pound of meat for each person.

Braised Venison

Use steaks cut ¾ to 1 inch thick. Pound flour into both sides with head of camp ax, and put in skillet or Dutch oven containing a small amount of hot fat. When one side is brown, season with salt and pepper, and turn. Brown the other side, season again, add ½ cup of water or tomato juice, cover tight, and simmer slowly until meat almost falls apart when pierced with a fork. This will take 2 to 2½ hours, and more water may have to be added at intervals to prevent burning.

Venison Stew

Use the least tender cuts—shoulder, brisket, or flank. Put 4 pounds of meat in a jar, and cover with equal parts of water and vinegar. Add 3 sliced onions and 6 bay leaves, and let stand in a cold place 2 days. Remove meat, wash in cold water, put in kettle, cover with cold water, add 4 teaspoons of salt and 1 teaspoon of pepper, and cook slowly until meat is tender. Thicken liquor in kettle with flour, and pour some of this gravy over venison when it is served. Or you can make a regular stew by adding potatoes, onions, and carrots 1 hour before meat will be done.

Pot Roast Woodchuck

Summer campers should not miss an opportunity to procure half-grown woodchucks. They should be "eating" size by early July and are delicious prepared this way.

Dress the chuck, cut in serving-size pieces, and soak 2 hours in cold salted water. Season with salt and pepper, and roll in dry flour. Put ½ cup of bacon fat in skillet or kettle; when hot, add meat, and brown on all sides. Then pour in 1 cup of boiling water, cover with lid, and cook slowly about 4 hours. This long, slow cooking makes tender meat without a strong or gamy flavor. Add more water at intervals if needed to prevent burning. Remove meat, and make gravy by thickening liquid in pot with flour.

If you cook an adult woodchuck, parboil it 45 minutes before the pieces are browned and reduce roasting time by 1 hour.

Game Birds

Coots

Much strong flavor can be eliminated if you save and eat only the legs, breast, and gizzard of these birds. Skin them; do not just pluck their feathers. Soak the dressed meat overnight in water containing a little vinegar and salt. Then wipe dry, season with salt and pepper, and brown in hot fat. When brown, add—for every pair of coots—a little water, a few slices of onion, the juice of ½ lemon, and a bay leaf. Simmer until tender. Hungry hunters usually eat a couple of coots apiece.

SMOTHERED CROW

Sportsmen learn yearly that, besides being a canny and an elusive target, crows are good to eat. Young birds are best; older ones may be tough and strong. So after dressing your kill, sort as to age and size. After they are cut in half, old crows should be soaked 4 hours in water containing a little vinegar and salt. Young birds do not need this soaking.

In a heavy skillet, brown a clove of garlic in ¼ inch of bacon fat. Remove garlic, and add the meat, which has been dusted with flour and seasoned with salt and pepper. Brown on both sides, turn fire low, cover skillet, and from time to time put in a little hot water. Cook very slowly until tender. Season with Worcestershire sauce and serve. Allow 1 crow per man.

GAME BIRD CASSEROLE

This could be the best of all methods of preparing game birds as well as domestic chickens. It is so easy that the rankest amateur cook would have to try extra hard to spoil it. Clean 3 or 4 pheasants, 5 or 6 grouse, quail, doves, or pigeons, or 2 half-grown chickens. Dismember, season with salt and pepper, and roll in flour. Brown pieces slowly in hot fat, and pack in a casserole or a Dutch oven; even a plain pot with a lid will do. Now put 1 can each of condensed cream of chicken and cream of mushroom soup in the skillet where meat was browned, add 1 soup can of hot water, and stir over heat until blended. Pour this over the meat, and bake slowly until tender— 1¾ to 2½ hours. The gravy forms automatically— and, man, is it good! This can be cooked on top of the stove if you lack an oven. Serves 4 to 6.

Sauerkraut-Stuffed Roast Duck

Prepare ducks the preceding day. Dress and soak 2 hours in cold water containing 1 cup vinegar. Then drain, wipe dry, sprinkle inside and out with salt and pepper, and set in a cold place until next day. To make stuffing for 3 average-size ducks, cook 1 quart of sauerkraut (either raw or canned) with 2 chopped apples, 1 chopped onion, and a 1-pound piece of pork spareribs. Cook until sparerib bones are loose and can be removed. Then put stuffing in the ducks, and lay a strip of bacon or salt pork over each bird. Brown in a hot, 400°F. oven for 20 minutes. If you suspect ducks have a fishy flavor, take them from the pan, and pour off and discard the accumulated grease Rinse pan with boiling water, replace ducks, and roast at 350°F. until tender. As much of a duck's strong flavor lies in its fat, discarding some at the start greatly improves the taste. About 2 hours total roasting time may be required. But do not overcook, or the duck meat may be dry.

Broiled Duck

Try this recipe with some of the wild fowl you have in the freezer. Young mallard are preferred. Split dressed ducks down the back, and open out flat. Rub with salt and pepper and with butter or bacon fat. Broil under a moderate heat, about 350°F. Turn once. Avoid overcooking. Serve with a sauce made of equal parts of melted butter and lemon juice or dry wine. One pound of wild duck is considered a serving portion.

Grouse Stew

A good way to cook old, tough birds. Clean and cut in fairly small pieces. Put in a kettle with enough water—containing a little salt and vinegar—to cover, and bring to a boil. Simmer 20 minutes; pour off water and add fresh. When meat is cooked enough to separate from bones, pick out the bones, and add 3 potatoes and 2 onions, all sliced fine. Cook until vegetables are done, season with salt and pepper, thicken with a little flour, and serve. Serves 2 or 3.

POT ROAST PHEASANT

Cut birds in pieces as you do chickens. Parboil an old cock 30 minutes with a little salt and vinegar in the water. Omit this step for a young cock or a hen. Season meat with salt and pepper, roll in flour, and brown in hot fat. When well browned, add 1 cup of sour cream and ½ cup of water. Cover and cook slowly until tender, about 1½ hours. Turn pieces occasionally, and add more water in small amounts if required. Dish up the meat, and thicken liquid in skillet for gravy. One pheasant serves 2 or 3.

DUTCH-OVEN QUAIL

Melt ½ cup of butter in oven, and put in 4 whole dressed quail. Brown birds on all sides. Add 1 sliced onion and enough water to cover quail. Simmer over low fire until meat is tender, about 1 to 1½ hours. Add water if required; otherwise, let the liquid cook down until it is only 1 inch deep. Remove quail. Add flour to liquid, and cook until thick and smooth; then add ½ cup of sour cream and ½ teaspoon of Worcestershire sauce. Pour some of this gravy over the quail; use the rest on potatoes, preferably baked. Allow 1 quail per person.

QUAIL ON TOAST

This is a traditional dish wherever these delicious game birds are hunted. Allow 1 quail per person.

Dress and cut in half by splitting down backbone and breast. Dust with salt and pepper, dredge with dry flour, and brown in hot cooking fat or butter. Add ½ cup of boiling water, cover skillet, and simmer until tender, 30 to 40 minutes. Now pour in 1 cup of sweet cream, and stir until slightly thick. Serve immediately on lightly buttered toast, and spoon a little gravy over each quail half.

Roast Wild Turkey

This is the only way you should even consider preparing this great American fowl which Ben Franklin once nominated our national bird. Dress turkey, season with salt and pepper inside and out, and weigh to determine cooking time—about 20 minutes per pound. Make a stuffing of:

1 chopped onion	¼ teaspoon pepper
1 pound pork sausage	2 teaspoons salt
1½ quarts soft breadcrumbs	3 tablespoons chopped parsley

Cook onion with sausage in skillet 5 minutes; then add other ingredients. Moisten with a little hot water if too dry. Put stuffed turkey breast down in uncovered pan, and roast for half the total required time. Then turn bird breast up; lay strips of bacon over breast, or cover with a piece of cloth dipped in fat. Finish roasting. If a cloth was used, remove it toward the last if a deeper brown is desired. Hen turkeys usually need 3½ to 4 hours; big toms, 4 to 4½ hours. Test by pushing sharp-tined fork into a thigh and the thick part of the breast. If fork enters easily and if the juice that runs out has no red tinge, the fowl is ready to serve.

26 - How to Use a Compass

Campers who confine their explorations to well-populated state and national parks will seldom, if ever, have occasion to use a compass. But for those adventurous outdoorsmen who want to hike beyond the limits of posted trails and paved roads and experience the thrill of wilderness discovery, a compass is a vital piece of equipment. Without one, camping in the undeveloped regions of the United States or Canada would be a foolhardy undertaking.

A compass doesn't automatically guide you to your distant camp or other destination. All it does is point toward the north. But with that essential information a man who knows how to use a compass can find his way across the most trackless and rugged country. With a good map of the area he can locate his position, find his way to any point he chooses, and return safely to his campsite.

TYPES OF COMPASSES

There are two basic types of compasses suitable for the outdoorsman—the needle compass and the revolving dial compass. Either one will serve as a satisfactory guide in the wilderness.

The Needle Compass

A needle, or stationary dial, compass consists of a case which houses a needle magnetized at one end mounted on a pivot so it can swing freely. The surface beneath the needle has a dial marked with the directions north, east, south, and west; it is also marked in degrees, 1 through 360. North is at 360 degrees, east at 90, south at 180, and west at 270. To obtain precise directions, the compass is read by these degrees; thus any direction—N, E, S, W, or any point in between—can be expressed by a degree. This number is called an azimuth.

To orient yourself with a needle compass, turn it until north on the dial lines up with the magnetized end of the needle (usually marked). Be sure that you are standing away from metallic objects that may tend to attract the needle. That is all there is to it. Now you know where north is, and accordingly the other directions.

Needle Compass

Once you have oriented your compass with your position, you can take an azimuth on a landmark. Do this by sighting over the top of the compass at a prominent tree or rock formation and noting the degree number your line of sight crosses.

Cruiser Compass

The Cruiser Compass.   A variation of the needle compass is the cruiser compass, which has an inner and an outer dial. The innermost dial is marked in directions, north, east, south, and west. To determine north you merely proceed as described above. Taking an azimuth on a landmark, however, requires a slightly different procedure. The outer dial on the cruiser compass is marked in directions and degrees, but the east and west markings are reversed, as are the degree markings. This is for a definite purpose. The cover is inscribed with a white line, which is used as a direction pointer. Point the line at the landmark on which you wish to take an azimuth. The needle will, of course, point north. But because the degree scale has been transposed, reading the degree number at the point the needle comes to rest gives you the correct azimuth of your line of sight.

To travel in a particular direction—east, for example—just turn yourself and the compass until east on the outer dial lines up with the needle. Then walk in the direction the white line is pointing.

Revolving Dial Compass

This compass has the degrees and direction markings printed on a dial which revolves freely on a pivot. The edge of the dial that is marked with an arrow is magnetized and acts like a needle; it always points north. A sighting device, similar to a gunsight, allows you to aim the compass at a landmark. Give the

Revolving Dial Compass

jiggling dial time to settle and read your compass bearing in degrees at the point the floating dial lines up with your sighting line.

For a quicker, more general reading, glance at the big letters on the dial. If the E on the dial is generally in line with the sighting slot as you aim at your landmark, the landmark is east of where you stand. This gives you a rough but quick estimate of your position.

Either compass—the needle or the floating dial—should have a sturdy case with a lid that snaps shut to keep the compass reasonably clean and dry. Brass or aluminum cases will take more knocks than most of the plastic ones, some of which chip and crack easily. Be sure the north end of the needle or the north edge of the floating dial is plainly marked with a big N or an arrow. Without that clear marking, all you have is a needle that lines up in a general north-south direction, and you want to know positively which is which. For that reason luminous markings, easy to see at night, are a big help. A sighting slot of the type shown on the floating dial compass makes readings more precise. Most of the better compasses have a device that locks the needle when the case is closed, thus saving continuous wear on the pivot post as the needle jiggles in travel. A ring on the compass case makes it easy to anchor the instrument to your belt or trouser loop, decreasing the chances of losing it.

Good compasses of the simple type outdoorsmen need are relatively inexpensive. A fine one can be bought for $5.00. Some of the tiny models sold for mounting in gunstocks and such work well enough, but most of them are too cheap in price and casual of craftsmanship to inspire confidence. That matter of confidence is vital. A faulty compass is a quick route to trouble in wild country.

MAGNETIC DECLINATION

The compass needle *does not* consistently point to true north, or the true north pole. This statement may come as a surprise to some readers, but an understanding of the vagaries of the compass in different areas is important to accurate and intelligent use of the instrument.

A magnetic field runs through the earth, with the

north magnetic pole located in the Arctic north of Hudson Bay and the other pole in the sea near Antarctica. Actually, the compass needle does not really point; it parallels that magnetic field in whatever area you happen to be. Due to variations in terrain, this field is not constant in its direction; hence

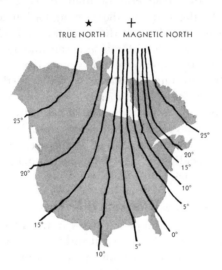

the deviation of the compass in different parts of the country. The accompanying map shows the variations in degrees east and west of true north that a compass needle takes in various areas of North America. If you were taking a reading in Oregon, your compass needle would point about 20 degrees east of true north. In Maine the needle would point about 20 degrees west of true north.

In using a map, then, it is important to take the magnetic declination of the area into consideration. Most Geodetic Survey maps have lines of magnetic declination running across the surface. Other maps list the magnetic declination for the area at the bottom.

ORIENTING MAP AND COMPASS

Supposing that you have a Geodetic Survey map similar to Fig. 1, orienting a map and a compass to compensate for magnetic declination is extremely simple. Lay the map on the ground, or on a level stump or rock, and place the compass on it. If you know your exact whereabouts and can find it on the map, place the compass on this point. Now line up north and south on the compass with the north-south grid lines on the map. Turn the map and compass until the needle parallels the line of magnetic declination, which in Fig. 2 is 17 degrees west. Your map and compass are then oriented to the area. You can now take a reading on any point on the map and by following it reach your objective.

STRAIGHT-LINE COMPASS TRAVEL

Suppose you are camped at Percy in the area shown on the map in Fig. 1. You want to hike to peak 2710. Place the compass directly on Percy, and draw a line from the center of it to peak 2710 (Fig. 2). Note that the line passes through 290 degrees NW.

Looking out over the terrain in the direction of peak 2710, you find that you can see it faintly in the distance. But you observe that your route will take you through heavily wooded areas, into valleys, and behind cliffs, during which time the peak will be obscured from sight. Or it may get dark before you get there. Taking a sight on the peak (Fig. 3), you observe that a tall tree stands directly on your course. Hike to that tree. You now find that, although you can't see the peak, the cliff in the distance is on your

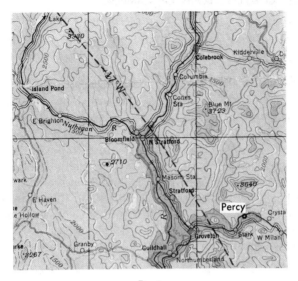

Fig. 1

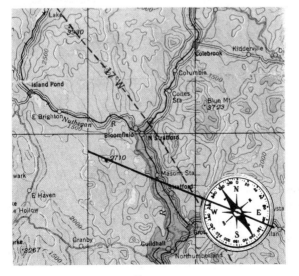

Fig. 2

course of 290 degrees. Head for the cliff. Thus, leap-frogging from landmark to landmark on your 290 degree azimuth, you eventually reach your objective.

TRIANGULATING YOUR POSITION

Perhaps before starting out you take another look at your map and consider that there may be some interesting country to explore east of peak 2710. Before you decide to explore that area, you can take precautions that will help you to return to your camp at Percy.

Locate another prominent landmark on the terrain; in Fig. 4 we have chosen Blue Mountain. Now draw a line on your map from your compass center to Blue Mountain. Your reading is 335 degrees. You now have taken a reading on peak 2710 and on Blue Mountain;

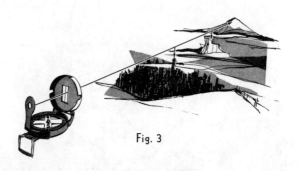

Fig. 3

where the two lines cross is your camp at Percy. As long as you can see one of those two landmarks, you can correct your direction by getting back on one of your azimuths. If you can see both landmarks, you can take a reading on each of them. Two lines drawn on the map through the two points in accordance with these readings will intersect at your present position. Checking your position on the map in relation to your camp should make your return relatively easy.

DELIBERATE COMPASS ERROR

It is advisable in certain situations to make a deliberate error in taking a compass bearing for a return

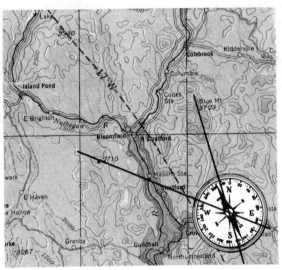

Fig. 4

trip to a base camp. For instance, suppose you are camped near a stream (Fig. 5) and have hiked away from camp through heavy timber (dotted line). You have taken an azimuth on your way and know the direction of your route. But if you try to follow that azimuth on the way back, you will probably deviate slightly from your exact course and emerge from the woods either above or below your campsite. How will you know which way to walk to reach it? You won't.

By making a deliberate compass error either above or below your camp (solid arrows), you will know, when you reach the stream, the direction you have to travel to find your camp.

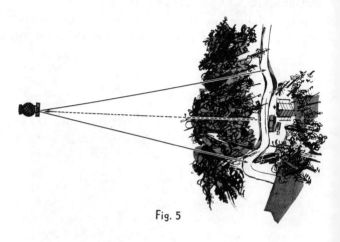

Fig. 5

27 - Plan to Get Lost
—Wilderness Survival

A WELL-KNOWN STORY QUOTES THE GREAT woodsman Daniel Boone as saying, "I was never lost in the woods in my life, but once I was mighty confused for three days."

Anyone who spends a lot of time in the back country of the world will have similar periods of "confusion." There is no truth in the notion that some people have a built-in sense of direction. The woodsmen who seem to get where they are going by instinct are in fact guided by such things as wind direction, the position of the sun or stars, the slope and drainage of the land—by a dozen natural clues the outsider would not notice. A born woodsman traveling in his home country keeps track of such things automatically. He may believe that he "just knows" the right direction to take, but he actually has developed to a high degree the habit of careful observation.

Army tests have shown that on a cloudy, windless day both the Indian guide and the city boy will walk in large circles when blindfolded and told to walk a straight course on an open plain. (Wind and sun are both direction signals.) Some men tested circled to the left, some to the right, but they all circled. These tests merely confirm what every well-traveled outdoorsman already knows—that no man can steer a sure course through strange country without relying on navigation aids. The plainsman will get lost in Maine's heavily wooded flatlands. The trapper who ranges Canadian wilds without a compass will only know two directions—up and down—in New York City on an overcast day.

So anyone can get lost. The camper who accepts that fact of outdoor life has taken a giant stride toward avoiding an unpleasant or a tragic period of "confusion" in the woods. Knowing that it can happen to him, he will take steps to avoid it. If he gets lost despite his precautions, he will have a sound and rehearsed recovery plan. Panic is the main killer of lost campers and hunters.

PLAN ON GETTING LOST

There is a great square of prime mule deer country in the Ochoco National Forest of central Oregon where local woodsmen hunt each year knowing that they will probably be lost for a few hours every day. They drive trucks or jeeps over a dim woods road that dead-ends in the center of this vast tract of jackpine thickets and tiny sagebrush clearings. Parking at the end of the road before daylight, the deer hunters fan out into the forest. There are no notable landmarks on this flat Oregon summit, and distant peaks are seldom helpful as guideposts; they can not be seen before daylight, in stormy weather, or from dense timber growing on a gently rippling flatland. Clouds often hide the sun. The wind, though usually blowing west to east, is unreliable as a direction finder. A compass would be sure in expert hands, but a hunter circling and dodging after deer would need a team of surveyors to keep precise track of his compass course.

So the competent woodsmen who hunt that Oregon highland take it for granted that they will be lost by the time they make a kill or quit for the day. But because they expect that, they know how to get out efficiently. They know that five or six miles of straight-line walking in any direction will bring them out on the signposted road that circles the sprawling thickets on the plateau. Straight-line walking is fairly easy, even in a driving snowstorm, if you locate *two* landmarks in line ahead of you, walk almost to the first one, then pick a third in line with the first two. Keep this up from landmark to landmark in a straight line until you reach your destination. In starting, do not assume that the spot where you are standing is one landmark; keep two in line in front of you and pick the third one before you actually reach the first.

A compass provides a quicker and more precise way out of that Oregon thicket; it gives you the extra advantage of being able to head for the north, south, east, or west stretch of the road and of knowing which side you are on when you arrive. Once on the road that runs along the hunting area, the hunter either waits to hitch a ride or hikes calmly along the road until he finds a signpost directing him to the dead-end road in the center of the hunting area. Knowing that it will take time to assemble the party at the end of the day, the hunters carry what they need to be comfortable for a long day—lunch, a couple of nut-rich candy bars, fruit juice or water, plenty of matches and tobacco, a rain jacket or an extra sweater, rope, knife, and perhaps a tiny block-and-tackle rig to hang a deer without help. Since many of these hunters also take a camera, field glasses, and extra ammunition, they carry all their gear in a light back pack, which leaves their hands free, their pockets and belt uncluttered. It is a pleasure to be "lost" for a few hours in this way. You have bet on yourself in a friendly contest with woods and weather, and in the end you feel pretty smug about the planning and prowess that have won the game.

Map Study

Knowing the general lay of the land in advance is the key to getting lost safely on that Oregan plateau. Men who hunt there regularly know the pattern of surrounding roads and landmarks from maps and personal observation. Any camper heading into strange country can gain the same advantage by going over a map of the region before he gets there. Fix the main features of the region in your mind. Are there tall peaks you can identify? Is there a major stream, and what would it lead to if you followed it? What roads or trails would you encounter if you headed straight north, south, west, east? Are there swamps or cliffs that would involve major detours? Do any of the major peaks have lookout towers on them? The camper can learn all this and much more by a few minutes' study of a good topographical map of the area he plans to visit. (See the chapter on maps for more information on maps and how to obtain them.) With a compass and a good detail map, an experienced woodsman can tour strange country as confidently as if it were his backyard. If you *do not* have a map (some campers persist in the silly notion that basic map reading is too complicated to bother with), at least ask someone at your jumping-off point about the general layout of the region you are going to enter. Lots of extremely helpful directions can be gained from watching a local resident scratch a crude map in the dirt while advising you that, "Mile north of the flat that's burned over—black burn from last fall, it is—you'll come to a rapids where you better pull out your canoe and carry around." There are lots of old-timers who draw and talk more than they know, of course, but it certainly pays to listen when you have no reliable maps of your own.

Get-Lost Kit

An outdoorsman in back country he does not know exceedingly well should carry a basic kit of get-lost items as a matter of routine. And he should carry it on jaunts that start out to be short ones, too, for as often as not it is the deer hunter spending the day in camp who wounds a buck in the clearing behind the tent and excitedly trails it until by nightfall he is hopelessly lost. This is also the man who does not come back because he is wearing camp slippers and has no gloves or coat, no compass, food, or matches. He will not last long in cold weather.

The best kit for the camper who sensibly plans on getting lost in remote country is a light back pack. It should have such items as follows, depending on the weather and type of country: waterproof matches; candle; 100 feet of strong fishing line or copper wire or both; map; compass; signal mirror; police whistle; such first-aid essentials as antiseptic and bandage material; small store of emergency food—candy bars, sardines, packets of dehydrated food, salt, teabags, cocoa; light shelter sheet 8 feet square (a plastic sheet weighing a few ounces and costing less than a dollar will do fine); a canteen cup or other metal cup large enough to boil water in; light hatchet of top quality; wool sweater, lightweight rain parka or poncho, and spare pair of socks. In hot desert country, spare clothing for wet or cold regions would be replaced by a canteen holding at least a quart of *reserve* water. If the outdoorsman is a hunter, a few spare rounds of ammunition to fit his weapon will be worth their weight in the get-lost kit. Include a few fishing hooks and flies, which amount to nothing in weight and bulk. A man who is miserable without tobacco should include a reserve supply; he will want it badly if he has to use his get-lost kit. Add or subtract from this list to suit yourself and your specific needs. Many items, such as binoculars, have routine uses that would justify their weight and bulk in the light pack you need for wilderness survival.

Marking Outgoing Trail

In addition to map study, the camper heading into territory where there is tall and uncut timber can do a great deal to avoid getting lost by marking and observing his route. You are courting trouble if you blithely forge ahead as fast as you can travel. Pause from time to time to turn around and see what the landmarks *behind* you look like; they are the ones you will see when you try to retrace your route. Make mental notes of how many streams or ridges you cross. If you are on a trail, mark the proper return route each time you come to a fork. An arrow dug in the dirt with your heel will show plainly for days. If you need a more permanent marker, make a small blaze on a tree or break a branch to show the proper return route. A good woodsman with no trail to follow can break the top twig of a bush or a thin tree limb every 25 or 30 yards and follow the route back and forth without hesitation. Light reflecting off the white inner wood of a broken twig catches the eye in a forest where all other twigs show dull natural colors. Leaves tipped bottom up are also attention catchers. Take note of unusual or incongruous things in the woods.

They serve as natural route markers. Keep track of the sun's position; it is east in the morning, south about noon, west at dusk. A steady wind from the west, say, is another natural compass; if it is in your face going out, keep it on your back as you return. The North Star is an age-old navigation guide at night. Use your pocket compass to check your general direction when natural signs are invisible (in fog, for example) and at other times when you have the least doubt about your course.

HOW TO COPE WITH PANIC

Thus, the cautious and meticulous route planner, trail marker, and compass checker rarely gets lost. His pessimistic caution, however, is foreign to the nature of most campers, so we deal now with the exuberant majority—the people who never think of back trails and compass bearings while the breeze is fresh and the sun is warm and the vale ahead full of promise.

The crucial moment with 90 per cent of all persons lost in the woods comes in that instant when they first realize they are lost. One minute the wanderer is merely puzzled, perhaps irritated at the delay in locating a trail or landmark. A second later the words "I'm lost!" flash through the mind—and they panic the novice beyond all reason. This is the point where intelligent thought can be swamped. There is an irrational urge to run after the missing trail as if it were a live thing that must be recaptured by headlong pursuit. The friendly forest is abruptly full of stalking phantoms, and flight is your only escape. The fresh breeze is a cold wind now, the yellow sun paler and plummeting toward dusk and darkness. Walk faster, faster! Run!

You will feel this panic the first time you are lost

in big woods. Perhaps it sounds improbable as you read about it in your own living room, but some sense of panic at being lost is as normal as shivering when you are cold. Be prepared to cope with it.

Stop traveling the instant those words "I'm lost" take shape in your thinking. If you are standing, sit down. If you smoke, light up. If you wear a pack, take it off. Get out a sandwich or candy bar if you have one. All of these are simple tricks to keep you rooted where you are until that urgent hurry, hurry mood passes. If you feel you are in serious trouble, build a fire. Nothing will calm and reassure you more quickly than to get a cheerful blaze going. The work involved keeps your mind from spinning aimlessly, and the fire gives you an established base. With the fire going, you have a camp right where you are, and the only problem now is to plan the best route back to the camp or trail you left in the beginning. In a sense you are not lost any more: that urgent need to escape is gone.

You are now in shape to use your head rather than your feet. Where were you last definitely on the right track? Think back step by step. Chances are your mistake will come to mind as vividly as the sudden realization that you were lost. You took the wrong fork in the trail, perhaps, or turned down the wrong slope of the ridge. Maybe camp is upriver, and you clung to the notion it was downstream from the point where you hiked out of the brush. The man who sits down and calms himself with familiar distractions such as pipe loading, eating, and fire building can nearly always think himself back to base camp.

When the solution is immediately and positively clear to you, put out your fire, gather up your gear, and be on your way. You are not lost at all. If you have the slightest doubt, however, mark your trail as you go so you can easily find your way back to the point where you stopped to collect your wits and directions. That is the closest spot to camp or trail that you know for sure.

Unless you see your mistake at once, do not move from the little camp you have established. Get out your map and compass. The map will show that horseshoe bend in the river below you. That tallest peak beyond the river bend is due west, your compass shows. The peak is on the map, too, and so is the road you are aiming for. It is about a mile south of the peak and river bend. You are just on the wrong side of the ridge. Climb to the saddle 200 yards south of you, and you will see the road in the valley beyond. Pack up and go there.

Lacking map and compass, try drawing a map of all you can remember in the dirt with a twig, with pencil and paper if you have them. No help? Climb the little butte to your right, marking a foolproof trail as you go, and look for something familiar from that vantage point. Listen for any sound in a known direction—say, the noon whistle of the sawmill in the valley to the east, the rumble of the ore train from the mine where your car is parked.

Still no luck? Well, you will now have to settle down to being lost overnight.

OVERNIGHT TACTICS

Making Camp

If it is near dusk, with a freezing night and possible rain or snow coming on, it is too late to travel. So get busy setting up a comfortable camp.

You will not have to walk far in most North American forests to find a good combination of water, fallen trees with dead and broken limbs, and a stand of evergreens to thatch a shelter and furnish boughs for a bed. Hike slowly and calmly to such a place (you can do with less, if you must) and get a good fire going at once. Pick a flat with a little elevation, not a marshy lakeshore or damp creek gorge. And do not start a wild-goose chase in search of a perfect site. Get settled as quickly as possible—well before dark.

Drop all your gear at the first suitable site, and get a good fire going on flat clear ground. Build up the fire so it covers an area about 6 feet long and 2 feet wide. With a freezing night and no blankets, that is where you are going to sleep. When the fire is going, turn at once to the job of gathering a night-long supply of dry branches from blow-downs and dead snags. In most forests you need neither an ax nor a saw to get a good supply of such squaw wood. Haul in the longest lengths you can manage. Let the fire cut them in half for you. Use the rest of your daylight to pack in evergreen boughs (a twist of the wrist will easily snap an evergreen bough half an inch thick). Collect half a dozen long limbs or poles to frame a lean-to shelter. You can put up the shelter by the light of your fire. Use your daylight to haul in firewood, shelter poles, and boughs—the more boughs and firewood, the better.

With king-sized mounds of fuel and shelter materials piled by the fire, the lost camper has invested time and labor in his emergency homestead which have kept his mind off his troubles and given him a sense of proprietorship over the place he at first wanted to flee from in panic. Now is the time to make the best meal you can from whatever you have in your pack and pockets. One night without food or water is not a real disaster, of course, but it is a wretched experience for a man in search of outdoor recreation. On the other hand, there is banquet satisfaction in such frugal fare as sardines and raisins with tea or coffee brewed in a canteen cup. Save a little for breakfast.

A couple of hours have passed by now, and that 6-foot fire has been burning hot and bright all the time, filling the ground beneath it with heat that will linger through most of the night. Push the burning limbs and hot coals of the fire 3 or 4 feet forward now, raking its previous bed fairly smooth and clean with the same long limb used to sweep the flaming wood and hot coals forward. If there is plenty of loose sand or mineral dirt underfoot, scrape an inch or so of that over the hot spot where the long fire has been to help hold in the heat. Then pile on evergreen boughs, angling the broken butts down. Build up a fluffy bough bed 2 feet high. (See Chapter 3.)

Rig a lean-to similar to the ones on the opposite page to cover the bough bed and reflect heat from the long fire, which is now about 3 feet in front of the bough bed. To shed heavy rain, a bough-thatched lean-to must have a roof 3 or 4 inches thick with a slope no flatter than 45 degrees. A thinner or flatter roof will hold off snow, but not a steady rain.

Bedding-Down

Burrow down in that bough bed under the rain-shedding, heat-reflecting roof. The fire-heated ground under the bed will send up warmth for hours. Use your coat, sweater, or other spare clothing as substitutes for whatever bedding you miss most—pillow, blanket, or mattress. Chances are you will want the coat and sweater spread blanket-fashion on top of you. Take off or at least unlace and loosen your shoes.

Two types of frame shelters with evergreen-bough roofs that a lost camper can build out of wilderness materials.

Get all the hard and lumpy objects out of your pockets. If you are wearing long underwear, you probably will be more comfortable sleeping in it alone and using pants and shirt as bedding. Any wet or damp clothing should be dried thoroughly before you turn in. Do not try to sleep in damp or tight and bulky clothing.

Now push a couple of the larger, slower-burning logs or limbs in your collection against the back of your night fire, positioning them to burn slowly and bounce heat into your shelter. Do not worry about rigging an intricate stack of backlogs unless they are plentiful and you have time and tools to handle them easily. You will need to tend the fire once or twice during the night with the most elaborate backlog set-up, unless you are uncommonly lucky in your guess about how the fire will burn. What you want is a hot and steady bed of coals with just enough flame to nibble slowly at the backlogs.

If the stars are out, locate and mark the direction of the North Star as a travel guide for the next day.

And then to bed. This bed, in all honesty, will have little in common with the innerspring comfort the average camper is conditioned to by home life. Plenty of rough edges and cool drafts will crop up before dawn. With the persistent uneasiness of being lost, or at least temporarily confused, the man in this out-camp shelter will not get his eight hours of blissful sleep. But he will get enough sleep and rest to make a healthy, hearty trip out of the woods the next day, and he will suffer no more than minor discomfort if the temperature dips toward zero—weather that will soon kill the lost person who lets panic drive him aimlessly through the woods until he drops from fatigue.

In the Morning

How to get out next morning? First, don't be in a rush to leave your temporary camp. If there is reason to think companions or guides from camp might be searching for you, build up your fire, adding green boughs to raise a good smoke signal, and do some scouting close to camp, being careful not to lose sight of your fire smoke or of a marked trail that will take you back to your emergency camp. Whistle or yell now and then if you think searchers may be out.

Three gunshots about five seconds apart are a standard emergency signal. So are three fires built to send up three columns of smoke in a neat row. Leave a note in the overnight camp to tell where you are if you make long side trips in search of the trail or certain landmarks. Move slowly, looking and listening carefully as you go. If the sun is visible, it is rising in the east. That orients you if you lack a compass and failed to find the North Star at bedtime.

Ninety per cent of the persons lost at dusk can soon unravel their confusion with an hour of calm, unhurried scouting the next morning. The solution usually seems ridiculously easy after a night's sleep and a calm appraisal—but not always.

FINDING YOUR WAY

If you are still lost next morning and have no reason to expect searchers to be looking for you, you will have no trouble getting out on your on in any region where well-traveled trails and roads are no more than ten miles apart. Leave a note in your outcamp to explain where you are heading and what time you left (scrawl a message in the dirt with a stick if you have no better way), as a guide to searchers who find your overnight camp. Put out your fire, pack all your gear neatly, and set out on a modified straight-line course toward the point where you *think* you will hit a road or major trail. There are a dozen things that will help you make a good guess about this route. A long, low ridge cutting through the forest for several miles will nearly always have a trail on top of it. Such long ridges offer fairly straight and level passages through rough country, and trails and roads in every country generally follow the path of least resistance.

Watersheds

Roads and trails follow creeks and rivers for the same reason. Any lost camper who simply keeps walking downhill in mountains cut by roads and trails will soon be out of the woods. Small creeks lead downhill to larger streams. The streams flow down into rivers, and rivers all over the world are the highways of human traffic. Trails, roads, and railroads follow rivers. The farms and ranches in remote regions are along the flats by rivers. As rivers run downstream, they have villages, towns, and major cities on their shores. Most of North America was first explored by men following rivers upstream to their sources. In reverse, campers lost at the headwaters can get out by following the water downstream. This plan will work for an aviator in the Amazon headwaters of South America or a traveler lost at the head of the Nile in Africa.

There are three things to remember about following watersheds downhill as a means of getting "un-lost."

1. Do not try to stay right beside the creek or stream if there is no good trail and if the streamsides are swampy or tangled with thick growth. Follow the

general course of the water by walking on trails or in open country along the side of a hill or on a low ridge top above the stream.

2. Do not take the watershed way out when there is a railroad or an auto road that can be reached by a much shorter and easier route of generally straight cross-country travel; many creeks and streams, especially those in fairly flat country, run through twenty miles of loops and bends for every two of straight-line progress.

3. Keep in mind the general pattern of the water-sheds where you are traveling. In the Rocky Mountains —the great range that runs down from Canada, through our far western states, and into Mexico—the camper near the Continental Divide, which stretches the length of the Rockies, needs to know that a water-course off the east slope of the divide would take him eventually to the Gulf of Mexico, while a west-slope creek starting 100 yards away will end up in the Pacific Ocean. Either one would eventually lead a lost man to some road or outpost, but why pop out of the woods in Montana when your car is parked in Idaho?

One area in North America where following water-courses is a doubtful escape method is northern Canada and Alaska. As a glance at a map will show you, the rivers up there are about the only ones in the world that take you out of civilization rather than into it. They dump into the Arctic Ocean and the northern reaches of Hudson Bay which are equally frigid and barren. A person stranded in the depths of that far northern wilderness by such a mishap as a plane crash will nearly always be better off if he stays where he is and relies on such long-range distress signals as smudge fires, flashing mirrors, and a giant SOS contrived to show up in a clearing or on the lake ice.

The Alaska Highway, running north and south through western Canada, gives a straight-line walker something to aim for in that part of the North. Lacking such a landmark whose position he knows and is fairly close, it would be foolhardy for a novice woodsman to try to walk out of northern Canada or Alaska. His chances of survival will be a hundred times greater if he makes the best camp he can and lives off the land until he is spotted from a plane or picked up by some northland native attracted by his signals.

Compass or Straight-Line Course

A straight-line course is the best way out of a flat and featureless swamp, thicket, or plains region that has no natural passages such as flowing streams or high ridges running cross-country. If you are in a walk-out situation in such terrain, choose the direction that—on the basis of what you know *for sure*—will be the quickest route to a river, trail, road, or settlement. If you have a compass, use it to keep on a generally straight line. (There is always some dodging and detouring in travel off a trail.) The sun will guide you on a general course on all but heavily overcast days. There is the North Star to give you a bearing at night. When none of these easy signposts can be used, look for two conspicuous trees, rocks, or other landmarks that are in line on your travel route, and start a straight-line course. This is a slow and frustrating way to travel in a dense swamp or thicket where you can not see far ahead, but it will prevent you from circling if you keep it up. Lost men have circled for days in swamps and thickets that cover only a couple of square miles. On the other hand, it is fairly difficult to draw a straight line through a map of ordinary camping and hunting country without hitting a road, trail, or obvious landmark every five or ten miles.

There is one mental hazard in following a straight course out of tangled woods with either compass or lined-up landmarks. Avoid becoming so wrapped up in your navigation that you pass an obvious guidepost or hike across a trail without seeing or recognizing it. Many a good woodsman has been "confused" for an hour or so because his compass course back to camp took him 50 yards west of his tent, and he straight-lined past it without taking the glance to the right that would have shown him a patch of white canvas peeking through the trees. Every year there are reports of lost men who become so intent on straight-ahead travel that they hike across trails and roads and plunge on into the woods. The cure for this is slow, methodical travel with frequent pauses to scan for landmarks.

A person completely confused about directions should stay on the first man-made trail or travel route encountered. This may be a blazed trapper's trail, a logging road, a line of telephone or power poles, a pack-horse route with the tracks of shod horses. Any such trail will eventually lead to a road, camp, or settlement. It is nearly always best to head downhill on any dim road or trail. Most major roads, houses, and villages are in valleys. A steady uphill course is almost certain to take a lost man farther into the wilds.

Establishing Direction without a Compass

Any person stranded without a compass can use one of the following natural guides to get his bearings.

Stars. At night the stars are the quickest and surest guide, and the most reliable star in the Northern Hemisphere is the North Star—easily located because two stars in the cup of the hard-to-miss Big Dipper point

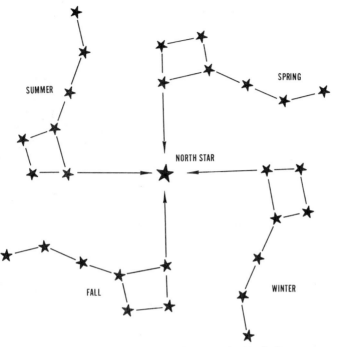

Positions of the Big Dipper in relation to the North Star at different seasons of the year.

right to it, as shown in the sketch above. Although the Big Dipper changes position in relation to the North Star, the two stars in the outer edge of the Dipper's cup remain lined up with the North Star. As you face the North Star squarely, south will of course be directly behind you, east to your right, west to your left. Mark those directions on the ground at your camp as soon as you establish them. The stars may be hidden by clouds when you look for them again, and it is faulty guesswork that keeps lost men lost.

There is no guesswork about North Star directions. That star, as seen by any observer in the Northern Hemisphere, is never more than one degree away from true north.

A watch accurately set according to the standard Greenwich time in a particular time belt will serve as a fairly accurate compass on a sunny day. Read it as follows: Place the watch flat and face up so the hour hand points directly at the sun. South will be halfway between the hour hand and 12 on the watch dial. Other directions can be figured accordingly—north in the opposite direction, east and west at right angles.

This watch compass works at any time of the day the sun is visible. When the hour hand is exactly at 12, *both* the hour hand and the numeral 12 will be aimed at the sun, which will be very close to due south.

A similar procedure allows the person with a compass to set a watch that has stopped. First use the compass to establish south. Next make a rough guess at what time it is and position the hour hand of the watch accordingly. Then turn the hour hand slowly, and keep it pointing at the sun while you rotate the watch itself. When south (established by your compass reading) is midway between the hour hand and 12 on the watch dial, push in the watch stem. That's approximately the right time. The accuracy of this system varies according to the season of the year and the latitude where the reading is taken, but it works far better than the average camper's guess.

Any lost camper who awakes with the morning sun

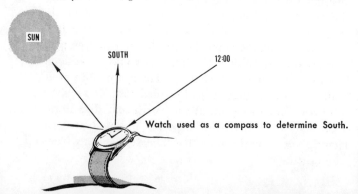

Watch used as a compass to determine South.

and needs sure bearings can get them exactly by driving three stakes into the ground as the sun passes over his camp during the day. Proceed as follows: Drive the first stake (about 1 foot long) around ten in the morning and note where its shadow falls. At the end of that shadow drive a second stake. Now use a string or boot lace hooked around the first stake to draw an arc on the ground the shadow's length from the pivot stake. The shadow of the pivot stake will shorten as noon approaches, then grow longer as the sun moves westward in the sky. Watch the lengthening shadow carefully as it starts to reach out toward the even arc you drew on the ground. At the moment it reaches the arc you drew in the morning, drive the third stake at the point where the afternoon shadow touches the arc. Now use your string or boot lace to measure the distance between the two stakes driven on the arc and then double the string to establish the halfway point between these two stakes. That halfway point, which can be marked on the ground or with a fourth stake, will line up with the pivot stake to give you a north-south line. South, of course, is in the direction of the pivot stake you drove first. And there is no guesswork about it; the system is precise.

Tree Moss and Other Natural Signs.   Many outdoor manuals and picnic woodsmen have pointed out that directions can be established by moss on the sides of trees and rocks, the common explanation being that moss growth will be heavier on the north side, which is more shaded from the sun. This is true only in a general way. Prevailing winds and adjoining bodies of water can throw the system out of whack. Trees near the coast or in swampy regions with heavy rainfall often are so heavily furred with moss that one side looks much like the other. The moss-on-the-north-side system can be demonstrated to be true in many areas by woodsmen who *know* their directions and the pattern of local growth. But moss on trees is always a doubtful direction guide for a person lost and confused in unfamiliar terrain.

Trees in many regions tend to tip toward the sun—southward—and have thicker south-side growth rings when a cross-section of the trunk is examined. The man who knows the region and its trees can tell directions by these clues. But he will not be the fellow who is lost there.

The same objection applies to directions judged by wind and the location on hillsides of certain types of growth. All those things are natural compasses for the local people familiar with the patterns. The tourist or outlander needs something more sure to steer by. He cannot go wrong with a bearing taken from the North Star at night or from the sun by day.

STAY PUT OR TRAVEL?

Let's now consider the person who is on his own in the middle of nowhere without the routine tools most campers and hunters carry. Planes go down in the wilds of northern Canada. Jeeps break down in desert storms which leave drivers stranded and confused as dim roads are obscured by drifting sand or rainstorm washouts. The one man who knows the way can be drowned in a white-water accident, which turns a wilderness trip into a survival problem. Sometimes it is the trail-wise Alaska guide, not the city-bred sportsman, who has the heart attack or accident ten miles from camp and fifty miles from the nearest outpost.

The best basic rule when stranded in real wilderness is to stay put rather than to try to walk out. Aerial searchers can spot a downed plane easily in most reg-

ions. A stranded automobile or truck is easily seen in
a desert. Stay with it unless you know a short, sure way
out. A canoe traveler piled up on a sand bar is far
easier to locate if he stays right there than if he starts
hiking. The one wilderness situation that ordinarily
calls for travel is the plane crash or emergency parachute jump that leaves the survivor stranded in the
tall, dense growth of a tropical jungle. That growth
will frequently swallow a downed plane like a dime
dropped in a wheat field. The tight canopy of trees
100 feet high springs back in place after the plane
crashes through, and it is extremely difficult for searchers to spot signs of the crash in the sea of green below
them. That same tight canopy of jungle growth breaks
up smoke signals and makes mirror signaling impossible. Unless there is a clearing close by where signals
can be seen, the survivor of a crash or bail-out in dense
jungle should make a pack of survival gear and try to
straight-line his way to a coastline or major stream.
Rivers are usually the highways in tangled tropical
jungles, and a raft drifting downstream is the logical
way out.

Whether traveling or camping in one spot to wait
for rescuers, the man lost in real wilderness without
routine camp equipment can survive indefinitely if he
knows what to do and calmly does it.

FIRE WITHOUT MATCHES

Electric Spark with Gasoline

Lacking matches for the fire that warms, signals,
and cooks your food, think first of the *easy* ways to
start a fire; most of the Boy Scout methods are extremely difficult with anything but ideal tools and
conditions.

Any person stranded by a disabled plane or engine-driven vehicle is likely to have gasoline and an electric spark as a fire starter. Wrap a rag around a stick end to make a large swab. Dip it in any gasoline left in or around the disabled craft or vehicle. If the engine ignition is still in order, hold the gas-soaked swab between spark plug and a loosened spark plug wire while the starter is worked and the ignition switch on. The electric spark jumping from the disconnected wire to the spark plug will start the gas-soaked swab flaming instantly. A wire hooked to one terminal of an auto-size battery will spark when the loose end of the wire is tapped on the other battery terminal. Any electrical system in a plane or vehicle may produce a spark after the machine is stalled or smashed. An electric spark coupled with a gas-soaked rag is as quick and sure a fire starter as a giant cigarette lighter. The gas-soaked rag will also be a great help in building a fire by other means when battery and ignition systems are destroyed or completely dead.

Burning Lens

A magnifying lens is the second quick and sure fire starter on any day when the sun is out. Just hold the glass steady a few inches above some inflammable tinder so that the sun's rays passing through the glass converge in a small, bright spot at the base of the tinder. Good tinder will start to smoke in a minute or two with a good glass and direct sunlight. In another minute or so it will be flaming. Blow or fan it gently to speed the flames if the tinder smolders without flaming promptly.

Most travelers will have something that will serve as a fire-starting glass: a camera lens, the lens from a telescope or binoculars, a convex watch crystal, or a flashlight lens. If the back is hollow, fill it with water. It is even possible to shape a fire-kindling lens from a piece of clear ice, forming the rounded convex surface by melting the ice with body heat from your bare skin. The weakness of the magnifying lens as a fire starter is that it requires bright sunlight and therefore is just another piece of glass at night or on an overcast day.

Fire with Firearms

The lost man with a firearm and cartridges has the means to start a fire quickly. The spark from any large-bore rifle, pistol, or shotgun cartridge will start a fire. Proceed as follows:

1. Get tinder and kindling ready to light—always the first step in fire building with improvised lighters.

2. Remove bullet or shot pellets and wadding from cartridge and sprinkle about two thirds of the powder in the cartridge on a fluffy "bullet" made from frayed cloth from a dry corner of a bandanna or shirt tail.

3. Poke the powder-loaded cloth loosely into muzzle of gun, and fire the cartridge with bullet and two thirds of powder removed, aiming straight up in the air or at some solid object a few feet from the muzzle.

The powder-laden cloth, either flaming or smolder-ing, will only go a few feet. Catch it in the air or pick it up quickly and stick it in the prepared tinder under your fire, blowing or fanning it gently to keep the spark or flame going. The cloth needs to be good and dry, and it needs to travel a few feet through the air to let the sparks fan into life. Chances are you will just scatter your tinder without getting a fire if you hold the gun muzzle against the main pile of tinder as you blow out the powder-dusted cloth.

Fire starting is fairly easy with a shotgun or a large-caliber pistol or rifle. It is difficult with the little rimfire .22 cartridges. Their mild primer charges *will* start a fire, but everything has to be just right for them to do so. Larger cartridges allow more margin for error.

Flint and Steel Fire-Starting

To put things in the proper order of their import- ance, this system should be known as the "flint and tinder method," for those are the two things that make this fire starter work; the steel (iron or another chunk of flint will do) presents no special difficulty.

A cigarette lighter is a common and extremely effi- cient example of a flint and steel fire starter. It works so well because the spark struck off the flint by the steel wheel hits a wick (tinder) saturated with highly inflammable liquid fuel. The outdoorsman working with flint and steel, however, seldom has tinder as efficient as that cigarette-lighter wick.

Charred cloth will neatly catch and hold a spark struck from flint, but the only fire maker who ordinar- ily has dry, charred cloth is the fellow who demon- strates for Boy Scouts or outdoor clubs at meetings in town. The man cautious enough to carry flint and steel seldom gets lost, and you can bet he will have waterproof matches in three different pockets if he does.

The man dumped in the woods has to make do with what he can find under conditions that are usually far less than ideal. First, the chunk of flint or quartz. Either will do, but both are difficult or impossible to find in many areas. A creek or river bed covered with stream-washed stones and gravel is a good place to look.

So is a hillside or mountain flat littered with similar stones. The flint most people know, the type from which most Indian arrowheads are made, is jet black and has a smooth, shiny, slick surface when freshly split. A chunk lodged in a stream or weathering on a hillside may be dull and pitted on its outside surfaces, however. Split it by pounding it against another rock to be sure you have found flint instead of some other black rock. Flint is very hard, but it cracks almost as easily as glass, which it resembles a great deal in that it has the same hard, slick look when freshly broken.

Quartz for the fire maker's purpose is just white or transparent flint. Most quartz looks a good deal like dull window glass, though it is often·with and colored by other minerals. Stream beds in mountain country are usually littered with chunks of quartz. So are rocky slopes ,and ridges. Half the rock formations in most major mountain ranges are streaked with whitish, glassy chunks of quartz.

The fire builder needs a chunk of flint or quartz big enough to grip securely in the palm of one hand—say, a piece the size of a flattened baseball. Any rough-edged piece of steel or iron that can be wielded easily with one hand will do as a spark knocker. So will a second piece of flint or quartz. The sparks fly when the steel is grated sharply across the face of the flint or quartz or when two chunks of flint or quartz are clashed together with a glancing blow.

The sparks must be showered into some inflammable tinder held right under the point where they spring from the flint. One good way to do this is to hold the flint in the fingers of the left hand with a wad of tinder in the cupped palm of the same hand. By striking downward with steel held in the right hand, the fire maker drives the sparks directly from the flint to tinder—and when a spark takes hold, he can quickly cup both hands around the tinder and gently blow it into a flame. A flint spark in woods-gathered tinder is an extremely precarious start toward a campfire. It must be shielded and breathed to life with the utmost care before it can be thrust under the previously prepared kindling to expand into a reliable fire.

The dry bark of cedar trees, birch trees, or sagebrush will catch a flint spark if it is broken into fibers thin as hair and wadded close beneath the sparking point. Dry cotton cloth frayed into fine fuzz is good improvised tinder. Any bone-dry and finely shredded wood or bark is worth trying. Downy bird feathers or a mat of dry hair barbered off your own body may be the best tinder available. If you have any inflammable liquid fuel, prime your tinder with that. Flint fires are a cinch with gas to prime the tinder. If you have cartridges, dump the powder from one of them over your tinder to speed your fire making. Lacking top-notch tinder, persistence is a helpful trait in the person working up a fire with flint and steel. It will be a miracle if you light unprimed tinder with your first shower of sparks. Fifty to a hundred strokes of the steel is about par for beginners with a fair amount of aptitude.

Bow and Drill

This is another fire-starting method that is easy with ideal conditions and material, but maddeningly difficult with poor wood and tinder. Using the best of everything, the famous writer-naturalist Ernest Thompson Seton could light a fire with bow and drill in less than a minute. The beginner gathering materials in the woods for a first effort will be lucky to get a fire within an hour with this system. But it is a means of starting a fire under conditions that may offer no other means.

The materials needed are a bow-shaped limb, a stout cord or leather thong, a drill stick, a fire board, a wooden socket to hold the drill stick, and a wad of tinder.

The fire builder holds the stick in place with one hand on the wooden socket, which protects his palm

Preparing to build a fire by the bow and drill method:

Woodsman collects ragged bark for tinder. It should be extremely dry.

B. Lacking a knife, he cuts sticks for the bow and drill on a granite rock.

C. He shapes the drill to proper size with a chipped piece of granite.

D. A knothole will be used to steady the upper end of the drill.

E. The bow is made from a slightly curved limb rigged with a rawhide lace.

F. Placing a notched stick over the tinder, he inserts one end of the drill in the notch. The length of rawhide, which is tied leaving some slack, is looped around the drill. His left hand presses the knothole on the top of the drill to hold it steady. He then saws the bow rapidly back and forth, whirling the drill in the notched stick.

G. A spark! It smoulders in the tinder.

I. Tinder begins to smoke and to give it more oxygen he swings it back and forth in the air.

H. Blowing on the tinder, he encourages the spark to catch fire.

from the friction of the drill stick, and uses his other hand to saw back and forth with the bow. This action twirls the drill stick in the notch cut in the fire board.

J. Fire!

K. He's got a real campfire now for cooking and warmth.

The friction of the drill stick against the fire board eventually showers hot sparks down onto tinder under the notch in the fire board. The smoldering tinder is then fanned or blown into flame and placed under prepared campfire kindling.

Since this is a friction fire, the drill stick must be whirled rapidly, the faster the better. This calls for a strong, properly adjusted bow and string. A hard, slick cord will slip. Rawhide boot laces have a good combination of grip and strength. Any wooded area will yield a sturdy limb with a natural bow curve. The bow string is rigged to make one turn around the drill stick; the tension is adjusted to twirl the stick as the bow is sawed back and forth. If grease or any slick lubricant is available, put some in the socket that holds the top of the drill stick to ease friction at that point.

The drill stick should be of dry wood that is soft and rather splintery. Cedar is good, as are poplar and willow. Dry limbs of the yucca tree found in southwestern desert regions are excellent (a favorite of lecture-hall demonstrators) but seldom available to the lost man who really needs them.

The fire board should be chosen by drill-stick standards—a slab of dry, rather soft wood that splinters easily. Place a square of bark, large chip, or thin stone under the fire board as a saucer to catch and hold some tinder and the smoldering dust and splinters that will fall through the notch in the fire board. When this litter is hot enough to be blown into life, use the crude saucer to shove it under the tinder and kindling stacked in readiness beside the fire board.

Speed and pressure on the drill stick are the secret of this system. Bear down and saw on that bow like a barn-dance fiddler. The system will build you a fire when there is no other way.

Hot Coals

All the primitive methods of starting a fire without matches are troublesome enough in ordinary field conditions to justify carrying hot coals to start a new fire at the end of each day's journey. Natives still do this in parts of the world where matches are scarce. American pioneers often carried hot coals rather than have to resort to flint and steel for each new fire. Hot coals bedded in rotten, punky wood that allows just a little air to reach them will hold a spark indefinitely. Ashes and dead coals from the fire will insulate and maintain the glow in a few hot coals bedded in a metal can or an improvised container made of bark. The idea is to surround the hot embers with some material that will smolder and glow without flaming. Dry moss will work. So will a dry mixture of partly decomposed leaves and pine needles scooped off the forest floor.

SOS SIGNALS

Signals are the quickest, surest means of rescue when a person is too confused to travel with assurance or unable to hike because of injuries or dangerous terrain. Searchers will nearly always pick up the lost man who signals properly, no matter where he is. With spotting planes and helicopters readily available all over the country, it is just about impossible to pick a part of North America where a lost person using standard emergency signals could stay lost for long.

The number three is basis of an emergency signal. The international distress signal is SOS—which is three dots, three dashes, three more dots. Three rifle shots are a distress signal known over most of North America. Three fires built in an even row will bring help. Three blasts of a whistle will attract attention.

Three smoke or signal flares fired into the air will be understood as a call for help.

Radio

The radio is the first thing to think of in any emergency involving a plane, boat, or vehicle that has one. If the radio still works, it will accomplish more faster than any other signal device. Try it whether or not you know the dials and procedure. Any garbled transmission may be picked up.

Mirror Signals

A pocket mirror or any shiny piece of glass or tin can flash a signal visible for miles on a sunny or even a hazy day. A plane thousands of feet above a stranded man can see mirror signals easily. Rescue pilots say the signal mirror is second only to a radio in attracting attention.

The beam of light from a standard signal mirror (in survival kits, sold by war surplus stores) can be aimed precisely. Look through the hole in the center of the mirror at the target, as shown in the drawing. A spot of sunlight coming through the hole will fall on your face so that you can see the spot reflected in the mirror. Adjust the angle of the mirror so that the spot lines up with the sighting hole as you aim at the target —say, the cockpit of a plane overhead. That will send a beam of light into the cockpit. Jiggle the mirror to produce three flashes, three more, another three.

A hole punched in a piece of bright tin will allow it to be aimed like a standard signal mirror.

Fire Signals

Fires built as distress signals should be fed fuel that will raise tall smoke columns during the day. Green grass or browse on a blazing fire does this. Oil and rubber make conspicuous smoke fires. Experiment with whatever is available. If fuel is too scarce for three fires in an even row, try sending up smoke puffs in three series by briefly trapping smoke with a blanket

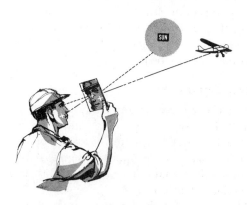

How to use a signal mirror: 1. Sight through the hole in the mirror at the cockpit of the plane. 2. Observe in your reflected image the spot of sunlight that shines on your face through the hole. 3. Adjust the mirror so that the spot lines up with the hole. You will then be flashing signals directly at the pilot.

or similar fire cover. This will work only with a good smudge fire and a reasonably windless day.

At night the signal fires should blaze brightly.

Always build signal fires in the most conspicuous place in easy reach of your camp and fuel supply—a clearing, an open ridge, a sand bar, or open beach. Tall trees obscure both smoke and flames.

Flags and Signal Panels

Three flags in tops of tall trees will attract attention in a thicket where aerial searchers could never see a man on the ground. White or bright clothing will make the flags. Hoist them in the tallest trees that can be climbed safely. Clothing or equipment can be spread on beach, a sand bar, a frozen lake, or any clear ground to spell out SOS in large letters.

Flashlight or Lantern

Either a flashlight or a lantern can be used to flash SOS (· · · — — — · · ·) at night from a high point. A signal lantern can be improvised with a candle and a tin can cut open along one side. Shield the beam of the candle lantern briefly with your hat to produce signal flashes.

Spell It Out

In many areas a lost person can spell out distress messages by writing out such words as "HELP" or "LOST" on snow field, beach sand, ice, or open grassland. Dark branches will spell out words on snow or white sand. A path stomped in deep snow will form conspicuous letters if the snow trail is deep enough to cast shadows. Contrast is the thing to strive for in catching attention—dark letters on snow or white sand, white clothing or peeled limbs on dark ground. The bigger the better.

SHELTERS

There are several types of shelter that can be readily improvised to protect a lost man from the elements while he is waiting for his distress signals to pay off. Conditions and available materials vary so much from hot desert to arctic cold that few general rules apply, but the following suggestions are subject to few exceptions.

A plane downed but intact or a disabled car will be a better shelter than any that can be quickly improvised. Stay with it. It is also a ready-made distress signal.

Do not waste time and energy searching for a great hollow tree or a dry and roomy cave. They exist, but they are never readily available in times of urgent need.

Adequate shelters *can* be put up in any forest with no tools of any kind. An ax, a hatchet, or a heavy knife is a great help, of course, and so is rope, wire, or strong fishing line to lash the frame together. But limbs for the frame can be picked up or broken off by hand, lashed together with tough vines, strips of pliable bark, willow shoots, or thin tree roots. (Many trees that have rather soft and brittle trunks and limbs have tough, flexible roots.)

Broken Evergreen Shelter

Cut or break the largest evergreen that can be easily cut or broken 4 or 5 feet above ground so that a strong strap of wood and bark holds the fallen trunk to the high stump. Break or cut out limbs on under side to make a hollow interior big enough for a bed. Use limbs from inside and from other evergreens to make the bough bed and thatch roof. A thick thatch with a roof slant of 45 degrees or steeper is needed to turn rain. A fire in front of the shelter will provide a great deal of reflected heat in the triangular interior. In extreme cold the shelter can be situated so that the bed can be laid on the warm side of the fire, as described earlier in this chapter.

Frame Shelters

Frame shelters closely follow patterns of canvas lean-to, campfire tent, and pup tent. Roofs and sides can be thatched with evergreens, leafy branches, broad tropical leaves, long grass, slabs of bark. Start at lower edge and work up in shingling fashion with any thatching material.

Snow Shelters

All snow shelters require two major precautions:

1. Be sure there is adequate ventilation, particularly when the inside is heated by a candle or a gas stove which will create poisonous carbon monoxide gas. Take care to select a site that is not vulnerable to snow slides or drifting snow that could choke off ventilation holes; do not build in a shallow ravine or on the downwind side of a knoll. You do not need a torrent of fresh air, but you do need a constant supply.

2. Work slowly enough in building the shelter to avoid sweating up your inside clothes. Snow is such a good windbreak and insulator that overheating will be more of a hazard than freezing cold in any tight snow shelter with a fire inside. A slow, methodical working pace will head off serious trouble resulting from sweaty clothes. Sweat will not dry without a great deal of artificial heat in arctic cold. Clothes full of frozen sweat are mankillers when the temperature is far below zero.

Tree-Base Snow Shelter.   A tree partly buried can be

Tree-base snow shelter shown in cross-section. Entire area above the hole is actually covered with limbs and snow.

trimmed so that the remaining limbs form a frame for the roof of a shelter dug around its base. A pole run up the trunk will form a ventilation chimney.

Snow Trench.   In shallow snow, a trench can be dug by cutting blocks of snow and using them as a roof. The shelter will break wind and hold heat.

Snow Cave.   A cave dug into the side of a deep drift makes a good emergency shelter. Dig in at right angles to prevailing wind to keep the entrance from being choked with drifting snow.

Snow trench shown in cross-section.

Igloo.   The most palatial of all snow shelters is the dome-shaped Eskimo igloo made of carefully fitted blocks of snow. But the igloo, like the Indian teepee, is not as simple as it looks. A good deal of know-how is needed to shape and fit the snow blocks. A novice working by himself, with no helper to hold roof blocks in place, will find it either extremely difficult or impossible to put up an igloo. A group of men with good building aptitudes can put up an igloo, but it will involve some time-consuming trial and error. A simpler snow cave or a roofed snow trench will ordinarily be better.

Desert Shelters

A person stranded in one of the world's big deserts in summer needs shelter almost as urgently as the traveler lost in the Arctic. Here are the rules:

Your clothes are a primary shelter. Keep on enough clothing to cover all of your body. A layer of clothing is basic protection from sunburn, helps ward off hot air, and forms a cooling wick for evaporating sweat.

Stay in the shade of your disabled plane or car if available.

Look for natural shade such as an overhanging cliff or the bank of a dry wash.

Improvise a lean-to for a sunshade with any spare fabric available or with any bushes or desert growth that can be gathered.

Lacking anything better, dig a sand trench deep enough to shade you from the sun as you lie in it during the heat of the day.

Remember these things about desert heat:

A patch of desert screened from the sun by solid shade will be as much as 36 degrees cooler than the same area without shade.

Where no shade is available, the air a foot above the sun-baked ground will be about 30 degrees cooler than the ground, so that at the elevation provided by a cot, a hammock, or a thick bed of brush you will be cooler than if you were sitting or lying on the ground.

Summer nights in the desert are a great deal cooler than days. Work or travel by night. Rest in the shade during the day. The authorities who have studied records of military men in desert conditions have concluded that a person will be able to travel exactly twice as far on a given amount of water if he hikes by night rather than by day. They figure the average man lost in a desert in summer needs a gallon of water for each twenty miles of hiking if he travels at night. A gallon of water will take him only ten miles in hot sun.

Most of the world's great deserts are either cool or actually cold during winter months. The great Gobi Desert of Mongolia, for example, has winter temperatures far below zero. A winter shelter in most deserts will need to meet the standards of a cool- or cold-weather shelter in any other area.

WHY WORRY?

The first and the final thing to remember about being lost is that 99 per cent of the real danger is from panic—unreasonable fear that causes intelligent people to injure or deplete themselves in their own foolish stampedes.

Most of the woods of the world, even wilderness areas, are far safer places for a calm and rational man than the streets of any major city. There is more real danger in passing another car on your county roads than there is in meeting a bear on a primitive trail. Mountain lions, wolves, coyotes, bobcats—all these creatures want nothing from man but to be left alone. Grizzlies, Alaska brown bears, and polar bears seldom bother people who do not bother them first.

No one who reads newspapers thoughtfully would flee from the woods to escape bodily harm from the creatures that live there. The stories in our newspapers every day tell us that our population centers are the hazardous places and that man is the only creature consistently dangerous to man.

There is considerable danger to anyone lost in such extreme climates as the torrid Death Valley or the Arctic. Even those formidable areas can be mastered by the stranded traveler who calmly rigs a good shelter and uses emergency signals efficiently.

The great majority of people who get lost are out in temperate climates and only a few miles from a good road or trail. With calm planning, this garden variety of "lostness" is no more than an inconvenience.

As the following chapter will explain, the average man can get by without most of the things he considers necessities in his everyday life. The city-pampered gourmet will eat a rabbit raw after two hungry weeks in the wilds. The man who considers two flights of stairs a hardship can carry a pack over a mountain pass if he has to. And the fellow who shivers each time his home furnace falters can survive in a lean-to in weather far below freezing. There is a tough and adaptable animal just beneath the pampered skin of modern man.

28 - Living Off the Land

WATER, NOT FOOD, IS THE FIRST CONSIDERATION for any person lost or stranded under circumstances that require living off the land. The average adult needs 2 quarts of water each day to operate at peak efficiency in moderate weather. In 100-degree heat he has an average life expectancy of five days without water if he is resting quietly, three days or less if he is exerting himself. Ten days without water will ordinarily kill a healthy man in temperatures ranging between 50 and 70 degrees, and the dehydration caused by lack of water will make a person inefficient or helpless long before it kills. There are countless reports of men going more than ten days without food, and some survive twice that long without a bite to eat.

Purifying Stream and Lake Water

Where water is plentiful in lakes or streams, the possibility of pollution often makes it dangerous to drink. The following methods solve that problem:

Boiling. Water boiled briskly for at least five minutes will be safe to drink. The flat taste of boiled water can be overcome by pouring it back and forth between two containers or shaking it in a container with a loosely closed top; this restores the air lost during the boiling. A bit of salt sprinkled in boiled water tempers the flat taste to suit some people.

Halazone Tablets. Halazone tablets will quickly kill all routine germs in water. They are sold in bottles at drug and sporting goods stores and cost little more than aspirin tablets. There are directions on the bottle. The general formula is two tablets for each quart of water; then wait half an hour to let the tablets do their work. When treating a canteen or water bag of doubful water with halazone or another chemical purifier, shake the container to slosh the treated water over the cap or cork and pouring spout.

Iodine. Two or three drops of tincture of iodine for each quart of water will make it safe. Allow thirty minutes for the iodine to do its work. Even better, Iodine Water Purification Tablets will do the same job more efficiently.

Chlorine. Chlorine, commonly sold for water treatment as chloride-of-lime, is a dependable purifier which is especially useful for treating large quantities of water. Directions on packages of different brands will vary slightly, but the general measurements are as follows: Mix 1 teaspoon of chloride of lime in 1 gallon of water as a treating solution; then use only 1 part (cup or gallon) of this solution to each 100 parts (cups or gallons) of water. Mix the treated water thoroughly and let it stand for thirty minutes before using.

Filtering. Dirty or discolored water can be cleaned—but not completely purified—by filtering it through layers of clean fabric or through fine sand. The more sand or fabric, the better. Boiling or chemical treatment will then kill germs in the strained water.

Natural Filtering. Along many flowing streams it is easy to spot a place where a shallow hole can be dug in a sand bar that is near and just above the flowing water. This hole will quickly fill with stream water filtering through the barrier of sand that separates your water hole from the stream. After it has settled for a few minutes, the water in the sand-bar reservoir will be cleaner and substantially safer to drink than water from a still pool in the main stream.

Naturally Pure Water

Spring water bubbling out of the ground in real wilderness country will almost invariably be safe to drink without treatment if it is dipped out at the source. The farther the water runs through country inhabited by men and animals (especially men), the more likely it is to be polluted. Still pockets of water formed by slow, seeping springs in arid regions are often contaminated in the pool where they rise out of the ground if they are much frequented by men and animals.

Water near its source and far from man's influence is usually pure enough to drink without treatment. High-country lakes and headwaters streams are seldom polluted. By contrast, lowland lakes and rivers in settled regions are nearly always polluted to some extent. Thousands of people drink polluted water without apparent harm, of course; in fact, it is unlikely that one drink of doubtful water will cause the slightest trouble. But do not gamble with the deadly diseases water *can* carry. Treat or boil it when in doubt.

Even in remote mountain or desert regions where man seldom travels there is a chance of water pollution by diseased animals which often will stagger to a stream or spring to drink and die there. The diseased carcasses are often washed into the stream by spring floods or rolled into the water by animals feeding on them.

One of the authors remembers sprawling on his belly to quench an all-day thirst at a cool trickle of spring water in a trackless part of northern Nevada. After drinking a quart of this clear and remarkably tasty water, he gratefully wiped his lips on his sleeve and glanced uphill. There was a peculiar mound of gray sprawling across the tiny brook 100 feet upstream. It was an unbranded range horse, lying dead in the only trickle of water within twenty miles. Water filtering through a dead horse does not automatically become a deadly potion, of course, but the flavor is disturbing after a man sees the cause of it. Such incidents encourage the habit of following trickles to their source and drinking where the water first surges out of the ground.

Locating Water in Arid Regions

There are a few general rules for finding your way to water in a desert or in the arid foothills that border most deserts.

First scan the country near you, with binoculars if you have them, for signs of vegetation that is conspicuously greener and taller than the sparse and scattered growth common in desert regions. This lush vegetation in the desert will ordinarily be in the bottom of a valley or canyon, perhaps at the base of a hill. Sometimes it is supported by a small spring rising on the flattened shoulder of a high hill. Some desert springs rise on slopes and seep back into the earth within a few yards, but a patch of abnormally lush growth will make their location obvious to a trained observer miles away.

If there is no water-nourished growth in sight, there are two choices left: either gamble on following a well-traveled trail or keep sloping downhill, following the natural run-off channels of the infrequent desert rains. There are a few places where the downhill course will lead down dry channels to a dead lake too salty or alkaline to drink, but nature seldom pulls such grim tricks. The downhill course will lead to drinkable water 99 per cent of the time, though the route may be too long for a man afoot to survive. Any trail or road with obvious signs of regular human traffic will as a rule be a shorter route to water. Major game trails aiming like spokes toward a hollow are a very good sign that water is there. Such desert trails can be seen for miles from higher elevations. In a few regions these water-hole paths have been used so much for so long that they have worn shallow paths in the solid rock they cross.

A still pool of desert water (it may be only rain water trapped in a large natural basin of rock) is likely to be polluted. Boil or treat it. Although "poison" springs are purely fictional, be cautious about drinking from any spring that has little green growth along its banks. The water probably has a high mineral content (alkali, sulphur, saltpeter) which will be unpleasant to taste and in some cases sickening to drink in quantity. But only in very rare cases is such mineral-tainted water too potent to quench the thirst—perhaps save the life—of the desert wanderer. Drink it slowly. Boiling may make it more palatable, or pouring it through the air from one container to another will "air out" some of the taint.

Digging for Water

The idea that water can be found by digging into the sand of dry desert stream beds has been over-stressed by motion pictures and other mediums concerned more with entertainment than with education. There are a few places in desert watercourses where water can be reached by digging into a dry stream bed with primitive hand tools. Success is far too rare, however, to recommend the practice to any outlander in urgent need of water. In most cases the body water lost though the sweaty work and desert heat would kill the digger before he got close to water. The water is more likely to appear at 20 feet than at 20 inches, and a 20-foot, or even a 10-foot, hole wide enough to avoid cave-ins is a formidable project. It seldom pays to dig for water when the need is urgent unless mud or wet sand is visible on the surface of the river bed. Even then, a lesser amount of time and effort spent walking downstream will probably lead you to a natural depression in the damp river bed where water is still pooled on the surface. It is usually futile to dig with hand tools in damp river beds composed of coarse gravel and sizable stones, as water sinks fast and deep through such porous stuff.

Water Beside Salt-water Beaches

On a long stretch of ocean beach that has no freshwater inlets fed by rivers or streams, wait for low tide and dig in the sand below high-tide mark. If fresh water is seeping out to the salt water through the beach sand, it will fill your scooped hole before the salt water, which is heavier, starts to seep in from the seaward side. This trick works *some,* not *all,* of the time.

Snow Water and Sea Ice

Snow, no matter how old and settled the drifts, will provide fresh water. Simply melt it—in your mouth if you lack the fire and container to hurry the job.

The major icebergs that drift southward into shipping lanes will melt into fresh, not salt, water. They are great slabs broken off northern glaciers that were formed inland by ice and snow.

Ice that is frozen sea water loses its salt content as it

ages. Ice more than a year old (rounded and pitted surfaces above water, a bluish color under water) has most of the salt leached out of it. Melted, it will serve as drinking water.

Water from Plants

The young nuts from coconut palms found in most of the world's moist tropical regions are full of juice with a high water content. Pick the immature coconuts for drinking. The juice of ripe ones contains enough oil to cause digestive upsets when taken in quantity.

The large vines, or lianas, of tropical regions yield sap that will satisfactorily quench the thirst. Cut out a 6-foot section of such a vine and, holding it overhead, let the sap trickle into your mouth. Avoid those vines with milky sap. The good ones have clear, watery sap with an agreeable taste. Large grapevines yield water in the same way.

The barrel cactus is an emergency source of moisture in North American deserts. Do not expect a gusher when you cut into one, but a substantial amount of water can be squeezed and drained out of the inner pulp when the cactus is split open.

Most other plants containing a high percentage of water yield too little for the amount of work involved to be of use to the thirsty man in an emergency.

Rain Water

Rain water is always fresh and safe to drink as long as it is collected in an uncontaminated container. Natural "tanks" of solid rock in desert regions often hold rain water for long periods after a rainfall. It can be collected as it falls by spreading a sheet of fabric (a water-repellent coat works fine) in lean-to fashion to funnel the run-off into a container. Any rooflike panel of metal or wood or a slab of stone can be rigged to channel rain into a container. Scoop a hole in the ground and channel little drainage ditches into it when water is precious and there is no other way to catch rain. Many desert areas have soil fine enough to hold rain water in a scooped-out hole without immediate loss through seepage. The mud in rain water ditched into a hole will settle eventually. Drink or collect it, mud and all, if it is draining off quickly through porous soil.

Broad leaves are natural rain catchers in regions of lush foliage.

Moisture from Condensation

Where water is desperately scarce, there is a long-shot chance that a useful amount can condense and be collected in the form of dew. Moisture in the air forms as dew on cold or cool surfaces that are abruptly warmed by sun or artificial heat. (Watch it appear on the metal of a rifle brought from zero cold into a warm cabin.) There is an authentic record of a sailor adrift on a raft who lowered a large panel of thin metal on a line into the cool depths of the sea, hauled it up into the hot sun, and collected the moisture that formed on the panel through condensation. He gathered enough water this way to live through rainless weeks and was eventually picked up in reasonably good health. The large metal panels of an airplane down in waterless country may collect enough dew to provide a worthwhile amount of water at dawn. A large rubber or plastic panel will hold dew. Condensed moisture is a last-ditch hope and is available only when you have some large, water-proof surface. The method is always slow and laborious, and it is futile in a region of dry air and warm nights.

NATURAL FOODS

A man hungry enough to eat any available food and informed enough to recognize offbeat natural foods will find it almost impossible to starve to death during a month or two in the wilderness. One field-trained expert in wilderness survival, the author Calvin Rutstrom, points out that the average American sportsman is so well fed when he enters the deep woods or back country that his general health is likely to *improve* during his first three days without food of any kind—assuming that he has all the good water he wants.

Actually there is no reason to go three days—or even one day—without food. With the exception of a few stretches of arctic or desert wastelands, wilderness areas are full of natural food from spring through autumn, and most of them will supply enough winter food for the man who works for it.

The traveler who is broad-minded—or too hungry to care—can eat nearly everything that swims, flies, walks, or crawls in the North American wilds. Grasshoppers, for example, are nourishing when strung on a wire and broiled or cooked in any of a dozen ways. How they taste depends mainly on your frame of mind. Both grasshoppers and dragonflies are considered delicacies in Japan. Locusts, crickets, and similar insects have been eaten by various tribes since the dawn of time. Earthworms and grubs are also nourishing foods.

All snakes, including the poisonous ones, are good to eat. Snake poison is stored in sacs in the head, not in the edible meat of the body. Lizards are good food—prized among some peoples.

Any bird or its eggs will furnish an emergency meal. Edible animals and fish are too numerous to mention. The plants man can eat and thrive on are legion.

The basic idea is to shake free of the prejudiced and routine notions about what constitutes good food. The crow, as well as the chicken, is an edible bird. And so are its eggs. A man can eat porcupines, muskrats, ground squirrels; he does not have to kill a deer-size animal to get meat. Fern sprouts are about as good as asparagus, and the formidable stinging nettles are a dandy substitute for spinach, after the skin-stinging hairs have been neutralized by a few minutes in boiling water.

Edible Wild Plants and Trees

A complete list of wild plants a man can eat to stave off starvation or vitamin deficiency is too long to cover except in a book devoted entirely to that subject. The following partial list of edible wild plants will give you a general idea of what is available.

Wild berries—raspberries, blueberries, huckleberries, cranberries; dandelions, pigweed, plaintain, fern sprouts, miner's-lettuce, stinging nettles (gathered with gloves and boiled), the reindeer moss and lichen of the far North, cattail sprouts and roots, water-lily bulbs, wild rice, camas roots. The berries and most of the leafy plants on this list can be eaten raw. Brief boiling may make them more to your taste. Boil the lichen moss and the roots and bulbs.

Mushrooms, common in most North American woods, have too little food value to justify the risk a novice takes of picking a poison one. Drawings and descriptions cannot be trusted to teach the difference between safe and deadly mushrooms.

Grass and grass seeds of any kind are edible and nourishing. Wheat, oats, rice, and other such well-known cereals are grass seeds, which feed most of the world's population, and grass may be boiled for greens. All the many grasses known are edible.

In addition to yielding edible fruits and nuts in late summer and fall, most trees have a thin inner bark that is edible and nutritious in the spring and early summer. Young pines and other evergreens are particularly good, while the inner bark of poplars, birches, or willows will do. This tender layer next to the firm wood of the tree can be eaten raw, boiled, or roasted over a fire. The less cooking, the less loss of food value.

Precautions: The few plants and fruits poisonous to man can almost certainly be avoided by following these two rules:

1. Avoid any unfamiliar fruit, plant stem, or tuber filled with a white, milklike fluid.

2. Don't eat any strange plant food that stings or burns the mouth when a sample taste is taken after it is cooked.

There are exceptions (coconuts have a somewhat milky fluid, and peppers are hot), but these two restrictions will cost you few good meals and save a great deal of avoidable trouble.

Fishing

The fish is frequently the easiest source of meat, and the wilder the wilderness, the easier the fishing. Fish can often be caught by hand or killed with a crude spear as they make spawning runs up shallow creeks. Crude nets and traps will take them. And a fishhook, line, and bait can be rigged with primitive tools and equipment.

Quick and Easy Ways. Start by scouting the shallows and small feeder streams to see if there are spawning fish or schools of fingerlings that may be caught in quantity with little effort. Sometimes a few rocks can be moved to dam up or divert a shallow stream and strand fish in the pools below the dam. Spawning fish in the shallows can often be caught by hand or speared.

A torch or flashlight held over a pool at night makes spearing easy. (Lighting a pool for spearing is illegal in most areas, but this ruling is not designed to keep a lost camper or a crash survivor from spearing fish in this fashion.) A dip net fashioned from any open-mesh fabric fitted on a forked stick can frequently be used to scoop up quantities of minnows. (Cook and eat the little ones whole, like French fries, if they are scarce.) A low-walled corral of rocks or close-spaced stakes built in the ocean shallows at high tide will frequently trap fish when the tide goes out.

Fish trap is made by driving stakes side-by-side into a river bottom and leaving a gap for the fish to enter.

A man who expects to be stranded on a lake, a stream, or a seacoast for a long time can build a fish trap that is likely to provide a stable supply of fish. Put the trap all the way across a narrow stream or in the shallows of lake or ocean. Leave fish alive in the trap until they are needed. Dead ones spoil quickly in weather above freezing.

The trap shown and others like it take advantage of the fact that a fish funneled through a narrow opening lacks the reasoning power to use that same entrance as an escape route. Most of the fish that work through the narrow gate will mill around aimlessly in the wide holding pool of the trap and will remain imprisoned indefinitely. Fish in narrow, fairly shallow streams can be herded into a trap by stirring up the water with a splashing drive toward the trap's open arms.

Snagging.   Fish that will not bite a baited hook or an artificial lure are often schooled in deep holes, where it is easy to snag them with sharp hooks lowered to the bottom and jerked upward sharply. A good improvised rig for snagging is a stiff sapling from 6 to 8 feet long with a stout line as long as the pole tied to the end. Tie as many as five or six hooks to the line, spacing them about 2 inches apart on the lower portion of the line. Knot the hooks so that the points aim out from the line. Tie to the lower end of the line a rock or other sinker heavy enough to take it down quickly. Swing this rig out over a deep hole, let the heavy sinker go to the bottom, then jerk sharply upward at regular intervals, moving the stiff pole to cover as much of the pool as possible. It is not necessary to see the fish in order to snag them efficiently when they are schooled together in a deep hole. When the fish can be seen in clear water, ease the line beneath them and jerk upward to snap the hook-studded line against them. A snag line moved very slowly is not particularly alarming to fish in deep holes, but most fish are wary and nervous in shallow water.

Spearing.   Improvise a sharp metal point and barb for your fish spear when possible. A large nail or a similar small bar of soft iron can be hammered and filed or ground into a good spear point. Lash the point to a sapling handle with string, wire, or leather. (Leather lashings that are put on soaking wet will shrink to form amazingly tight bonds when dry. This is particularly true of rawhide laces and other thongs that have had a minimum of tanning or commercial processing.)

Lacking a sharp metal point, try to find a *dry* limb or

sapling that can be whittled to a sharp point. Dry wood will always form a harder, sharper point. Some green woods can be hardened by scorching them with fire.

The spear trap shown below can be made by splitting the end of any springy green sapling about a foot. Use a small stick to prop the split open to a width of about 6 inches at the bottom. When the spear trap is jammed down over a fish, the small prop stick will be knocked loose by the impact, letting the split ends of the sapling snap sharply together and grip the fish. Small barb notches cut on the inside surfaces of the split ends will help grip the fish.

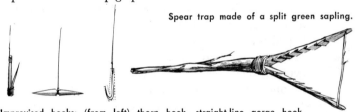

Spear trap made of a split green sapling.

Improvised hooks: (from left) thorn hook, straight-line gorge hook, branch-fork hook.

Bamboo poles make good double-point fish spears. Dry bamboo makes particularly hard points. Cut to the shape shown below.

Improvised Fishhooks. The baited hook or artificial lure is likely to be the slow, hard way to take fish if your situation is desperate. Spearing, snagging, and trapping—all illegal in most waters under ordinary circumstances—are likely to take more fish with less time and effort. Yet the baited hook or artificial lure will take loads of fish when they are in a biting mood, and there is usually an ample supply of hungry fish in wilderness waters.

The simplest of the improvised hooks that will efficiently catch fish is a gorge made of hard wood, bone, metal, sea shell—almost any tough material that can be worked with a knife or other simple tool. The gorge will sink one of its two points in a fish long enough for the fish to be yanked out of the water on a strong line. Allow the fish plenty of time to take the bait, which should be big enough to cover most of the gorge hook. Let the fish swallow the whole hook if he will. Then he is caught for sure. Natives all over the world use this simple hook.

The fork of a dead branch of tough wood can quickly be whittled into a workable fishhook. The smaller branch of the crotch forms the barb.

A sharp thorn lashed to a slender wooden shank makes a fairly good emergency hook. Hooks can be carved from bone. The wishbone of a bird is easily shaped and sharpened into a hook.

Most people have a half a dozen bits of wirelike metal in their clothes and equipment that will make suitable fishhooks. Wire buckles are easily bent and sharpened into a hook shape. (A barb is not essential if the fish is hoisted out at once, which is the safest and fastest way to "play" a fish with strong survival tackle.) Bent nails make good fishhooks, and of course any bit of stiff wire is suitable. Shape the improvised hooks to suit the size of the fish, using the largest hook the fish can and *will* gulp down easily.

Natural Bait. Bait for hook fishing is nearly always harder to come by than hooks to hang it on. Here are some things that are likely to work, one or several of which will be available near any fishing water: earthworms (dig and tip over rocks in rich, moist soil); wood grubs (rip open rotten logs); grasshoppers, dragonflies, locusts, and any similar bulky-bodied insects (on grass, reeds, brush); small frogs, toads, salamanders (scout for them in marshy areas); any small fish or minnow (in shallow water); the meat of crawfish, clams, oysters, mussels (on bottom in shallow water); chunks of flesh from any animal; bits of ripe fruit or berries.

Artificial Lures. Fish will frequently hit bits of white or colored cloth used like bait on a hook, particularly when the hook is in motion. Feathers, fur, or pieces of bright metal tied to hooks make workable artificial lures. Move them around in the water (just jiggling them up and down will often be enough), and strike back quickly when a fish takes the lure. Fish will commonly swallow a hook baited with real food in a leisurely way, but they spit out artificial lures fairly quickly.

Set Lines. If fish are hard to catch, toss out as many baited hooks as can be rigged conveniently, and tie the lines to limber saplings or some other anchor point on the shore. An untended line with a good bait on it will catch about as many fish as one held in the hand constantly. Toss the bait on these set lines into deep stream holes or lake or sea water more than 5 feet deep. Sizable fish are seldom found in shallow water unless they are spawning or feeding on something special. A bait near the bottom in fairly deep water will ordinarily outfish a shallow bait 10 to 1.

If you are on a lake or sea inlet or a fairly narrow river you can cross, rig a heavy line with a dozen baited hooks on dropper lines, and string this line across the river or inlet. Anchor the ends to the tops of tough, springy saplings that will absorb some of the shock of heavy fish tugging against the main line. Take off hooked fish, and rebait the rig as needed.

Set lines fish for you while you do some other chore, and are on the job all night while you sleep. Not many fish escape from such untended lines if lines and hooks are sturdy and hitched to something that will give and take like a limber sapling or a green tree limb. The crude efficiency of set lines has made them illegal for routine fishing in most states, but the man fishing to save his life is not going to be prosecuted.

Fishing Lines. A factory-made fishing line is just a convenience, not a necessity, for survival fishing. A much thicker and cruder line will usually catch the unsophisticated fish in wilderness waters. Lacking line, string, or cord of any kind, search your clothing and equipment for some spare items made of thread that can be unraveled or cut into thin strips and braided into a stout line. Thin strips of leather (cut a leather panel in ever smaller circles from outer edge to center to get a continuous length of leather line) will make a suitable fishing line. Strips of strong plastic will do. Threads of flexible bark or split tree roots can be braided into a makeshift line.

Preserving Fish. Since fresh fish spoil quickly without refrigeration, it will at times be wise to cure an emergency supply for future use. Smoking as much moisture as possible out of the fish is the easy way to do this. Proceed as follows:

Clean the fresh fish, remove heads, and split them up the spine almost to the tail—leaving just enough "hinge" flesh to hold the fish on a pole, one half dangling on one side, one half on the other. Rig the long pole that will hold the fish horizontally about 4 feet above a smoky fire. Keep fire heat very low. Use any wood in a pinch, but avoid the resinous evergreens when possible. Use enough green wood to keep smoke going. A crude tent of bark or fabric over the fish will speed the job considerably by holding in smoke and keeping off rain and dew. Keep the smoky fire going steadily until fish are dehydrated enough to crumble like dry cheese. Curing will take from one to two days, depending on how well smoke is confined, on dampness of weather, and on size of fish. Once they are thoroughly cured, smoked fish will keep for months in a cool, dry container.

Shooting Game

Getting game is a comparatively easy matter for the lost or stranded traveler who has a high-powered rifle, a shotgun with both birdshot and buckshot, or even a little .22 rifle—assuming that anyone who has one of those weapons knows how to use it as he ought to. Any high-powered rifle handling a cartridge in the .30/06 class (give or take a little power) will kill any big game animal in the world with a solid hit into the chest cavity, the neck column, or the brain cavity. A prudent hunter would hesitate to shoot an elephant with a .30/06, but lighter rifles in expert hands have killed hundreds of elephants. This elephant example is just to make the point that a good and careful marksman with a big-game rifle can feast on anything he encounters at reasonable range. He can easily convert a moose standing 100 yards away into a month's supply of meat. The big rifle will also take the head off a grouse or a rabbit ten steps away. No competent hunter with a big-game rifle will go hungry in a region that holds game of any kind.

The shotgun or little .22 rifle should down enough birds, rabbits, and other small game to keep a lost man going. With rifled slugs or buckshot, the shotgun will kill big game. It is a moose gun up to 25 yards with such loads, and it will knock down deer up to 50 yards or more. The .22 is a big-game weapon only in a desperate emergency. Indians and other everyday backwoodsmen have been known to kill animals as dangerous as the grizzly bear with close-range head or heart shots from a .22 rifle, but we do not hear about—or from—those who try such a stunt and fail. At a range of 50 feet or less, a .22 bullet taken squarely between the eyes or behind the ear is a terrible health hazard to elk, moose, caribou, deer—even to a grizzly bear. But it is futile, possibly dangerous, and always criminally wasteful for any person to plunk .22 bullets into the bodies of big game animals at random. Solid body hits as a rule will cause only wounds from which the animal may die painfully a week later in a thicket miles away.

The .22 is a good survival weapon for the collecting of rabbit-size game. It will kill fish that are within a few inches of the surface, and with a straight-down shot, it may get a fish under a foot of water. Aim a few inches beneath where the fish appears to be if shooting at an angle, since refraction of light makes the fish appear higher in the water than it really is. Never shoot at a fish between you and another person. Bullets fired at an angle will glance off the water. The shock of a bullet from a high-powered rifle will kill a fish near the surface whether or not the bullet actually hits it. A near miss will kill any fish of ordinary size.

Where to Hunt.   Fringe or border areas are generally the best bets to look for any game—that is, the places where dense woods meet clearings, where open plains meet brushy foothills, along natural borders formed by lakes, streams, trails, or ridges. Game is very difficult to locate in a dense thicket of woods or a sea of tall brush. Hunt the fringes and edges, the dim trails. Wait by well-tracked game trails or water holes in dry country. Early morning and late evening are the prime times to hunt most game animals, as they move more then. They are usually holed up or bedded down in heavy cover while the sun is high. Waiting and watching at strategic points ordinarily gets more game than prowling and searching. For the lost man, a patient ambush beside a game trail, feeding area, or water

ch-up snares hoist the game beyond the reach of predators.

hole has the added advantage of conserving energy and avoiding risk of even further confusion about directions and escape routes.

Anchored snare tightens when animal tries to get free.

Trapping and Snaring Game

A roll of light wire or strong twine will make loop snares, which are a sure-fire way to keep meat in camp in a region full of rabbits. Scout for well-used runways along brush bottoms—or wherever tracks show the rabbits are traveling—and put up all the snares time and material allow. Since a single snare may hang in the trail a week before a rabbit hits it, with seven snares out you should get a rabbit a day.

Either of the simple snares shown will catch rabbits. (They stick their heads through them as they come along the trail, and tighten the noose with their struggles to get lose.) The twitch-up snare with a trigger stick has the advantage of hoisting the captured rabbit high in the air where a rabbit-eating predator will not beat you to your meal. It kills tougher game than rabbits quicker and more surely.

When setting wire or cord snares, adjust size and loop of the snare to suit the standing height and head size of the game you are after. (A deer, as well as a rabbit, can be snared with suitable tackle.) The loop should be large enough to admit the animal's head easily and naturally as it hikes along the trail but small enough to tighten against the animal's shoulders. The snared animal's attempts to escape will work the strangling snare down around its neck. Make the set look as natural as possible. If the trail is wide, use rocks or limbs to block part of it, forcing the animal into the clear passage where the snare noose hangs.

In subzero weather the springy green saplings that make good twitch-up snares may freeze into a bend and lose their spring. In that event use heavy logs or rocks on snare wires or cables run pulley fashion over stout tree limbs. These weighted pull-up snares will work in any weather.

Birds can be snared where there is a concentration of such feed as wild grain or berries which can be used as bait. Animal fat or bacon will bait some birds. The basic idea is to arrange stones or branches to form cubbyholes into which the birds must reach to get the bait. Fit nooses of light cord or strong bark over the entrance holes so that the noose will catch in the neck feathers of the bird as it reaches through the loop for the bait. A large square of bark with a hole broken in it and a noose around the hole will catch a bird reaching down for bait placed under the bark.

Where flocks of birds commonly congregate in a certain small area—say, ducks on a small sand bar—two or three nooses can be placed on the sand bar and linked to a long line running back to a hiding place. When the ducks (or other flocking birds) return to this favored spot and stand over the nooses, yank the long connecting string to jerk the nooses tight around their feet.

Birds can also be trapped by rigging a box of saplings with an open door that will drop when a baited release trigger inside is moved or a long cord leading to a blind is yanked.

A trail of bait leading into the trap will lead birds (or animals) into the trap, where a tempting mound of bait can be seen by the quarry.

Deadfall Traps. The deadfall traps are designed to crush any animal that jiggles the trigger device while trying to get the bait lashed to it. Fill in the sides of the trap so that the animal must be squarely under the heavy fall log when it grabs the bait. Weight the log to suit the size of the animal you are after.

Box Trap. Box traps are effective, but involve quite a lot of labor. Baited with grain, fruit, or berries, they will catch birds and maybe rabbits. Meat on the trigger bar will pull in a great variety of animals, some of which are hard to hold. A fox, a mink, a marten, a bobcat, or any similar sharp-toothed and active animal will quickly bite and tear out of any box trap made of thin saplings. A box trap can be made sturdy enough to hold a bear, but it is not the sort of quick and easy trap that is most useful in a survival situation.

Last and Least—The Porcupine

Outdoor writers have for half a century been pointing out that the porcupine is one animal a lost man can easily kill with rock or club—a lifesaving meal that requires almost no effort or thought to capture. That is true. There are some important qualifications, however. Porcupines, though distributed over most of North America, are scarce or almost unknown in many very large regions. Even where porcupines are fairly plentiful they can be very difficult to locate.

Those you see are often high up in trees or within waddling distance of a safe retreat in a cliff crack or an abandoned burrow. It is therefore foolish to assume that porcupines will be steadily available as emergency food in any region where you are lost.

Deadfall trap is supported by notched stick arrangement that collapses when animal nibbles bait impaled on the sharpened end.

If you *do* find one, on the ground or in a low or easy-to-climb tree, it will in fact be easy to kill the slow-moving, dim-witted animal. Despite the formidable quills on its back and tail, a porcupine can be skinned and dressed out by starting the incision on the belly, which is free of quills. There is a lot of nourishing meat and fat on a big porky. The dressed carcass can be roasted on a spit over a low fire, boiled, fried, or cut into chunks for a stew.

29 - Insects and Other Pests

A HUNGRY OR CURIOUS BEAR CAN WRECK AN unguarded camp. Wolverines, though not as common or powerful as bears, can also despoil a wilderness cache or cabin. Skunks or porcupines blundering into camp can cause trouble that you will not laugh about till much later, and pack rats, ground squirrels, and mice can chew up a good bit of grub and gear.

We will describe how to cope with these animal pests later in this chapter, but first we will deal with insects, the most common and annoying of outdoor pests. Northern woodsmen who scoff at bears will cache their gear to make a fast escape from a valley clouded with mosquitoes. When deerflies swarm into summer camps in the Rockies and similar high country, they can make outdoor living utterly miserable. The same is true of black flies, no-see-ums, chiggers, and a dozen kinds of ticks. There are times and places when a camper needs to be armed against fleas, hornets, wasps, bedbugs, and even scorpions and tarantulas.

MOSQUITOES AND OTHER WING PESTS

There are three effective ways to deal with mosquitoes, black flies, no-see-ums, deerflies, and other flying pests; (1) avoid them; (2) screen them out; or

(3) kill or ward them off. When these pests are really plentiful, the camper should use all three methods.

Avoiding Mosquitoes

Consider the natural elements that are hostile to these insects. Dry and open ground is unattractive to them, and they breed in marshy flats. Wind, even a soft breeze, hampers their flight. Cold weather kills them. Thus, the main swarms can be dodged in summer by choosing high, dry, and breezy places to pitch your tent. (A mosquito-free camp on a knoll is well worth the extra effort of hauling water from a stream or lake 200 yards below.) The less green grass or dense foliage near camp, the better. Rank growth attracts and holds mosquitoes. In permanent camps it pays to cut tall grass and pour a little oil on nearby pools of still water; oil forms a thin film over still water which suffocates mosquito larvae. Do not let any water stand about, as even a tin can full of rain water can attract enough mosquitoes to give you a week of insomnia. Finally, the fact that frosty fall nights put an end to the yearly crop of mosquitoes, as well as other summer insects, is worth considering when scheduling a camping trip.

Screening out Mosquitoes

Loose clothing snugly buttoned or snapped at the collar and wrists will protect most of the camper's body from mosquitoes. Unlined leather gloves and a head net will protect the head and hands. The best head net—they are all rather awkward—is designed to tie snugly around the body beneath the armpits, rather than cinching around the neck. A broad-brimmed hat under the head net will keep the mesh away from the face. Some models have an elastic hole in front, which is a boon to smokers. The net ports are made for pipe smokers, but cigarette users can get their smoke through the net if they use a holder. A black or dark brown head net is easier to see through than a white or light colored one.

The trouble with some tent netting is that either the net is cut so skimpily that gaps open along joints and edges, or the mesh is too coarse to keep out the smallest of the winged marauders. The woven bars of some netting are as open as a parrot cage to no-see-ums and other tiny flies.

Bobbinet, which has a finer and stronger mesh, is the best all-round insect netting for campers.

Regular mosquito netting is a poor choice for general camp use. It is too coarse, too easily torn and stretched.

Cheesecloth has just one advantage: the weave or mesh is an effective barrier against the tiny pests that can squeeze through mosquito netting or bobbinet. Cheesecloth is fragile, however, and the tight weave blocks the flow of air. Since insects are usually at their worst during hot and humid weather, there is a great advantage in have compromise screening (bobbinet) that will let cooling air in and keep insects out. If a few small insects are squeezing through your medium-mesh netting, the mesh can be tightened by soaking it with water, which will swell any ordinary cotton fiber. As nylon and Dacron nettings do not swell and tighten with moisture, they must be sprayed or painted with insect repellent to keep out tiny bugs.

Chemical Repellents

Chemists have replaced such old backwoods reme-dies as pine tar and citronella with modern potions that are painless and inoffensive to humans and intolerable to mosquitoes. Several of the new mosquito repellents are almost foolproof protection against mosquito attacks on the face, neck, and hands. These liquid repellents are easy and pleasant to use: you simply wipe on enough of the liquid to dampen the skin. It will not irritate normal skin; the odor is not unpleasant, and there is no grease or mess. Unless the solution is washed off by sweat, rain, or water, it will keep mosquitoes at bay for several hours. It can be replenished as needed.

The trade-names of some effective mosquito repellents are Off!, 6-12, and Pellent. Off! is comparatively new and is sold by the makers of Johnson's Wax. Its basic formula—N, N-diethyl toluamide—was recently endorsed by the U.S. Department of Agriculture.

The following preparations are old-timers that are effective against mosquitoes, flies, and most other insects. Although they are generally messy and unpleasant to use, they save the day where more modern repellents are not available.

1. Blend 1 part of carbolic acid with 9 parts of sweet oil. Rub the mixture on exposed skin as often as required to keep bugs at bay.

2. Mix 1 ounce pure pine tar and 1 ounce oil of pennyroyal with 3 ounces of Vaseline, and smear on skin as needed.

3. Mix 1 ounce oil of citronella, 1 ounce spirits of camphor, and ½ ounce oil of cedar. Smear on skin or on netting or clothing where insects are trying to penetrate.

4. A backwoods formula that will make a season's supply of bug repellent: Mix 2½ pounds tallow with ½ pound black tar. While mixture is warm, stir in 3 ounces oil of citronella and 1½ ounces of pennyroyal.

Insect repellents containing tar will form a sort of glaze over the skin, making a physical as well as a chemical barrier. The glaze is more comfortable in cool northern regions, where trappers and prospectors often use tar repellent. But the tar-baby appearance and stunning aroma that result from using the tar and oil repellents will not be welcomed by warm-weather weekend campers. They will want such clean and inoffensive commercial repellents as Off!, Pellent, and 6-12.

Bug Bombs

All the repellents and methods just described will cope with mosquitoes and other flying pests, but they are only repellents—defensive weapons. In fixed camps the camper can head off a lot of trouble with such offensive weapons as sprayed insecticides, chemical dusts, and the old reliable smudge fire.

The modern "bug bombs"—pressure cans of insecticide which spray at the push of a button—are ideal for killing mosquitoes in a tent before bedtime or wiping out bugs in a cabin.

DDT is probably the most common insecticide used in bug bombs. It is deadly against mosquitoes and most other winged pests, though alone it needs time to take effect. A combination that kills almost instantly is DDT and malathion or lindane. Look for these ingredients on the label if you want a quick-acting bug bomb. The pressurized cans with DDT as the main ingredient are ineffective against some ticks and crawling mites. DDT will wipe out bedbugs, for instance, but chiggers seem to thrive on it. Use DDT with reasonable care. Keep it away from food, avoid prolonged exposure to the fumes, and do not rub strong solutions on the skin.

Smudge Fires

Smudge fires, given time to take effect, will at least cut the traffic in winged insects raiding a woods camp. To prevent annoying smoke, build smoldering fires in metal buckets or tin cans, and place them about 50 feet upwind from the camp, so that the smoke will not bother you. A bed of glowing coals and ashes covered with green evergreen needles or green grass will make a potent tin-can smudge. Set up the cans on wet or mineral soil where there is no fire danger, and let the smoke drift through your campsite. Do not expect insects to buzz off in alarm at the first whiff. But the steady irritation of the smudge will soon move out most of the resident bugs and keep newcomers at bay.

Emergency Measures

A bug-plagued camper who has nothing else can defend himself with plain kerosene, which all of the troublesome insects hate. There is the drawback, however, that a camper sponged with kerosene is almost as miserable as one harassed by bugs. Kerosene irritates the skin, has an unpleasant odor, and is dangerously inflammable to use around campfires or open flames.

A makeshift bug repellent can be contrived by soaking tobacco in warm water to produce a strong nicotine solution, which is deadly to nearly all insects. There is no particular risk or discomfort in smearing this solution on the skin, but it must be replenished almost constantly to ward off flying insects. It will quickly kill those crawling bugs that have already gained a toehold on the skin. Pipe tobacco or strong cigars will make stronger nicotine water than will cigarettes.

A person who is lost or stranded where clouds of mosquitoes are an actual threat to life has one effective defense—mud. Any mixture of soil and water that can be plastered thickly over exposed skin will act as a repellent. Animals rely on mud for protection when mosquitoes are out in blood-draining hordes. A thick layer replenished as needed (often, in warm weather) is sure protection.

CHIGGERS

Chiggers, also called "jiggers," "red bugs," or "chigoes," are tiny red mites which harass outdoorsmen in the South. Various kinds are found in the warmer regions in Mexico and Central America. They come off grass and foliage and attach themselves to the skin, where they soon dig in. They look like pinhead dots of red, and a stranger to chiggers could easily mistake them for some sort of skin rash. A chigger causes no sharp pain, as does the bite of a deerfly, say, but a good crop of chiggers thoroughly dug in will keep the average camper scratching and squirming. Scratching can infect the places where chiggers are submerged in the skin.

Chiggers are best avoided by dusting or spraying the skin and clothing that may come into contact with grass or foliage infested with them. Powdered sulphur or dimethyl phthalate is effective against chiggers. Napthaline or kerosene on clothing at crucial points will ward them off. Clothing saturated with strong smoke, particularly tobacco smoke, keeps them away. Some Southerners even smoke their clothes over fires of tobacco stems and scraps. After such a treatment, the clothes will repel people as well as chiggers.

A bath with salt water or strong soap every evening will keep chiggers in check. Those that sink in despite precautions can be killed by sealing them with a drop of clear nail polish. Itching can be relieved with calamine or benadryl hydrochloride lotion. A solution of ammonia or baking soda will help curb itching if the chigger is dealt with promptly; once he is firmly entrenched, neither will help.

TICKS

Various kinds of tick are a painful and sometimes dangerous menace to campers in mild weather. In the west—and in isolated cases in other parts of the country—tick bites may cause Rocky Mountain spotted fever, a disease that in the past was often fatal. An effective serum is available now, and a series of shots before tick season is a sound precaution in the Rocky Mountain states.

Prompt treatment with the so-called "miracle drugs" has sharply cut the number of spotted-fever fatalities in recent years, but ticks are still a hazard as well as a nuisance. Strip each night, and have a companion search you for ticks when camping during spring or early summer in western states that are known to have ticks. Sometimes it is possible to feel the ticks crawling on the skin and to pick them off immediately. Just as often they settle and dig their heads into the skin without causing a bit of pain or other sensation. Check hairlines and folds of skin.

A tick dug in can be removed quickly and in one piece by daubing it with alcohol, kerosene, gasoline, or strong nicotine solution made from tobacco. Heat from a match head or a cigarette will make a tick release its grip. Do not try to pull it out, for its head is likely to break off, with the possibility of infection.

The dopes and powders effective against chiggers will ward off most ticks.

Mexico has a particularly vigorous and bloodthirsty assortment of ticks and ticklike pests. If you are planning back-country trips in Mexico or Central America, take a good supply of repellents from the States, and inquire about local remedies at your destination south of the border.

The Spanish adventurer Hernando Cortes, the first white man to explore the interior of Mexico, spoke of the ferocity of the region's insects as if they were greater hazards than Indians or jungle beasts. That condition is unchanged in the humid back country today. Delbert L. Chears, a California archer who was hunting jaguars in Nayarit, Mexico, in 1959, was calm enough about the big cats to dispatch two of them with bow and arrows. He speaks emotionally of the insects, however. Telling his story for *Outdoor Life,* Chears says: "The tiny bug the natives call the ja-jen is the most vicious insect nature ever devised. You can hardly see them, but they are all biting mouth. If they were as big as bumble bees, I think they would rule the world."

The moral of these Mexico stories? Take plenty of bug dope on south-of-the-border trips that involve travels beyond the tourist towns. And do not scoff at such local and seemingly primitive measures as dusting with sulphur powder or dabbing with kerosene. The person with only one bottle of modern repellent will not go far in fertile bug country before he finds some insect that eats through all-purpose repellent as if it were cake icing.

WASPS, BEES, AND HORNETS

All these stinging insects, particularly wasps, are

at times attracted to campsites by exposed food. Keep food covered, and bury or burn scraps to avoid attracting wasps, bees, or hornets.

Campers with young children run some risk that the children, particularly boys, will deliberately stir up a nest of hornets out of a misguided sense of adventure. That is an educational problem that solves itself. The hornets will give those small campers the best instruction they could possibly receive.

The stinging insects of this class are nearly always defensive fighters. They sting when they are molested or when they think that they are. Avoid trouble by keeping a respectable distance from nests, hives, or concentrations of these stinging flyers. A lone wasp or hornet exploring a camp seldom stings anyone who sits or stands quietly. The fellow who slaps at it is its prime target.

A fresh fish skinned and hung up some distance from camp will help keep a hungry den of wasps away from camp tables. At times the wasps will so gorge themselves on the fresh fish that they will fall into a pan of water placed as a trap under the fish. This device may sound like a tall tale, but will actually work where stinging insects are hungry enough to form nuisance swarms about camp food.

Insect sprays and repellents rubbed on the skin are flimsy defenses against hornets, bees, and wasps, which do not seek to settle on the skin. Insect repellents are offensive to them, but not enough so to keep them from darting in and sinking a stinger into a repellent-smeared hide. Attempts to shoot them down with blasts of spray from a pressurized can will often result in the sprayer's being stung.

All in all, the best way to deal with such stinging insects is to leave them strictly alone.

BEARS

Pampered by tourists and protected by state and national parks, black bears are potential camp wreckers in many summer camping areas which are as busy and crowded as the grounds of a county fair. Grizzly bears are a threat to untended camps in the wilder parts of Canada and Alaska.

Bear raids on camps are prompted by a combination of hunger and curiosity, not by any animosity or violent intent toward people. The tourist-spoiled black bears in and around Yellowstone National Park, for example, are much given to night strolls through tents and over sleeping campers to explore grub boxes. Rattling tins wake up the sleepers, and all sorts of things can be broken and disheveled as the frightened bear and terrified campers maneuver in the dark tent. If the campers are not home when the bear arrives, he will chew and rip up everything that tempts his taste or arouses his curiosity, and then will leave quietly.

The best way to head off bear damage is to keep food in sacks that can be suspended out of reach from tree limbs or on a rope strung between two trees.

Food that smells attractive to a bear will not be safe untended in a light wooden box or a frame shack—and is not always safe even in a locked car trunk, for a bear's teeth and claws are incredibly powerful. Yellowstone Park black bears have many times proved that they can flip off trunk lids like bottle caps, if there is a crack for their claws to latch onto and a pound of bacon for incentive.

Northern trappers, prospectors, and hunting party outfitters often protect gear and grub left in bear-country camps by building storage shacks or cache platforms on stilts of tall poles. A couple of joints of stovepipe fitted over each pole makes it impossible for bears or most other clawed animals to climb to the supporting poles.

Untended cabins in grizzly or Alaska brown bear country need formidable door and window barricades to be safe. Old-timers stud their doors and window boards with sharpened spikes, crisscross patterns of barbed wire, or saw blades. The only sure protection for the tent camper's grub and gear is to keep it hoisted high between trees when it is to be left unguarded for any length of time. Possible snow depth must be considered when any cache is strung up for winter storage, for a short-legged predator can stand on 6 feet of snow and reach a cache that swung 8 feet above bare ground when the camper put it up before the snow fell.

WOLVERINES

The wolverine, a king-size member of the weasel tribe, is an efficient camp wrecker but a scarce one. A few are left in the wilder portions of the states bordering Canada, and perhaps a few stragglers are in remote parts of the high country farther south of the Canadian border. The same tricks that foil bears work with wolverines, though extra effort is required to defeat the wolverine's superior climbing skill and his ability to squeeze through small openings.

PORCUPINES

The porcupine is only a gnawing nuisance—unless a camper stumbles into him in the dark or a dog challenges his right to gnaw on camp gear. Then there will be quills to pull. And those quills can be dangerous. They work into the flesh gradually, and a face full of quills can blind or kill an animal ten times the porcupine's size. The porcupine does not throw his quills, by the way. Some may flip loose and rattle to the ground as he swishes his tail in defensive fright, but they have no harmful momentum. Those that drive home are implanted by a direct blow from that lashing tail. They will go deep.

Some people have recommended vinegar to soften quills for easy pulling. Others suggest cutting off the ends of the hollow darts to deflat and flatten them. Actually the time lost fiddling with such methods is probably better spent yanking quills with both hands. The longer they stay in, the more blood and body fluid seem to swell and tighten them. Get them out in a hurry. Pliers may be needed for those stuck deep and tight.

Grub boxes, leather goods, and wood-handled tools salted by sweaty hands should be boxed or hung out of reach where porcupines are plentiful. They are fair climbers, but not tightrope walkers by any means. They cannot get into tight wooden boxes or crates except by slow gnawing. Tin or other metal containers defeat them.

A salt block put out near a permanent or a semipermanent camp may satisfy the salt hunger of porcupines that would otherwise work on camp gear. Or it may merely attract and hold more porcupines in the area. There are two schools of thought on that, both valid at times.

Some campers paint things with a strong mixture of linseed oil and red pepper to discourage porcupines, which do not like the mixture; but it is a troublesome and messy routine to keep up.

Shouts, curses, and direct hits with rocks are no help whatever in persuading a porcupine that your camp is inhospitable. A porcupine has only brain enough to hold a grudge for seconds. It will come waddling back, full of appetite and good humor, five minutes after you drive him off your camp knoll with a fire log. Most working woodsmen are short on humor and patience where porcupines are concerned. They kill every one they see.

CHIPMUNKS, RATS, MICE

Campers making one-night stands or short-term stays will have little serious trouble with the small rodents. They are a threat mainly to cabins or semipermanent camps, where they can cut up stored mattresses and sleeping bags and can spoil food at a great rate. Tin or metal containers thwart them. So do cloth sacks hung on wires out of their jumping range. Regular mouse or rat traps will keep down the rodent population at a permanent cabin. And while campers are in residence in the cabin, there is no better rodent-control device than an active house cat. But take him with you when you leave: an abandoned house cat will soon become one of the worst pests and predators in the woods.

30 · First Aid for Campers

A SOUND KNOWLEDGE OF FIRST AID IS AS MUCH a part of the camper's equipment as are matches and knife. The man who ranges far from roads and telephones cannot depend on the brisk arrival of a doctor in the event of an emergency. He must be able to take care of himself or of someone else until medical help is available. And he should be able to deal with minor injuries which, although not demanding a doctor's care, might spoil a camping trip unless promptly and properly treated.

The first-aid instructions in this chapter are particularly appropriate for outdoorsmen. Endorsed by the official manual of the U.S. Forest Service, these sound rules are tailored to the needs of the thousands of professional outdoorsmen who work in the nation's national forests and they will meet situations with which campers have to cope.

GENERAL RULES

Follow this six-step sequence in dealing with any person who appears to be seriously ill or injured:

1. Examine the patient carefully.
2. Treat immediately those things that can cause

immediate death. The quick killers are, in this order: arterial bleeding, stoppage of breath, poisoning, and shock. (Proper treatment of each is described in detail in this chapter.)

3. Send or signal for help. If you are alone, you may be able to attract attention by building a smoky fire that a fire-tower lookout will report. Rifle shots —three close together are a common distress signal —may bring help.

4. Do not let the patient drink anything if you suspect internal injuries. Do not pour any liquid in the mouth of an unconscious patient.

5. Make the patient as comfortable as possible. That includes such considerations as a blanket or a coat for warmth, head rest, or sunshade. It also includes a calm and cheerful attitude on your part when the patient is conscious. Keep onlookers away if there is a large group present. Do not let the patient look at a serious wound.

6. Carefully consider the question of whether or not the patient should be moved. It is generally inadvisable to move any seriously injured person if a doctor or an ambulance crew can reach the scene of the accident quickly. Never make a quick decision about moving the patient in any circumstances. A person with a broken neck or back, for example, can be killed by careless handling. Many wilderness areas are served by rescue units with helicopters or doctors who parachute to the scene of an accident. In Montana, for instance, Forest Service smokejumpers have for years maintained a wilderness rescue unit that can safely move a desperately injured person from wilderness to hospital in hours, once they know the location of the accident. They use helicopters, parachuting

doctors, and a stretcher team of young smokejumpers trained and toughened for mountain rescues.

BLEEDING

Arterial

The symptom of this bleeding is blood spurting or welling up strongly. This is a quick, sure killer and demands attention ahead of anything else.

First Aid:

1. Quickly remove any obstructing clothing, and supply pressure directly over the wound with a bandage pad held in the hand. Use the best bandage pad that is instantly available, whether or not it is clean.

The first step in controlling bleeding is to apply pressure over the wound, preferably with a sterile gauze.

Seconds count with arterial bleeding. Pressure of a bandage pad directly over the wound will stop most bleeding.

2. If this fails, apply firm pressure with fingers at a pressure point that will check flow of blood to affected area.

3. A tourniquet is a last resort in checking arterial bleeding. It should be put on tightly above the wound and *kept tight* until a doctor can be reached. Use it only when continued loss of blood seems sure to kill the patient. The tourniquet can save a life, but the limb it is used on will often be lost. Never think of

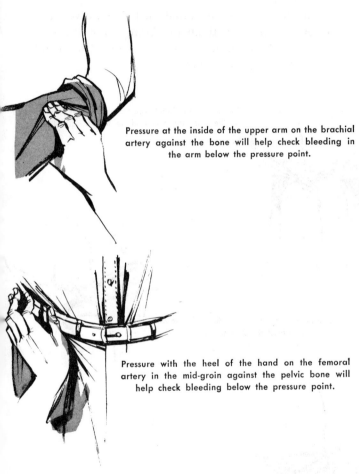

Pressure at the inside of the upper arm on the brachial artery against the bone will help check bleeding in the arm below the pressure point.

Pressure with the heel of the hand on the femoral artery in the mid-groin against the pelvic bone will help check bleeding below the pressure point.

the tourniquet as a routine device for the control of minor or even fairly profuse bleeding from the veins.

Minor External Bleeding

When dealing with a bleeding wound that is not immediately dangerous, take precautions to guard against infection. Such wounds include most vein cuts, which ooze blood without the strong pulse of arterial bleeding. If possible, wash the hands thoroughly before treating the wound.

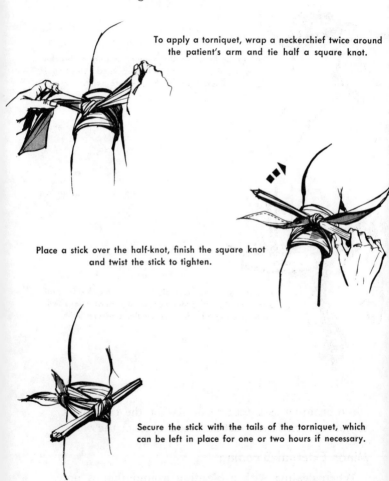

To apply a torniquet, wrap a neckerchief twice around the patient's arm and tie half a square knot.

Place a stick over the half-knot, finish the square knot and twist the stick to tighten.

Secure the stick with the tails of the torniquet, which can be left in place for one or two hours if necessary.

First Aid:

1. Wash wound with soap and water when practical, and cover it with a sterile bandage. Cloth can be sterilized by boiling, dipping in alcohol, or scorching with a flame.

2. Do not breathe on an open wound, and do not touch it with anything but a sterile bandage after it has been cleaned with soap and water.

3. A drop of iodine or similar disinfectant and a neat stick-on bandage of tape and gauze is a sound precaution with small nicks and scrapes.

Internal Bleeding

A violent blow may produce internal bleeding without breaking the skin. The symptoms are restlessness, thirst, pale face, weak and rapid pulse, over-all weak feeling.

First Aid:

1. Keep patient flat on his back unless that hampers his breathing, as it may with a punctured lung.

2. Prop him up slightly to ease breathing when necessary.

3. Stand by to turn his head to the side for vomiting, which may occur.

4. Keep patient quiet, and reassure him.

5. Keep him flat on his back or propped only slightly if he must be moved.

Nosebleed

First Aid:

1. Have patient sit or recline with head back.

2. Bleeding can frequently be stopped by holding finger pressure on outside of nostril for about five minutes; release it gently after the blood has clotted.

Mouth-to-Mouth (Also Mouth-to-Nose) Method
of Artificial Respiration

A. Remove foreign matter from the patient's mouth with your fingers.

B. Tilt the head back so the chin is pointing upward (Fig. 1). Pull or push the jaw into a jutting-out position (Fig. 2 and 3). The objective is to relieve obstruction of the air passage by moving the base of the tongue away from the back of throat.

C. Open your mouth wide and place it tightly over the patient's mouth and pinch the nostrils shut (Fig. 4), or close the nostrils with your cheek (Fig. 5). Or close the patient's mouth and place your mouth over the nose (Fig. 6). Blow into the patient's mouth or nose. Determine from the first blowing whether any obstruction exists.

D. Remove your mouth and listen for the return rush of air that indicates air exchange. Repeat blowing. For an adult, blow vigorously at the rate of about 12 breaths per minute. For a child, take relatively shallow breaths, at the rate of about 20 per minute.

E. If you are not getting air exchange, recheck the head and jaw position. If you still do not get air exchange, quickly turn the victim on his side and administer several sharp blows between the shoulder blades to dislodge any foreign matter in the throat (Fig. 7). Try again, and keep trying for several hours if a doctor does not arrive sooner. If you do not wish to come in contact with the person, hold a cloth over his mouth or nose and breathe through it. The cloth does not greatly affect the exchange of air.

F. When the patient revives, keep him lying quietly. Offer him warm water, milk, tea, or coffee unless he is nauseated. He should rest quietly for twenty-four hours.

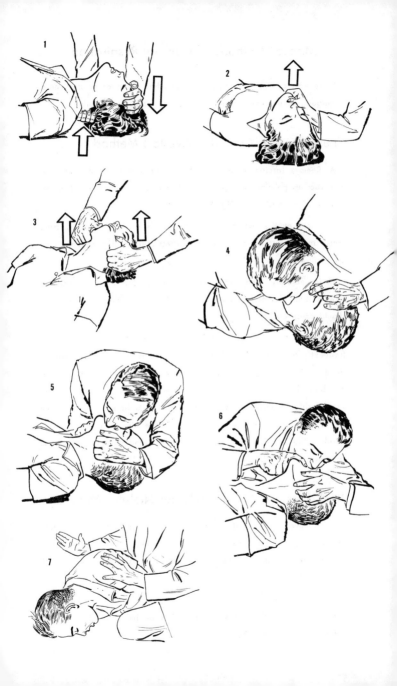

Manual Methods of Artificial Respiration

Those who cannot, or will not, use mouth-to-mouth or mouth-to-nose techniques, should use a manual method of artificial respiration.

Chest-Pressure Arm Lift (Silvester) Method

A. Remove foreign matter from the patient's mouth and place him in a face-up position with something under his shoulders to allow the head to drop backward (Fig. 8).

B. Kneel at the patient's head, grasp his arms and wrists, cross them, and press them over the lower chest (Fig. 9). This should cause air to flow out.

C. Immediately release this pressure and pull the arms outward and upward over his head and backward as far as possible (Fig. 10). This should cause air to rush in.

D. Repeat this cycle about 12 times per minute, checking the mouth frequently for obstructions. When the patient is in a face-up position, there is always danger of aspiration of vomitus, blood, or blood clots. This hazard can be reduced by keeping the head extended and turned to one side. If possible, the head should be a little lower than the trunk. If a second rescuer is available, have him hold the patient's head so that the jaw is jutting out (Fig. 11), and have him check the presence of any stomach contents in the mouth.

Back-Pressure Arm Lift (Holger-Nielsen) Method

A. Remove foreign matter in the patient's mouth and place him face down. Bend his elbows and place his hands one upon the other, turning his head slightly to one side and making sure that the chin is jutting out (Fig. 12).

B. Kneel at the patient's head and place your hands on the flat of his back so that the palms lie just below an imaginary line running between the armpits (Fig. 13).

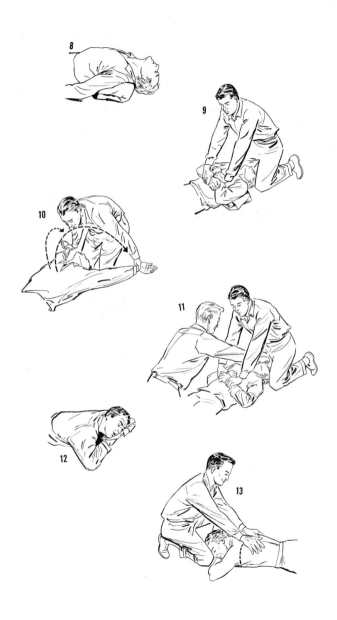

C. Rock forward until the arms are approximately vertical and allow the weight of the upper part of your body to exert steady, even pressure downward upon the hands (Fig. 14).

D. Immediately draw his arms upward and toward you, applying enough lift to feel resistance and tension at his shoulders (Fig. 15). Then lower the arms to the ground. Repeat this cycle about 12 times per minute, checking the mouth frequently for obstruction. If a second rescuer is available, have him hold the victim's head so that the jaw continues to jut out (Fig. 16). The helper should be alert to detect any stomach contents in the mouth and keep the mouth as clean as possible at all times.

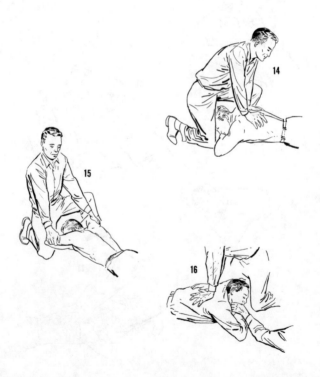

3. Cold wet cloths applied to nose, face, and neck help.

4. Pack sterile gauze in nostrils if milder methods fail.

ARTIFICIAL RESPIRATION

The following four fairly common accidents may stop breathing and call for artificial respiration: drowning, the most common; smoke and gases; shock from electric power lines or lightning; throat obstruction or smothering. The symptoms will be much the same in all four: the patient will be unconscious and not breathing; face and lips will be blue, and the face either flushed or pale; pulse will be weak or absent.

Electric Shock

An electric-shock victim who has stopped breathing must be approached cautiously. Use a dry wooden pole or a rope to pull the electric wire away from him. Give artificial respiration as in breath stoppage due to drowning, smoke, or gas. A victim of high-voltage shock will usually have serious burns to treat (burn treatment is discussed later in this chapter), but artificial respiration is the first consideration.

Choking

A person choking on some object or matter lodged in his throat should be held upside down or bent sharply forward from the waist and given a sharp slap on the back. If that fails, try to clear his throat with your fingers. Use mouth-to-mouth artificial respiration in any case where breathing has stopped.

POISONING

Any camper, especially a young child, runs some risk of poisoning. The symptoms are: pain in stomach, headache, nausea, vomiting, flushed or bloated face, possible burns inside mouth, convulsions, loss of consciousness.

First Aid:

1. Dilute poison by having patient drink all the fluid he can. A good mixture is 1 teaspoon of either salt or baking soda in warm water or milk. Milk is best if the poison is one of the caustics such as lye or ammonia. Get four to seven glasses of fluid down the patient if possible.

2. Induce vomiting by tickling patient's throat with finger. This will bring up the poison that has been diluted by fluid consumed in step 1.

These are the urgent steps in cases where the symptoms suggest serious poisoning and the exact nature of the poison is not known. If the poison is known to be an acid or an alkali, it is better not to encourage vomiting. Instead, neutralize the acid or alkali. Good antidotes for acid poisoning are baking soda, magnesia, or chalk mixed with water. Then give milk, olive oil, or egg whites to protect digestive tract lining. Alkali poisoning can be neutralized by drinking a glass of water and then such weak acids as lemon juice or vinegar. Follow with milk, olive oil, or egg white.

Get any poisoning case to a doctor or a hospital as soon as possible. If a doctor is coming to the patient, keep him lying down and warm.

Snake Bites

A person can be struck by a poisonous snake without knowing it—say, in a fall down a steep hill where the snake's strike is only one of several cuts and bruises. The symptoms are: immediate pain, swelling and purple discoloration, over-all weakness, rapid pulse, vomiting in some cases. The puncture points of the snake's fangs will usually show clearly—two punctures ordinarily, but possibly only one due to a broken fang or a strike partially blocked by clothing.

First Aid:

1. Get the victim—who will ordinarily be excited —to sit or lie down and remain quiet. Do that yourself if you are the victim.

2. If strike is on arm or leg, as most are, tie a belt, handkerchief, or bandage above the wound to slow circulation and spread of poison. *Do not* tie this band so tight or leave it on so long that the limb becomes cold or numb. Remove the band for a minute every fifteen minutes.

3. Sterilize knife or razor blade (with flame, alcohol, iodine, merthiolate), and make shallow cross incisions a quarter of an inch long through each puncture. Slant these incisions to avoid cutting a major tendon or blood vessel.

4. Apply suction to incision with suction cup or mouth. There is little risk that enough venom will be sucked into the mouth (spit it out promptly) to cause any serious trouble, even if there are a few raw spots in the mouth or on the gums. Continue suction for thirty minutes unless a doctor arrives or is reached sooner.

5. Move the constricting band on the limb higher if the swelling spreads up to the band. Make more incisions and apply suction wherever major swelling and discoloration appear.

6. Give plenty of drinking water but no strong

stimulants. Whisky, jokingly known as snake-bite remedy to many outdoorsmen, is not recommended.

7. Get the patient as quickly as possible to a doctor or a hospital, by a method that causes him the least possible exertion and excitement. If you are the victim and are alone, give yourself the first-aid treatments—constricting band, cuts, and suction—then walk slowly toward help.

Bee, Wasp, or Hornet Stings

First Aid:

1. Remove stinger if it is stuck in puncture.
2. Apply paste of baking soda and water or soda and cold cream.
3. Use cold packs to ease pain.
4. Apply calamine lotion to relieve itching.

Black Widow Spider Bite or Scorpion Sting

First Aid:

1. Keep victim warm and lying quietly.
2. Give hot bath to relieve any cramps that may occur.
3. Get professional medical treatment as soon as possible.

Chigger and Red-Bug Bites

First Aid:

Apply calamine lotion or a similar lotion recommended by a druggist or a doctor in a region where these annoying insects are common. A good preventive measure is to coat socks and ankles with dimethyl phthalate before hiking into chigger or red-bug country.

Ticks

The dangerous tick in this country is the one that transmits Rocky Mountain spotted fever. As the name suggests, Rocky Mountain tick or spotted fever usually occurs in the Rocky Mountain states, but there are scattered cases in states far removed from the Rockies.

A sound preventive measure is vaccination with spotted-fever serum in advance of the spring and summer tick season. Examine clothes and body at least once a day when camping in that region in tick season. Have a companion inspect your back. A tick can dig its head into your back or the back of your neck without your being aware of it. They can usually be felt crawling on bare skin—but not always.

First Aid:

Ticks burrow their heads in the skin. Jerking one off, however, may make the head break off under the skin, with risk of infection. Ticks are dislodged safely by any of the following methods:

1. Hold heated metal or a lighted match or cigarette close enough to the tick to force it to withdraw.

2. Cover the tick with grease, gasoline, or kerosene. Such treatments usually cause the tick to withdraw within a few minutes.

3. After removal, wash bite with soap and water or treat with a drop of a potent antiseptic.

Pajaroella Tick Bite

These ticks are particularly troublesome in the oak forests of southern California, and they are relatively new even there. They will bite, causing a slight prickling sensation at the time, and then drop off.

In six to twenty-four hours the bite will begin to

itch and ooze serum. A dark circle will form around the bite. The bite area becomes a running sore very vulnerable to infection for about a month.

First Aid:

1. Make a shallow incision in the bite at once, and apply suction for twenty minutes.

2. Apply such an antiseptic as merthiolate, zephiran, or alcohol and a bandage.

Poison Oak, Ivy, Sumac

The skin affected by any of these plants will be red, swollen, and sprinkled with small blisters and will itch violently.

First Aid:

1. Wash affected area with soap and hot water, then with alcohol.

2. Apply a thick paste of melted soap to the rash; let it dry and remain on the skin overnight.

3. Treat rash with calamine lotion thereafter.

Campers can now build up resistance to these plant rashes by taking pills or injections for a prescribed period before going into the woods. Learn to recognize and avoid the plants. Stay away from the smoke of a fire burning among these plants.

Poison ivy grows as a small plant, a vine, or a shrub everywhere in the United States except California and parts of adjacent states. Leaves consist of three glossy leaflets.

Western poison oak grows in shrubs or vine form in California and parts of adjacent states. Leaves consist of three leaflets.

Poison sumac grows as a woody shrub or small tree in most of the eastern third of the United States.

SHOCK

Shock is an over-all loss of efficiency in bodily functions due to an injury, and it can kill a person who would not otherwise die from the injury that has triggered it. It is likely to result from serious burns, internal injuries, broken bones, loss of blood, extreme pain, exposure, extreme fatigue. The symptoms, which ordinarily develop gradually, are as follows: the skin becomes pale, moist, cold, and clammy; the eyes lose their luster, and the pupils become dilated; breathing is shallow and irregular; the patient feels faint, perhaps nauseated; the pulse is weak, rapid.

First Aid:

1. Get patient to lie flat.
2. Use blanket or other cover to warm patient just enough to prevent shivering.

3. Give patient a cup of warm water, milk, tea, or coffee unless he is nauseated, unconscious, or there is reason to expect he will soon undergo surgery.

4. Get a doctor's help as soon as possible. If the doctor is coming to the patient, send word that plasma may be needed. While waiting for the doctor or during stretcher trip to hospital, keep the patient lying down and as quiet and comfortable as possible.

BURNS AND SCALDS

Burns break down into three degrees of seriousness. A first-degree burn only reddens and irritates the skin. A second-degree burn blisters the skin. A third-degree burn cooks or chars the skin and often damages underlying tissue.

First Aid:

For small first- and second-degree burns:

1. Place sterile gauze over burn.

2. Bandage snugly.

3. Rebandage after three days, at which time healing should be well under way.

For widespread burns of any degree:

If doctor or hospital can be reached within an hour, treat the patient for shock and rush to doctor or hospital without attempting to treat the burns yourself.

In an isolated area:

1. Cover burned area with eight or ten layers of sterile dressing, making no attempt to clean the area.

2. Bandage area snugly.

3. Treat patient for shock.

4. Give patient all he can drink of a solution of ½ teaspoon of baking soda and 1 teaspoon of salt to 1 quart of water.

5. Notify doctor that plasma may be needed.

With burns, do not:
1. Touch burn with fingers.
2. Breathe on burn.
3. Apply antiseptic.
4. Break or drain blisters.
5. Change dressing—a doctor's job.

Keep in mind that burns cause great loss of salty fluids which must be replaced. Thus the patient should have all of the solution of salt and soda in water that he can drink. This helps to ward off shock, which is the first danger in cases of serious burning or scalding.

Chemical Burns

Treatment for chemical burns differs in that the burned area should be flushed with water to remove as much of the chemical as possible. Then treat like any other burn.

Sunburn

Use petroleum jelly or moist skin lotion to relieve dryness in minor cases. Extreme cases should be treated the same as other widespread first- or second-degree burns.

SUNSTROKE

The symptoms are: headache, dizziness, red face, hot and dry skin, rapid pulse, high temperature, loss of consciousness.

First Aid:
1. Place victim on back in the shade with clothing loosened and head and shoulders elevated.
2. Apply cool, wet cloths to entire body.
3. Rub limbs toward heart.

4.   Give cool drinks slowly (no strong stimulants) .

5.   Call doctor.

FROSTBITE

There will be considerable pain if frostbite is in the hands or feet. Nose, cheeks, and ears may become frostbitten without that warning. Grayish white skin is a warning sign.

First Aid:

1.   Cover the affected part with warm, soft insulation, and get the patient into a heated shelter as soon as possible.

2.   Give the patient warm drink.

3.   Thaw the affected area gradually in a warm room or in lukewarm water.

4.   Massage area near frosted part to increase circulation, but *do not* rub frosted area at any time. (Such treatments as rubbing with warm hand or with snow may increase circulation *before* frostbite has actually occurred. Do not use snow, direct heat, or massage on any area where tissue is actually frozen before first aid is started.)

5.   Extensive frostbite requires a doctor's treatment, perhaps hospital care.

COLD EXPOSURE

These are the symptoms: the victim becomes drowsy and numb; loss of co-ordination; fading eyesight, eventual loss of consciousness.

First Aid:

1.   Bundle the patient warmly or get into a warm shelter if that can be done at once.

2.   Use mouth-to-mouth artificial respiration immediately if breathing has stopped.

3.   When the patient responds, give him hot coffee and a long rest in a warm bed.

SNOWBLINDNESS

Snowblindness is caused by prolonged exposure without dark glasses or snow goggles to bright sun reflected off snow.

First Aid:

Cover the eyes with cold compresses and get the victim out of sun glare. Wash the eyes with boric acid solution. A drop of mineral oil in the eyes will sooth the gritty feeling. Wear dark glasses until the eyes are again normal.

BONE FRACTURES

You can recognize a broken bone by one or several of the following: The victim may hear or feel the bone snap. There will be pain and tenderness at the broken point. The patient usually loses ability to move the injured part. The area near the break will usually become swollen and discolored and may appear deformed. The bone will break through the skin, often with severe bleeding, in compound fracture.

First Aid:

1. Where a doctor is near, do not move either the broken limb or the patient.

2. If there is profuse bleeding over the break area, control it with pressure of sterile compress. Use tourniquet only when arterial bleeding cannot be stopped by compress or pressure points.

3. If it is necessary to move patient, immobilize broken part and adjacent joints with padded splints, being careful to disturb broken ends of bone as little as possible. Do not try to set a broken bone yourself.

4. If patient with break in long leg bones must be moved a considerable distance, he will be more com-

fortable if a traction splint is applied to pull and hold the leg taut.

5.   Check splinted limb every twenty minutes to be sure swelling has not cut off circulation. Loosen splint bindings enough to cope with swelling.

6.   Get the patient to a doctor or a hospital as fast as possible without needlessly disturbing broken bones.

Skull Fracture and Concussion

Look for lump or cut on head. Victim is usually dazed or unconscious. There may be bleeding from ears, mouth, or nose. Pupils of eyes may be of unequal size.

First Aid:

1.   Keep patient lying down but with head and shoulders raised slightly if the face is either normal in color or flushed. Lower the head if the face is pale.

2.   Move the patient in horizontal position if a move is necessary.

3.   Bandage open wounds.

4.   Be alert to lower and tip the head of patient strangling on blood. Turn his whole body to do this when possible; avoid needless neck motion in any case where there is a possibility of the neck's being broken.

5.   Give no stimulants.

6.   Get a doctor as soon as possible.

7.   Do not leave patient alone.

Spine or Neck Fracture

A symptom is pain in spine or neck. If victim can not close his fingers firmly, the neck may be broken. If fingers work but toes do not, back may be broken. Patient with broken back or neck usually is in severe shock.

First Aid:

1. Treat all doubtful cases as if the neck were fractured: do not let victim move, lift, or tip his head.

2. Cover with blankets.

3. Get doctor or ambulance.

4. In remote area where victim must be moved, he must be lashed face up to rigid stretcher, board, or poles. Utmost care must be taken to avoid moving neck or spine during stretcher loading or transportation. Pad and lash the carrying platform as shown, to hold patient flat and motionless. A twist or bend of neck or spine can kill the patient when there is a break in either place. Never try to move a patient with suspected neck or back break until the most competent aid available is there to help.

CRACKED OR BROKEN RIBS

The symptoms are: Pain and possibly a lump or a gap in the break area which you can feel with your fingers; severe pain when the patient takes a deep breath or coughs. Shallow breathing—shock may occur in serious cases. Patient may cough up frothy blood if lung is punctured.

First Aid:

1. With serious breaks or a punctured lung, have the patient lie quiet. Transport him lying down with a minimum of motion to hospital or doctor. Do not use bandages around the chest.

2. With cracked or greenstick fracture of rib, place a thick pad over the break area, and bandage snugly in place with cloth bands reaching all the way around the chest. The object here is to ease pain by restricting rib motion.

Pelvis Fracture

The symptoms are: much pain in pelvic region if victim stands (which he may be able to do) or tries to walk, and severe shock in some cases. Pain and shock may not be conspicuous if victim is lying down and does not try to stand up after injury.

First Aid:

1.   Tie knees and ankles together.

2.   Move the patient on his back on stiff stretcher, door, or board to hospital or doctor's office.

Jaw Fracture

The term "broken jaw" refers, in general use, to a break in the hinged lower jawbone; as the upper teeth are imbedded in the skull, a fracture there is essentially a skull fracture.

First Aid:

1.   Place palm of your hand under the patient's chin, and raise broken jaw gently to bring teeth together.

2.   Tie the jaw in place with a wide cloth band running under jaw and over top of head.

3.   If the patient starts to vomit, which may happen, loosen the bandage and support the jaw with the hand; then rebandage when throat is clear. A tight bandage that could not be loosened would cause vomiting patient to strangle.

4.   Get the patient to a doctor.

Collarbone Fracture

The symptoms are: The shoulder on the injured side will often be lower than the other. A break in the collarbone can sometimes be felt with light finger pres-

sure. The patient usually cannot raise his arm above
the shoulder.

First Aid:

1. Put the arm on the side where the break occurs
in a sling, with the sling adjusted so the hand is slightly
higher than the elbow.

2. Tie the arm snugly to the body to avoid undue
motion.

3. Get the patient to a doctor.

DISLOCATION OF JOINTS

The symptoms are: intense pain, deformity, swelling, loss of movement.

First Aid:

1. Apply cold compresses to help ease pain.

2. If the victim must be moved, support the area
of dislocation with sling or bandages to prevent needless motion.

3. Do not try to put serious dislocation back into
place; that is a doctor's job.

SPRAINS AND BRUISES

First Aid:

1. Elevate injured part when practical.

2. Apply ice, cold cloths, or running cold water at
once.

3. After six or eight hours of cold applications,
which will often retard swelling and discoloration,
switch to hot applications or heat treatments and rest
the injured muscles.

4. Gentle massage to increase circulation will help
as bruised or sprained muscles lose swelling and discoloration.

5. When skin is broken over bruise or sprain, treat

it as an open wound: cleanse with soap and water or antiseptic and bandage.

PUNCTURE WOUNDS

There is danger of fatal tetanus or lockjaw with any puncture wound on a person who has not had a recent tetanus inoculation. Small, deep puncture wounds always pose the danger of infection.

First Aid:

1. Encourage bleeding by mild squeezing to flush out wound.

2. Apply sterile pad and bandage. (Surface washing or antiseptic treatment will not reach into puncture wound.)

3. Get a doctor to clean out wound and administer tetanus shot if needed. If puncture wound is from an animal bite, be sure to tell doctor. A rabies shot may be indicated.

4. With a major puncture or a cut through the abdomen, keep the victim on his back, giving him nothing to drink. Do not try to clean the wound; just cover it with a sterile bandage. If the intestines are exposed, keep a wide bandage over the opening moist with warm water containing 1 teaspoon of salt per quart. Raise the patient's knees, and keep him on his back while you transport him to hospital quickly.

BULLET WOUNDS

First Aid:

1. Stop blood flow.

2. Apply sterile dressing and bandage.

3. Immobilize broken bones.

4. Keep the patient quiet, warm, and comfortable to head off shock.

5. Get the patient to a doctor soon as possible.

EYE WOUNDS

First Aid:

1. Cover the eye with a sterile pad and bandage—not too tight if eyeball is injured.

2. Get the patient to a doctor at once.

An irritating particle of foreign matter in the eye can be removed by lifting the eyelid and dabbing out the particle with the corner of a clean handkerchief. Irritation can be eased by flushing out the eye with half a teaspoon of boric acid in a glass of water. A drop of pure mineral oil in the eye will ease discomfort when the speck cannot be located and removed.

OBJECTS UNDER SKIN AND NAILS

First Aid:

1. Sterilize needle, knife point, or pointed tweezers, and pry out object. (Trim and scrape top of nail thin to allow small V incision when necessary.)

2. Disinfect wound with antiseptic such as tincture of iodine, merthiolate, or alcohol.

BLISTERS

First Aid:

Wash with soap and water and cover with sterile bandage if fresh blister is broken and raw skin is exposed.

Though some first-aiders advocate opening and draining of blisters caused by friction, the skin and fluid over a blister is actually a safer and better bandage than any the camper can apply. When in doubt, leave an unbroken blister alone. It will frequently cause less trouble and heal faster if you let nature take its course.

INFECTED WOUNDS

The symptoms are: throbbing pain and heat near wound; unusual swelling and redness with pus and red streaks leading out from wound.

First Aid:

1.   Keep the patient resting quietly.

2.   Make solution of hot water with 2 teaspoons of salt to each quart, and apply to wound for an hour at a time, allowing intervals of three or four hours between treatments. If possible, as with hand or foot, soak infected part in the hot salt water. Keep the water hot.

3.   Elevate infected area between treatments if possible.

4.   Repeat steps above until doctor arrives or patient can be delivered to doctor.

HEART FAILURE

The symptoms are: The patient may appear to faint. His face will usually be pale (sometimes flushed), pulse weak. There may be pain around the heart and down the arms. The patient will not recover rapidly, as will a healthy person who faints, and will usually be considerably alarmed about his condition.

First Aid:

1.   Keep the patient quiet and lying down; elevate head and shoulders if he has trouble breathing lying down.

2.   Give coffee or tea.

3.   Keep the patient warm and try to reassure him.

4.   Get quickest possible medical attention.

FAINTING

The symptoms are: pale face, sweating, drooping eyelids.

First Aid:

The victim can be helped at once if you sit him down with his head between his knees or get him to lie down. This can prevent a falling faint which may cause serious injury.

After a person faints:

1. Keep him lying down with clothing loose and his head slightly lower than his body.

2. To revive him, sprinkle cool water on face or put an ammonia inhalant under his nose.

3. Keep patient resting until fully revived.

EPILEPSY

The symptoms are: The patient turns pale, his eyes roll, he falls—usually with a hoarse cry. He turns blue, bites tongue, loses consciousness, froths at mouth. His head, arms, and legs will jerk wildly.

First Aid:

1. Prevent the patient from biting his tongue by putting a cloth in his mouth.

2. Put a pillow or a coat under his head, but do not restrain patient's thrashing; the phase will pass.

3. Give no stimulants when patient revives.

4. Let patient rest undisturbed after he recovers from attack.

APPENDICITIS

The symptoms are: pain *all over* abdomen but usually unusual pain and tenderness on lower right portion; the patient will probably be nauseated, vomiting.

First Aid:

1. Put the patient to bed.
2. Apply cold pack or ice bag to relieve pain.
3. Do not give food, water, or laxative.
4. Get medical help soon as possible.

DIARRHEA

Put the patient on a diet of tea or hot water and toast until he has no bowel movement for twenty-four hours. Then gradually resume normal diet, starting with easily digestible foods.

EARACHE

Caution patient against hard nose-blowing. Put a few drops of warm mineral oil in ear. Hot packs or a hot water bottle on the ear may ease discomfort. If that fails, try cold pads on the ear.

TOOTHACHE

If the ache can not be traced to a cavity, try hot or cold application on outside of the jaw. When the pain is traced to a cavity, clean the cavity with cotton on a toothpick or a wood sliver, and then pack cavity with cotton saturated with oil of cloves.

STIES AND RED EYES

Clean eye or eyes with solution of half a teaspoon or boric acid in a glass of water. Apply hot compresses for five or ten minutes at a time until condition is relieved.

POINTS TO REMEMBER

1. Keep yourself up to date on the standard rules of first aid and the periodic improvements—such as mouth-to-mouth breathing for artificial respiration.
2. Carry a good book of first-aid rules on any wilderness trip. The most complete and thorough book

on that subject alone is the manual put out by the American Red Cross. It costs seventy-five cents and is available through local Red Cross offices or from the publisher, Doubleday & Company, Garden City, New York. A first-aid rule book is worth ten times its weight, especially for campers with children.

3. Carry a good standard first-aid kit. All drug stores and big sporting goods stores sell them. Check your kit before each trip to be sure some vital item has not been taken out for home use. Ask your doctor's advice about what to take into the woods to deal with any known and persistent medical problems you have. He can suggest such drugs as oral penicillin for a wilderness jaunt where the party will be out of reach of medical attention for a long time. Ask your doctor about remedies for afflictions that are common in some places where you may plan to travel. Tourists headed into the back country of Mexico, for example, can almost always count on two troubles: bloodthirsty insects and some variety of diarrhea.

4. Be very cautious about playing doctor with your first-aid treatments. Guesswork is usually worse than no treatment at all.

5. Never be in a rush to move a seriously injured person. Doctors are also avid campers, fishermen, and hunters. A bone specialist may be camped around the bend from the wilderness trail where a member of your party suffers a severe back injury or some other bone break. Helicopters and parachuting doctors can often get into wilderness areas in a remarkably short time.

6. Finally—and this above all—be careful. It is the habit of deliberate caution that allows trappers, prospectors, and other professional woodsmen to stay alive in the wilds where doctors and hospitals are days and miles away.

31 - Knots and Hitches

THE CAMPER NEEDS TO KNOW WELL ABOUT A dozen of the best knots, slings, and hitches. A simple clove hitch, for example, will anchor a rope to a tent pole just as efficiently as a topsail halyard bend. The camper who really knows the halyard bend only loses time by tying it on a tent pole. The novice who insists on tying simple knots in a complicated way usually fumbles his big-name hitch, and his tent blows down.

The following instructions will be clearer if the beginner knows the basic rope terms. Ropes fall into two general classes—laid and braided. In a laid rope the strands are twisted together in the same direction. The three-strand laid rope is the most common. In a braided rope the strands are interwoven. Depending on its size and use, a rope may also be called a "line," a "sheet," a "hawser," or a "cord."

In describing knots, the free end of the rope, which you will be manipulating, is known as the "running" end. The other end, usually secured to some object, is called the "standing" part.

A "bend," as in sheet bend, is a knot that joins two ropes or the ends of the same rope.

A loop in a rope is called a "bight."

The term "hitch" means that the rope is fastened

to something else—a pole, a ring, sometimes another rope.

A "round turn" is a complete turn of the rope around some object.

"Lashings" are multiple turns of a rope around raft logs or a tripod of tent poles; the ends of the lashing rope are secured by knots or hitches.

"Whipping" on a rope end is a series of turns with string or thread to prevent the strands from unraveling.

A "sling" is a loop, or multiple loops, rigged to suspend or hoist something.

FACTS ABOUT ROPES

Here are the materials most commonly used in ropes sold for camp use: (1) hemp, which is available in various grades and types ("manila" is a common designation for a certain type of hemp rope); (2) cotton strands of regular cotton fiber treated in various ways; (3) nylon; (4) Dacron; (5) polyethylene.

It is also worth mentioning that some of the cheapest and shoddiest camp equipment is fitted with ropes or tying cords made of twisted and treated paper; there is nothing good to say about paper cords or ropes for outdoor use. In pack-horse country the camper now and then encounters ropes of braided rawhide and sometimes one made of braided horsetail hair—usually the painstaking work of a ranch hand in a winter camp, where nights between trips to town are long and plentiful. Skillfully braided rawhide or horsehair ropes make strong and dressy halters or bridle reins. The good ones are too rare and expensive for general camp use.

Synthetic rope (nylon, Dacron, polyethylene) has the following advantages: (1) It is from 50 to 100 per cent stronger than hemp rope of the same diameter; (2) Its waterproof fibers keep it from swelling or kinking when wet; (3) it is not affected by dry rot, mildew, or fungus; (4) polyethylene rope floats—an advanatge to boatmen—and it comes in bright colors, which appeal to many mariners.

What are the disadvantages of synthetic rope? It costs ten times as much as cotton rope of the same diameter and at least three times as much as hemp rope. Knots do not hold as well in the slick, hard synthetics. Nylon rope will stretch as much as 20 per cent of its total length. Dacron does not stretch enough to be particularly troublesome.

Nylon rope is the strongest of the synthetics—twice as strong as top-grade hemp and a third stronger than Dacron. Polyethylene rope is the weakest; it is only slightly stronger than hemp.

Here are the safe load limits for typical hemp and synthetic ropes. The advertised breaking strength of each rope will be a good deal higher, of course, but the camper wants to be sure his rope is loaded to hold, not to break. The following chart allows a substantial margin of safety.

SAFE ROPE LOADS

Rope Diameter

(*inches*)	*Hemp*	*Nylon*	*Dacron*	*Polyethylene*
¼	100	350	250	125
½	500	1,200	900	700
1	1,800	5,000	3,000	2,000

CARE OF ROPES

Moisture is the main enemy of hemp rope. Keep it as dry as possible, both in use and in storage. Hang it in a cool, dry place out of reach of mice or rats. Rodents may chew it up, attracted by the traces of sweat salt left from handling, or chop it up for nest material. Synthetic rope requires no special care, but it should be guarded from direct contact with potent oils, acids, and extreme heat. Abrasion against sharp or rough edges will cut it. Flame will melt it. Some acids weaken it. But these are extreme situations. Salt water, hot sun, or fungus growth do not affect it. There is no point, however, in abusing a rope just because it is tough, and synthetic rope should be kept clean and coiled.

HOW TO KNOT, HITCH, AND LASH ROPE

The illustrations that follow show clearly how to knot, hitch, and lash ropes for all routine outdoor jobs. Practice the unfamiliar ones with a short length of rope until the proper moves seem easy and natural.

Whipping

A whipping, made with turns of strong thread, keeps the end of a rope from unraveling. Synthetic rope can be sealed at the ends by melting it with a small flame. A cigarette lighter does this job neatly. Rope ends can also be sealed by dipping them in quick-setting liquid glue, sold for all-purpose household use.

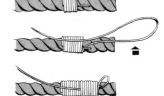

Whipping a Rope End

There are variations in whipping methods, but the one shown is both simple and reliable. Keep the thread taut during the wrapping turns. The portion of the thread indicated by the arrow is given five or six turns after the pull-through loop is formed. Pull the loop snug, and trim the end to complete the job.

Stopper Knot

The stopper knot can be used either as a substitute for whipping to keep a rope end from unraveling, or as a "stopper" to keep an object or another knot from slipping up or down on a rope. The figure 8 knot is a quick stopper knot which is far more reliable than the overhand knot commonly used as a stopper.

Figure 8 Knot

Clove Hitch

The clove hitch is good for securing a rope end to a pole or a tree, and it is ideal for hitching it to the top of a post or a stake. The hitch can be made in the middle of a long rope while both ends of it are loosely tied to other objects.

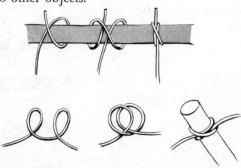

Clove Hitch

Square Knot

This common knot, also called the "reef knot," is good for joining two ropes or lines of similar size or tying together the two ends of the same rope. It will not slip, as will the similar granny, or thief knots, and it is easy to untie.

Square Knot

Bowline

This is a secure, non-slip knot for tying a loop around an object. It is a good knot for leading or hitching horses with ropes around their necks. The bowline is easy to untie—a requisite of all good camping knots.

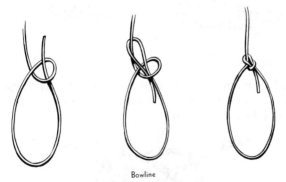

Bowline

Turns With Half Hitches

This combination—so simple that any novice can do it in the dark—will hold a rope end to a pole or a ring as well as any complicated knot. Two turns and half hitches are needed for a secure job. Take more of each for extra strength.

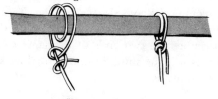

Half Hitches with Round Turns

Double Sheet Bend

This knot is for linking two ropes of different diameter. Always make the simple loop in the larger of the two ropes, using the thinner one to make the turns. A single sheet bend made with one turn is commonly used, but the double, or two-turn, version is a much safer knot and takes only a fraction of a second longer to tie.

Double Sheet Bend

Carrick Bend

This is the knot for joining ropes to tow or support heavy loads. It holds well without jamming so that it is not difficult to untie.

Carrick Bend

Guy-line Hitch

This hitch, as the name suggests, is for tightening

tent and other guy ropes that may need to be adjusted. The hitch involves two simple overhand knots, the rope running through the top knot. The lower knot will slide up or down to take or give slack on the tent rope or guy line. This hitch is not intended for towing or extremely heavy strains, but it will keep a tent as taut as it can be stretched without ripping the fabric.

Guy-line Hitch

Timber Hitch

This is the hitch for towing logs or hitching to a tree or a pole a rope that will have strong and steady pressure on it. The hitch ties quickly and will not jam under pressure, which is what is needed in a timber-towing hitch. It is not a secure slack-rope hitch or permanent knot.

Timber Hitch

Horse Hitch

Here is a quick and positive way to tie a horse (or a boat line) to a ring, a tree, or a pole. The short, running end of the rope is passed through a fairly open loop at the completion of the hitch to make the hitch more secure. When the running end is pulled out of the loop and jerked, it will loosen the hitch, which saves the trouble of fumbling with knots jammed by a restless horse tugging against its halter rope.

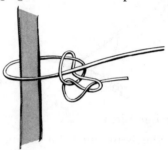

Horse Hitch

Ring Knot

Though it will work other places, this knot is at its best when tied to a ring. Fishermen can use it for swivel ends or the metal loops in lures. Do not trim the loose end too close if the knot is used with hard and slick monofilament fishing line. Monofilament slips much more than do linen, silk, or braided synthetic lines. A knot-holding bulge can be put on the end of a monofilament line by touching the free end

Ring Knot

with a cigarette coal or a hot match head after the knot is tied and the free end trimmed. Heat applied with slight pressure melts the monofilament enough to form a rounded ball at the end, and the ball cools and hardens in a second.

Slip Knot

The simple slip knot, which can be made more secure with half hitches around the standing part of the line or rope, is a fine permanent or semipermanent knot. It will jam and hold tight enough to suit anyone when the half hitches are added. Loosening the knot is another matter. Do not use it where the rope or line needs to be untied quickly.

Slip Knot

Water Knot

This knot does a neat job of joining fishing lines, leaders, small cords, or ropes. An overhand knot is loosely made in the end of one line; the running end of the other line is poked through and secured with an overhand knot around the standing part of the first line. Then the two overhand knots are pulled together. The knot can be made more secure by adding half hitches on either side after it is pulled tight. Trimmed, the knot will slide through fishing rod guides without catching.

Water Knot

Figure 8 Knot

There are a hundred ways to tie a line to a hook. This is one good and simple way. Do not trim the free end too short if monofilament line is used. Pull knot as tight as possible.

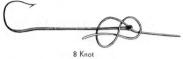

8 Knot

Dropper Loop

This method will make a dropper loop in the standing part of a rope or a fishing line without cutting the main line. Form the loop in the standing line as if starting a half hitch; then bend the line through the loop, and pull tight.

Dropper Loop

Bow Knot

Since a certain percentage of fishermen are sure to scorn the one hook-eye knot shown already, here is another that is quick and secure. Be sure to pull it tight if you use it with monofilament.

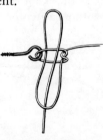

Bow Knot

Lashing for Shear Poles

The system shown here is as good as any and better than most for joining shear poles to hold up a tent or other camp equipment. Take three or four turns around the poles while they are held close together and parallel. Bring the loose rope ends between poles from opposite sides, and tie with a square knot. The lashing is fairly loose at this point. The key to the system is the way the lashing tightens when poles are spread scissor fashion. It loosens and unties easily. Three-pole shear lashing is essentially the same, except that rope ends are given one or more turns on each side of the center pole before they are tied together.

Tripod Lash

Shear Pole Lash

Malay Hitch

The simple Malay hitch is excellent for lashing together the ends of poles for an improvised camp table or a shelter wall. Bundles of grass or reeds can be lashed the same way to form a wall or a mat. Double the rope or cord to form a loop at one end at the start. Push that loop over the end of the first pole and work down the exposed ends, pushing on open hitches as you go. Pull the hitches as tight as is necessary. The whole hitch comes off without a knot or tangle.

Malay Hitch

Paling Hitch

This is an Indian system for lashing stakes to a crosspiece to form a fence or a shelter wall. Though it may look flimsy, try to substitute a system of your own that holds as well with the same economy of rope and labor. Gradually it will dawn on you that it must have taken a lot of fences, Indians, and years to boil the hitch down to its essentials. Wet rawhide is the prime lashing for this work. As it dries, it shrinks to hold the stakes as rigid as if they were nailed.

Paling Hitch

GUIDE TO CAMPGROUNDS IN THE UNITED STATES

The following guide to U.S. campgrounds lists the vast areas for recreation throughout this country that have been made available by the state and national governments. Included are State Parks (SP), National Parks (NP), State Forests (SF), National Forests (NF), and State Recreation Areas (SRA). All provide camping areas ranging from forest wilderness to campgrounds with flush toilets, electricity, shelters, showers, and laundry. Information about facilities available at each campground can be obtained by writing to the address provided at the head of each state listing.

ALABAMA *Department of Conservation*
Montgomery 4

GULF SP—45 miles southeast of Mobile on Ala. 3.

WILLIAM H. BANKHEAD NF—Northwestern Alabama, southwest of Decatur.

CONECUH NF—Florida border.

TALLADEGA NF—Central and east central Alabama, 20 miles northeast of Greensboro on Ala. 92.

ARIZONA *Tourist Bureau*
Phoenix

APACHE NF—East central Arizona along the New Mexico border.

COCONINO NF—Central Arizona surrounding Flagstaff.

CORONADO NF—Southeastern Arizona along Mexico border.

CROOK NF—Southeastern Arizona bordering New Mexico.

KAIBAB NF—North central Arizona near Utah border.

PRESCOTT NF—Central Arizona southwest of Flagstaff.

SITGREAVES NF—East central Arizona southeast of Flagstaff.

TONTO NF—South Arizona northeast of Phoenix.

GRAND CANYON NP—North central Arizona.

ARKANSAS   *State Highway Commission*
Little Rock

ARKANSAS POST SP—100 miles southeast of Little Rock off Ark. 169.

BUFFALO RIVER SP—120 miles northwest of Little Rock on Ark. 14.

CROWLEY'S RIDGE SP—145 miles NE of Little Rock, off Ark. 25.

DEVIL'S DEN SP—180 miles northwest of Little Rock on Ark. 74.

LAKE CATHERINE SP—56 miles southwest of Little Rock off U.S. 270.

NOUNT NEBO SP—91 miles northwest of Little Rock off Ark. 7.

PETIT JEAN SP—60 miles northwest of Little Rock on Ark. 154.

OUACHITA NF—West central Arkansas bordering Oklahoma.

OZARK NF—Northwest Arkansas.

HOT SPRINGS NP—Central Arkansas near Little Rock.

CALIFORNIA   *Division of Beaches & Parks*
721 Capital Ave., Sacramento

ANZA DESERT SP—90 miles NE San Diego on Cal. 78.

ARMSTRONG REDWOODS SP—77 miles northwest of San Francisco off Cal. 12.

BIG BASIN REDWOODS SP—60 miles south of San Francisco off Cal. 9.

D. L. BLISS SP—190 miles northeast of San Francisco on Cal. 89. (Lake Tahoe).

CALAVERAS BIG TREES SP—150 miles northeast of San Francisco off Cal. 4.

CARPINTERIA BEACH SP—85 miles northwest of Los Angeles on U.S. 101.

CASTLE CRAIGS SP—270 miles northeast of San Francisco on U.S. 99.

CUYAMACA RANCHO SP—50 miles

DOHENY BEACH SP—55 miles southeast of Los Angeles on U.S. 101.

FREMONT PEAK SP—100 miles southeast of San Francisco off U.S. 101.

GRIZZLY CREEK REDWOODS SP—260 miles north of San Francisco on Cal. 36.

EDWARD R. HICKEY SP—190 miles north of San Francisco on U.S. 101.

HUMBOLDT REDWOODS SP—240 miles north of San Francisco on U.S. 101.

MCARTHUR-BURNEY FALLS SP—11 miles northeast of Burney.

MORRO BAY SP—200 miles northwest of Los Angeles on Cal. 1.

MOUNT DIABLO SP—44 miles east of San Francisco off Cal. 21.

MOUNT SAN JACINTO—120 miles southeast of Los Angeles on Cal. 74.

MOUNT TAMALPAIS SP—15 miles north of San Francisco off Cal. 1.

NEW BRIGHTON BEACH SP—6 miles east of Santa Cruz.

PALOMAR MOUNTAIN SP—100 miles southeast of Los Angeles off U.S. 71.

PATRICK'S POINT SP—20 miles north of Arcata on U.S. 101.

PFEIFFER-BIG SUR SP—32 miles south of Monterey on Cal. 1.

PISMO BEACH SP—180 miles northwest of Los Angeles on Cal. 1.

PORTOLA SP—40 miles south of San Francisco off Cal. 5.

PRAIRIE CREEK REDWOODS SP—6 miles north of Orick on U.S. 101.

RUSSIAN GULCH SP—130 miles north of San Francisco on Cal. 1.

SAN CLEMENTE BEACH SP—42 miles southeast of Los Angeles off U.S. 101.

SEA CLIFF BEACH SP—8 miles east of Santa Cruz on Cal. 1.

JEDEDIAH SMITH REDWOODS SP—9 miles northeast of Crescent City on U.S. 199.

SONOMA COAST SP—86 miles northwest of San Francisco on Cal. 1.

SUNSET BEACH SP—5 miles west of Watsonville.

TAHOE SP—$\frac{1}{4}$ mile east of Tahoe City on Cal. 28.

SAMUEL P. TAYLOR SP—35 miles northwest of San Francisco off Cal. 1.

VAN DAMME BEACH SP—14 miles south of Fort Bragg on Cal. 1.

ANGELES NF—Southern California, east of Los Angeles.

CLEVELAND NF—Southwestern tip of California.

ELDORADO NF—Northeastern California, east of Sacramento.

INYO NF—East central California along the Nevada border.

KLAMATH NF—Northern California along the Oregon border.

LASSEN NF—Northern California bordering Lassen Volcanic Park.

LOS PADRES NF—Southwestern California along the Pacific Coast.

MENDOCINO NF—Northern California, northwest of Sacramento.

MODOC NF—Northeastern corner of California.

PLUMAS NF—Northern California, southeast of Lassen Volcanic Park.

SAN BERNARDINO NF—Southern California, east of Los Angeles.

SEQUOIA NF—South central California, south of Sequoia National Park.

SHASTA NF—North central California near the Oregon border.

SIERRA NF—East central California.

SIX RIVERS NF—Northwestern corner of California.

STANISLAUS NF—Central California, north of Yosemite National Park.

TAHOE NF—Northeastern California, northeast of Sacramento.

TRINITY NF—Northwestern California, east of Eureka.

KINGS CANYON NP—East central California.

LASSEN VOLCANIC NP—Northeastern California.

SEQUOIA NP—East central California.

YOSEMITE NP—East central California.

COLORADO   *State Park and Recreation Board*
Capital Building, Denver 2

ARAPAHO NF—North central Colorado west and south of Rocky Mountain National Park.

GRAND MESA NF—West central Colorado.

GUNNISON NF—West central Colorado.

PIKE NF—Central Colorado, southwest of Denver.

RIO GRANDE NF—South central Colorado.

ROOSEVELT NF—North central Colorado, north of Rocky Mountain National Park.

Routt NF—Northern Colorado, northwest of Rocky Mountain National Park.

San Isabel NF—South central Colorado, south of Pueblo.

San Juan NF—Southwestern Colorado, northeast of Mesa Verde National Park.

Uncompahgre NF—Southwestern Colorado near the Utah border.

White River NF—West central Colorado, southwest of Denver.

Mesa Verde NP—Southwestern Colorado.

Rocky Mountain NP— North central Colorado, northwest of Denver.

CONNECTICUT
State Park and Forest Commission
165 Capital Ave., Hartford 15

Black Rock SP—10 miles north of Waterbury on Conn. 109.

Hammonasset Beach SP—25 miles east of New Haven off U.S. 1.

Housatonic Meadows SP—50 miles west of Hartford on U.S. 7.

Indian Well SP—15 miles northwest of New Haven on Conn. 34.

Lake Waramaug SP—40 miles west of Hartford off Conn. 45.

Macedonia Brook SP—50 miles west of Hartford off U.S. 7.

Mashamoquet Brook SP—40 miles northeast of Hartford on U.S. 44.

Rocky Neck SP—50 miles southeast of Hartford on Conn. 156.

Squantz Pond SP—60 miles southwest of Hartford on Conn. 39.

Wharton Brook SP—13 miles northeast of New Haven on U.S. 5.

Pachaug SF—Southeastern section of Connecticut.

DELAWARE
State Park Commission
Faulkland Road, Wilmington 8

Assowoman Bay SP—47 miles southeast of Dover on north end of Assowoman Bay.

Indian River Inlet SP—50 miles southeast of Dover.

Trap Pond SP—40 miles south of Dover near Laurel.

FLORIDA   *Board of Parks and Historic Memorials*
204 Center Building, Tallahassee

FLORIDA CAVERNS SP—70 miles northwest of Tallahassee off U.S. 90.

FORT CLINCH SP—35 miles northeast of Jacksonville off Fla. 200.

GOLD HEAD BRANCH SP—40 miles southwest of Jacksonville off Fla. 21.

HIGHLANDS HAMMOCK SP—80 miles southeast of Tampa off U.S. 27.

HISSLBORO RIVER SP—20 miles northeast of Tampa on U.S. 301.

MYAKKA RIVER SP—17 miles southeast of Sarasota on Fla. 72.

O'LENO SP—71 miles southwest of Jacksonville off U.S. 41.

TORREYA SP—40 miles northwest of Tallahassee off Fla. 12.

APALACHICOLA NF—Northwestern corner of Florida.

OCALA NF—Central Florida.

OSCEOLA NF—North central Florida about 50 miles west of Jacksonville.

EVERGLADES NP—Southern tip of Florida.

GEORGIA   *Department of State Parks*
418 State Capitol, Atlanta

CHEWA SP—160 miles south of Atlanta on U.S. 19.

CLOUDLAND CANYON SP—125 miles northwest of Atlanta off U.S. 11.

CROOKED RIVER SP—315 miles southeast of Atlanta off U.S. 17.

JEFFERSON DAVIS MEMORIAL SP—185 miles southeast of Atlanta on Ga. 90.

FORT MOUNTAIN SP—90 miles northwest of Atlanta on U.S. 76.

GEORGIA VETERANS MEMORIAL SP—160 miles southeast of Atlanta on U.S. 280.

HARD LABOR CREEK SP—2 miles north of Rutledge off Ga. 12.

INDIAN SPRINGS SP—53 miles southeast of Atlanta on U.S. 23.

KOLOMOKI MOUNDS SP—3 miles northeast of McRae on Ga. 31.

MAGNOLIA SPRING SP—80 miles south of Augusta on U.S. 25.

FRANKLIN D. ROOSEVELT SP—80 miles southwest of Atlanta off U.S. 27.

ALEXANDER H. STEPHENS MEMORIAL SP—100 miles southeast of Atlanta on Ga. 12.

Vogel SP—95 miles northeast of Atlanta on U.S. 19.

Laura S. Walker SP—10 miles southeast of Waycross off U.S. 1.

Chattahoochee NF—Northern Georgia.

IDAHO *Department of Public Lands*
Boise

Heyburn SP—7 miles from Plummer on U.S. 95.

Lawyer's Canyon SP—3 miles from Craigmont on U.S. 95.

Ponderosa Camp SP—110 miles north of Boise off U.S. 95.

Salmon River Bridge SP—200 miles north of Twin Falls on U.S. 93.

Spaulding Memorial SP—7 miles from Lewiston on U.S. 95.

Boise NF—Southwestern Idaho northeast of Boise.

Caribou NF—Southeastern Idaho bordering Wyoming.

Challis NF—Central Idaho.

Clearwater NF—Northern Idaho along the Montana border.

Coeur d'Alene NF—Northern Idaho, northwest of Coeur d'Alene.

Kaniksu NF—Extreme northwestern Idaho.

Minidoka NF—South central Idaho bordering Nevada and Utah.

Nezperce NF—North central Idaho.

Payette NF—West central Idaho along the Oregon border.

St. Joe NF—North Idaho near the Washington border.

Salmon NF—East central Idaho along the Montana border.

Sawtooth NF—South central Idaho.

Targhee NF—Eastern Idaho bordering Montana and Wyoming.

ILLINOIS *Division of Parks and Memorials*
Room 100, State Office Building
400 South Spring St., Springfield

Apple River Canyon SP—60 miles northwest of Rockford off Ill. 78.

Cahokia Mounds SP—10 miles northeast of East St. Louis on U.S. 40.

Cave-in-rock SP—170 miles southeast of East St. Louis on Ill. 1.

Channahon Parkway SP—42 miles southwest of Chicago off U.S. 6

DIXON SPRINGS SP—150 miles southeast of East St. Louis on Ill. 146.

FORT KASKASKIA SP—60 miles southeast of East St. Louis off Ill. 3.

FORT MASSAC SP—170 miles southeast of East St. Louis on U.S. 45.

FOX RIDGE SP—64 miles southeast of Decatur on Ill. 130.

GIANT CITY SP—108 miles southeast of East St. Louis off U.S. 51.

ILLINI SP—60 miles southwest of Chicago off U.S. 6.

ILLINOIS BEACH SP—50 miles north of Chicago off Ill. 42.

JUBILEE COLLEGE SP—15 miles northwest of Peoria on U.S. 150.

KICKAPOO SP—150 miles south of Chicago on U.S. 150.

LOWDEN MEMORIAL SP—100 miles northwest of Chicago on Ill. 2.

MISSISSIPPI PALISADES SP—75 miles southwest of Rockford on Ill. 80.

PERE MARQUETTE SP—50 miles northwest of East St. Louis on Ill. 100.

STARVED ROCK SP—70 miles southwest of Chicago on Ill. 71.

WHITE PINES FOREST SP—110 miles northwest of Chicago off Ill. 2.

SHAWNEE NF—Southern Illinois.

INDIANA   *Department of Conservation*
              311 W. Washington St., Indianapolis 9

BASS LAKE BEACH SP—47 miles southwest of South Bend on Ind. 10.

BROWN COUNTY SP—50 miles south of Indianapolis on Ind. 135.

CLIFTY FALLS SP—7 miles west of Madison on Ind. 107.

INDIANA DUNES SP—12 miles east of Gary on U.S. 12.

LINCOLN SP—38 miles northeast of Evansville on Ind. 162.

MCCORMICK'S CREEK SP—59 miles southwest of Indianapolis on Ind. 46.

MOUNDS SP—40 miles northeast of Indianapolis on Ind. 32.

MUSCATATUCK SP—66 miles southeast of Indianapolis on Ind. 7.

POKAGON SP—45 miles northeast of Fort Wayne on U.S. 27.

SCALES LAKE SP—20 miles northeast of Evansville near Ind. 61.

SHADES SP—56 miles northwest of Indianapolis off Ind. 234.

SHAKAMAK SP—30 miles southeast of Terre Haute on Ind. 48.

SPRING MILL SP—85 miles southwest of Indianapolis on Ind. 60.

TIPPECANOE RIVER SP—100 miles northwest of Indianapolis on U.S. 35.

TURKEY RUN SP—35 miles northeast of Terre Haute on Ind. 47.

VERSAILLES SP—75 miles southeast of Indianapolis on U.S. 50.

IOWA *State Conservation Commission*
East 7th and Court Ave., Des Moines 9

BACKBONE SP—55 miles north of Cedar Rapids off Iowa 13.

BELLEVUE SP—75 miles north of Davenport on U.S. 67.

BLACKHAWK SP—120 miles northwest of Des Moines on U.S. 71.

AMBROSE A. CALL SP—130 miles northwest of Des Moines off U.S. 169.

CLEAR LAKE SP—125 miles north of Des Moines off U.S. 18.

DOLLIVER MEMORIAL SP—90 miles northwest of Des Moines off Iowa 50.

FORT DEFIANCE SP—180 miles northwest of Des Moines off Iowa 9.

GULL POINT SP—99 miles northeast of Sioux City on Iowa 32.

LACEY-KEOSAUQUA—135 miles southeast of Des Moines off Iowa 1.

LAKE AHQUABI SP—25 miles south of Des Moines off U.S. 69.

LAKE KEOMAH SP—65 miles southeast of Des Moines off U.S. 69.

LAKE OF TREE FIRES—120 miles southeast of Des Moines on Iowa 49.

LAKE WAPELLOW—100 miles southeast of Des Moines off Iowa 2.

LEDGES SP—45 miles northeast of Des Moines off U.S. 30.

MAQUOKETA CAVES SP—45 miles north of Davenport off U.S. 61.

OAK GROVE SP—50 miles north of Sioux City off Iowa 10.

OAKLAND MILLS SP—90 miles southwest of Davenport off U.S. 218.

ORLEANS HATCHERY SP—110 miles northeast of Sioux City on Spirit Lake.

PALISADES-KEPLER SP—16 miles southeast of Cedar Rapids off U. S. 30.

PAMMEL SP—38 miles southwest of Des Moines off Iowa 92.

PILOT KNOB SP—125 miles north of Des Moines off Iowa 9.

PINE LAKE SP—75 miles northeast of Des Moines off Iowa 57.

SPRINGBROOK SP—60 miles northwest of Des Moines off Iowa 25.

STONE SP—On northwest edge of Sioux City.

WALNUT WOODS SP—6 miles southwest of Des Moines on Iowa 90.

WAPSIPINICON SP—24 miles northeast of Cedar Rapids on U.S. 151.

WAUBONSIE SP—160 miles southwest of Des Moines off Iowa 2.

WILDCAT DEN SP—20 miles southwest of Davenport off U.S. 61.

KANSAS *State Highway Commission Topeka*

BUTLER COUNTY SP—18 miles east of Wichita on Kan. 96.

CLARK COUNTY SP—135 miles southwest of Wichita off U.S. 54.

CRAWFORD COUNTY NUMBER ONE SP—4 miles north of Pittsburg on U.S. 69.

CRAWFORD COUNTY NUMBER TWO SP—2 miles north of Farlington on Kan. 7.

DECATUR COUNTY NUMBER ONE SP—1 mile north of Oberlin off U.S. 83.

DECATUR COUNTY NUMBER TWO SP—1 mile northeast of Oberlin on U.S. 36.

FINNEY COUNTY SP—200 miles northwest of Wichita off U.S. 50N.

KEARNY COUNTY LAKE SP—230 miles west of Wichita on U.S. 50S.

KINGMAN COUNTY SP—50 miles west of Wichita on U.S. 54.

LEAVENWORTH COUNTY SP—30 miles west of Kansas City off Kan. 16.

Lyon County SP—112 miles northeast of Wichita on Kan. 99.

Meade County SP—195 miles southwest of Wichita on Kan. 98.

Miami County SP—12 miles southeast of Paola off U.S. 69.

Nemaha County SP—75 miles northwest of Topeka on Kan. 63.

Neosho County SP—150 miles southeast of Wichita off U.S. 59.

Ottawa County SP—5 miles north of Bennington off Kan. 93.

Pottawatomie County SP—5 miles west of Westmoreland on Kan. 11.

Republic County SP—160 miles northwest of Wichita off Kan. 28.

Rooks County SP—220 miles northwest of Wichita off Kan. 28.

Scott County SP—12 miles north of Scott City off U.S. 83.

Sheridan County SP—2 miles east of Quinter off U.S. 40.

Woodson County SP—100 miles northeast of Wichita off U.S. 54.

KENTUCKY *Division of Parks*
Department of Conservation
New Capitol Annex, Frankfort

General Butler SP—60 miles northeast of Louisville off U.S. 42.

Carter Caves SP—100 miles northeast of Lexington on Ky. 182.

Columbus-Belmont Battlefield SP—300 miles southwest of Lexington on U.S. 51.

Cumberland Falls SP—18 miles southwest of Corbin.

Levi Jackson SP—3 miles south of London.

Kentucky Dam Village SP—28 miles southeast of Paducah.

Lake Cumberland SP—115 miles southwest of Lexington on Ky. 35.

Natural Bridge SP—57 miles southeast of Lexington on Ky. 77.

Pennyrile SP—9 miles south of Dawson Springs.

Pine Mountain SP—1 mile south of Pineville.

Cumberland NP—Eastern Kentucky.

Mammoth NP—Southern Kentucky, south of Louisville.

LOUISIANA *State Parks and Recreation Commission*
3170 Florida St., Baton Rouge

ABITA SPRINGS SP—60 miles north of New Orleans on La. 114.

AUDUBON MEMORIAL SP—155 miles northwest of New Orleans off U.S. 61.

BOGUE FALAYA SP—58 miles north of New Orleans off La. 7.

CHEMIN-A-HAUT SP—10 miles north of Bastrop.

CHICOT SP—8 miles north of Ville Platte.

FONTAINBLEAU SP—50 miles north of New Orleans off U.S. 190.

LAKE BISTINEAU SP—30 miles southeast of Shreveport off U.S. 79.

LONGFELLOW-EVANGELINE SP—12 miles north of New Iberia on La. 25.

MARKSVILLE PREHISTORIC INDIAN SP—160 miles northwest of New Orleans off U.S. 90.

KISATCHIE NP—Central Louisiana.

MAINE *Maine Development Commission*
Augusta

AROOSTOOK SP—165 miles northeast of Bangor on U.S. 1.

BAXTER SP—26 miles northwest of Millinocket.

BRADBURY MOUNTAIN SP—20 miles northeast of Portland on Me. 9.

CAMDEN HILLS SP—80 miles northeast of Portland on U.S. 1.

FORT KNOX SP—20 miles south of Bangor off U.S. 1-A.

LAKE ST. GEORGE SP—17 miles west of Belfast.

MOUNT BLUE SP—14 miles northwest of Wilton.

SEBAGO LAKE SP—2 miles south of Naples.

ACADIA NP—Island 47 miles southeast of Bangor.

MARYLAND *Department of Forests and Parks*
State Office Building, Annapolis

ELK NECK SP—50 miles northeast of Baltimore off U.S. 40.

PATAPSCO SP—1 mile northwest of Elkridge.

SANDY POINT SP—6 miles northeast of Annapolis on U.S. 50.

CEDARVILLE SF—14 miles from Washington, D.C. border, off U.S. 301.

DONCASTER SF—1½ miles east of Doncaster on MD. 6.

GREEN RIDGE SF—15 miles east of Comerland along U.S. 40.

POCOMOKE SF—Southern Maryland.

Potomac SF—Western Maryland, bordering on Virginia.
Savage River SF—Western Maryland.
Swallow Falls SF—Western Maryland, bordering on Virginia.

MASSACHUSETTS *Department of Natural Resources*
Division of Forests and Parks
15 Ashburn Place, Boston 8

Roland C. Nickerson SP—90 miles southeast of Boston on U.S. 6.

Deer Hill SR—38 miles northwest of Springfield on Mass. 9.

Misery Island SR—20 miles northeast of Boston off Mass. 127.

Monument Mountain SR—4 miles north of Great Barrington.

Mount Greylock SR—60 miles northwest of Springfield off U.S. 7.

Mount Sugarloaf SR—30 miles north of Springfield on Mass. 116.

Mount Tom SR—10 miles northwest of Springfield off U.S. 5.

Salisbury Beach SR—40 miles northeast of Boston off Mass. 1-A.

Wachusett Mountain SR—15 miles north of Worcester off Mass. 31.

Bash Bish Falls SF—67 miles west of Springfield off Mass. 23.

Granville SF—20 miles west of Springfield off Mass. 57.

Mohawk Trail SF—60 miles northwest of Springfield on Mass. 2.

Otter River SF—65 miles northeast of Springfield off U.S. 202.

Harold Parker SF—18 miles north of Boston off Mass. 114.

Sandisfield SF—60 miles west of Springfield off Mass. 57.

Savoy Mountain SF—60 miles northwest of Springfield off U.S. 2.

Myles Standish SF—55 miles southeast of Boston off Mass. 58.

Tolland SF—35 miles west of Springfield off Mass. 23.

Willard Brook SF—30 miles north of Worcester off Mass. 31.

Windsor SF—43 miles northwest of Springfield off Mass. 9.

MICHIGAN *Department of Conservation*
Lansing 26

ALGONAC SP—45 miles northeast of Detroit on Mich. 29.

ALOHA SP—9 miles south of Cheboygan on Mich. 212.

BARAGA SP—125 miles northwest of Escanaba on U.S. 41.

BAY CITY SP—5 miles north of Bay City.

BENZIE SP—11 miles northwest of Frankfort.

BLOOMER SP—8 miles southwest of Pontiac.

BRIMLEY SP—12 miles southwest of Sault Ste. Marie.

BURT LAKE SP—225 miles northeast of Muskegon on U.S. 27.

D. H. DAY SP—1 mile south of Glen Arbor.

DODGE BROTHERS SP—2 miles south of Utica.

EAST TAWAS SP—170 miles northwest of Detroit on U.S. 23.

FORT WILKINS SP—220 miles northwest of Escanaba on U.S. 41.

GLADWIN SP—146 miles northwest of Detroit on Mich. 18.

GOGEBIC SP—158 miles northwest of Escanaba off U.S. 2.

GRAND HAVEN SP—1 mile southwest of Grand Haven.

HARRISVILLE SP—204 miles northwest of Detroit on U.S. 23.

HARTWICK PINES SP—8 miles northeast of Grayling.

W. J. HAYES SP—9 miles west of Clinton.

HIGGINS LAKE SP—9 miles southwest of Roscommon.

P. H. HOEFT SP—5 miles northwest of Rogers City.

HOLLAND SP—35 miles south of Muskegon off U.S. 31.

INDIAN LAKE SP—5 miles west of Manistique.

INTERLOCHEN SP—15 miles southwest of Traverse City.

LAKEPORT SP—10 miles north of Port Huron.

LUDINGTON SP—70 miles north of Muskegon off Mich. 116.

F. J. MCLAIN SP—7 miles west of Calumet on Mich. 203.

CHARLES MEARS SP—48 miles north of Muskegon on U.S. 31.

MICHILIMACKINAC SP—250 miles northeast of Muskegon on U.S. 31.

WILLIAM MITCHELL SP—2½ miles west of Cadillac.

MUSKEGON SP—7 miles west of Muskegon on Mich. 20.

ONAWAY SP—6 miles north of Onaway.

ORCHARD BEACH SP—2 miles north of Manistee.

OTSEGO SP—7 miles south of Gaylord.

PORCUPINE MOUNTAINS SP—20 miles west of Ontonagon on Mich. 107.

SILVER LAKE SP—7 miles west of Hart.

ALBERT E. SLEEPER SP—5 miles northeast of Caseville.

STRAITS SP—143 miles east of Escanaba off U.S. 2.

TAHQUAMENON FALLS SP—12 miles west of Paradise.

TRAVERSE CITY SP—156 miles northeast of Muskegon on U.S. 31.

J. W. WELLS SP—30 miles southwest of Escanaba on Mich. 35.

WHITE CLOUD SP—42 miles northeast of Muskegon on Mich. 20.

WILDERNESS SP—8 miles west of Mackinaw City.

WILSON SP—1 mile north of Harrison.

YOUNG SP—1½ miles north of Boyne City.

BRIGHTON SRA—3 miles southwest of Brighton.

HIGHLAND SRA—17 miles west of Pontiac.

ISLAND LAKE SRA—39 miles northwest of Detroit on U.S. 16.

ORTONVILLE SRA—40 miles northwest of Detroit on Mich. 15.

PROUD LAKE SRA—39 miles northwest of Detroit off U.S. 16.

WATERLOO SRA—39 miles northwest of Detroit off U.S. 16.

YANKEE SPRINGS SRA—12 miles southwest of Hastings.

Lower Peninsula

ALLEGAN SF—Southwest corner between Holland and Kalamazoo.

ALPENA SF—Northeast shore line.

AU SABLE SF—North central part of lower peninsula.

BLACK LAKE SF—Northeast section of lower peninsula.

FIFE LAKE SF—Northwestern section of lower peninsula.

HARDWOOD SF—Northwestern corner of lower peninsula.

HIGGINS LAKE SF—North central part of lower peninsula.

HOUGHTON LAKE SF—Central part of lower peninsula.

OGEMAW SF—East central part of lower peninsula.

PIGEON RIVER SF—North central section of lower peninsula.

PRESQUE ISLE SF—Northeastern part of lower peninsula.

Upper Peninsula

ESCANABA SF—Central portion of upper peninsula.

GRAND SABLE SF—East central section of upper peninsula.

LAKE SUPERIOR SF—Eastern part of upper peninsula.

MACKINAC SF—Eastern section of upper peninsula.

STURGEION RIVER SF—Central section of upper peninsula.

MINNESOTA   *Department of Highways*
1246 University Ave., St. Paul 4

Beaver Creek Valley SP—4 miles northwest of Caledonia.

Camden SP—7 miles southwest of Marshall.

Jay Cooke SP—25 miles southwest of Duluth off U.S. 61.

Flandrau SP—98 miles southwest of Minneapolis on U.S. 14.

Fort Ridgely Memorial Park SP—7 miles south of Fairfax.

Gooseberry Falls SP—40 miles northeast of Duluth on U.S. 61.

Interstate SP—54 miles northeast of Minneapolis on U.S. 8.

Itasca SP—180 miles northwest of Duluth off U.S. 71.

Kilen Woods SP—7 miles northwest of Jackson.

Lac Qui Parle SP—8 miles northwest of Montevideo.

Lake Bemidji SP—108 miles southwest of International Falls off U.S. 59.

Lake Bronson SP—163 miles west of International Falls off U.S. 59.

Lake Carlos SP—10 miles north of Alexandria.

Lake Shetek SP—3 miles north of Currie.

John A. Latsch SP—14 miles north of Winona.

McCarthy Beach SP—20 miles northwest of Hibbing.

Monson Lake Memorial Park SP—3 miles southwest of Sunberg.

William O'Brien SP—2 miles north of Marine-on-St. Croix.

Old Mill SP—10 miles east of Argyle.

Alexander Ramsey SP—120 miles west of Minneapolis off U.S. 71.

St. Croix SP—20 miles east of Hinckley.

Scenic SP—6 miles southeast of Bigfork.

Sibley SP—7 miles west of New London.

Whitewater SP—100 miles southeast of Minneapolis on Minn. 74.

Chippewa SF—North central state.

Superior SF—Northwestern corner of state.

MISSISSIPPI   *Park Service*
1104 Woolfolk, State Office Building
P.O. Box 649, Jackson

Shelby Lake SP—12 miles south of Hattiesburg.

Tombigbee SP—6 miles southeast of Tupelo.

BIENVILLE NF—South central part of state.
DELTA NF—50 miles northwest of Jackson.
DE SOTO NF—Southeast corner of state.
HOLLY SPRINGS NF—North central part of state.
HOMOCHITTO NF—Southeast of Natchez.

MISSOURI   *State Park Board*
                    P.O. Box 176, 1206 Jefferson Building
                    Jefferson City

ALLEY SPRING SP—200 miles southwest of St. Louis off Mo. 19.
SAM A. BAKER SP—120 miles south of St. Louis off Mo. 34.
BENNETT SPRING SP—12 miles west of Lebanon.
BIG LAKE SP—100 miles northwest of Kansas City off U.S. 60.
BIG SPRING SP—190 miles southwest of St. Louis off U.S. 60.
CROWDER SP—2 miles west of Trenton.
CUIVRE RIVER SP—60 miles northwest of St. Louis on Mo. 47.
KNOB NOSTER SP—65 miles southeast of Kansas City off U.S. 50.
LAKE OF THE OZARKS SP—200 miles southwest of St. Louis off U.S. 54.
LEWIS AND CLARKE SP—53 miles northwest of Kansas City on U.S. 59.
MARK TWAIN SP—10 miles west of Perry.
MERAMEC SP—75 miles southwest of St. Louis off U.S. 66.
MONTAUK SP—168 miles southwest of St. Louis off Mo. 32.
PERSHING SP—120 miles northeast of Kansas City on U.S. 36.
ROARING RIVER SP—7 miles south of Cassville.
ROUND SPRING SP—200 miles southwest of St. Louis on Mo. 19.
VAN METER SP—25 miles east of Kansas City off Mo. 41.
WALLACE SP—50 miles northeast of Kansas City off U.S. 69.
WASHINGTON SP—55 miles southwest of St. Louis on Mo. 21.
CLARK NF—Southeastern corner of Missouri Ozark mountains.
MARK TWAIN NF—South central and southwestern part of state.

MONTANA   *Highway Commission*
                   Helena

BEAVER CREEK SP—20 miles south of Havre.
GOOSE BAY SP—20 miles south of Kalispell.

HELL CREEK—34 miles north of Jordan.

ROCK CREEK SP—56 miles northwest of Circle.

YELLOW BAY SP—12 miles northeast of Polson.

GLACIER NP—Northwestern Montana.

BEAVERHEAD NF—Southwestern Montana.

BITTERROOT NF—West central Montana.

CABINET NF—Northwestern corner of Montana.

CUSTER NF—Southeastern Montana.

DEERLODGE NF—West central Montana.

FLATHEAD NF—Northwestern Montana.

GALLATIN NF—South central Montana.

HELENA NF—Surrounding Helena on the Continental Divide.

KOOTENAI NF—Extreme northwestern part of Montana.

LEWIS AND CLARK—Central Montana.

LOLO NF—West central Montana.

NEBRASKA   *Game, Forestation and Parks Commission, State Capitol Building, Lincoln 9*

CHADRON SP—9 miles south of Chadron.

FORT KEARNY SP—10 miles southeast of Kearny on Neb. 10.

NIOBRARA ISLAND SP—124 miles northwest of Omaha on Neb. 12.

PONCA SP—155 miles northwest of Omaha off Neb. 12.

STOLLEY SP—3 miles southwest of Grand Island.

VICTORIA SPRINGS SP—8 miles north of Merna on Neb. 80.

NEBRASKA NF—North central Nebraska.

NEVADA   *State Park Commission State Capitol, Carson City*

HUMBOLDT NF—Northeastern Nevada.

NEVADA NF—East Central Nevada.

TOIYABE NF—Central Nevada.

NEW HAMPSHIRE   *Recreation Division Concord*

BEAR BROOK SP—18 miles northeast of Manchester off N.H. 28.

BELKNAP SP—40 miles northeast of Concord off U.S. 3.

CRAWFORD NOTCH SP—14 miles south of Twin Mountains.

FOX FOREST SP—2 miles northwest of Hillsboro.

FRANACONIA NOTCH SP—6 miles north of Woodstock.

MILAN HILL SP—2 miles west of Milan.

MONADNOCK SP—4 miles north of Jeffry Center.

MOOSE-BROOK SP—2 miles west of Gorham.

PILLSBURY SP—35 miles west of Concord off N.H. 31.

SUNAPEE SP—33 miles northwest of Concord on N.H. 103.

WHITE LAKE SP—68 miles northeast of Manchester off N.H. 16.

WHITE MOUNTAIN NF—Northern New Hampshire.

NEW JERSEY   *Department of Conservation and Economic Development*
520 East State St., Trenton 7

HIGH POINT SP—8 miles northwest of Sussex.

PARVIN SP—6 miles west of Vineland.

JENNY JUMP SF—45 miles northwest of Newark off U.S. 46.

LEBANON SF—30 miles east of Camden on N.J. 40.

STOKES SF—50 miles northwest of Newark off U.S. 206.

NEW MEXICO   *State Park Commission*
P.O. Box 958, Santa Fe

BOTTOMLESS LAKES SP—10 miles southeast of Roswell off U.S. 380.

KIT CARSON SP—71 miles northeast of Santa Fe, at Taos.

CONCHAS DAM SP—176 miles northeast of Albuquerque off U.S. 66.

HYDE SP—9 miles northeast of Santa Fe.

CARSON NF—North central New Mexico.

CIBOLA NF—Southwest of Albuquerque.

GILA NF—100 miles north of the Mexican border.

LINCOLN NF—Southeast of Albuquerque.

SANTA FE NF—Vicinity of the Rio Grande River Valley.

NEW YORK   *Conservation Department*
State Office Building, Albany 1

Allegany Area

ALLEGANY SP—10 miles southwest of Salamanca on N.Y. 17.

LAKE ERIE SP—7 miles southwest of Dunkirk on N.Y. 5.

Central New York Area

CHENANGO VALLEY SP—13 miles north of Binghamton on N.Y. 369.

GILBERT LAKE SP—7 miles northwest of Oneonta on N.Y. 205.

GREEN LAKES SP—10 miles east of Syracuse near Fayetteville.
SELKIRK SHORES SP—3 miles west of Pulaski on N.Y. 3.

Fingerlakes Area

BUTTERMILK FALLS SP—2 miles south of Ithaca on N.Y. 13.
CAYUGA LAKE SP—3 miles east of Seneca Falls on N.Y. 89.
FAIRHAVEN BEACH SP—2 miles north of Fairhaven on N.Y. 104-A.
FILLMORE GLEN SP—1 mile south of Moravia on N.Y. 38.
NEWTON BATTLEFIELD RESERVATION SP—5 miles southeast of Elmira on N.Y. 17.
STONY BROOK SP—3 miles south of Dansville on N.Y. 36.
TAUGHANNOCK FALLS SP—8 miles north of Ithaca on N.Y. 89.
ROBERT H. TREMAN SP—7 miles southwest of Ithaca on N.Y. 13.
WATKINS GLEN SP—At Watkins Glen.

Genesee Area

LETCHWORTH SP—At Castile

Long Island Area

HITHER HILLS SP—8 miles east of East Hampton on N.Y. 27.
WILDWOOD SP—73 miles east of New York City on N.Y. 25-A.

Palisades Area

HARRIMAN SP—35 miles northwest of New York City on U.S. 17.

Taconic Area

CLARENCE FAHNSTOCK MEMORIAL SP—9 miles east of Cold-spring on N.Y. 301.
LAKE TAGHKANIC SP—14 miles south of Hudson on N.Y. 82.
MARGARET LEWIS NORRIE SP—9 miles north of Poughkeepsie on U.S. 9.
RUDD POND SP—2 miles north of Millerton on N.Y. 22.
TACONIC SP—At Copake Falls on N.Y. 22.

Thousand Islands Area

BURNHAM POINT SP—3 miles east of Cape Vincent on N.Y. 12-E.
CANOE-PICNIC POINT SP—Grindstone Island, reached from Clayton.
CEDAR ISLAND SP—Reached from Chippewa Bay.
CEDAR POINT SP—6 miles west of Clayton on N.Y. 12-E.
GRASS POINT SP—1 miles east of Fisher's Landing on N.Y. 12.

KRING POINT SP—At Redwood.

LONG POINT SP—14 miles from Three Mile Bay.

MARY ISLAND SP—Wellesley Island.

Adirondack-Catskill Area

JOHN BOYD THATCHER SP—15 miles southwest of Albany on N.Y. 157.

CAROGO LAKE SF—9 miles north of Gloversville on Route 29A.

CRANBERRY LAKE SF—3 miles south of Cranberry Lake near Route 3.

CROWN POINT RESERVATION SF—9 miles north of Crown Point on Route 8.

CUMBERLAND BAY SF—1 mile north of Plattsburg on Route 9.

EAGLE POINT SF—2 miles north of Pottersville on Route 9.

EEL WEIR SF—6 miles south of Ogdensburg near Route 87.

EIGHTH LAKE SF—5 miles west of Raquette Lake on Route 28.

FISH CREEK PONDS SF—12 miles east of Tupper Lake on Route 10.

FORKED LAKE SF—West of Deerland on Route 10.

GOLDEN BEACH SF—3 miles north of Raquette Lake on Route 28.

HEARTHSTONE POINT SF—2 miles north of Lake George on Route 9N.

LAKE DURANT SF—2 miles east of Blue Mt. Lake on Route 28.

LAKE EATON SF—2 miles west of Long Lake on Route 10.

LAKE GEORGE BATTLEGROUND SF—$\frac{1}{4}$ mile south of Lake George on Route 9.

LEWEY LAKE SF—14 miles north of Speculator on Route 10.

LITTLE SAND POINT SF—3 miles west of Piseco on Route 8.

MEACHAM LAKE SF—19 miles north of Lake Clear Jct. on Route 10.

MEADOWBROOK SF—4 miles east of Saranac Lake on Route 86.

MOFFITT BEACH SF—4 miles west of Speculator near Route 8.

PARADOX LAKE SF—2 miles east of Severance on Route 73.

PIXLEY'S FALLS SF—6 miles south of Boonville on Route 46.

POINT COMFORT SF—4 miles west of Piseco on Route 8.

PAKAMOONSHINE SF—6 miles south of Keesville on Route 9.

POPLAR POINT SF—2 miles west of Piseco on Route 8.

ROGERS ROCK SF—2 miles north of Hague on Route 9N.

ROLLINS POND SF—Same as Fish Creek Pond.

SACANDAGA SF—4 miles south of Wells on Route 30.

SHARP BRIDGE SF—5 miles north of Schroon River on Route 9.

WHETSTONE GULF SF—6 miles south of Lowville on Route 12D.

WILMINGTON NOTCH SF—3½ miles west of Wilmington on Route 86.

BEAVERKILL SF—7 miles northwest of Livingston Manor near Route 17.

DEVIL'S TOMBSTONE SF—4 miles south of Hunter on Route 214.

NORTH LAKE SF—3 miles northeast of Haines Falls near Route 23A.

WOODLAND VALLEY SF—6 miles southwest of Phoenicia near Route 28.

NORTH CAROLINA
Department of Conservation and Development, Raleigh

CLIFFS OF NEUSE SP—65 miles southeast of Raleigh on N.C. 55.

CRABTREE CREEK SP—10 miles northwest of Raleigh on U.S. 70.

HANGING ROCK SP—25 miles north of Winston-Salem on N.C. 89.

MORROW MOUNTAIN SP—47 miles northeast of Charlotte off U.S. 52.

MOUNT MITCHELL SP—35 miles northeast of Asheville off N.C. 80.

BLUE RIDGE PARKWAY NP—Follows crest of the Blue Ridge Mountains.

CAPE HATTERAS NATIONAL SEASHORE NP—Outer Banks of North Carolina.

CROATAN NF—East central part of state.

NANTAHALA NF—Western part of state.

PISGAH NF—West central part of state.

NORTH DAKOTA
Greater North Dakota Association 311 Broadway, Fargo

FORT LINCOLN SP—15 miles southwest of Bismark off N.D. 6.

LAKE METIGOSHE SP—210 miles northeast of Bismark off N.D. 14.

TURTLE RIVER SP—20 miles west of Grand Forks on U.S. 2.

OHIO   *Department of Natural Resources*
1106 Ohio Depts. Building, Columbus 15

BLUE ROCK STATE RESERVE SP—65 miles east of Columbus on Ohio 77.

JOHN BRYAN SP—12 miles south of Springfield off U.S. 68.

EAST HARBOR SP—45 miles east of Toledo off Ohio 2.

GUILFORD LAKE SP—70 miles southeast of Cleveland off U.S. 30.

HARRISON LAKE SP—50 miles west of Toledo off U.S. 20.

HOCKING SP—50 miles southeast of Columbus off U.S. 33.

HUESTON WOODS SP—37 miles northwest of Cincinnati off U.S. 27.

INDEPENDENCE DAM SP—50 miles southwest of Toledo on U.S. 24.

INDIAN LAKE PARK SP—42 miles north of Springfield off U.S. 33.

JACKSON LAKE SP—100 miles southeast of Columbus off U.S. 35.

JEFFERSON LAKE SP—15 miles northwest of Steubenville.

KISER LAKE SP—32 miles northwest of Springfield off U.S. 36.

LAKE ALMA STATE RESERVE SP—87 miles southeast of Columbus off U.S. 50.

LAKE HOPE SP—65 miles southeast of Columbus off Ohio 56.

LAKE WHITE SP—70 miles south of Columbus off U.S. 23.

LORAMIE LAKE PARK SP—55 miles northwest of Dayton off Ohio 66.

MADISON LAKE SP—25 miles southwest of Columbus off U.S. 42.

MOHICAN SP—75 miles southwest of Cleveland off Ohio 3.

MOUNT GILEAD SP—55 miles northeast of Columbus on Ohio 95.

NELSON AND KENNEDY LEDGES SP—30 miles southeast of Cleveland off U.S. 422.

PIKE SP—80 miles southwest of Columbus off Ohio 41.

PORTAGE SP—40 miles south of Cleveland off U.S. 21.

PYMATUNING SP—64 miles east of Cleveland off U.S. 6.

ROOSEVELT SP—100 miles south of Columbus off U.S. 52.

Scioto Trail SP—60 miles south of Columbus off U.S. 23.

South Bass Island SP—50 miles east of Toledo.

Tar Hollow SP—55 miles southeast of Columbus off Ohio 56.

Van Buren Lake SP—40 miles south Toledo off U.S. 68 at Van Buren.

Wayne-Hoosier NF—Southern Ohio and southern Indiana.

OKLAHOMA *Oklahoma Planning and Resources Board Room 500, State Capitol Building, Oklahoma City*

Beavers Bend SP—270 miles southeast of Okla. City off U.S. 70.

Boiling Springs SP—6 miles northeast of Woodward.

Lake Murray SP—7 miles southeast of Ardmore.

Osage Hills SP—15 miles northeast of Pawhuska on Okla. 35.

Quartz Mountain SP—18 miles north of Altus.

Robbers Cave SP—6 miles north of Wilburton on Okla. 2.

Roman Nose SP—7 miles north of Watonga on Okla. 8A.

Sequoyah SP—17 miles west of Taklequah.

Texoma SP—18 miles west of Durant.

Platt NF—South central part of state.

OREGON *State Highway Department Travel Information Division, Salem*

Alderwood SP—15 miles southwest of Junction City.

Armitage SP—5 miles north of Eugene.

Benson SP—28 miles east of Portland on U.S. 30.

Booth SP—13 miles west of Lakeview.

Cascadia SP—14 miles east of Sweethome.

Catherine Creek SP—8 miles southeast of Union on Ore. 203.

Champoeg SP—7 miles southeast of Newburgh.

Chandler SP—16 miles north of Lakeview.

Cline Falls SP—4 miles west of Redmond.

Cove Palisades SP—5 miles west of Culver.

Dabney SP—4 miles east of Troutdale.

Ben and Kay Dorris SP—3 miles west of Vida.

Ecola SP—2 miles north of Cannon Beach.

Emigrant Springs SP—26 miles east of Pendleton.

Hendricks Bridge Wayside SP—13 miles east of Eugene.

Hilgard Junction SP—8 miles west of La Grande.

Honeyman SP—2 miles south of Florence.

HUMBUG MOUNTAIN SP—6 miles south of Port Oxford.

NEPTUNE SP—3 miles south of Yachats.

PAINTED HILLS SP—9 miles northwest of Mitchell.

GOVERNOR PATTERSON MEMORIAL SP—1 mile south of Waldport.

RED BRIDGE SP—15½ miles southwest of La Grande.

REDMOND BEND-JUNIPER WAYSIDE SP—5½ miles north of Bend.

SADDLE MOUNTAIN SP—70 miles northwest of Portland off U.S. 26.

SHELTON SP—10 miles southeast of Fossil.

SHORT SAND BEACH SP—10 miles south of Cannon Beach.

SILVER FALLS SP—26 miles east of Salem.

UKIAH-DALE FOREST WAYSIDE SP—50 miles south of Pendleton.

VIENTO SP—55 miles east of Portland on U.S. 30.

WALLOWA LAKE SP—6 miles south of Joseph.

MAUD WILLIAMSON SP—12 miles north of Salem.

DESCHUTES NF—West central Oregon.

FREMONT NF—Southern Oregon, bordering on California.

MALHEUR NF—East central Oregon.

MOUNT HOOD NF—Northwestern Oregon.

OCHOCO NF—Central Oregon.

ROGUE RIVER SP—South of Crater Lake National Park.

SISKIYOU NF—West central Oregon.

SIUSLAW NF—West central Oregon.

UMATILLA NF—Northeastern Oregon.

UMPQUA NF—Northwest of Crater Lake National Park.

WALLOWA NF—Northeastern corner of Oregon.

WHITMAN NF—Northeastern Oregon.

WILLAMETTE NF—West central Oregon.

CRATER LAKE NF—Southwestern Oregon.

PENNSYLVANIA   *Department of Forests and Waters*
Harrisburg

ALLEGHENY NF—Northwestern Pennsylvania.

BLACK MOSHANNON SP—10 miles east of Philipsburg.

OLE BULL SP—1 mile south of Oleona.

BUSHY RUN BATTLEFIELD SP—22 miles southeast of Pittsburgh off Penn. 180.

CALEDONIA SP—55 miles southwest of Harrisburg on U.S. 30.

CLEAR CREEK SP—95 miles northeast of Pittsburgh off Penn. 36.

COLERAIN SP—100 miles northwest of Harrisburg on Penn. 45.

COLONEL DENNING SP—40 miles northeast of Harrisburg on Penn. 233.

COLTON POINT SP—3 miles southwest of Ansonia.

COOK FOREST SP—95 miles northeast of Pittsburgh on Penn. 36.

COWANES GAP SP—55 miles southwest of Harrisburg off Penn. 75.

S. B. ELLIOTT SP—130 miles northeast of Pittsburgh on Penn. 153.

FORT NECESSITY SP—10 miles south of Uniontown.

FOWLER HOLLOW SP—40 miles west of Harrisburg off Penn. 274.

FRENCH CREEK SP—8 miles southeast of Reading.

HALFWAY DAM SP—90 miles northwest of Harrisburg on Penn. 95.

HICKORY RUN SP—125 miles northeast of Harrisburg off Penn. 940.

KOOSER SP—57 miles southeast of Pittsburgh on Penn. 31.

LAUREL HILL SP—12 miles west of Somerset.

LINN RUN SP—60 miles southeast of Pittsburgh off Penn. 381.

OWEGO SP—37 miles east of Scranton off U.S. 6.

PARKER DAM SP—125 miles northeast of Pittsburgh off Penn. 153.

PECKS POND SP—45 miles southeast of Scranton on Penn. 402.

PINE GROVE FURNACE SP—35 miles southwest of Harrisburg on Penn. 233.

PROMISED LAND SP—10 miles northeast of Canadensis.

PYMATUNING SP—90 miles northwest of Pittsburgh on U.S. 332.

RACCOON CREEK SP—30 miles west of Pittsburgh on Penn. 18.

REEDS GAP SP—60 miles northwest of Harrisburg off U.S. 322.

SHAWNEE SP—90 miles southeast of Pittsburgh off U.S. 30.

SIZERVILLE SP—12 miles northeast of Emporium.

TROUGH CREEK SP—6 miles south of Marklesburg on Penn. 26.

VALLEY FORGE SP—8 miles west of Norristown.

WORLD'S END SP—120 miles northeast of Harrisburg off U.S. 220.

RHODE ISLAND
Division of Parks and Recreation
State Office Building, Providence

BURLINGAME RESERVATION SP—44 miles southwest of the State House.

GODDARD SP—15 miles southwest of the State House.

SOUTH CAROLINA
Commission of Forestry
P.O. Box 357, Columbia

AIKEN SP—40 miles southwest of Columbia off S.C. 215.

BARNWELL SP—50 miles southwest of Columbia on S.C. 3.

CHERAW SP—75 miles northeast of Columbia on U.S. 1.

CHESTER SP—3 miles southwest of Chester.

CROFT SP—6 miles south of Spartanburg.

EDISTO BEACH SP—20 miles south of Adams Run.

GIVHANS FERRY SP—8 miles west of Summerville.

GREENWOOD SP—5 miles east of Ninety Six.

HUNTING ISLAND SP—16 miles southeast of Beaufort.

KINGS POINT SP—12 miles north of York.

LEE SP—55 miles northeast of Columbia on S.C. 156.

MYRTLE BEACH SP—3 miles south of Myrtle Beach.

OCONEE SP—8 miles northwest of Walhalla.

PARIS MOUNTAIN SP—7 miles north of Greenville on county road.

POINSETT SP—8 miles south of Wedgefield.

RIVERS BRIDGE CONFEDERATE MEMORIAL SP—7 miles east of Sycamore.

SANTEE SP—6 miles east of Elloree.

TABLE ROCK SP—16 miles north of Pickens.

FRANCIS MARION NF—Southeastern part of state.

SUMTER NF—Northwestern part of state.

SOUTH DAKOTA
Department of Game, Fish and Parks
State Office Building, Pierre

BAD RIVER SP—94 miles east of Rapid City on U.S. 14.

BEAULIEU SP—5 miles southeast of Winner.

CLEAR LAKE SP—18 miles west of Sisseton.

CUSTER SP—10 miles east of Custer.

DE SMET FOREST SP—110 miles northwest of Sioux Falls off U.S. 14.

DURKEE LAKE SP—3 miles south of Faith.

DOG EAR LAKE SP—14 miles south of Winner.

FARM ISLAND SP—5 miles southeast of Pierre on S.D. 34.

FISHER GROVE SP—7 miles east of Redfield.

HARTFORD BEACH SP—12 miles north of Milbank.

HICKMAN DAM SP—9 miles south of Britton.

LAKE BURKE SP—200 miles southwest of Sioux Falls on U.S. 18.

LAKE BYRON SP—12 miles northeast of Huron.

LAKE CAMPBELL SP—4 miles northwest of Mound City.

LAKE HANSON SP—1 mile south of Alexandria.

LAKE HENDRICKS SP— 11 miles northeast of White.

LAKE HERMAN SP—2 miles west of Madison.

LAKE HIDDENWOOD SP—7 miles northeast of Selby.

LAKE HURLEY SP—15 miles northwest of Gettysburg.

LAKE PLATTE SP—150 miles west of Sioux Falls off U.S. 281.

LAKE SIXTEEN SP—5 miles east of Kimball.

LAKE SULLY SP—6 miles west of Onida.

LAKE WILMARTH SP—12 miles northwest of Plankinton.

MINA LAKE SP—13 miles east of Ipswich.

NEWTON HILLS SP—7 miles south of Canton.

OAKWOOD LAKES SP—10 miles north of Volga.

PIERPONT LAKE SP—3 miles south of Pierpont.

RAHN LAKE SP—18 miles south of Winner.

ROY LAKE SP—3 miles southwest of Lake City.

STICKNEY WAYSIDE SP—95 miles west of Sioux Falls on S.D. 41.

UNION COUNTY SP—11 miles south of Beresford.

WIND CAVE NP—Southwestern corner of the state.

BLACK HILLS NF—Directly south of Spearfish.

HARNEY NF—Southwestern part of state.

TENNESSEE   *Department of Conservation*
            203 Cordell Hull Building, Nashville

BIG RIDGE SP—25 miles north of Knoxville on Tenn. 61.

CEDARS OF LEBANON SP—50 miles southeast of Nashville on Tenn. 10.

CHICKSAW SP—112 miles southwest of Nashville on Tenn. 100.

CUMBERLAND MOUNTAIN SP—50 miles west of Knoxville on Tenn. 28.

FALL CREEK FALLS SP—100 miles southeast of Nashville off Tenn. 30.

HARRISON BAY SP—140 miles southeast of Nashville off Tenn. 61.

Montgomery Bell SP—40 miles west of Nashville on U.S. 70.

Natchez Trace SP—113 miles southwest of Nashville off Tenn. 20.

Norris Dam SP—30 miles northwest of Knoxville on Tenn. 71.

Paris Landing SP—100 miles northwest of Nashville off U.S. 79.

Pickett SP—150 miles northeast of Nashville off Tenn. 52.

Shelby Forest SP—190 miles southwest of Nashville off U.S. 51.

Standing Stone SP—110 miles northeast of Nashville on Tenn. 52.

Warrior's Path SP—120 miles northeast of Knoxville on U.S. 23.

Great Smoky Mountains NP—East central Tennessee.

Cherokee NF—Eastern Tennessee.

TEXAS   *Highway Department*
        Houston

Stephen F. Austin SP—3 miles west of Sealy.

Bastrop SP—1 mile east of Bastrop

Blanco SP—45 miles north of San Antonio on U.S. 281.

Buescher SP—1 mile northwest of Smithville.

Cleburne SP—12 miles southwest of Cleburne on Texas 174.

Daingerfield SP—2 miles southwest of Daingerfield.

Fort Griffin SP—15 miles north of Albany.

Frio SP—12 miles south of Pearsall.

Garner SP—30 miles north of Uvalde.

Goose Island SP—12 miles northeast of Rockport.

Huntsville SP—6 miles south of Huntsville.

Inks Lake SP—10 miles west of Burnet on Texas 29.

Kerrville SP—3 miles southeast of Kerrville.

Lake Corpus Christi SP—4 miles southwest of Mathis.

Possum Kingdom-East SP—90 miles west of Fort Worth off U.S. 180.

Tyler SP—10 miles north of Tyler.

Big Bend NP—Southwestern Texas.

Agelina NF—Eastern Texas.

Davey Crockett NF—East central Texas.

Sam Houston NF—Eastern Texas, north of Houston.

Sabine NF—Eastern Texas along Sabine River.

UTAH   *Tourist and Publicity Council*
              210 State Capitol Building, Salt Lake City

Bryce Canyon NP—Southwestern Utah.

Zion NP—Southwestern Utah.

Ashley NF—Northeastern corner of Utah.

Cache NF—North central Utah.

Dixie NF—Southwestern Utah.

Fish Lake NF—South central Utah.

Manti-Lasal NF—Central Utah.

Uinta NF—North central Utah.

Wasatch NF—Northern Utah.

VERMONT   *Department of Forests and Parks*
                Montpelier

Allis SP—12 miles north of Randolph.

Ascutney SP—4 miles south of Windsor.

Darling SP—4 miles south of East Burke.

Gifford Woods SP—12 miles northeast of Rutland on U.S. 100.

Mount Philo SP—15 miles south of Burlington off U.S. 7.

Sandbar SP—15 miles north of Burlington on U.S. 2.

Calvin Coolidge SF—35 miles east of Rutland off Vt. 100.

Groton SF—25 miles east of Montpelier off U.S. 302.

Maidstone SF—8 miles south of Bloomfield.

Mount Mansfield SF—31 miles northwest of Montpelier on Vt. 108.

Townsend SF—18 miles northwest of Brattleboro on Vt. 30.

Green Mountain NF—Southern Vermont.

VIRGINIA   *Division of Parks, Department of Conser-*
                vation and Development
                820 State Office Building, Richmond

Claytor Lake SP—57 miles southwest of Roanoke off U.S. 460.

Douthat SP—40 miles north of Roanoke off U.S. 60.

Fairy Stone SP—50 miles southwest of Roanoke on Va. 57.

Hungry Mother SP—100 miles southwest on Va. 16.

Seashore SP—10 miles east of Norfolk on U.S. 60.

Staunton SP—73 miles southeast of Lynchburg off U.S. 360.

Westmoreland SP—80 miles northeast of Richmond on Va. 3.

Blue Ridge Parkway NP—Follows the crest of the Blue Ridge Mountains.

SHENANDOAH NP—Northern Virginia.

JEFFERSON NF—Southwestern Virginia.

GEORGE WASHINGTON NF—Northwestern Virginia.

WASHINGTON *State Parks and Recreation Commission*
100 Dexter Ave., Seattle 9

BEACON ROCK SP—35 miles east of Vancouver.

BOGACHIEL SP—6 miles south of Forks.

BROOKS MEMORIAL SP—58 miles southwest of Yakima on U.S. 97.

CAMANO ISLAND SP—65 miles northwest of Seattle on Camano Island.

DECEPTION PASS SP—12 miles south of Anacortes.

FAY-BAINBRIDGE SP—West of Seattle via ferry.

FIELD'S SPRING SP—24 miles south of Asotin.

ILLAHEE SP—3 miles northeast of Bremerton.

LAKE CHELAN SP—9 miles west of Chelan.

LAKE SYLVIA SP—1 mile north of Montesano.

LARRABEE SP—7 miles south of Bellingham.

LEWIS AND CLARK SP—12 miles south of Chehalis.

LEWIS AND CLARK TRAIL SP—5 miles east of Waitsburg.

MILLERSYLVANIA SP—11 miles southwest of Olympia.

MORAN SP—90 miles northwest of Seattle on Orcas Island.

MT. SPOKANE SP—34 miles northeast of Spokane.

OSOYOOS LAKE SP—191 miles northwest of Spokane on U.S. 97.

RAINBOW FALLS SP—88 miles southwest of Tacoma on Wash. 12.

RIVERSIDE SP—3 miles northwest of Spokane.

SCHAFER SP—8 miles north of Satsop.

SEQUIM BAY SP—3 miles south of Sequim.

SUN LAKES SP—6 miles southwest of Coulee City.

TWANOH SP—10 miles southwest of Belfair.

TWIN HARBORS SP—21 miles southwest of Aberdeen.

WENATCHEE LAKE SP—22 miles north of Leavenworth on Wash. 150.

WENBERG SP—47 miles north of Seattle off U.S. 99.

YAKIMA SP—3 miles southeast of Yakima on Wash. 11A.

MOUNT RAINER NP—Southwestern Washington.

OLYMPIC SP—Northwestern Washington.

CHELAN NF—North central Washington.

COLVILLE NF—Northeastern Washington.

Mount Baker NF—North central section of state.

Olympic NF—Northwestern Washington.

Gifford Pinchot NF—Southwestern part of state.

Snoqualmie NF—Central Washington.

Wenatchee NF—In geographic center of state.

WEST VIRGINIA *Conservation Commission*
Charleston

Holly River SP—61 miles southwest of Clarksburg on W. Va. 20.

Monongahela NF—Eastern part of the State.

WISCONSIN *Conservation Department*
State Office Building, Madison 1

Big Foot Beach SP—1 mile south of Lake Geneva on Wis. 120.

Brunet Island SP—2 miles north of Cornell.

Copper Falls SP—3 miles north of Mellon on county road.

Devil's Lake SP—3 miles south of Baraboo on Wis. 123.

Nelson Dewey Memorial SP—1½ miles north of Cassville.

Interstate SP—120 miles northwest of Eau Claire on U.S. 8.

Merrick SP—2 miles northwest of Fountain City.

Pattison SP—12 miles south of Superior.

Peninsula SP—25 miles north of Sturgeon Bay.

Perrot SP—70 miles south of Eau Claire on Wis. 93.

Potawatomi SP—12 miles northwest of Sturgeon Bay.

Rib Mountain SP—100 miles east of Eau Claire off U.S. 51.

Terry Andrae SP—6 miles south of Sheboygan.

Tower Hill SP—5 miles west of Arena.

Wildcat Mountain SP—110 miles northwest of Makison on Wis. 33.

Wyalusing SP—100 miles west of Makison off U.S. 18.

American Leigion SF—18 miles northwest of Rhinelander.

Brule River SF—30 miles southeast of Superior.

Council Grounds SF—120 miles northeast of Eau Claire on Wis. 64.

Flambeau River SF—12 miles west of Phillips.

Mauthe Lake and Kettle Morraine SF—23 miles southeast of Fond du Lac.

Northern Highland SF—170 miles northeast of Eau Claire off U.S. 51.

Point Beach NF—145 miles northeast of Madison off Wis. 42.

Chequamegon NF—Northwestern Wisconsin.

Nicolet NF—Northeastern Wisconsin.

WYOMING *Travel Commission*
Capitol Building, Cheyenne

Grand Teton NP—Northwestern Wyoming.

Yellowstone NP—Extreme northwestern corner of the state.

Big Horn NF—North central Wyoming.

Bridger NF—West central Wyoming.

Medicine Bow NF—Southeastern Wyoming.

Shoshone NF—Northwestern Wyoming.

Teton NF—Northwestern Wyoming.

DIRECTORY OF EQUIPMENT SOURCES

The following list includes names and addresses of manufacturers and distributors of products mentioned in this book.

Alaska Sleeping Bag
   Company
334 N. W. 11th Avenue
Portland 9, Oregon

Aluma Craft Boat Company
1547 Central Avenue N. E.
Minneapolis, Minnesota

Burgess Battery Company
Freeport, Illinois

Coleman Company
250 North St. Francis Street
Wichita 1, Kansas

Eureka Tent Company
35-41 State Street
Binghamton 1, N. Y.

Eddie Bauer
417 East Pine Street
Seattle 22, Washington

Fulton Cotton Mills
P. O. Box 1726
Atlanta, Georgia

Gene Portuesi's Cycle Shop
6447 Michigan Avenue
Detroit 10, Michigan

Highway Cruisers
Travelcraft Sales of
   California, Inc.
8117 East Slauson Avenue
Montebello, California

Himalayan Pak Company
800 Cannery Row
Monterey, California

Hudson's
105 Third Avenue
New York, New York

Kar Kamp
8925 East Garvey
South San Gabriel, Calif.

Laacke Company
1023 West Walnut
Milwaukee 5, Wisconsin

Morsan Tents, Inc.
808 State Highway 17
Paramus, New Jersey

Old Town Canoe Company
Old Town, Maine

Sandvik Company
Saw and Tool Department
1702 Nevins Road
Fair Lawn, New Jersey

Sky-Vue Sleeper
22800 Buckingham
Dearborn, Michigan

Smilie Company
536 Mission Street
San Francisco 5, California

Thermos Company
Norwich, Connecticut

Vesely Manufacturing Co.
Box 151
Lapeer, Michigan

Western Cutlery Company
Boulder, Colorado

Index